US Consular Representation
in Britain since 1790

US Consular Representation in Britain since 1790

Nicholas M. Keegan

ANTHEM PRESS

Anthem Press
An imprint of Wimbledon Publishing Company
www.anthempress.com

This edition first published in UK and USA 2018
by ANTHEM PRESS
75–76 Blackfriars Road, London SE1 8HA, UK
or PO Box 9779, London SW19 7ZG, UK
and
244 Madison Ave #116, New York, NY 10016, USA

British Library Cataloguing-in-Publication Data
A catalogue record for this book is available from the British Library.

Library of Congress Cataloging-in-Publication Data
Names: Keegan, Nicholas M., 1939– author.
Title: US consular representation in Britain since 1790 / Nicholas M. Keegan.
Other titles: United States consular representation in Britain since 1790
Description: London, UK; New York, NY: Anthem Press, 2018. |
Includes bibliographical references and index.
Identifiers: LCCN 2017059995| ISBN 9781783087433 (hardback) |
ISBN 9781783087440 (paperback)
Subjects: LCSH: United States – Foreign relations – Great Britain. |
Great Britain – Foreign relations – United States. | Diplomatic and consular
service, American – Great Britain – History. | BISAC: POLITICAL SCIENCE /
International Relations / Diplomacy.
Classification: LCC E183.8.G7 K44 2018 | DDC 327.73041–dc23
LC record available at https://lccn.loc.gov/2017059995

ISBN-13: 978-1-78308-743-3 (Hbk)
ISBN-10: 1-78308-743-9 (Hbk)

ISBN-13: 978-1-78308-744-0 (Pbk)
ISBN-10: 1-78308-744-7 (Pbk)

This title is also available as an e-book.

To Elizabeth

CONTENTS

ILLUSTRATIONS

FOREWORD

Walls on either side of the main entrance to the US Department of State bear memorial plaques carrying the names of American diplomats who have died abroad while serving the country. As I write, there are 248 names on these memorials, a number which will sadly grow as time goes by. The first is that of William Palfrey, lost at sea in 1780 on his way to take up duties as the US Consul General to France. Not far behind comes the name of Abraham Hanson, who immigrated from Great Britain to the United States as a young man and died of African Fever in 1866 while serving as Consul General to Liberia. More recently, Marie Burke, a consular officer assigned to London, was stabbed to death in 1989 in a crime that remains unsolved.

The memorials bear testament to the dangers often faced by US representatives abroad. Looking at the walls and reading the causes of death, the trials and tribulations were particularly acute for our consuls, who lived in the most far-flung parts of the earth. They were posted in most major foreign ports and trading centres performing a critical role in promoting American commerce and influence. Officially, consular officers were responsible for safeguarding seamen and shipping, providing notarial services, and on occasion acting as estate executors for deceased Americans. In actuality, these men and their families were our original diplomatic expeditionary force – working with the US Navy to free the Mediterranean of Barbary pirates, negotiating early trade treaties, and representing the US government around the world.

In recognition of the important role these early diplomats played, I am delighted to have been asked to write the foreword for Nicholas Keegan's book, *US Consular Representation in Britain since 1790*. As president of the American Foreign Service Association, it has been my mission and privilege to explain the work of the State Department; the role American diplomats have played historically and continue to play today in advancing US strategic interests; and to advocate on behalf of the Foreign Service, our dedicated corps of diplomats who ably represent US interests around the world.

Today's Foreign Service Officers are consummate professionals, selected through a rigorously competitive examination process, and shaped by demanding tours in posts that span the globe. Like military officers, Foreign Service Officers have commissions from the president and take an oath to protect and defend the Constitution. Our nation's diplomats serve the president elected by the people of the United States, as well as the officials appointed and confirmed to help formulate and execute our country's foreign policy and international relations.

This was not always the case. In the early days of the US Department of State, our diplomatic corps and consular service were two separate entities, and the consular service vastly outnumbered our handful of diplomats. With the US government providing minimal salaries to either service, appointments primarily went to those with the financial means to be self-sufficient in their work abroad. This, combined with a government-wide practice of political appointments based on patronage rather than merit, overwhelmingly led to careers for those with connections and wealth rather than skill and knowledge. Perhaps not surprisingly, the quality of our first consuls and diplomats varied greatly.

As the United States began to play a more active role on the world stage, there was greater scrutiny of the qualifications of those engaged in diplomacy, as well as recognition of the need to appropriately fund this sector of government. The period of time immediately following World War I, when the State Department's inherent deficiencies became widely apparent, was a pivotal moment. The modern, professional diplomatic corps, or Foreign Service, was ushered in by Congress in 1924 through the Rogers Act.

The Rogers Act brought substantial restructuring and reform to the State Department. It combined the Diplomatic and Consular Services into one entity and established a career organization based on competitive examination and merit promotion. The Act also established or extended allowances and benefits that prior to this either did not exist or were completely inadequate, and opened up the Foreign Service to women and African Americans. There have been further improvements along the way, such as the establishment of standards for entry tests, clarification of the requirements for entry into the Foreign Service, creation of the Foreign Service Institute to train our nation's diplomats, and an ongoing effort to ensure that the US diplomatic corps better reflects the full diversity of the nation.

Nearly a century later, the Rogers Act still serves as the foundation of the current Foreign Service. This is the Foreign Service I joined back in 1985. I stand on the shoulders of women such as Lucile Atcherson, the first woman in the Foreign Service; Pattie H. Field, the first woman to enter the Foreign Service following the passage of the Rogers Act; and Frances E. Willis, the first female Foreign Service Officer to become an ambassador.

It was as a student at the University of Florida that I first became fully aware of the possibility of diplomatic service. The idea of the Foreign Service immediately captured my imagination. Working as a diplomat sounded like the most purposeful possible way to spend my life, and I jumped at the opportunity to serve my country while living in different places, learning new languages, and experiencing different cultures. This career has provided me the opportunity to travel the world, to represent all that is best about the United States of America, and to work to make the world a safer, better place.

First and foremost, diplomacy is about protecting the lives and interests of US citizens overseas. Our 270 missions around the world take this responsibility tremendously seriously, 24 hours a day, 7 days a week. We do this through routine and emergency services, assisting our fellow citizens during their most important moments – births, deaths, arrests, disasters and medical emergencies. We formulate and implement policy related to immigration and travel to the United States, and serve as the first line of defense for our citizens at home.

Diplomatic engagement on the part of the United States is also critical to ensuring international and domestic stability and prosperity. The expertise honed by Foreign

Service officers over the course of a career is an integral part of our government's national security architecture. Challenges such as terrorism, the global refugee and migration crises, global economic stability, and fragile or repressive societies cannot be addressed without sustained and robust US diplomatic leadership. Our nation's security and prosperity depend on having partners and allies who share our interests and values, and these partnerships are nurtured through US diplomatic engagement.

For three years it was my very great privilege to serve at the US Embassy in London, where preserving and promoting our 'Special Relationship' was something I worked at every single day. The United States has no closer ally than the United Kingdom. Bilateral cooperation reflects the common language, ideals and democratic practices of our two nations. As this book so well demonstrates, our official connections are long-standing, varied and rich in nature. At one point we had a network of up to ninety consular offices throughout the UK, stretching from the Orkney Islands to the Channel Islands. I would have appreciated similar resources during my time in the United Kingdom!

Ours is a remarkable story of service, of delivering for our country in the face of unique challenges. *US Consular Representation in Britain since 1790* opens the door to forgotten and untold accounts of America's presence in the United Kingdom – telling stories our early consuls never told about themselves or even dreamed would be of interest to modern readers.

Ambassador Barbara Stephenson
President, American Foreign Service Association

An active-duty member of the American Foreign Service for over 30 years, Barbara Stephenson was elected President of the American Foreign Service Association in 2015. Previously, she served as Dean of the Leadership and Management School at the Foreign Service Institute where she launched and co-chaired the Department-wide Culture of Leadership Initiative. In 2008, she was appointed Ambassador to Panama and later became the first female Deputy Chief of Mission and Chargé d'affaires at the US Embassy in London. Among other assignments, Ambassador Stephenson also served as the American Consul General in Belfast, Northern Ireland, from 2001 to 2004, and as desk officer for the United Kingdom in Washington, DC. Ambassador Stephenson holds a PhD in English Literature, writing her dissertation on the plays of Tom Stoppard.

PREFACE

Growing up in Edinburgh, I was always fascinated by the colourful national flags and coats of arms of the many consulates in the city. I was also struck by the unusual, at the time, sight of the left-hand drive chauffeur-driven car conveying the American consul around town. Years later, when working as a civil servant, a colleague and I took the American Consul General Norman Singer for an official lunch at one of Edinburgh's top hotels. This was my first encounter with a consul.

I maintained my interest in the consular world over the years and on leaving the civil service decided to examine the topic in more depth. I undertook graduate research at Durham University into a history of every country that has ever had a consulate in the United Kingdom, from earliest times until the year 2000. This was a unique project and included a major survey of all existing consulates, conducted by means of an extensive questionnaire. Cathy Hurst, the American consul in Edinburgh at the time, was kind enough to do a 'test drive' of the draft questionnaire to check for possible flaws in its design. More than two hundred career and honorary consuls representing almost seventy countries participated in the survey. This was about 60 per cent of the total number of consulates, and the data produced results that gave for the first time a detailed picture of the activities and duties of consuls working in the UK.

Having successfully put my PhD behind me, I wanted to continue with my interest in consular relations. At first I thought about researching the French Consular Service and, equipped with my undergraduate degree in French, felt confident enough to read official archives. But after some preliminary research I found that the topic did not hold enough appeal. My thoughts turned again to that lunch with the American consul in Edinburgh and led to an extended visit to Washington, DC, and to College Park, Maryland, where the State Department archives are stored, and to visits to the Department and the embassy in London. I also combed numerous other archives throughout the United States and Britain and corresponded with many officials and private individuals, some of whom were retired diplomats. This book is the result.

PREFACE

ACKNOWLEDGEMENTS

This book has taken almost ten years to research and write, during which time I have been greatly assisted by many individuals in Britain, the United States and elsewhere.

In Britain, I received a great deal of help from librarians and archivists. They include Alison Cullingford, Special Collections Librarian, J. B. Priestly Library, University of Bradford; Alison Fraser, Principal Archivist, the Orkney Library and Archive, Kirkwall; Barbara Sharp, Senior Archivist, Nottinghamshire Archives, Nottingham; Catherine Taylor, Team Historian, Central Library, Aberdeen; Christine Scott, Carol Attewell and staff of the reference section, Clayport Library, Durham; Nick Hodgson, Hon. Secretary, the Society of Antiquaries of Newcastle upon Tyne; Edward Hampshire, Modern Records Specialist, Research Knowledge and Academic Services, and Tim Padfield, Information Policy Consultant and Copyright Officer, National Archives, Kew; Jennie Grimshaw, British Library, London, and Kathryn M. Taylor, British Library Document Supply, Boston Spa, Wetherby, West Yorkshire, both of whom were particularly helpful in providing microfilms of US consular despatches; Katie Petty, Archives Assistant, Bristol Record Office, Bristol; Maureen Reid and Eileen Moran, Library and Information Assistants, Local History, Central Library, Dundee; staff of the National Archives of Scotland, Edinburgh; staff of the National Library of Scotland, Edinburgh; Paul Webster, Librarian, Liverpool Record Office; Robert Cole, User Services Librarian, Harold Cohen Library, University of Liverpool; Roger Hull, Researcher, Liverpool Record Office; Ruth Barriskill, Guildhall Library, London; Sarah Mulligan, Library Information Officer, City Library, Newcastle upon Tyne; staff of the Edinburgh Room, Edinburgh Central Library; Sue Hill, Archivist, Southampton City Council, Southampton; Julia Holmes, Archives Department, Wirral Museums, Birkenhead; Joan Mitchell, Special Collections, the Mitchell Library, Glasgow; Laura Walker, Surrey History Centre, Woking; Amy Proctor, London Metropolitan Archives.

In the US Embassy, London, Anna Girvan, Director of the Information Resource Center, was particularly helpful both during my time at the embassy and in later correspondence. Jeremy Dawe, Consular Operations Manager, managed to locate a decommissioned consulate shield. Chrystal Denys, Commercial Specialist, pointed me to several sources on US states' interests in Europe. Eric A. Johnson, Minister Counselor for Public Diplomacy, was enormously encouraging and supportive. His successor, Courtney Austrian, was equally supportive and spared an hour out of her busy schedule to meet with me at the embassy and also facilitated the submission of the Foreword. Ghazala Malik, Eric and Courtney's assistant, was helpful. I am honoured that Ambassador Barbara Stephenson agreed to provide the Foreword.

I also received assistance from Normand Redden, retired US Foreign Service Officer, London; Johanna Booth, Photo and Repro Administrator, Walker Art Gallery, National Museums Liverpool; John Mohin, Stone, Staffordshire; John Winrow, Assistant Curator, National Museums Liverpool, Merseyside Maritime Museum, Liverpool; Bob Jones, Local Historian, Liverpool; Pamela Raman, Footwoman, the Lord Mayor's Office, Liverpool; Jurgen Wolff, author, London; and Nick Utechin, Historian of the Sherlock Holmes Society.

In the United States, I wish to thank the staff at the National Archives II in Maryland, where State Department archives are held. During my extended visit they guided me patiently through the sometimes arcane cataloguing system of the archives. At the State Department, Linda S. Schweizer, in the Ralph J. Bunche Library, made my visit enjoyable as well as informative, and introduced me to her colleagues Hugh Howard, Sara Schoo, Lorna Dodt and Fran Perros. In the Office of Historian, Mark T. Hove, Tiffany T. Hamelin, Lyndsay Krasnoff, Evan Dawley and Emily Horne answered my often tedious questions with endless patience. Others in the Department who provided assistance were William E. Todd and Zipora Bullard in the Office of Inspector General; John F. Hackett, Director, and Tyler Brothers in the Office of Information Programs and Services; Kathryn W. McNamara in the Bureau of Overseas Building Operations; Charlotte W. Duckett, Program Analyst, Alan McKee, FOIA Reviewer, and Michael D. Caramelo in the Bureau of Diplomatic Security. In the Defense Intelligence Agency I would like to thank Alesia Y. Williams, Chief, FOIA and Declassification Services Office.

Throughout the United States there is a rich variety of enthusiastic local history societies, which are assiduous in gathering the personal archives of their citizens who became consuls. I was probably the first person for many years to seek and request most of these archives. I received assistance from many of these societies and am grateful to the following officials: Debbie Vaughan, Director of Research and Access and Chief Librarian, Chicago Historical Society, Chicago, Illinois; Allison DePrey and Corinne Nordin, Indiana Historical Society, Indianapolis; Jocelyn Koehler, Camden County Historical Society, Collingswood, New Jersey; John McClure and Katherine Wilkins, Virginia Historical Society, Richmond, Virginia; the staff at Ocean County Library, Toms River, New Jersey; and Nancy Bierbrauer, Ocean County Historical Society, Toms River, New Jersey. Librarians were also an essential and helpful source of information and documentation. They include Archives Services staff, Texas State Library and Archives Commission, Austin, Texas; Bonnie Lease, Information Services, Enoch Pratt Free Library, Central Library/State Library Resource Center, Baltimore, Maryland; Christopher A. Pembelton, Archives Technician, George H. W. Bush Presidential Library, College Station, Texas; David Kessler, the Bancroft Library, University of California–Berkeley, Berkeley, California; John M. Hoffman, Librarian, and John Franch, University of Illinois at Urbana–Champaign, Illinois; Frank Gagliardi and Renata Vickery, Elihu Burritt Library, Central Connecticut State University, New Britain, Connecticut; Helen E. Weltin, Senior Librarian, Manuscripts and Special Collections, New York State Library, Albany, New York; Jeffery T. Hartley, Chief Librarian, Archives Library Information Center, and Rodney A. Ross, Center for Legislative Archives, National Archives and Records Administration, Washington, DC; Jill Palmer, Library Assistant, Western History,

Manuscripts Department, and Lita Garcia, Library Associate, Huntington Library, San Marino, California; Jim Gerencser, Archives and Special Collections, Dickinson College, Carlisle, Pennsylvania; Julia Gardner, Reference and Instruction Librarian, Special Collections Research Center, University of Chicago Library, Chicago; Lisa Wilson, Archives Technician, the Library at the Mariners' Museum, Newport News, Virginia; Margaret Jerrido, Urban Archives Center, Temple University Libraries, Philadelphia; Michael Carroll Dooling, Librarian, Republican-American, Waterbury, Connecticut; Nan Card, Curator of Manuscripts, Rutherford B. Hayes Presidential Center, Fremont, Ohio; Nicholas Scheetz, Manuscripts Librarian, and Scott S. Taylor, Manuscripts Processor, Georgetown University Library, Washington, DC; Robert Bohanan, Deputy Director, Jimmy Carter Library and Museum, Atlanta, Georgia; the Digital Reference Team and the Reference Section of the Prints and Photographic Division in the Library of Congress, Washington, DC; Jill Kloberdanz, Lake Blackshear Regional Library, Americus, Georgia; Amanda Strauss and Laurie S. Ellis, Schlesinger Library, Radcliffe Institute for Advanced Study, Harvard University; and Jennifer Callaway of Denver Public Library, Colorado.

I was fortunate enough to correspond with a number of retired Foreign Service Officers and their relatives, all of whom were keen to assist me. These include Ambassador Peter Bridges, Arlington, Virginia; Ambassador William N. Dale, Durham, North Carolina; Charles Stuart Kennedy (he is also Director of the Foreign Affairs Oral History Program at the Association for Diplomatic Studies and Training, Arlington, Virginia); Henry E. Mattox (also lately Editor of *American Diplomacy*), Chapel Hill, North Carolina; J. Edgar Williams, Carrboro, North Carolina; Helga Ruge (widow of Consul Neil Ruge), Chico, California; Rev. Dom Julian Stead OSB (son of the late William F. Stead), Portsmouth Abbey, Rhode Island; and Robert W. Maule, Poulsbo, Washington.

Others in the United States who provided information and assistance include Alicia Clarke, Curator, Sanford Museum, Sanford, Florida; Carl Malamud, President, public.resource.org, Sebastopol, California; David McCullough, author, West Tisbury, Martha's Vineyard, Massachusetts; David Morrell, author, Santa Fe, New Mexico; Francis Lackner, Webmaster, Chicago Literary Club, Chicago, Illinois; J. Robert Moskin, author, New York; John Secor, Editor in Chief, *The Evening Bulletin*, Philadelphia; Emeritus Professor Howard Stone, Texas Christian University, Fort Worth (for expert advice on vintage radios); Michael Robert Patterson, Webmaster, Arlington National Cemetery website; Nadine Holder, Sierra Vista, Arizona; Sean Furniss, Reston, Virginia; Stacey Peeples, Curator, Pennsylvania Hospital, Philadelphia; Steven A. Honley, Editor, *Foreign Service Journal*, and Dmitry Filipoff, Publications Coordinator, American Foreign Service Association, Washington, DC; Carole Nasra, Rochester, New York; Alice Y. L. Burkholder, Harmony Foundation, Estes Park, Colorado; Doug and Susan Burgess, Fremont, California; Karen Griffin, Bartleby Books, Chevy Chase, Maryland; Peter E. Blau, Bethesda, Maryland; Phil Cohen, Bismarck, North Dakota; and Phillip L. Kaplan, *The Blade* newspaper, Toledo, Ohio.

I also received assistance from individuals and institutions in other parts of the world. They include American Resource Center, US Embassy, Prague, Czech Republic; Bruno Gravellier, Cultural and Commercial Delegate, US Consulate, Bordeaux, France; and

Manuela Kirchberg-Welby, German Foreign Office Help Desk, Berlin. In Canada, the following were helpful: Catherine Mills Rouleau, Québec; Francis M. Carroll, University of Manitoba, Winnipeg; Renu Barrett, Archivist, Mills Memorial Library, Archives and Research Collections, McMaster University, Hamilton, Ontario; Scott French, *Québec Chronicle-Telegraph*, Québec City; services aux usagers, Bibliothèque et Archives nationales du Québec, Montréal; and Astrid C. Black, Public Diplomacy/Political/ Econ-commercial Assistant, US Consulate, Hamilton, Bermuda.

The book was improved by the comments of the three anonymous peer reviewers and I am grateful to them for their time and their helpful contributions. At Anthem Press I am grateful to Tej Sood, Publisher and Director of the Press, and to the entire team at Anthem and to the copyeditor, Dana Richards, for carefully and patiently guiding the manuscript to publication. In Durham, my thanks to Brian and Margaret Taylor of Durham City Studios for their professional and friendly assistance in preparing high-resolution images of the book's illustrations.

My family, especially Lesley, was also hugely supportive throughout. However, above all, I should like to thank my wife Elizabeth for her constant encouragement and support over the years and for giving me the time to pursue what is essentially a selfish occupation. At times she must have felt that she was married to an American consul.

INTRODUCTION

'The vaguest of ideas are still [...] prevalent as to the functions and life of a consul, and as to the constitution, organisation, and general administration of the consular service.'[1] So wrote Joseph H. Longford, a retired British diplomat and later inaugural professor of Japanese at King's College London, more than a century ago when referring to British consular representation. But his words are just as relevant today to describe popular knowledge of the existence and extent of consular representation and the functions undertaken by consuls. Indeed, some people confuse consulates with embassies and use the terms interchangeably and often wrongly. This may be because they have no contact with consulates; yet, if they get into difficulties abroad they will expect their consul to help them out. It does not seem to occur to them that foreign consulates also operate in their own country. This book focuses on one country, describing for the first time the history and activities of the American consular presence in Britain from 1790 to the present day.

Differing claims have been advanced for the first appearance of consuls, and this is recognized in the preamble of the 1963 Vienna Convention on Consular Relations, which states simply that 'consular relations have been established between peoples since ancient times'.[2] It is generally accepted, however, that the Italian city states were the first examples of the modern consular institution, notably Venice with its impressive naval supremacy, although some maintain that Constantinople, the Byzantine capital, saw the first appearance.[3] The oldest among the modern Consular Services are those that were established by France, Britain, Portugal, Spain and the Netherlands. Although Eurocentric in its concept and form, the consular system has endured and spread throughout the world. Extraterritorial judicial powers were an early feature of consular functions, especially those imposed by European countries in China and the Ottoman Empire. Under this arrangement, foreign nationals were brought before their own consular courts to be tried and punished for offences committed in the host countries rather than allow them to be tried and punished by the local legal authorities. Extraterritorial judicial powers no longer exist.

All countries had separate diplomatic and consular services. Diplomats represented the person of their king, which gave them some claim to equality of status when engaging with the host king. Diplomats were drawn from the upper echelons of their societies and they dealt with high-level policy matters, such as negotiating treaties between countries and holding discussions with royalty and heads of state. Many diplomats regarded consuls as members of an inferior class and lacking in social skills. 'Certainly for the nineteenth and early twentieth centuries, when high social position was regarded as indispensable for diplomacy, the social gulf between the diplomats and consuls was enormous, practically unbridgeable.'[4] In the 1920s, Hugh S. Gibson, a senior American diplomat, remarked disdainfully that 'the best picture of a sweating man was a consul at a diplomatic dinner'.[5] And, in 1939, Sir Hughe Knatchbull-Hugessen, a senior British diplomat, said: 'Although we should be far from suggesting that personality, "address", and *savoir faire* are not of great importance in the Consular Service, it is in the Diplomatic Service that these rather intangible qualities are most essential.'[6] Consuls were drawn from the commercial or merchant classes and concerned themselves with trade matters and protecting the affairs of their citizens abroad, who, in the early days, were usually sailors and traders. Diplomats and consuls therefore not only moved in completely different worlds, both professionally and socially, rarely encountering each other, but also belonged to separate services, each with its own system of recruitment, training and distinctive career paths. This gradually changed during the twentieth century, and today most countries have unified Foreign Services whose personnel move freely between diplomatic and consular duties.

Consular services and their staffs throughout the world have generally been neglected by historians, and in the case of the former British Consular Service, have at times been described as Cinderella Services[7] and 'the step-child of the Foreign Office'.[8] There are several reasons for this. Although consuls were official overseas representatives of their countries, they were almost always overshadowed by high-flying diplomats who, as mentioned earlier, dealt with foreign governments, royalty and heads of state; negotiated important treaties relating to peace or war; and were drawn from the upper echelons of their societies. Many diplomats became famous, and their activities attracted the interest of historians; others wrote biographies or accounts of important aspects of their careers, which ranged from interesting stories to self-aggrandizing reminiscences. Consuls, on the other hand, in the early days, represented the commercial interests of their countries and were treated as second-class officials in comparison with diplomats. The work was not glamorous; they met only local officials and merchants, and dealt with the practical problems of sailors and the travelling public. Few wrote accounts of their careers, and fewer still became famous. There is relatively little literature therefore relating to the activities of consuls, whether American or otherwise.

Consuls are grouped into two categories: career and honorary, although the United States has consular agents rather than honorary consuls. Career consuls are full-time, permanent members of their country's Foreign Service and are posted to various countries throughout their careers, usually moving from one country to another every three or four years. Honorary consuls and consular agents are drawn from the ranks of business and the professions and are generally nationals of the countries in which they reside rather than of the countries they represent. They also bring with them the experience and expertise of their principal professions and provide governments with a very cost-effective means of overseas representation. Most are paid a small honorarium, in return for which they provide their own office accommodation and support staff; but American consular agents are regarded as part-time Foreign Service employees and receive a salary. However, many honorary consuls receive no payment and cover their operating costs from their own resources; for some, the social cachet in their communities of holding the appointment is sufficient reward. All consuls combine the roles of, among other things, lawyer, customs officer, social worker, shipping and trade expert and counselor. They deal with such diverse issues as visa questions, passport applications and renewals, child custody, abduction, prison visits, notary services, citizenship, and safety and security. They no longer perform marriages. A convenient shorthand description for their work is contained in the US State Department's 2012 Budget Request for the running costs of its Bureau for Consular Affairs: 'Consular Affairs provides services around the cycle of life, from certifying the birth of US citizens born abroad, to assisting family members when a US citizen dies overseas.'[9]

What is the difference between a consulate and an embassy? A consulate is generally located in a town or city other than the capital. In the case of the United States in Britain, the consulates are currently located in Edinburgh and Belfast. A consulate may be headed by a consul general, consul or occasionally by a principal officer, and its functions are as previously described. An embassy is almost always located in a country's capital city and is headed by an ambassador, also called the chief of mission.[10] Ambassadors are the link between their government (known as the sending state) and the state to which they are accredited (known as the receiving state). They negotiate with the government of the receiving state on all matters representing the interests of their country. In the United Kingdom, the Foreign and Commonwealth Office is the principal point of contact for ambassadors and their staff, although direct contact with certain other departments is common. Within the US embassy in London there are sections representing a number of federal departments or agencies. These include Commercial Service; Defense Attaché; Department of Homeland Security (which encompasses Customs and Border Protection, Immigration and Customs Enforcement, Citizenship and Immigration Services and the US Secret Service); and Departments of Justice, Economic Affairs, Foreign Agricultural Service, Internal Revenue Service and Public Affairs. There is also a very large consular section that deals with all of the functions that are undertaken in the Edinburgh and Belfast consulates, although the volume of work is much greater. Accredited embassy staff and consular staff are both members of the Foreign Service, and all may be described as diplomats though not all have full diplomatic immunity. Immunity is governed by two international conventions: the Vienna Convention on Diplomatic Relations 1961 and the Vienna Convention on Consular Relations 1963. Consular officers and consular employees have immunity only in respect of their consular functions, whereas diplomatic agents have immunity in respect of both their official and private activities. The term diplomatic agent is defined as 'the head of the mission or a member of the diplomatic staff of the mission'.[11]

During the nineteenth century, the American public very often attached more importance to the commercial activities of their consuls than to the political work of their diplomats. There were several reasons for this. Diplomats were fairly remote figures who dealt largely with foreign policy and affairs of state, activities that seldom impacted on the day-to-day lives of the public, unless of course the foreign policy led to a possible outbreak of war, minor hostilities or trade embargoes. On the other hand, consuls were generally well known to the public because many were ambitious or prominent local politicians or business people who had sought an overseas appointment as a consul, and their activities were frequently reported in the local press. They also dealt with issues that directly affected local companies, therefore the most vocal criticism of consuls and the functions they delivered or did not deliver came from the business sector, which frequently called for the reform of the Consular Service. Businessmen expected consuls to aid with the promotion of their goods in the country in which they served and to be kept abreast of developments in that country, particularly if these developments could lead to openings for their products, or have a detrimental effect on them. They felt, with some justification, that too often many consuls were dilettantes or opportunists who were not doing enough to assist them. As well as consulates, there were a few commercial agencies that dealt solely with commercial matters. Headed by a commercial agent, their activities were also of greater interest to the American public than those of diplomats. In the nineteenth and early twentieth centuries there were at one time up to eight American commercial agencies in the United Kingdom, located in towns that had important industries, such as Bradford (wool) and Nottingham (lace). Commercial agencies and 'the grade of commercial agent, which had existed as a separate rank and title in the US Consular Service since the Revolutionary period', were abolished as part of the Act of April 5, 1906, which dealt with the reorganization of the Consular Service.[12] It was only in the early part of the twentieth century that the United States and other governments began to see the value of having their overseas representatives engaged fully in trade promotion and market intelligence gathering. Often these officers were designated as commercial attachés, although the term seems to have fallen out of use. Nowadays, it is taken for granted that all countries will have in their embassies and consulates specialist personnel who are responsible for promoting their exports, carrying out market intelligence, dealing with economic affairs, promoting inward investment and so on. These may sometimes be designated as commercial officers.

Over the years, from the early days of its establishment in the late eighteenth century, the American Consular Service has been a source of many interesting and diverse themes and topics. These are identified and discussed in the book and are based on extensive research in national and local archives in both the United States and Britain. The book has also benefited from transcripts of oral histories of retired American diplomats pioneered by Charles Stuart Kennedy, a retired US consular officer and the author of an interesting book about the Consular Service.[13] Unlike this book, his deals with the Service worldwide and stops in 1924; this book concentrates on Britain (and Ireland up to independence) and comes up to the present day; it is in three parts.

Part 1 begins with a reminder of the early days of American independence and the formation of the new nation and is a useful backdrop to the rest of the book. This was a period of rapid growth, which saw the creation and development of the State Department and the Consular Service. In Part 1, accounts are given of the frequent legislative changes; major weaknesses of the early Consular Service; the recruitment and training of consuls; the spoils system, which ensured that political allies or presidential fundraisers were appointed as consuls or were able to influence the appointments of their friends or relatives; the constant turnover of the majority of consuls every time there was a change of administration in Washington; calls for reform; how the Consular Service lost its separate identity in 1924 when it merged with the Diplomatic Service into the unified Foreign Service; the role of women; and the amalgamation of the State Department and the Foreign Service following the recommendations of the Wriston Report of 1954.[14]

Parts 2 and 3 form the major sections of the book and deal with activities in Britain and pre-independence Ireland. Part 2 concentrates on the consulates and the people who served in them. It is an overview of the American consular presence in the country from 1790 to the present day. Topics covered include the wide-ranging extent of the consular network in the country; the difficulties of communicating with the State Department when it took several weeks for despatches to be shipped across the Atlantic; the often hazardous travel that early consuls encountered; the physical disabilities of some consuls; the illnesses and health problems that a few consuls and their wives suffered due to climate and occasionally to the effects of pollution in heavily industrialized areas; amputees from the 1812 War with Britain and the American Civil War who became consuls; British nationals who served as American consuls; consular families; office accommodation, furnishings and equipment of consulates; espionage activities conducted in Britain during the American Civil War; how Texas and Hawaii had consulates in Britain before they became states; inspections of consulates in order to raise standards and make consuls more efficient; the dangers consuls faced during the First and Second World War blitzes; food rationing during and after the Second World War; and consuls who on retirement decided to settle in Britain.

Part 3 consists of detailed histories of consulates in 15 towns throughout Britain (and one in pre-independence Ireland): Belfast, Birmingham, Bradford, Bristol, Cardiff, Dublin, Dundee, Dunfermline, Edinburgh and Leith, Falmouth, Liverpool, London, Newcastle upon Tyne, Southampton and Stoke on Trent. The descriptions of these consulates include the dates on which the offices were operational, short biographies of staff who served in them and an indication of their routine activities, including a few noteworthy incidents or highlights. The accounts are of varying length, reflecting the duration of the consulates' presence. Of the two remaining consular offices, the account for Edinburgh is longer than that for Belfast because its history has only very briefly been written about before – see, for example, the consulate general's website.[15] On the other hand, the account for Belfast is shorter, not because it is of less importance (arguably it is of more importance because of the political troubles there throughout the twentieth century) but because a comprehensive history of it has been given by Francis Carroll and Bernadette Whelan in their excellent books.[16] The extent and scale of the former consular network can be appreciated from the list of locations and categories of consular offices shown in the Appendix. The concluding chapter reflects on the long history of the American Consular Service, from its time as a separate service to its amalgamation in 1924 with the Diplomatic Service to establish the present-day Foreign Service. Examples are given of how it has evolved over the years, making use of new technological advances to keep up with changing times and demands. Although the former Consular Service took the lead early in the twentieth century to abolish the spoils system for its posts, one such appointment remains, that of consul general in Hamilton, Bermuda, a post that comes within the responsibility of the US Embassy in London. Elsewhere in the Foreign Service the spoils system flourishes for many ambassadorial appointments.

For most countries, distinctions between diplomats and consuls have largely disappeared, and nowadays staff are usually accredited as both diplomats and consuls. Despite this, in the current edition of that long-established and respected handbook *Satow's Diplomatic Practice* only 38 pages are devoted to consular matters, whereas 246 are devoted to diplomatic matters.[17] My intention in writing this book is to alter that balance, at least insofar as it relates to our knowledge of the history, presence and activities of US consuls in Britain. I hope that it may also encourage other researchers to consider this as a potential topic area.

Part 1

Chapter One

EARLY COLONIAL HISTORY
AND AMERICAN INDEPENDENCE

Britain was not the only European country that acquired territory in North America. Spain, France and the Netherlands also made significant inroads. Spain's interests continued until the early nineteenth century when they were passed to Mexico. Place names today, for example Los Angeles, San Francisco, Louisiana, New Orleans, Baton Rouge and, in Canada, Québec, Montréal and Trois-Rivières, give an indication of their colonial roots. The Dutch had New Amsterdam, which became the present New York City. With the exception of Canada, the interests of Spain and France in those places would later be acquired by the United States through war, diplomacy or outright purchase. Britain's possessions in America, the 13 colonies, were confined to the East Coast where the settlers gave their towns the names of familiar English towns, for example Boston, Cambridge, Portsmouth and Rochester. The 13 colonies eventually broke away from Britain and declared their independence in 1776 to form the United States.

Queen Elizabeth I of England died in 1603 and was succeeded by her Scottish cousin James VI of Scotland who also took the title James I of England, thereby uniting the crowns of the two nations. These were the heady days of exploration beginning to open up the New World, and after moving to England James did not allow the dust settle in his new role. On 10 April 1606, in one of his earliest acts, he granted royal charters to two companies – the London Company and the Plymouth Company – for the purpose of founding colonies in Virginia.[1] The charters allocated territory to each. The London Company was quick off the mark and in 1607 established the first permanent British settlement at a site that it named, somewhat sycophantically, Jamestown. The Plymouth Company made an unsuccessful attempt to establish a colony in Maine. However, in 1620, after several years of inactivity, it received a new charter and a new name, the Council for New England. By then, other settlers from Britain had set sail, the best known being the Puritans, the so-called Pilgrim Fathers, who arrived at Plymouth, Massachusetts, on the *Mayflower* in 1620. By 1624, Virginia had outlived the original purpose of the London Company, which was dissolved, and became a full-fledged crown colony. The British presence in America increased dramatically, and by 1733 there were 13 colonies, all on the East Coast. In order of founding these were Virginia, Massachusetts, New Hampshire, New York, Connecticut, Maryland, Rhode Island, Delaware, Pennsylvania, North Carolina, New Jersey, South Carolina and Georgia.

Distance from London, long delays in receiving and sending communications and hazardous sea voyages for administrators and military personnel all contributed to the necessity of having devolved colonial administrations run by local politicians and officials.

So, in many respects, the American colonies ran their affairs relatively independently while still being ruled from London and under the Westminster Parliament's jurisdiction. But they still needed to make their voices heard in London, so they appointed Colonial Agents to represent their interests to the British government in England.[2] They were usually merchants or politicians and could be either individuals sent out from the colonies on a temporary basis to reside in London or Englishmen who had never been to America. After the end of the seventeenth century the colonial governments realised that their interests would be better served with permanent representatives in London to serve as their lobbyists. Some, like Benjamin Franklin, represented more than one colony. This arrangement ended after independence.[3] However, by 1763 the seeds of revolt and a campaign for independence from Britain were already evident. A remarkable, for the time, feature was the extent of debate and counterargument within the colonies about rule from London that was expressed in written publications, for example in newspapers 'of which by 1775 there were thirty-eight in the mainland colonies. [...] Above all, there were pamphlets [...] [and it] was in this form [...] that much of the most important and characteristic writing of the American Revolution appeared.'[4]

Taxation is never a popular measure, and it became the major source of resentment for the colonists because it did not give them representation in the Parliament in London. As taxpayers, they felt that they ought to be represented, hence their popular slogan 'No taxation without representation.' The American colonies were regarded solely as an easy source of income for British governments, particularly to meet the ever-increasing costs of maintaining the locally based military establishments. The colonists' resentment was understandable, because the legislation passed by the British government, beginning with the Navigation Acts (1651–1696), the Sugar Act (1764), the Stamp Act (1765), the Townshend Act (1767) and the Tea Act (1773), most certainly favoured the economic and trade interests of Britain and not those of the colonies. During the first half of 1774 the Coercive Acts, known in America as the Intolerable Acts, were passed. These were designed to punish Massachusetts for the so-called Boston Tea Party in 1773 when in an act of defiance against duties imposed on tea under the Tea Act of that year crowds boarded ships in Boston and dumped their cargoes of tea into the harbour. The Coercive Acts covered a wide range of topics, such as the government and administration of justice in Massachusetts, stopping the port of Boston from trading until compensation had been paid for the dumped tea, powers relating to the quartering of troops and almost as an afterthought the regulation of government in Québec. This raft of legislation was the last straw to the colonists. In September 1774, representatives of 12 of the colonies met together in Philadelphia for the First Continental Congress. Despite the strength of their feelings, their demands were surprisingly moderate; they did not, as might have been expected, call for independence from Britain but sought only to assert what they saw as their rights as colonies, and to express their opposition to this latest round of oppressive legislation. They did however agree to boycott the importation of British goods until their demands were met. The British government refused to meet their demands and in a fit of pique introduced further repressive legislation. The Navigation Acts of the previous century had already banned the colonies from trading with countries that were not part of the British Empire, but the noose was tightened even further by this latest

New England Restraining Act of 1775 (the title gives an idea of how Britain felt about its unruly and disruptive colonies). Henceforth they could trade only with Britain and were also banned from access to the rich fishing grounds off the coast of Newfoundland until the differences were settled. Effectively, this legislation completely isolated the colonies and was clearly unacceptable to them. Although the initial reaction cannot have come as a surprise to the authorities in London, even the most far-sighted politician at the time could not have envisaged the historic outcome. It was the catalyst that would create the United States.

The first shots in the American Revolution were fired in April 1775 in skirmishes against British troops in Lexington and Concord, Massachusetts. The following month, the Second Continental Congress met again in Philadelphia and agreed that the local militias should form a Continental Army to represent the 13 American colonies and that it should be commanded by George Washington. The first major clash between the colonists and British forces took place on 12 June at Bunker Hill in Boston. In October that year, the Congress authorized the establishment of a navy and in the following month appointed a committee to deal with foreign affairs. All the colonies had independent arrangements for territorial governance but these were still fairly fragmented and patchy, although many colonies had begun to introduce constitutions. It was time, therefore, to consolidate matters. So, meeting in May 1776, the Congress instructed those that had not yet drawn up constitutions to expedite their introduction. The fact that the colonies were prepared to be tasked in this fashion showed that they accepted the authoritative and overriding role of Congress. It represented a coming of age, a recognition that 'Americans were one people and must behave as such: if Congress could not act without the states, the states could not, in this matter, act without Congress.'[5] At the same meeting, Congress appointed a committee of five leading politicians (John Adams, Benjamin Franklin, Thomas Jefferson, Robert R. Livingston and Roger Sherman) to draft a declaration of independence; the committee chose Jefferson to write the first draft. The final version was approved, and on 2 July, Congress voted in favour of independence. Two days later, on 4 July, the formal version of the Declaration of Independence was approved and signed. The colonies had now become the United States of America.

However, the existence of a Declaration of Independence did not mean that there were no further obstacles in the path of the new nation. Several major problems remained to be resolved. The country still did not have a national government, Britain did not recognize its changed status and the hostilities between both countries that had begun in 1775 continued. In the absence of a national government, the Continental Congress took on the role, and a week after the Declaration of Independence it considered the first draft of a constitution setting out the respective roles and responsibilities of the states and of Congress. This document was the Articles of Confederation, or to give it its full title 'Articles of Confederation and Perpetual Union between the States of [...]' (which were then listed individually).[6] It was adopted by Congress on 15 November 1777 but not finally ratified by all the states until 1 March 1781. The two remaining questions – recognition by Britain and the cessation of hostilities – were settled in September 1783 when, under the terms of the Treaty of Paris, the war was ended and Britain recognized the new nation.

The Articles of Confederation served their original purpose of providing a frame-work constitution for the fledgling nation, but very soon needed a complete revision. Following calls from leading politicians, a Constitutional Convention began work on a constitution in Philadelphia in May 1787. The Convention has been described as 'a unique occasion in American history [...]. It was the crowning act of the American Revolution; next to the declaration for independence, it was the most important; and it was a huge, though not unqualified, success.'[7] After several revisions, a draft constitution was ready by September and eventually received the necessary ratification by nine of the thirteen states on 21 June 1788. Ratification by the other four states followed between 25 June 1788 (Virginia) and 29 May 1790 (Rhode Island). The first elections for the new executive were held in February 1789, George Washington was elected president and took office on 30 April 1789. Two years later, in a circular to consuls and vice consuls, Thomas Jefferson, when Secretary of State in Washington's cabinet, summed up the optimism of the new nation: 'In general our affairs are proceeding in a train of unpar-alleled prosperity [...] So that I believe I may say with truth that there is not a Nation under the sun enjoying more present prosperity, nor with more in prospect.'[8]

So, what had begun fairly modestly with King James I of England giving two pri-vate companies the right to establish colonies in Virginia led ultimately to what became the United States of America. Geography dictated that rule from Britain would always be distant and this gave the colonists an early taste of what it might be like to be inde-pendent. However, their early demands were not for independence, but rather for what has become known nowadays as devolution of powers. But Britain handled things badly and this led to resentment. At the first stirrings of revolt it turned the screws and introduced harsh laws on the recalcitrant colonists. Inevitably, as later history shows only too clearly in other colonial countries, it was only a matter of time before the colonists had had enough, broke free and fought a bitter war. Perhaps if Britain had treated them more fairly or sympathetically the course of history would have changed. But that is straying into the realm of counterfactual history. The Declaration of Independence in 1776 set the seal. The genie was out of the bottle and there was no going back. Seven years later, Britain bowed to reality and recognized the new nation. The next chapter describes the creation and development of the major department that would oversee the country's foreign policy, the Department of State.

Chapter Two

CREATION AND GROWTH
OF THE STATE DEPARTMENT

Given that America had been a group of British colonies until the end of the third quarter of the eighteenth century, it obviously neither sent nor received consuls. The overseas interests of its sailors and merchants was the responsibility of British consuls. All that changed when the colonies achieved independence and nationhood. The United States now had to be responsible for its own diplomatic and commercial relations with other countries. Therefore, an executive department for administering this had to be created. The colonists were well aware of this and had taken the first steps towards doing so shortly before the Declaration of Independence.

In November 1775, the Second Continental Congress appointed a secret committee, chaired initially by Benjamin Franklin, to correspond with friends and sympathizers in Britain, Ireland and other parts of the world.[1] This was the Committee of Secret Correspondence, which was renamed the Committee for Foreign Affairs in April 1777, with Thomas Paine as its first secretary.[2] However, this committee system of government, and particularly of running foreign affairs, was frequently criticized, and in January 1779 Congress instructed the committee to obtain information about the ways in which other countries administered not only their foreign policy but also other topics. As a result, the committee had a further name change on 10 January 1781 to the Department of Foreign Affairs, headed by a Secretary for Foreign Affairs. The first holder of the office, Robert R. Livingston, was not offered the post until August and mulled it over before accepting it on 20 October. He held the appointment until 4 June 1783 before resigning.[3] He was succeeded almost a year later by John Jay, who served from 7 May 1784 until 4 March 1789. On 27 July 1789 Congress formally established the department, but less than two months later, on 15 September, gave it a number of additional domestic responsibilities, such as custody of the Great Seal of the United States. As a consequence of these new functions it was renamed the Department of State, and was headed by a secretary of state.[4] The first holder of this office was Thomas Jefferson, who was appointed on 26 September 1789 but did not take up his duties until almost six months later, on 22 March 1790.[5] As there were considerable delays before Jay and Jefferson took up their appointments, it would appear that continuity at the top of the department was not regarded as important.

At that time, the government and the department were located temporarily in New York City. They moved to Philadelphia in 1790 and remained there until early 1800 before moving finally to the new capital of Washington, DC. The department was also frequently on the move, and between 1789 and 1866, when it relocated to the

Figure 2.1 State Department staff, early 1900s.

Women were employed as clerks in the State Department as early as 1874, much earlier than their British counterparts. This photograph of a State Department office in the early 1900s shows male and female clerks. Office equipment on the rather untidy desks includes typewriters, glue pots, a rocker blotter, rubber stamps, staplers and inkwells. The high filing cabinets on the left are accessed by two stepladders; presumably in those days the upper ones would be accessed only by the male clerks. [Author's collection.]

Washington City Orphan Asylum building, it had been housed in 17 buildings.[6] From 1875, it shared its headquarters accommodation with the War Department, the Navy Department and, for a short time, part of the Treasury, in what is now known as the Old Executive Office Building. Increased responsibilities led to its moving from there in 1947, this time to the Foggy Bottom district in a new and larger building that had been earmarked originally for the War Department, which had decided instead to move to the purpose-built Pentagon building in nearby Arlington, Virginia. The Department gradually outgrew the old War Department building but avoided moving once again; instead, a large new section incorporating the existing building was constructed around it and was completed in 1960. In 2000, this extended headquarters building was named the Harry S. Truman building.[7]

As the new country's foreign responsibilities increased so, too, did those of the Department. In 1833, the diplomatic and consular bureaus were established to administer those arms of the service, and a further reorganization took place in 1870, which reorganized the Department's administration into nine bureaus and two agencies.[8] The next change was in 1909 when a major reorganization brought new responsibilities

Figure 2.2 State Department group photo, 4 August 1922.

Taken on 4 August 1922, this shows Secretary of State Charles Evan Hughes and Chief of the Consular Bureau Wilbur Carr standing on the steps of the then State Department with a group of consuls general. Those shown are: front row, from left to right, Roger C. Tredwell, Ralph J. Totten, Carr, Hughes, Charles C. Eberhardt, Nathaniel B. Stewart (who has an empty left sleeve tucked into his jacket pocket; as a young he was injured in a railway accident which resulted in the amputation of his arm). Back row, from left to right, Edward J. Norton, Nelson T. Johnson, William Dawson, Arthur Garrels, Robert Frazer Jr. [National Photo Company Collection, Library of Congress, Prints & Photographs Division, reproduction no. LC-DIG-npcc-23237.]

for administering the diplomatic and consular services, and a further expansion of the politico-geographical divisions.

In 1924, the Rogers Act created a unified Foreign Service, composed of the former separate Diplomatic and Consular Services. However, personnel of the Foreign Service and of the Department of State largely functioned in a non-integrated fashion, almost as separate branches; staff of the Department were members of the Civil Service and did not leave Washington. The upheavals of both world wars entailed further responsibilities and challenges, but despite several initiatives in 1949 and 1951 it was not until the Wriston Report of 1954 that agreement was reached to integrate the staffs of the Department and the Foreign Service. The Foreign Service now numbers more than eleven thousand employees and there are also over nine thousand Civil Service personnel, mainly in Washington, DC, who are involved

Figure 2.3 Secretary of State Charles Evans Hughes sitting at his desk with a radio.

Secretary of State Charles Evan Hughes at a desk in the State Department in 1922. He is wearing headphones connected to a battery-operated 2-tube amplifier, housed in a wooden cabinet, probably a SE 1000. The top item on his left is a variable capacitor and his hand is on what is probably the radio detector. The capacitor and detector knobs are for tuning in to stations and the amplifier amplifies the signal. These three separate items make up an early radio and nowadays are parts of a simple radio. [Author's collection.]

in almost every aspect of its work. For example, within the Department's Bureau of Consular Affairs, the Passport Services Directorate issues passports and visas, a function that in other countries is not part of the responsibility of ministries of foreign affairs. Civil Service staffs are regarded as the 'domestic counterpart to consular officers abroad'. A further important group of staff are the 37,000 Foreign Service Nationals who work in embassies and other posts abroad and are citizens of the countries in which they serve.[9] In addition, there are increasing numbers of federal government officers based in American embassies. For example, in the London Embassy in 2015 there were representatives of the State Department and 25 other US government agencies.[10]

The Department has continued to grow in response to additional responsibilities and tasks. In recent years it has seen its traditional role as the sole public face of the nation's foreign policy reduced by influences not from outside government but from within it. Two such challenges are the increasing number of political appointments to senior posts within the Department and the increasing militarization of foreign policy. After secretary of state, senior posts in the Department are deputy secretary of state, under secretaries, assistant secretaries and deputy assistant secretaries. The secretary post is traditionally a non-career appointment, that is, a political appointment, but the others are usually filled

Figure 2.4 Secretary of State Charles Evans Hughes and Ambassador George Harvey.

Secretary of State Charles Evans Hughes and Ambassador George Harvey, in Hughes' office in the State Department on 13 June 1923. Prior to his appointment in 1921, Hughes had been an attorney, governor of New York, and a Supreme Court judge. Harvey, whose background was in journalism and publishing, was ambassador to the United Kingdom until approximately five months after the photograph was taken. Both men, together with Robert Peet Skinner in London, were actively involved in the acrimonious exchanges with the Foreign Office that led to the closure, for two years, of the consulate in Newcastle upon Tyne. [Author's collection.]

by career and political appointees. However, there has been a trend, particularly during the Obama administration, to increase the number of political appointees. In 1975, 37 per cent of these senior posts were filled by political appointments and 60 per cent career Foreign Service staff; in 2014, political appointees held 51 per cent of these posts and 30 per cent were held by career Foreign Service staff. In addition, in early 2016 there were 63 diplomatic functions headed by individuals titled special envoys, special representatives, ambassadors-at-large, coordinators, special advisors, senior advisor, personal represen- tative and senior representative.[11] These 'often bring numbers of staff from outside the Department, operate in a closed loop with other non-career staff, and pursue their issues without integrating the larger national interests that *must* inform responsible foreign policy decisions and implementation'.[12] During President Obama's first term only 5 of the then 35 such posts were filled by Foreign Service officers.[13] Administrations are there- fore relying to a much greater extent on getting foreign policy advice from individuals who have little or no experience in such matters, rather than from career professionals who have greater direct experience and knowledge in the field. This is a further, per- haps unintended, consequence of the spoils system so prevalent in the United States.

Figure 2.5 Wilbur J. Carr, 1924.

Wilbur J. Carr was the legendary chief of the Consular Service, holding posts successively as chief of the Consular Bureau, director of the Consular Service, and assistant secretary of state. He was an opponent of political patronage and a long-time campaigner for a professional consular service. A State Department official from when he joined in 1892, his only consular or diplomatic post came at the end of his career when he was appointed minister to Czechoslovakia, a post he held from 1937 until his retirement in 1939. [National Photo Company Collection, Library of Congress, Prints & Photographs Division, reproduction no. LC-DIG-npcc-11647.]

Matters will not improve until such time as the whole idea of such a practice is drastically overhauled, and this seems unlikely to happen. This is discussed further in Chapter 22. A noticeable feature of President Trump's first year is the number of vacancies among the Department's senior posts.

There has also been an increasing role played by the military in foreign policy, what has been described as 'mission creep'.[14] This is nothing new, but its scale has increased, with the Department of Defense and its worldwide regional commands frequently playing a role in foreign policy implementation. For example, the military are often called on to carry out aid projects to civilian populations around the world, a role that was in the past handled more by the US Aid agency. Ironically, the first warnings about the increasing militarization of foreign policy came from the military themselves, from then Defense Secretary Robert Gates and Admiral Mike Mullen, Chairman of the Joint Chiefs of Staff. Gates said: 'Broadly speaking, when it comes to America's engagement

Figure 2.6 Herbert C. Hengstler.

Herbert C Hengstler was born in Middletown, Ohio, in 1876 and entered the State Department in 1898. He succeeded Carr as chief of the Consular Bureau from 1907 until 1921, and in 1924 was appointed chief of the Division of Foreign Service Administration. Apart from various other assignments between 1931 and 1936 he held the post more or less continuously until 1937 when he was appointed consul general in Toronto, retiring from the service there in 1941. [Author's collection.]

with the rest of the world, it is important that the military is – and is clearly seen to be – in a supporting role to civilian agencies.' He continued: 'Nevertheless, in Iraq, Afghanistan and beyond, the U.S. military is increasingly involved in activities once handled by civilian agencies. This has led to concern among many organizations, about what's seen as a creeping "militarization" of some aspects of America's foreign policy. This is not an entirely unreasonable sentiment.'[15]

In a Guidance document in November 2008, Mullen wrote:

> We are a global force with global responsibilities and will continue to be so. The sustained presence and persistent engagement of our forces are the most effective way to develop the lasting relationships and cooperation necessary to secure our vital national interests. We have the most combat-hardened forces in history. Our Navy and Air Force are unmatched, although our advantage could easily slip. Reenlistments are up; the all-volunteer force is sound. However, we cannot meet the challenges of today and those of tomorrow with military power alone. We must guard against further militarization of our foreign policy. To achieve our strategic object-ives in Iraq and Afghanistan, to reset, reconstitute, and revitalize the force, and to rebalance strategic risk, it is vital that we not only develop our military capabilities, but also strengthen capacity of other government agencies and that of our foreign partners.[16]

The Obama administration attempted to face this challenge by introducing a concept based on a model employed by the United Kingdom. Its aim was to create a 'whole of government' fund, – in other words, a true '3D' fund (diplomacy, development and defense) to achieve foreign policy objectives.[17] In US terms, this is a pooling of State Department, USAID and Department of Defense resources.

In addition to facing new challenges, the Department has always sought ways to increase the efficiency of its internal policy and administrative procedures. Responsibility for long-term policy initiatives is undertaken by the Policy Planning Staff, created in 1947, whose role is 'to take a longer term strategic view of global trends and frame recommendations for the Secretary of State to advance US interests and values'.[18] Examples of two shorter-term initiatives that have been introduced in recent years are International Cooperative Administrative Support Services (ICASS) and Transformational Diplomacy. ICASS is the system for ensuring that each government agency that has a presence in or involvement with more than two hundred diplomatic and consular posts abroad is charged for the actual cost of common shared services incurred by their presence at these posts. Before this system was introduced, the State Department met these relatively significant costs.[19] The objective of Transformational Diplomacy was defined by former Secretary of State Condoleezza Rice:

> To work with our many partners around the world, to build and sustain democratic, well-governed states that will respond to the needs of their people and conduct themselves respon-sibly in the international system. Let me be clear, transformational diplomacy is rooted in partnership; not in paternalism. In doing things with people, not for them; we seek to use America's diplomatic power to help foreign citizens better their own lives and to build their own nations and to transform their own futures. In extraordinary times like those of today, when the very terrain of history is shifting beneath our feet, we must transform old diplomatic institutions to serve new diplomatic purposes.[20]

This new policy was a vital part of the Department's policy rethinking in response to the events of 11 September 2001, and was an attempt to engage with people in parts of the world that the United States had perhaps neglected. As a result, many staff at the larger embassies in, for example, Europe were repositioned to more frontline posts in Africa, the Middle East and Asia, some of which are regarded as war zones.

The Department has therefore come a long way since the Founding Fathers established the fairly modest Committee for Foreign Affairs in 1777 and has successfully managed to adapt and change according to the shifting demands of foreign policy. In the next chapter we consider how the Department established and developed the Consular Service, particularly how it dealt with the considerable early weaknesses of the consular system and the many criticisms that were directed against it.

Chapter Three

ESTABLISHMENT AND DEVELOPMENT
OF THE CONSULAR SERVICE

The first American consul, as opposed to commercial agent, was Colonel William Palfrey, appointed by the Continental Congress in November 1780 to reside in France. However, transatlantic crossings were extremely hazardous ventures in those times, and the unfortunate Colonel Palfrey was lost at sea very soon after leaving America. He was succeeded in June 1781 by Thomas Barclay an American merchant living in France who, more than a year previously, had been recommended by John Adams for the post of consul general in London.[1] However, the first consular appointments under the United States Congress did not take place until 1790, and this marked the establishment of the Consular Service. But considerable improvements were needed which required the introduction of frequent new legislation up to the beginning of the twentieth century.

The Early Days: A Time of Frequent Legislative Change

On 9 August 1785, the Continental Congress ordered John Jay, Secretary for Foreign Affairs, to report on the number of consuls and vice consuls that Congress should appoint, and their locations.[2] Jay reported on 19 September that, in the case of Britain, he thought there ought to be a consul general in London who should nominate the number of consuls required in the country. However, he concluded his report by advising that in order to avoid the not inconsiderable expense of appointing a consul general it might be more prudent to give the Minister in London powers as a consul general.[3] In a further report on 13 October, he recommended that the Minister should have the powers of a consul general for the whole of Britain. At the same time, he felt there was little use for consuls until such time as the United States had a commerce treaty with Britain. But, like a good diplomat, he hedged his bets, adding that if he were mistaken in his opinion then he thought consulates might be established in London, Bristol, Dublin and Cork. He was unsure about having consulates in Scotland, as 'the far greater part of the American trade to Scotland [was] carried on in British vessels.'[4] Congress resumed consideration of the report on 24 October, debating an amendment that consuls general or consuls should not receive salaries or fees; they referred it for further debate, which took place three days later when the proposed ordinance failed to get the necessary votes and was lost.[5] However, a compromise resolution was passed on 28 October. It said that American Ministers Plenipotentiary in Europe should exercise the powers of a consul general for the country in which they resided, but with no additional salary for doing so.[6]

The first United States Congress met in 1789 under the presidency of George Washington. In September of that year the 'freckled and sandy-haired, rather tall and awkward' Thomas Jefferson was appointed Secretary of State, the first holder of this new post in charge of the country's foreign relations.[7] A year earlier, when Minister in Paris and negotiating a consular convention with France, he had informed Count Armand Montmorin, the Minister of Foreign Affairs, rather disdainfully that 'we [the United States] do not find the institution of consuls very necessary. Its history commences in times of barbarism and might well have ended with them. During these they were perhaps useful, and may still be so in countries not yet emerged from that condition.' One wonders what the urbane Montmorin made of Jefferson's haughty observation, considering that France had had an efficient and thriving consular service since the seventeenth century. For example, it had a consulate in London as early as 1668.[8] Undaunted, Jefferson continued, 'we carry on commerce with good success in all parts of the world: yet we have not a consul in a single port, nor a complaint for the want of one, except from the persons who wish to be Consuls themselves.' He favoured instead the system adopted by 'every mercantile house', which 'has correspondents in almost every port [...] who are found to take better care of their interests and to obtain more effectually the protection of the laws of the country for them than the consul of their nation can.'[9] This unenthusiastic viewpoint did not augur well for the nascent consular service. Yet, despite such a discouraging start, the United States gradually built up an extensive, and eventually efficient, consular service. Incidentally, Jefferson was splitting hairs about not having a consul in a single port, perhaps carried away by his own rhetoric. In fact, the first American 'consular' post was established in the port of Bordeaux in March 1778, headed by John Bondfield who was appointed as commercial agent for the Continental Congress. A commercial agent, even at that time, had consular functions.[10] Also, Samuel Shaw and Thomas Randall were appointed consul and vice consul respectively in the Chinese port of Canton on February 1786. Shaw was reappointed to the post on 10 February 1790, making him the first consular officer appointed under the Constitution.[11]

George Washington made 19 consular appointments between February and August 1790, 13 of them with the rank of consul and 6 with the rank of vice consul.[12] Four of the appointments were in Britain, at Liverpool (June), Dublin (June), Cowes (June) and London (August). Cowes was a vice consulship, the other three were consuls. The Cowes nominee Thomas Auldjo was not, however, recognized by the British government on the grounds that there had never previously been a consul in that port. A compromise was reached the following year, which recognized him at Poole, although he continued to reside in Cowes.[13] All the appointments were unsalaried, the holders being expected to gain their livelihoods from business activities and from the fees they charged for providing consular services. On 26 August 1790, Secretary of State Jefferson sent his first circular to consuls, which instructed them to send him reports every six months of US ships entering and leaving their ports (together with details of the names and types of vessels, their captains and owners, numbers of seamen, description of cargoes). They were also to send information about any military preparations or other indications of war, to notify local American merchants and vessels about the imminence of war, to forward any political and commercial intelligence they thought might be of interest, and were also given authority to appoint their own agents within their districts who would report only to them.[14] That the consular service had been established on a fairly piece-meal basis can be seen from the opening lines of Jefferson's 26 August 1790 circular. He began, apologetically, by saying:

> I expected 'ere this to have been able to send you an Act of Congress, prescribing some spe-cial Duties and Regulations for the Exercise of the Consular Offices of the United States; but Congress not having been able to mature the Act sufficiently, it lies over to the next Session. In the mean while I beg Leave to draw your Attention to some Matters of Information which it is interesting to receive.[15]

At the same time, he was anxious to rein in the consuls, cautioning them:

> It will be best not to fatigue the Government in which you reside, or those in authority under it, with applications in unimportant cases. Husband their good dispositions for occasions of some moment, and let all representations to them be couched in the most temperate and friendly terms, never indulging in any case whatever a single expression which may irritate.[16]

It was now time to put the service on a more regular, established basis. The first attempt to do so was the Act of 1792 whose purpose was to carry into full effect the 1788 con-sular convention between the United States and France. The Act defined and established the functions and privileges of each country's consuls and vice consuls and set out the duties and responsibilities of American consuls when dealing with US citizens who were seafarers, merchants, commercial persons or private individuals. Fees could be charged for providing services such as authenticating documents ($2) and winding up personal estates of deceased persons (5 per cent of gross amount of estate). No mention was made of salaries for the consuls except in the case of those who resided on the Barbary Coast who were to be given an annual salary of $2,000.[17] Consuls and vice consuls would receive only fees as compensation and they were to provide a bond with sureties 'in a sum not less than two thousand nor more than ten thousand dollars'. This was held as insurance against their failing to carry out their duties efficiently and with financial correctness. No mention was made of consuls' nationality, their qualifications for office or how they should be recruited.[18] Other legislation affecting consuls was introduced between then and 1855 that largely reinforced their duties in respect of seafarers and the movements of American shipping, for some of which they could make a charge, and made it an offence to knowingly issue an alien with a US passport. Under Treasury Acts of 1818 and 1823, rather than consular legislation, they were also given a major new role relating to the export of goods from their districts to the United States. This made them responsible for certifying the values of goods on invoices so that the correct duty could be charged on their arrival in the States. They were authorized to charge fees for doing this, which not only offset the cost of maintaining consulates but also formed a vital source of income for a non-salaried consul.[19] Even though it created income for unsalaried consuls it was not universally popular. Writing in 1897, Samuel E. Morss, who had just relinquished the post of consul general in Paris, bemoaned: 'the work connected with the certification of invoices […] is very heavy and takes precedence of all other Consular duties … [it] … is not imposed upon the Consular officers of other countries. Our system of Consular certification of invoices is peculiar to the United States.'[20]

Consular instructions were used as a means of notifying consuls of their duties and functions, and so on. However, these tended to be issued on a fragmented and ad hoc basis, and it was not until 1833 that Secretary of State Edward Livingston (1831–1833) drew up the first set of general consular instructions. He attached these to a highly critical report on the consular establishment which he presented to President Andrew Jackson. This report, he began, 'may show the inconveniences of our present system, if one it may be called.' Consuls, in the various acts they performed, had 'no legal adviser, and no rule prescribed by law to guide them in the delicate and important questions that are continually calling for their decision.' He contrasted this with the situation 'at home', where 'every officer has his duties prescribed and marked out by law'. He also had 'no hesitation in giving a decided opinion that the exaction of fees has been the source of misunderstanding between our consuls and the masters of vessels, injurious to the reputation of the country'. He was sympathetic to the financial status of consuls, saying 'I cannot avoid expressing the opinion that these officers, like all others, should be compensated by adequate salaries, and should be prevented from engaging in commerce.' If salaried, consuls 'will never, then, by their countrymen, be suspected of acting towards them as their commercial interest, not as their duty requires'. Without salary, and 'at a distance from all superintendence, they have greater opportunities for illegal exactions, and that very circumstance makes them more liable to suspicion'.[21] Jackson submitted the report and instructions to the Senate on 2 March 1833. Although Congress took no action on the report, a number of Livingston's recommendations were included in the 1856 Act.[22] Livingston's *General Instructions to the Consuls and Commercial Agents of the United States* were extensive, running to nine pages, and gave consuls for the first time a comprehensive guide to their duties and responsibilities. There were 51 articles, arranged 'under proper heads, for the purpose of making them easily referred to, and producing uniformity in all the consular proceedings'.[23] They dealt with the following topics: duties of a consul on his appointment; formalities to be observed after entering upon their duties; the records and papers that should be kept in the consulate; duties in relation to intestates' estates, to wrecks, to masters of American ships and to seamen of the United States; duties in granting certificates and passports; the appointment of consular agents; rules for the general conduct of consuls; the consular uniform; contacts between consuls and the officers of the US Navy; and the expenses to be allowed to consuls. Livingston's 1856 instructions went through several editions; the third edition was published in 1868 and was also aimed at merchants, shipowners and masters of American vessels.[24] This was followed in 1908 by a Digest of Consular Instructions to Consular Officers, which brought together all the instructions that had been issued between 1 January 1897 and 25 May 1908. A lack of instructions regarding the nature of support that consuls should give to promoting the American merchant marine was at the heart of the dispute in 1922 which led to the closure of the Newcastle consulate. This is described in Chapter 19, the Newcastle upon Tyne consulate chapter. Over the years, instructions for use by consuls continued to be revised and amended as necessary. Nowadays, their duties and functions are set out in the Department's Foreign Affairs Manual, Chapter 7, Consular Affairs, which is regularly updated and is available online.[25]

Thomas Wilson, the consul in Dublin, for one, was unhappy about the proposal to pay salaries to consuls and restrict them from trading. By the time he received his copy of the proposals Livingston had been replaced as secretary of state by Louis McLane (1833–1834). Wilson wrote to McLane saying why he thought the proposal was unrealistic, and describing himself as: 'the son of one who risked his life in the Revolutionary War, and who was afterwards appointed by his Friend [underlined by Wilson] General Washington (under whom he served in that War) to the Office of Consul of this district'. He conceded condescendingly that 'It will no doubt be possible to obtain men and respectable men too,' as consuls and vice consuls for the respective salaries of $2,000 and $1,000 and who would agree not to engage in trading, 'but certainly not of the same class or rank in Society as those who now fill these situations'. He himself was a shipowner. Wilson also thought that, in the case of a vice consul, while $1,000 might be sufficient for 'a person already possessed of an independent property, residing in the country and not engaged in business' it would be too small a sum 'to induce a "respectable" citizen to leave his home and settle in a strange country'.[26] Wilson seemed fixated on 'respectable'. Despite his claims of strong American links and sentiments, he was not an American citizen. When he was replaced by Hugh Keenan in 1847 the reason given was that, where practicable, consulships should be held by American citizens. Keenan was a naturalized American citizen.[27]

In 1847, the Select Committee on the Revision of the Consular System brought forward a bill proposing the level of annual fees that the following consuls in Britain should receive by way of compensation: Liverpool and London (each $4,000); Cowes, Glasgow and Belfast (each $2,000). However, the bill was tabled, which meant it was killed and not enacted.[28] By 1853, the fees for consuls in Britain were as shown in the following table.

1853 Annual fees for consuls in Britain and Ireland											
	$250	$300	$500	$700	$800	$1000	$1500	$1600	$1800	$2000	$4000
Belfast		X									
Bristol							X				
Cork								X			
Dublin			X								
Dundee			X								
Edinburgh									X		
Falmouth						X					
Galway	X										
Glasgow		X									
Leeds								X			
Liverpool											X
London										X	

(continued)

1853 Annual fees for consuls in Britain and Ireland										
	$250	$300	$500	$700	$800	$1000	$1500	$1600	$1800	$2000	$4000
Londonderry				X							
Manchester									X		
Plymouth					X						
Southampton & Cowes									X		

Note In addition to these fees, the London consul is also permitted to retain whatever other fees he collects, which are considerable. Blue Book for 1853, containing the salaries of all the United States Ministers to foreign courts, and the fees of the United States consuls in all parts of the world, Philadelphia, 1853.

The next significant legislation came in March 1855 with an act to remodel the diplomatic and consular services.[29] This was a very detailed measure and, for the first time, proposed that the consuls at London and Liverpool should receive annual salaries of $7,500, the highest in the US consular service. The next tier of consuls should receive the following salaries: Glasgow, $4,000; Dundee, $2,000; Belfast, $2,000; Newcastle, $1,500; and Leeds, $1,500; none would be allowed to transact business, either in their own name or through the agency of others. The penalties for failing to observe this were being recalled and fined not less than $2,000. Finally, the consuls and commercial agents elsewhere in Britain were to receive annual compensations as follows: Bristol, Cork, Dublin, Galway, Leith and Southampton, $1,000 each but, more importantly, they were allowed to transact business. The act set out regulations for the location and hours of business of offices, the requirements for bonds, the amount of fees to be charged for itemized services and the records to be kept. It restricted the posts of consul, commercial agent, vice consul, consular agent and clerk to US citizens and only they were to have access to the archives. In a throwaway section at the end of the act, the president was authorized to bestow the title of consul general on any consul in Asia or Africa 'when in his opinion such title will promote the public interest.'[30] There were no US consuls general in Britain or elsewhere in Europe at the time. However, the act never got off the ground, immediately encountering procedural difficulties, and was repealed the following year by the 1856 Act.[31] This was as wide-ranging as the 1855 Act but there were a number of important changes. Under the 1856 Act, salaries would be introduced for the consuls at Liverpool and London ($7,500 each), Glasgow ($3,000) and $2,000 each for those at Belfast, Cork, Dundee, Leeds, Manchester and Southampton, but they were not permitted to engage in business, an undertaking they had to give in their bond. Instead of a salary, the other consuls at Bristol, Dublin, Galway, Leith and Newcastle were to receive only the fees that they collected from their consular functions, but they were permitted to engage in business. The proposal to bestow the title of consul general on an existing consul only in Asia or Africa was amended; the geographical restriction was removed and if it was thought that the public interest would be served, a consul general could be appointed instead of a consul or commercial agent who need not necessarily be an existing officer. There were still no consuls general in Britain, but there were two in the

British Empire, in Québec and Calcutta. The requirement to appoint only American citizens was dropped but replaced by one with similar effect that said no compensation was to be given to non-American citizens. Presumably, therefore, a foreigner could hold a post but not be paid for doing so. Fees charged for consular services were standardized and had to be submitted regularly to the Treasury, thus putting an end to the practice of some consuls who charged what they thought fit, a convention that had come in for much criticism. The 1856 Act was a watershed and remained in force until 1906.

Unlike the consular services of countries such as Great Britain and France, and most other European countries, the US Consular Service remained largely staffed by unqualified individuals, many of whom had gained their positions through patronage. The first tentative steps towards putting the service on a permanent, career basis were taken when the 1856 Act proposed that up to 25 'consular pupils' should be appointed, subject to satisfactory evidence by examination or otherwise of their qualifications and fitness for office, and assigned to various consulates. However, the proposal was repealed by the Appropriation Act of 1857 and thus never implemented.[32] Nevertheless, the idea was resurrected in 1862 and 1864 by Secretary of State William Seward (1861–1869), who drew attention to the additional duties imposed on consuls by the current Civil War, and was included in the 1864 Act.[33] This authorized the appointment of 13 'consular clerks', over the age of 18 years, who were American citizens and had been shown after due examination and report by an examining board to be qualified and fit for the duties. They would receive annual salaries of $1,000. The act also increased the annual salary of the Manchester consul to $3,000 and provided office rent allowances for consuls who were not engaged in business, but they were not permitted to employ clerks at public expense.[34] It was intended, therefore, that while learning the general duties of the consular service the 'consular clerks' could 'thereby relieve the consuls in a degree from the charge of clerk-hire, which, when taken from the compensation of those officers, leaves the latter quite inadequate for an economical support of themselves and their families in expensive foreign capitals'.[35] In 1874, one of the 13 consular clerks, Charles D. Atwood of Wisconsin, was serving in the Liverpool consulate.[36] It was also expected that the consular clerks could be trained to eventually attain posts as consuls, but this idea proved unsuccessful as most consuls lost their posts every four years on the change of administration. For example, in 1897 when President McKinley's (1897–1901) administration took over, 238 of the 272 consuls in the Service lost their jobs in order to make way for new appointments.[37] Unsurprisingly, few consular clerks were willing to risk giving up their secure, albeit lower level, posts in order to become consuls who had no long-term job security. Some of the clerks grew: 'to be old men, serving for thirty years without a change of status. One who accepted promotion [to consul] was removed at the next succeeding change of administration; the nomination of another was rejected by the Senate. None is willing to give up the security of his clerical post; this has been the end of the experiment.'[38] During the period from 1864 to 1896, only eight of the sixty-four clerks appointed were promoted to consul.[39] The author Nathaniel Hawthorne was a keen advocate of consular clerks and several years after leaving his post as consul at Liverpool he suggested that all clerks in consulates should be appointed directly by the Department and not by consuls. He pointed to the risks of financial irregularities when consuls appointed their own clerks. 'With clerks of my own selection, I would [be tempted to] engage to commit defalcations to the extent of at least one-half of the receipts of the office, without the possibility of proof against me. No man ought to be exposed to so great a temptation as this. Many men will certainly yield to it; and those who do not yield will find it difficult to make their integrity manifest.'[40] Consular salaries were never high, and many consuls who had become salaried under the 1856 Act but no longer permitted to trade saw a reduction in their incomes. The incomes of those at busy ports such as Liverpool had been higher when their compensation had been on a fees-only basis. Moreover, many complained that they had to pay their clerks' salaries and other office expenses out of their own reduced salaries.

In June 1874 two acts relating to the diplomatic and consular services were issued. The first divided the consulates into seven classes for salary purposes. Under these, the consul general in London and the consul in Liverpool each received a salary of $6,000. Liverpool alone had a consular clerk who was paid $1,000 from State Department funds; all the other consuls received salaries of between $1,500 and $3,000 but for the first time a number of the busier ones were allowed sums for the hire of clerks. This amounted to $2,000 for London, $3,000 for Liverpool and $1,500 each for Belfast, Birmingham, Bradford, Leith, Manchester, Sheffield and Tunstall. The other act that month dealt with a number of miscellaneous personnel topics such as absences from post, corresponding without official permission with private persons or newspapers on topics relating to the public affairs of the government of the host country, or recommending persons for employment or trust with that government.[41]

A Major Weakness in the Early Consular Service

The widespread use of patronage to fill vacancies was a major weakness in the early Consular Service. As we have seen, under that practice, known as the spoils system, whenever there was a change of government almost the entire consular establishment (and other branches of government) was replaced, and there was no shortage of people putting themselves or their protégés forward to fill the vacancies. President Andrew Jackson (1829–1837) was an enthusiastic proponent of the spoils system and 'believed Government duties could be "so plain and simple" that offices should rotate among deserving applicants.'[42] Of course, it all depends upon how one defines 'deserving'. Under the spoils system, almost anyone, if they had political, social or business connections could seek and obtain a consulship. No entrance qualifications or knowledge of languages were required. It was often sufficient merely to write to one's senator or congressman to express an interest in a post, and this would then be forwarded to the president or the secretary of state with a recommendation, usually with a reminder that a political favour was owed. For example, Abraham Lincoln wrote on 15 March 1861: 'Mr Senator Fessenden is exceedingly anxious that Hon. Freeman H. Morse shall be consul to London.'[43] A few days later he wrote: 'On this 27th of March 1861 Hon. Mr [Samuel S.] Blair of Pa. calls and presses that Thomas P. Campbell Esq. of his District shall be consul to Glasgow, or have some other eligible appointment. Mr Blair says his District does a large share of the voting, and never receives anything. Therefore he is very anxious in this matter.'[44] Some bolder souls bypassed their representatives and wrote directly to the president or secretary of state. William Wharton, a former Assistant Secretary of State, writing in 1894, said: 'It seems to be the common opinion that anybody can fill a consular office, and it is curious to note how the character of the applicants for these offices has reflected the popular sentiment.'[45] Wharton was correct; many of those appointed as consuls were bungling amateurs.

The spoils system was described by George M. Towle, a former consul in Nantes and commercial agent in Bradford, as 'the great bane of our political life, the corrupting consequences of an irresponsible executive patronage'. Consuls were 'the nominees of Congressmen, the personal pets or political managers of Presidents and Secretaries [of State]', and their positions were rewards for 'persistent flattery' or 'past devotion'. In some cases consulships were given 'to propitiate and get rid of' certain individuals.[46] Henry White, former secretary of the Embassy in London, felt that the chief obstacle to a reformed consular service: 'appears to me to lie in the sacrifice likely to be entailed upon the political party which, being in possession of the executive branch of the government when [any] proposed reform goes into effect, is compelled to leave a considerable number of the opposite party's appointees in office'.[47] Francis Loomis, US minister to Venezuela, was unimpressed by the criticisms aired by businessmen and he gave a spirited defence of the Consular Service. In his view, many American businessmen were: 'too inactive, too ill-informed or too stupid to take advantage of the opportunities for increasing export trade which the Government is persistently setting before the people of the United States. Businessmen who fail in the foreign markets become very severe critics of the United States Consul.'[48] A letter in the *New York Times* in 1893 was equally blunt:

> What an army of greedy men are now in Washington, according to newspaper reports, making an eager rush for those places; how very few can be successful, how few have considered the qualifications required, and how ignorant are these office seekers of the vocation to which they aspire! [...] Better men than political waifs should certainly be our commercial representatives in foreign countries.[49]

Nowadays, only one consular appointment remains open to patronage, that of the Consul General in Hamilton, Bermuda. However, the spoils system remains alive and well. Individuals, known familiarly as 'bundlers', who contribute to presidential electoral campaigns are often rewarded with various federal appointments, including ambassadorships, if their candidate attains office. In the summer of 2008, a group of retired senior diplomats, including all living former secretaries of state, wrote to the two presidential candidates, Barack Obama and John McCain, urging them to reduce the number of politically appointed ambassadors if either of them became president. Unsurprisingly, neither candidate commented, as that might have put at risk the millions of dollars that were being raised for their campaigns. According to the group, non-career ambassadors since President Kennedy's time averaged 33 per cent of the total.[50]

Consular Uniforms

Before moving on to the important questions of calls for reform and first attempts at professionalising the Consular Service it is interesting to note briefly another topic, unimportant in itself but an indication of the early Service's seeking to emulate some European practices. Diplomats represented monarchs and were usually members of the aristocracy and so were accustomed to wearing some kind of uniform, military or civil, when attending court or other formal social functions. European consuls also wore uniforms. The founders of the American republic were anxious to avoid copying these practices but nevertheless recognized that their representatives would look out of place at formal diplomatic gatherings if they were not wearing some kind of uniform, so they arrived at a compromise. In 1790, Secretary of State Thomas Jefferson sent a circular to consuls informing them that: 'The Consuls and Vice-consuls of the United States are free to wear the uniform of their navy, if they chuse [sic] to do so. This is a deep blue coat with red facings, lining and cuffs, the cuffs slashed and a standing collar; a red waistcoat (laced or not at the election of the wearer) and blue Breeches; yellow buttons with a foul anchor, and black cockades and small swords.'[51] The consular uniform described in the circular was in vogue until 1815 when the Department issued a further circular abolishing it and substituting an even more elaborate one. This included a single-breasted coat of blue cloth, with 10 navy buttons; the front, cuffs and pocket flaps were embroidered in gold, with button holes worked with gold thread. The outfit was finished off with a white vest (waistcoat), white 'small clothes' (close-fitting knee breeches), cocked hat, small sword and buckled shoes.[52] It was to be worn 'on all visits of ceremony to the authorities of the place, and on all proper occasions.'[53] Until 1817, American diplomats, as opposed to consuls, had generally invented their own uniforms but, as may be imagined, this had led to a wide variety and types being worn.[54] The Department therefore issued a circular that year standardizing diplomats' uniforms, basing them on those that American representatives had designed for themselves in 1814 to wear at the conference in Ghent.[55]

Despite the fledgling republic's external image of an egalitarian society, enshrined in its 1776 Declaration of Independence by the affirmation that 'all men are created equal', it did not regard its consuls as the equals of its diplomats. Inequalities were reflected in differences between their uniforms. In 1853, Secretary of State Marcy issued another circular, which encouraged the wearing of 'the simple dress of an American citizen'.[56] Note the word 'encouraged', but by 1915 American diplomats were still wearing uniforms although they had been simplified. They were described as:

Full-dress jacket: Stand-up collar with gold-metallic embroidered leafage panel and border trim. Black wool flannel fabric, with front closure of 8 gilt brass US State Eagle buttons. Tails and applied cuffs similarly decorated. Silk twill lining. Coordinate trousers with side stripes of applied gold leaf-pattern bands. Bicorne hat in black, with black feathered trim, metallic gold embroidery, single gilt button, black gros-grain ribbon bands, and red, white and blue appliqués. Complete with pearl-handled dress sword; leather scabbard, gilt-metal fittings.[57]

It is not clear when American officials ceased wearing uniforms, but in 1937 President Franklin D. Roosevelt issued an order 'directing that no person in the diplomatic or consular service should wear a uniform or official costume not previously authorized by Congress', although this was 'something that Congress never did.'[58] Nowadays,

American Foreign Service officers do not wear uniforms, although one American ambassador in the 1990s reflected that his attendance at a diplomatic function in Buckingham Palace

> done up in my best finery was a deflating experience. Surrounded by my fellow ambassadors in gold-braided diplomatic uniforms, all festooned with brilliant sashes across their fronts and glittery decorations the size of hub caps (the smaller the country, the bigger the medals), I felt pretty plain. I always attended these functions with a quiet apprehension that someone would mistake me for a footman and ask me to fetch him a drink.[59]

Calls for Reform and First Attempt at Professionalizing the Service

Over the years, many of the calls for reform came from the business sector, represented by chambers of commerce and boards of trade throughout America, and from the civil service.[60] For example, George McAneny, Secretary of the Civil Service Reform League, writing in 1899 said, changing 'the whole personnel of the corps whenever there is a change in the political character of the government at Washington […] must be regarded not only as an absurdity, but as a serious injury to our developing interests, the correction of which cannot with safety be long deferred.'[61] Almost despairingly, he catalogued the previous unsuccessful attempts at reform:

> The defects in the consular service of the United States have figured as a matter of public discussion for many years. They have been set forth in the messages of the Presidents, reviewed in a multitude of congressional and departmental reports, treated in magazine articles and standard works on administration, and deplored in the formal resolutions of every commercial body of consequence in the country. The result, to the present time, is virtually nothing. The system stands uncorrected.[62]

However, he managed to end on an upbeat note: 'Certain it is that the party or the administration which shall first place the consular establishment of the United States on a footing with those of other great nations of the world will give to our commerce an inestimable advantage and win distinction.'[63] Even Wilbur Carr, the legendary Chief of the Consular Bureau and the first (and only) person to be appointed Director of the Consular Service, acknowledged the failings of the Service: 'the fact remains that our service has been uneven in point of efficiency; there has been no satisfactory organization; little care has been exercised in the selection of persons for appointment; and the salaries and equipment have been far from adequate'.[64] Carr echoed McAneny's view about lack of progress: 'Repeated attempts to correct these defects have been made during a period dating almost from the beginning of government, but, with the exception of the improvements made in 1856, all these attempts have failed largely because they lacked the support of any considerable public sentiment.'[65] Other calls for reform came from men who had themselves been diplomats or consuls and whose experience working alongside their European counterparts had highlighted the deficiencies of the US Consular Service. A further cause for criticism was the practice of sending naturalized Americans back to their country of origin as consuls. Questions were raised about where their true loyalties might lie if they had to deal with disputes between their native country and their adopted one. Also, as their vice consuls would almost certainly be non-Americans it meant that the consulate, and therefore American interests, was in the hands of 'foreigners'.

The constant turnover of consuls contributed to the general decline in standards of many posts. Indeed, it would have been surprising if the result had been otherwise. Inefficient consuls bided their time, knowing that they would return home after spending what, at least for many of them in Europe, was a relatively pleasant interlude in their lives. Efficient ones were removed just when they had gained a good knowledge of their duties, their locale and the people in it. For example, between 4 March and 31 December 1893 in Britain alone the consul general and 18 of the 24 consuls were replaced.[66] Henry White, the former secretary of the Embassy in London, stated the obvious: 'It is impossible to suppose that such an upheaval was intended to benefit the Consular Service, or that it could have been otherwise than exceedingly detrimental to its efficiency.'[67] This example was replicated throughout the Consular Service. Efficient consuls lived with the constant threat of removal hanging over them every four years. The method of their removal also left much to be desired. George Towle, commercial agent in Bradford, described the procedure as an 'affront – for it is nothing less – which is offered to him by a removal, not only without explanation, but without the least notice, a removal effected simply by the appearance at his desk of his successor demanding his chair'.[68] And if the consul had been in post for a few years he probably would have established good relations with the local community.

> Even those who are his friends and have esteemed him are constrained (arguing from their own official system) to suspect him of having forfeited the confidence of his government. Is he inefficient, has he embezzled, what can be his fault? Only a very few, abroad, understand the 'rotation-in-office' system; and the effect is that the removed consul's reputation is in jeopardy when so curtly dismissed without a reason.[69]

Little wonder, therefore, that morale in the Service was low. Towle was taken aback at the manner in which he was replaced and sent an urgent cable to Secretary of State Hamilton Fish (1869–1877), saying 'Reported suspended, why? Assured safe through [Senator] Fessenden.' He was unaware that his successor, W. Yates Selleck, had been given the post a month earlier.[70] Handovers were often not smooth and David Gould complained that when he tried to take up his appointment in Leith his predecessor, Neil McLachlan, 'declined to accede to my request and became very angry and offensive, virtually excluding me from the office.' This may, however, have been caused by the usual delay in the new consul receiving his exequatur, or official approval, from the British authorities.[71] David C. Davies, commercial agent at Swansea, was another who did not take kindly to the manner of his removal. In a lengthy letter to the Department he said: 'I wish to enter my solemn PROTEST against this act of eviction,' adding, 'I incurred expenses that I would not have done, had I believed the office subject to the caprice of political exegences [sic].' He refused to hand over the consulate to his successor and became embroiled in an increasingly bitter exchange of correspondence with the Department, the Board of [Civil Service] Commissioners, his successor and the vice consul. His successor, Griffith W. Prees, informed the Department that 'there was nothing left for me to do, but to assert my authority in a gentlemanly but firm manner and take possession of everything [...] and I am [now] in full control of the Consulate'.[72]

Those calling for consuls to be appointed only after undergoing rigorous written and oral examinations complained of the inadequacies of the American system, comparing it unfavourably with the high standards required by the major European countries. Some attempts had been made to introduce examinations but the standards and qualifications required were relatively low. In 1866 candidates for the Consular Service were supposed to sit examinations, 'Yet only one such examination was given, and then no more was heard of the matter.'[73] State Department regulations laid down that 'No candidate [for a consulship] will be appointed until he has been examined and found qualified by a board consisting of three examiners, selected by the head of the department.'[74] The regulations also specified topics for the written examination. At last, it seemed that only suitably qualified candidates would be eligible for appointment. Not so, however, according to a consul writing in 1872. The board of examiners was non-existent, and 'it would be difficult to find any American consul appointed within twenty years, who had ever seen this board, or who had ever heard of it outside of the [consular] manual'. Moreover, no written examination was proposed to this particular consul and he knew of no consul who had ever undergone one.[75] He describes how he was received when presenting himself at the State Department, expecting to be examined by the board. Anticipating some official welcome after having been appointed to high office he was met instead by an uninterested clerk who paused in his task of 'putting enormous wax seals on an enormous white package' long enough to direct him to the consular bureau. There, 'a pleasant gentleman' chats with him 'about his consulship, dilates on the climate, the wines, the people, the theatres' at the proposed consular post. When 'asked about the examinations and instructions' the gentleman 'laughs a subdued, amiable laugh' and says 'here are the late consul's despatches, you may look through them if you like; and here is the manual, which you had better run your eye over at the hotel in the course of to-night or to-morrow.' 'Is that all', the consul enquired. 'Well, yes, about all.'[76] Henry White, while criticizing the general standards of consuls, had nothing but praise for those appointed to Britain, many of whom he had known and regarded as efficient. He added: 'We usually send, however, men of ability and good standing to that country, where in any case their efficiency cannot be impaired by ignorance of the language.'[77] In 1895, an Executive Order was issued requiring that certain consular vacancies had to be filled by examination. However the standard of the examination was gradually lowered and 'the oral and most important part [...] was [...] later discontinued altogether'.[78] In the written examination, 'questions were simple. A candidate might be asked to define a consular invoice or to name the capital of the country to which he was about to be assigned. It was said that only one man failed out of the 112 who were sent to be examined.'[79]

In 1906, almost 130 years after appointing its first consular officer, the United States finally began to put its Consular Service on a professional footing and to bring it largely into line with the long-established consular services of the major European powers. On 5 April 1906, Congress approved 'An Act to provide for the reorganization of the consular service of the United States.'[80] The driving forces behind this were the newly appointed Secretary of State Elihu Root (1905–1909) and Senator Henry Cabot Lodge of Massachusetts.[81] The act's main provisions were: consuls general and consuls were grouped into classes of seven and nine respectively; a corps of five consuls general was created who would conduct inspections of consulates at least once in every two years; consuls general, consuls or consular agents receiving salaries of more than $1,000 a year were not permitted to engage in trade or practise as lawyers; fees received by all consular officers (with the exception of consular agents) had to be paid to the Treasury, their sole compensation was to be their salaries; in the case of consular agents, they were to be paid one half of the fees received in their agencies, up to a maximum of $1,000. The grade of commercial agent was abolished. In the case of staff based in Britain and Ireland, the consul general in London was graded as class one, at an annual salary of $12,000. The classifications and salaries of the consuls were as follows:

	1906 Classes and salaries of consuls in Britain and Ireland								
Town	One $8K	Two $6K	Three $5K	Four $4.5	Five $4K	Six $3.5K	Seven $3K	Eight $2.5K	Nine $2K
Belfast			X						
Birmingham				X					
Bradford						X			
Bristol									X
Burslem							X		
Cardiff								X	
Cork								X	
Dublin					X				
Dundee					X				
Dunfermline							X		
Edinburgh						X			
Glasgow				X					
Huddersfield							X		
Hull								X	
Leeds								X	
Liverpool	X								
Manchester		X							
Newcastle upon Tyne							X		
Nottingham				X					
Plymouth								X	
Sheffield							X		
Southampton				X					
Swansea							X		

Source: Compiled by author from State Department Registers.

President Roosevelt issued an Executive Order on 27 June setting out regulations for the selection of consuls general and consuls that laid down that vacancies for consuls general and consuls above class eight would be filled by promotion from the lower grades, based upon ability and efficiency as shown in the service. Vacancies for classes eight and nine consuls would be based on promotion of clerks, vice consuls, deputy consuls, consular agents, student interpreters and interpreters in the consular or diplomatic services who had been appointed after examination. A board of examiners for admission to the consular service was established, candidates had to be American citizens between 21 and 50 years of age, and entrance examinations would include at least one foreign language, commerce of the United States, political economy, elements of international, commercial and maritime law. In making appointments, regard would be made to ensuring proportional representation of all the states, and no account would be taken of candidates' political affiliations. Regulations governing the examinations were issued later in the year, which stated that candidates who achieved an average mark of 80 per cent would be placed on a list for two years from which appointments would be made, and any who had not been appointed after two years would have to go through the whole process again. Detailed information about consular duties was also issued. A little-heralded but important improvement was the introduction of a uniform tariff of fees that consuls could charge for services they performed. This was reinforced by issuing them with adhesive official stamps printed with the equivalent money value of the fees; these had to be affixed to all documents, and then cancelled and were to be accounted for quarterly. Their introduction was intended to stop the fairly widespread practice of consuls deciding the level of fees they should charge. As fee revenue was an important part of some consuls' incomes, therefore the practice was open to abuse. The stamps, whose values ranged from 25 cents to $20, were used from 1906 until 1955, when they were discontinued.

Shortly after taking office, Secretary of State Elihu Root (1905–1909) established an efficiency record for each consul and this was the yardstick against which an individual's career prospects were measured. Wilbur Carr, Chief of the Consular Bureau, and a long-time campaigner for a professional Consular Service, was in no doubt about the value of the efficiency record.

> It is no longer sufficient that a consul should be able merely to exhibit a clean record free from complaints or criticisms. He must now produce positive results of more than average character if he would be rated relatively high in the scale of efficiency. He may no longer rest content in the knowledge that his friends at home will aid him in a desire to reach higher rank. [...] The only friend of real service to him now is a record of efficient and faithful performance of duty.[82]

We shall see in the next chapter how the inspection reports carried out by the consuls general at large took account of a consul's efficiency at his post. At last, the tide was turning and the Consular Service was beginning to attract and retain able men, many of whom were not replaced when the administration changed. A secure career path opened for able individuals. Wilbur Carr took a strong stand against patronage, which, although it did not disappear completely, began to reduce. Consuls began to play a positive role in encouraging and promoting trade and the overall improvement was welcomed by the business community. One senior businessman, Edward N. Burns, wrote to William Jennings Bryan (1913–1915) the newly appointed secretary of state who had a reputation for forcing officials to resign: 'Such a vast improvement has taken place in the personnel and ability of our Consuls, due we believe largely to the efforts of the present head of that service, Mr Wilbur Carr, that we urge you to continue him in that position.'[83] Almost ten years after the 1906 Act, several changes were made by the 1915 Act.[84] For example, some improvements were made to salaries, consuls general and consuls could be seconded to the State Department for a three-year period without, as previously, having to resign from the Service then seek reappointment at the end of the secondment, and consuls general and consuls were appointed to classes rather than to posts.

A Unified Foreign Service

Morale in the Service had begun to increase, to the extent that one official felt able to write to Carr in 1922: 'The British have Lloyd's agents scattered throughout the world [...]. We have no such agencies but we have the most efficient consular service in the world.'[85] The 1906 Act remained essentially unchanged until 1924. In that year a major piece of legislation was enacted, which radically changed the organizational structure and working practices of the diplomatic and consular services, which continues to the present. As has been mentioned earlier, these were discrete services, with little or no cross-transferability of personnel. The question of having a unified foreign service had been under consideration for some time, particularly by Republican Representative John Jacob Rogers of Massachusetts who had introduced bills on this in 1919 and 1921, neither of which had been successful. Undaunted, he resubmitted an amplified version of his bill in 1922, which, after considerable and protracted deliberation, was passed on 24 May 1924.[86] Rogers was assisted throughout the passage of the bill by Wilbur Carr, who was a keen advocate of an amalgamated service, and he also had the strong support of Secretary of State Charles Evans Hughes (1921–1925) and Robert Peet Skinner, the consul general in London. It was not all plain sailing, however. The bill was opposed by many officers in the diplomatic service. One minister 'reflected the common opinion among most of the diplomatic secretaries' that 'the Rogers bill was the destruction of the diplomatic service'. His view remained unchanged some 30 years later; as he saw it, 'the difficulty was a difficulty of vanity'. This was 'Largely due to the social ambitions of the wives of some consular officers, who did not receive the recognition accorded to diplomatic officers and their wives in foreign capitals.'[87]

The most important and lasting effect of the act was amalgamating the separate Diplomatic and Consular Services into a single Foreign Service on an interchangeable basis. Staff below the grade of minister were designated as Foreign Service Officers and were graded into nine classes (and one unclassified) for salary purposes, the salaries ranging from $9,000 to $1,500; all appointments would be to a class and not as before to a particular post, which meant that staff would be able to transfer from one post to another without suffering a reduction in salary, as in the past. Officers could be assigned for duty to the State Department without loss of their class or salary; and the grade of consular assistant was abolished. For the first time, a retirement and disability system was established; the absence of a previous scheme explains why so many consuls up to that time had felt obliged to work well beyond a normal retirement age. The position of Director of the Consular Service, which Carr had held from 1909, was abolished and replaced by an additional assistant secretary of state post to which he was appointed. The practice of requiring all officers to give a bond was retained against sureties who would be liable for a sum not less than the officer's annual compensation if his performance failed to measure up. Remarkably, the bond requirement was not abolished until 1956.[88] Before the act, the practice in capital cities was to have separate consular and diplomatic offices, but under the new unified system both offices were brought together in the same building. The consulate general in the capital became the embassy's consular section. Foreign Service staff could now be commissioned as diplomatic or consular officers, or both, and depending on their roles would hold the titles of counselor and consul general, first secretary and consul, or third secretary and vice consul. The first part of the title denoted their diplomatic rank, the second their consular rank. By the early 1980s, the chief of an embassy consular section, in other words the consul general, held the title of counselor for consular affairs, and by the late 1980s this was changed to minister-counselor for consular affairs. This is the current practice.[89] Rogers unfortunately did not live long enough to see the successful impact of his bill; he died 10 months later on 28 March 1925.[90] Traditions die hard, however, and the new unified Foreign Service took several years to bed in. Many members of the former Diplomatic Service, in particular, were unhappy with the new system but eventually general acceptance was gained.[91]

The Role of Women

Just as in many other areas of public life, women were not allowed to enter government service, especially to a branch whose staff were employed mainly overseas. Several had tried to join the Department as early as 1833 and the Consular Service as early as 1867, but were refused. There were two isolated examples of a woman acting in a temporary capacity for a few weeks. During the Civil War, Thomas H. Dudley, the consul at Liverpool, asked E. S. Eggleston, the consul at Cadiz, Spain, 'to assist him in obtaining evidence regarding the iron rams being built in Glasgow for the Confederacy'. Further discussion on this topic is set out in Chapter 5. Since Dudley wanted Eggleston without delay, Eggleston notified the Department that 'I shall take the liberty of leaving my Consulate for that purpose. [...] The Consulate will be under the superintendency of Mrs H S Eggleston during my absence.'[92] And when Bernard Peel Chenoweth, the consul in Canton, China, in 1870, died, his wife Mrs C. V. D. Chenoweth took over for a week and submitted the required quarterly reports.[93] However, the situation within the Department slowly changed; in 1874, 5 of the 13 clerk positions were filled by women, and between 1878 and 1909, 31 further women were hired as clerks, one of whom had attended college in Edinburgh. One woman who entered the Department in 1901 recalled working with 'three elderly ladies wearing powdered blond wigs and colorful Victorian-style dresses with long, sweeping trains'.[94]

As far as working in consulates was concerned, by 1918 a number of women were employed as clerks in consulates, but they were not permitted to be appointed as vice consuls.[95] By early 1922 it was noted that a number of women had applied for positions in the Consular Service and the Diplomatic Service but none had passed the entrance examinations. However, in July of that year three women were deemed eligible to take the Diplomatic Service examination. One of them, Lucile Atcherson, was successful in both the written and oral parts, and thus became the first woman Diplomatic Service officer in the history of the Department. She was assigned initially to the Division of Latin American Affairs until 1925 when she was posted to the Legation at Berne, Switzerland. In 1927 she was posted to Panama and later that year resigned in order 'to make final preparations for her January [1928] wedding'.[96] The first examination after the 1924 Rogers Act merging the Consular and Diplomatic Services into a unified Foreign Service was held in January 1925. One woman, Pattie Field, passed the examinations and was assigned as vice consul at the Consulate General in Amsterdam.[97] William H. Gale, the consul general had read newspaper reports of the appointment before he received notification from the Department, and in a telegram on 3 September 1925 to the Department said: 'If true earnestly advise reconsideration and suggest assignment to a post having larger staff where appropriate duties could be arranged. A woman would not fill the requirements here and would be worse than useless.'[98] His objections were overruled and he was informed that Miss Field 'was believed qualified to perform the duties of a vice consul, and she neither expects nor should receive special treatment in the selection of these duties'.[99] Under Secretary Joseph C. Grew, wrote to Gale on 5 September in an attempt to soften the blow, saying: 'Miss Field is particularly fortunate in going to such a Chief as yourself, and I know that whatever may be your personal views with regard to the principle involved in the admission of women to the Foreign Service you will none the less give her the same sympathetic advice and support that you would give to any young man on your staff.'[100] What a diplomat! Pattie Field remained in Amsterdam until 1929 when she resigned to take up a position with the National Broadcasting Company.[101]

A slow trickle began, and in 1928 Frances E. Willis, the third female Foreign Service Officer to be appointed (on 29 August 1927) was assigned as vice consul at Valparaiso. She had an impressive career and later held ambassadorships to Switzerland, Norway and Ceylon.[102] Also in 1928, Margaret Warner passed the Foreign Service examination and was assigned to Geneva where she remained until resigning in 1931.[103] In 1929, Nelle Blossom Stogsdall was appointed a vice consul in Beirut, at that time in Syria. While there, she met and married John P. Summerscale, a vice consul in the British Consulate General, and resigned in 1931 to accompany him on his next posting.[104] He had a distinguished career in the British Foreign Service and was knighted on his retirement; Nelle therefore became Lady Summerscale. Constance Ray Harvey was assigned to Ottawa in 1930 as a vice consul; she retired in 1964 as consul general in Strasbourg and has the distinction of being the first woman to hold the rank of consul general.[105] Between 1930 and 1941, more than two hundred women were classed as eligible to take the Foreign Service examinations, however none passed both parts.[106] In the meantime,

Figure 3.1 Lucille Atcherson, first woman appointed to the US Diplomatic Service in 1922. She was born in 1894 in Columbus, Ohio. After graduation she worked as a university secretary before moving to France where she served from 1917 to 1921 with the American Committee for Devastated France, an aid organization. She sat and passed the Foreign Service examinations in 1922, becoming the first woman Diplomatic Service officer in the history of the Department. Her first assignment was in the Division for Latin American Affairs in Washington, DC, where she served until 1925 when she was transferred to the Legation in Berne. In February 1927, she was posted to the Legation in Panama but resigned a few months later in order to marry George Curtis, an American surgeon whom she had met while he was in Berne as part of a two-year research fellowship. They had two daughters. She died in 1986. This photograph was taken on 20 December 1922 and shows her outside the State Department dressed stylishly for a cold winter's day. [National Photo Company Collection, Library of Congress, Prints & Photographs Division, Reproduction Number LC-DIG-npcc-07575.]

the situation in the Department had continued to improve, and by 1940 there were 552 women employed there. After the Second World War, Betty Ann Middleton was the first woman to successfully complete both parts of the examination and was assigned as a vice consul in Hong Kong in November 1945.[107] From then onwards, women have continued

Figure 3.2 Pattie Hockaday Field, first woman to hold a consular appointment in 1925: a portrait. Field was born in Denver, Colorado, in 1901. After graduating from the University of Colorado, Radcliffe College, and the Ecole Libre des Sciences Politiques in Paris she passed the Foreign Service examinations in 1925. She was assigned as vice consul at the Consulate General in Amsterdam despite the objections of the Consul General, William H. Gale, who was overruled by the Department; she thus became the first woman to hold a consular appointment. She resigned in 1929 in order to accept a post with the National Broadcasting Company (NBC). This photograph shows her as the lone woman in a group of graduating consular officers. It was taken on the steps of the then State Department on 5 June 1925, although the graduation was on 1 September. [National Photo Company Collection, Library of Congress, Prints & Photographs Division, Reproduction Number LC-DIG-npcc-27089.]

to play an increasing role in the Foreign Service and to hold senior appointments at all levels.

In terms of their appointment to consulates in Britain women gradually entered as vice consuls. The first to do so was Imogene E. Ellis who was appointed to Belfast in October 1944 at the relatively old age of almost thirty-eight. Although she was born in Kansas she went to the University of Montana for her Bachelor's degree, then to Columbia University in New York for her Master's and finally to American University in Washington, DC. She moved once more, to Spokane, Washington, where she was a teacher for 12 years, then back to Washington, DC, as an assistant librarian in the Library of Congress and finally as an assistant in the Navy Department before joining the State Department as a clerk in the Foreign Service Auxiliary. After Belfast her postings were to

Figure 3.3 Pattie Hockaday Field. This photograph is dated 2 September 1925 and shows her outside the then State Department shortly before her assignment to Amsterdam. [National Photo Company Collection, Library of Congress, Prints & Photographs Division, Reproduction Number LC-DIG-npcc-14433.]

consulates in Europe but, despite her impressive university education, she never attained a higher position than that of vice consul for the rest of her career. The next women were Nathalie Boyd and Edith A. Ingle (later, Edith Stensby) who were assigned as vice consuls to London in January and May 1945, respectively. Frances Meadows was assigned to Manchester in July 1945, and in May 1946 Norah Alsterlund was assigned to London, both as vice consuls. The following month, also in London, Kathleen Molesworth was the first to be appointed to the more senior rank of second secretary/consul and in 1949 was promoted once more, to first secretary/consul and held this rank until she retired from the Foreign Service in 1955 while in London.[108] In 1947, two more women were appointed: Frances E. Willis as first secretary/consul in London and Mary E. Volz as vice consul in Liverpool. Nina Belle Bradley and Harriet C. Thurgood were appointed as vice consuls in London in 1949, and in the following year Mary W. Mackenzie was appointed vice consul in Liverpool. Other women were appointed in 1954 and 1956 as vice consuls in London. In 1959, Ange Belle Hassinger was appointed as vice consul in Liverpool and Alice T. Curran as consul in Manchester. Marguerite Whitehead was appointed as vice consul in Birmingham in 1960. After this the appointment of women to consular posts was unremarked and was taken for granted.[109] Curran, recently widowed, transferred to Birmingham in 1963 and was promoted to consul general in 1965, becoming the first woman to hold that rank in an American consulate in Britain and at the time one

Figure 3.4 Nelle Blossom Stogsdall and Margaret Warner, both early consular appointees. Stogsdall, on the left, was born in Omaha, Nebraska, in 1905. After graduating from Wellesley, the Ecole Libre des Sciences Politiques in Paris, Columbia University and Columbia Law School she worked for a year as researcher for the Council on Foreign Relations. In 1929, she passed the Foreign Service examinations and was assigned to the Foreign Service School. Her first, and only, assignment was as vice consul in Beirut from 1929 until 1931. While there, she met and married John P. Summerscale, a vice consul in the British Consulate General, and resigned in order to accompany him to his next posting. He had a distinguished career in the British Foreign Service and was knighted on retirement. Nelle therefore became Lady Summerscale. Warner, on the right, was born in Lincoln, Massachusetts, in 1904. After graduating from Radcliffe College she passed the Foreign Service examinations in 1929. Like most new entrants, she was assigned briefly to the Foreign Service School before transferring to Geneva, where she served from 1929 until she resigned in 1931. This photo taken on 10 May 1929 shows both women sitting outside the then State Department building shortly before being transferred overseas. [National Photo Company Collection, Library of Congress, Prints & Photographs Division, Reproduction Number LC-DIG-npcc-17526.]

of only two women in the Service to hold that rank; the other was Eileen Donovan in Barbados.[110] The Edinburgh consulate general has been headed by women since 1992 when Bobette Orr was appointed. The Belfast consulate general has also regularly been headed by women, one of whom, Barbara J. Stephenson, later held the top US diplomatic post in the United Kingdom; she was Deputy Chief of Mission at the Embassy in London until August 2013.[111] She was succeeded in that post by another woman, Elizabeth L. Dibble.

Throughout the history of American overseas representation, women have played an important and unsung role in supporting their consul and diplomat husbands socially, as well as acting as housekeeper and hostess managing a household, often with young children and on a fairly limited budget. Some paid a price for making hazardous transatlantic crossings which could take several weeks. Their stay in Britain was often dogged with ill health caused by the differences in climate and environmental conditions between the two countries and several had to return to the United States. A few died, as did some of their young families, but their stories were seldom recounted or recorded. A relatively recent one was written by Helga Ruge, whose husband, Neil, was consul in Cardiff from 1956 to 1958. She recalls: 'I did my share of entertaining, opening bazaars, making speeches to women's clubs, presenting diplomas, hoisting the Pakistani flag on their national day, and picking up a few words of Welsh from our Welsh friends. The gossip columnist of the local newspaper was so hard up for news she visited me several times.'[112]

Amalgamation of the State Department and the Foreign Service

During World War Two the Foreign Service was enlarged and encountered many new challenges, and it was clear that after hostilities had ended further change was required. The Foreign Service Act of 1946 was a codifying act, replacing all previous legislation.[113] Many of its provisions were administrative and organizational structural improvements. For example, the post of Director General of the Foreign Service was created; there were improvements in recruitment and training of personnel, and improvements in salaries and allowances. The next significant change was the amalgamation of the State Department and the Foreign Service. The majority of the Department's staff were members of the Civil Service, although, as we have seen, Foreign Service Officers could be seconded to the State Department, but the two bodies continued to function as separate entities. It did not make sense, however, for the department responsible for the nation's foreign policy to be separate from the service and staff who implemented that policy around the world. Change was needed. In 1954, a committee chaired by Henry Wriston, issued a highly critical report of this arrangement and of the management of the Foreign Service and recommended integration of the State Department and the Foreign Service.[114] Departmental staff whose jobs involved foreign policy (such as geographical desk officers) would become Foreign Service Officers; staff who did not come within this definition (such as administrators or librarians) would remain as members of the Civil Service. The merger of the State Department and the Foreign Service was completed in 1957.[115] Several Foreign Service acts followed, dealing with topics such as improvements and amendments to conditions of service, salaries, increases in the number of classes of Foreign Service Officers, medical benefits and retirement and disability provisions. The next major legislation was the Foreign Service Act of 1980.[116] It is the last major legislative reform of the Foreign Service, incorporating the reforms of the 1924 and 1946 Acts and bringing the terms and conditions of service up to the standards required of a modern service. The 1980 Act, as amended, remains the legislative bedrock of the Foreign Service.

The Present Day

Fairly recent developments have included the creation of American Presence Posts (APP) and Virtual Presence Posts (VPP), both of which are offshoots of local embassies. These are cost-effective initiatives to show the flag in places beyond capital cities where it might not otherwise be financially viable to do so. Use is made of modern information technology and both initiatives have dedicated websites. APPs began in 1998 and are the brainchild of Felix Rohatyn when he was Ambassador to France. They are operated by one diplomat and are regarded as consulates under the Vienna Convention on Consular Relations 1963. They provide limited consular assistance to American citizens, explain US policy locally and assist American businesses that may be trying to break into the local market. There are no APPs in the United Kingdom. VPP are not regarded as consulates and have no resident staffs but receive regular visits from a designated officer from the embassy. They do not provide any visa or passport services or American citizens services. There is one VPP in the United Kingdom, in Cardiff, which receives regular visits from an embassy officer designated as Welsh Affairs Officer.[117] Writing about the Cardiff VPP in 2001, Ambassador Philip Lader described the benefits thus:

> Under an arrangement with a business center, the VPP has a permanent local address and telephone number linked to the Embassy. It is staffed by a Foreign Service officer based in London, who travels to the VPP region on a regular basis, using an office in the business center to hold meetings, conduct seminars, and carry out other contact activities. When the officer is in London, phone inquiries and correspondence are automatically forwarded to his or her desk. A VPP webpage on the Embassy website lists contact information and publishes outreach information.

He also listed the financial benefits. 'The VPP Cardiff offers focused local representation at an annual operating cost of less than $30,000 per year, considerably less than an estimated $650,000 required to operate a consulate or $134,000 for an American Presence Post.'[118]

One retired senior Foreign Service Officer has floated the idea of the Foreign Service reverting to pre-Rogers days and re-creating a separate Consular Service. He sees the advantages being that consular work would be run entirely by consular officers, that income from visa fees would enable it to be self-financing and promotion prospects would be improved. Unsurprisingly, his suggestion has not been taken up. His case is rather weakened by the fact that he cites as exemplars the United Kingdom and Germany, both of which, he said, have separate diplomatic and consular services. On the contrary, neither of these countries has had such a system for very many years.[119]

We have seen, therefore, that after its shaky start at the end of the eighteenth century the Consular Service was immediately faced with a considerable number of problems, such as the cronyism rife under the spoils system, the relatively high number of unsuitable and unqualified candidates seeking and obtaining consular appointments under that system, frequent criticism from the public and the business world of the standards of the services provided by consuls and the almost total change of personnel every time that there was a change in the administration in Washington. Things had to change. The Department and the early Consular Bureau did manage eventually to deal with all of these difficulties. Carrying out the necessary changes required frequent legislation, beginning in 1792 and continuing up to the twentieth century. Other challenges faced along the way and dealt with successfully included frequent calls for reform, professionalizing the service by introducing entrance examinations for persons interested in a consular career, changing the piecemeal system of payments to consuls, introducing an inspection system to check the efficiency of consuls and their consulates, integrating with the separate Diplomatic Service to form the unified Foreign Service, admitting women to what had traditionally been a male career organization and embracing new technologies. Consuls today still continue to carry out many of the functions and duties undertaken by their earlier colleagues but against a modern backdrop. The next chapter focuses on American consular activities in Britain, when they began, how they expanded and later contracted, the nature of consuls' duties, the problems they and their families experienced, as well as other aspects of the consular life.

Part 2

Chapter Four

US CONSULAR REPRESENTATION IN BRITAIN

The American Constitution came into effect in 1789. On 4 June of the following year, the first nominations for consular appointments to Britain were made. These initial appointments were the forerunners of a network of offices that would eventually extend from the Orkney Islands in the north of Scotland to the Channel Islands off the south coast of England. The activities of the consuls brought new challenges for the Consular Service, many of them dealing with topics that nowadays would be described as personnel or human resource related. Later, consuls would experience the same dangers as the British population during two world wars. This chapter discusses a number of topics that taken together give a broad overview of the many different facets of American consular activities and life.

The Extent of the Consular Network

The first American consular appointments to Britain were approved by the Senate in June 1790. They were James Maury of Virginia as consul at Liverpool; William Knox of New York as consul at Dublin; and Thomas Auldjo, an Englishman, as vice consul at Cowes. Two months later, in August, Joshua Johnson of Maryland was approved as consul at London. However, Auldjo faced two additional hurdles. First, his nomination was postponed by the Senate because of initial concerns about appointing foreigners as consular officers – Auldjo was a British subject – but they gave their approval on 17 June. Second, his appointment was not recognized by the British government because there had never been a previous consular appointment in Cowes. Instead, it was intimated to him that if he were appointed to the nearby port of Poole his appointment would be recognized and the fact that he was living in Cowes 'would not be noticed'. He was therefore reappointed to Poole on 24 February 1791.[1] The honour of being first operational consul in Britain falls to Maury, who began reporting from Liverpool in September 1790, while Knox did not arrive in Dublin until November of that year.[2] Johnson in London did not begin reporting until 2 November.[3] By 1801, there were 16 consulates and consular agencies throughout Britain and Ireland.[4] Numbers increased slowly and in 1859 there were 21, but only 13 years later, in 1872, they had increased by an astonishing 148 per cent, to 52. This was due to two factors: the expanding influence of the United States and the continued increase in trading and mercantile activity between the two countries. Overall trading between them increased from £58.7 million in 1859 to £100.6 million in 1872.[5] The consul in Southampton alone reported that the tonnage of United States ships entering the port increased from 82,000 in 1852 to more than 100,000 two years later.[6]

Within the constituent regions of the United Kingdom the main increase in the consular presence took place in England, where the number of consulates and agencies functioning in 1859 increased from 11 to 34 by 1872; Scotland increased from 3 to 5 and Wales from 2 to 6, but Northern Ireland remained unchanged.[7] The total cost of administering the consular service in Britain in 1872 was just over $49,000.[8] The consular presence reached its peak by 1902, with a total of 61 offices, due largely to a doubling in Scotland (from 5 to 10). The extensive consular network (which included agencies) would eventually stretch from the Orkney Islands in the north of Scotland to the Channel Islands south of the English coast. However, as can be seen in the following table, numbers steadily decreased until the closure of the historic Liverpool consulate general on 28 May 1976 after 186 years of continuous service reduced the number to three.

Decline in numbers of American consular posts in the UK, 1902–1976

1902	1912	1922	1932	1942	1952	1962	1965	1975	1976
61	40	27	17	13	12	9	7	4	3

The surprisingly brief official announcement of the Liverpool closure said: 'The United States greatly values its long association with the city of Liverpool, but the Department of State regretfully has concluded that the post must be closed for reasons of economy.'[9] The consulate at Liverpool had been the premier post in the American Consular Service's firmament. Indeed, 'it was commonly understood that the Liverpool consulate paid more than any other United States foreign post and that only the ambassadorship to Great Britain had greater prestige'.[10] The generous level of remuneration may be gauged from the following remarks about US consular salary levels in 1871: 'The highest salary paid to [US] Consular officers is 7,500 dol., at the posts of London and Liverpool. [...] The lowest salary [...] is at Amsterdam and Stuttgardt [sic], being 1,000 dol.'[11] A proposal to close the consulate general in Edinburgh in 1995 was strongly opposed both in Scotland and the United States. Among those who voiced their opposition were former presidents Jimmy Carter and George H. W. Bush.[12] Three years later, a report by the US Audit Office suggested that Edinburgh was one of a number of low priority posts that could be considered for replacement by a consular agency, which would have been a much cheaper option but this too was resisted. The duties of consular agents are virtually identical to those of an honorary consul, an appointment that the United States does not have. However, an important difference is that unlike most countries' honorary consuls, American consular agents are regarded as part-time Foreign Service employees and receive a salary 'paid between 20 percent and 95 percent of one of the 14 step rates of class 06 of the Foreign Service Schedule'.[13] In 2017, the class 06 scale ranged from $39,954 to $58,674.[14] In 2017, apart from the consular section in the embassy (headed by the minister counselor for consular affairs/consul general), only the consulates general in Belfast and Edinburgh are still functioning. They celebrated their bicentenaries in 1996 and 1998, respectively.

Figure 4.1 Every consulate and embassy displays an official coat of arms at or near its entrance. It consists of the Coat of Arms of the United States with the designation of the post. These photographs show examples for a consulate and a consulate general. [Consulate: Anna Girvan, Information Resource Center, US Embassy, London; Consulate General, author's collection.]

Appointments

As we have seen, consuls received their appointments as a result of unashamedly touting for them, either personally or through the intervention of others, and by calling in political favours. This produced a rash of candidates who were completely unqualified for their duties. Many were unable to speak or understand the language of the country to which they were sent, and relied totally on their local clerk who often in effect ran the office for them. At least for those candidates sent to Britain there was no language problem and the calibre of candidates was generally higher than those sent elsewhere. However, the formal written and oral tests introduced in 1895 did much to weed out ungifted, unsuitable amateurs and to introduce professional standards that are the hallmark of today's Foreign Service Officers.

Consular officers were appointed to grades that reflected the importance of their positions in their consular post. In descending order these were consul general, consul, commercial agent, vice consul, deputy consul, vice commercial agent, consular agent and consular clerk. Consuls general, consuls and commercial agents were appointed by the president and received commissions from him, while all other post holders were appointed by the consular officer in charge of their office. Thomas Auldjo, the vice consul at Poole mentioned earlier, was an exception, as he was appointed by the president. How this relatively unknown merchant in Cowes, on the Isle of Wight, had come to the president's notice is explained by the fact that Thomas Jefferson on relinquishing the post of Minister Plenipotentiary to France on 26 September 1789 stopped off at Cowes the following month on his return journey to America and stayed with Auldjo who 'had not only entertained and lodged Jefferson, but had also helped procure protection for Jefferson's belongings from the prying eyes of the Cowes customs service. Jefferson commented that Auldjo had given him "every possible attention and friendly assistance" and was sufficiently impressed to recommend him [to the president] as Consul for the United States at Cowes.'[15] Jefferson became the first secretary of state in March 1790 and it was he who wrote to Auldjo offering him the consular post. Clearly on good terms with Jefferson, Auldjo wrote to him on 4 November 1790 'to offer to you my sincere thanks for your kindness and friendship in recommending me to the Service of the United States of America'.[16] And on 14 September 1801, by which time Jefferson had become president, he wrote to him again, beginning his letter: 'Having had the honor & advantage of your friendship & protection now for a considerable number of years.'[17] Although from the outset it was laid down that only American citizens could be appointed to the senior grades this did not always prove practicable or possible. As we have seen, Auldjo was a British citizen as were members of the Fox family in Falmouth. Concerns about employing foreign nationals as consuls or their deputies began to exercise the State Department. During the Civil War, Secretary of State William H. Seward drew attention to the large volume of confidential correspondence between the Department, its consuls and the Navy Department about 'rebel privateers, the fitting out of blockade runners, and equipping of vessels-of-war in foreign countries'. For this reason he stressed that it was imperative that 'the chief clerk in each of the principal consulates should be a thoroughly loyal American citizen, fitted at any moment, in case of the sickness, absence, death, or temporary disability of the consul, to take his place and discharge faithfully his duties'.[18] Nothing was done about this, and indeed during Consul Thomas Dudley's temporary absence from the highly important Liverpool consulate during the war he asked his British deputy, Henry J. Wilding, to give all the evidence collected about the infamous *Alabama* warship to the local customs collector.

Bonds for the faithful performance of duties were required for grades from consul general to vice commercial agent inclusive, but not for consular agents and below. In 1871 the amounts ranged from $10,000 to $3,000 for senior grades, and $2,000 for vice consuls and vice commercial agents. The bonds were in the names of two guarantors, or sureties, who were liable financially for the amount of the bond if the consular officer's performance fell below the level expected. These documents were not merely formalities. Occasionally, but not often enough given the level of incompetence of some consuls, action was taken when it was thought that a consul had not carried out his duties satis-factorily, particularly in relation to financial matters. In 1886, Adam Badeau, formerly consul general in London, successfully contested an action on his official bond brought against him by the State Department. The Department sought to recover from him approximately $10,500 that he had received as fees while serving as consul general in London from 1870 to 1881. However, Badeau proved that these were for notarial fees, which were unofficial and therefore belonged to him. They were for 'services done for private individuals in private business and not under the authority of the US govern-ment, and were for use in the individual states of the Union, and under the state laws'.[19] It was a good example of the difference between his status as a federal officer of the United States undertaking official duties and as a private individual undertaking non-official work for gain. This distinction is no longer permitted. Surprisingly, the bond requirement was not abolished until as late as 1956. Appointments were usually cleared in advance with the Foreign Office in London; the State Department then issued the individual with a consular commission (often via the legation or embassy) and the Foreign Office arranged for an exequatur signed by the monarch or a senior official to be issued to the individual (again, via the legation or embassy).[20] In the case of consuls, the Home Office would then notify the mayor or, in Scotland, provost of the town or city in which the consulate was located, and request them to arrange for the various local civic and commercial authorities to recognize the consul.

Consuls' Functions and Duties

Broadly speaking, consuls' duties relate to protecting US citizens, 'showing the flag', and monitoring American commercial and political interests in their districts. Other duties include issuing passports, performing notarial functions relating to the personal estates of deceased Americans, and granting and attesting various certificates. From the outset, however, duties were linked inextricably to shipping and mercantile matters. A few examples will show how varied and detailed these were. Consuls were responsible for the relief of shipwrecked or destitute sailors, were obliged to pay them a small daily main-tenance sum and to arrange for masters of American ships sailing for home to trans-port them free of charge. Healthy individuals were required to work for their passage. The arrivals and departures of American ships and their cargoes had to be reported. If a mutiny or serious disturbance occurred on an American vessel, consuls had to take depositions and arrange for offenders to be sent to America for trial. They were also responsible for arranging the salvage of shipwrecked American vessels and making an inventory of their cargoes. Masters of American ships were legally obliged to hand over ships' papers, which included the register and the crew list, to the consul on arriving in the port. The consul issued a receipt and retained the papers until the captain received a clearance certificate from the port's authorities; on presenting this to the consul he received his ship's papers and could then be on his way once a consular fee was paid. As part of safeguarding seamen's rights and responsibilities consuls had to certify whether the men had been discharged, taken on or deserted. There was also a document known as a Seamen's Protection Certificate, which proved that the individual was an American citizen and included distinguishing details to identify him. This was a vitally important document because of the Royal Navy's wartime practice in the late eighteenth and early nineteenth centuries of boarding foreign vessels, removing any crew members it suspected of being British and pressing them into service, which, for some, could lead to their deaths. In June 1792 Secretary of State Thomas Jefferson warned Thomas Pinckney, the newly appointed American Minister in London, that 'the peculiar custom in England, of impressing seamen on every appearance of war, will occasionally expose our seamen to peculiar oppressions and vexations. These will require your most active exertions and protection, which we know cannot be effectual without incurring considerable expence'. Jefferson was, however, strongly opposed to the idea that seamen should 'carry about them certificates of their citizenship' which, he said, was 'a condition never yet submitted to by any nation'.[21] Many American seamen were originally British and had settled in America; some were deserters, but without a formal certificate proving they had become naturalized American citizens they were seized. It has been estimated that 'about 6,500 US citizens were pressed into the Royal Navy, of whom about 3,800 were subsequently released.'[22] Based on that estimate, some 2,700 US citizens served in the Royal Navy because they did not have acceptable proof of their citizenship. Impressment, as it was known, was one of the factors that led to the United States declaring war on Britain in 1812. Dealing with the consequences of impressment was a regular feature of American consuls' responsibilities, particularly in large ports such as Liverpool and London. Where they had satisfactory documentary proof that individuals were American, they took up cases with the Admiralty to secure their release. Two such individuals who had been seized and were serving on HMS *Victory* were released after the London consul success-fully proved their American citizenship.[23] It is tempting to wonder if later in life those two men regretted missing out on the *Victory*'s historic engagement at Trafalgar. The war between the United States and Britain was ended by the Treaty of Ghent in 1814, and led to considerable numbers of American prisoners of war being held in Britain.[24] Such was the volume of work involved in dealing with their repatriation that a consul with specific responsibility, Reuben G. Beasley, was appointed in London as Prisoner of War Agent.[25] Impressment ended in 1815, but the Seamen's Protection Certificates continued in use for other reasons until the twentieth century.

A major part of consuls' duties was compiling reports on their consulate district, showing its principal industries and exports, the surrounding climatic and social conditions, the general cost of living and similar information. These reports were sent to the Senate and were frequently published. There are too many to list, but two examples will suffice to show the nature of these reports. In the one for 1885, which gives reports from consulates around the world, there are four from Britain: Sheffield, Hull, Bristol and Belfast. The report from consul C. B. Webster of Sheffield, dated 10 October 1884, gives information about the nature and extent of local trade with the United States and includes a detailed report on the decline of the English steel industry. Consul Edward Howard's report from Hull, dated 24 December 1884, gives similar information about trade but includes additional information on numbers of ships owned in Hull, the fishing trade, water communication, street lighting, the Hull and Barnsley Railway and Dock Company, emigration, the state of public health and local industries. Consul Lorin

A. Lathrop of Bristol in his report dated 5 February 1885 gives a very detailed 11-page report on municipal government in England. Consul Arthur B. Wood of Belfast, in his report dated 19 January 1885, gives an equally detailed 10-page report on flax and linen statistics.[26] The format of the 1902 report is different, although it continues to cover all the Consular Service's offices worldwide. In the case of Britain and Ireland (at that time part of Britain) it gives information about offices in 57 towns. In addition to the usual trade and local industries figures it provides very detailed information about the consulates and their subordinate consular agencies: for example, their addresses and office hours, furniture and the educational and career backgrounds of all members of staff.[27]

A further important function, which continued well into the twentieth century, involved certifying the value of goods being shipped from consular districts to the United States. Lists of 'prices current' for local freight rates were displayed in the consulates, and exporters were required to submit detailed invoices giving a description of the goods, the name and location of the manufacturer, the name and location of the American recipient, the port of destination and the value of the goods. The consul had to certify that the values were correct so that the appropriate customs duty could be charged when the goods arrived in the United States. They charged a fee for this service, and at some posts the income from this could be considerable, especially for a non-salaried consul who was compensated solely from fees. For example, in the relatively small consular offices of Leith and Bradford, Leith collected $3,700 in 1866 and Bradford collected $15,500 in 1869 – sums equivalent to $56,900 and $278,000, respectively, in 2014.[28]

The focus of consuls' work has shifted since the Second World War from the mercantile trade to the interests of Americans living and travelling abroad. More Americans travel on holiday and on business than in past years and consuls now concentrate on providing 'citizen services'. This includes consular protection for US citizens; visa enquiries (this service is not provided at the Edinburgh Consulate General); processing passport applications; registering the births and deaths of American citizens; assisting families caught up in child abduction and custody cases; arrests and trials of American citizens; visiting Americans in prison; offering assistance and support to bereaved families in cases where an American citizen dies abroad; keeping the local American community updated on topics such as voting in presidential elections, social security, income tax, welfare matters, other federal benefits, news of cultural events and emergency arrangements. Consular fees remain an essential component of the State Department's annual revenue and are established primarily on a cost-recovery basis. Political reporting by consuls is equally important, particularly regarding topics within their consular district that might affect US policies or interests. They keep the political section of the embassy up to date on these matters.

In the early days of the consular service, supervision was fairly relaxed, with consuls reporting variously to the minister in London, the consul general in London, the secretary of state, and even on occasion the president. This probably reflected the political influence that some consuls had in the United States. While such a disorganized practice may have been acceptable when the consular establishment was small, it clearly was unacceptable and inefficient when the service grew larger. A formal procedure was therefore introduced. Up to the early 1920s there was only one consul general in Britain, based in London, who acted as superintending consul, and all consuls throughout the country were required to report to him or, in his absence, to the minister; those below the rank of consul reported to the consul in charge of their district. From the 1920s onwards, consuls general began to be appointed in other parts of the country; in date order these were at Liverpool, Belfast, Southampton, Glasgow, Edinburgh, Birmingham and Manchester. They reported to London, but also had the right to report directly to the State Department with copies to London. Nowadays, the ambassador ultimately oversees the consulates general in Edinburgh and Belfast and the Virtual Presence Post in Cardiff. Less well known, perhaps, is that he also oversees the consulate general in Hamilton, Bermuda.[29]

Inspection of Consulates

As has been mentioned, up to the early twentieth century there were no formal entrance requirements for consuls; they came from a variety of backgrounds and obtained their posts through political patronage. Also, there was a constant turnover because their appointments ceased whenever there was a change of administration. Their suitability, temperament and fitness for consular work were never questioned, and the manner and effectiveness of their conduct of consular business often left a great deal to be desired. Very little was done to monitor the administration of their consulates or to identify mismanagement, fraud and waste, although the Act of 1856 made a token gesture in this regard by setting out detailed regulations about how consular fees were to be recorded by consuls.[30] However, the Treasury Department had begun to send agents to audit the collection of fees and other financial revenue. Although the agents began to widen the scope of their investigations and looked at other aspects of the running of the consulates there were still no formal inspections of the work of consuls and their staffs. Nevertheless, they submitted critical reports about a number of consulates throughout the world. The consul in Liverpool from 1857 to 1861, Nathaniel Beverley Tucker, was severely criticized on several occasions. Writing in November 1861, the then Auditor John C. Underwood commented:

> Although [consuls] are required by law to report quarterly, I found [...] that the last salary report of the consul of so important a port as Liverpool was made March 31, 1858. [...] Since then he had strangely been permitted to hold on without reporting, spending all the funds he could reach, neglecting the payment of claims for food, clothing, and medical attendance of our sick and destitute seamen, and, by a course of plunder and profligacy unequaled in our consular history, contracting public and private debts, which I am informed by a neighboring consul probably exceed $200,000. It is perhaps some consolation to know that this plunderer no longer disgraces the Government abroad.[31]

The same consul was also singled out by Treasury Agent De B. Randolph Keim who reported in 1872 that:

> The conduct of Mr Tucker [...] was a subject of comment in the report of the Fifth Auditor of the Treasury [Underwood] for the year 1861. [...] The report does not do justice to the

subject in exposing that most notorious of official delinquents. I note this case especially in order to show what a consular service we have; that the highest and most responsible consulate should not only be given to the most eminently disqualified person, but that he should be permitted to hold it and plunder at will, until arrested in his iniquitous career by a timely change of administration at home.[32]

In a supplementary report he added:

Accountability to the Government was evidently the last consideration which entered his mind, and with a degree of extravagance perfectly astounding he squandered not only large sums of the public money, but contracted debts, both public and private, which must long remain a disgrace to the consular service for being capable of harboring such a person for so long a time.[33]

Such was the lack of personal accountability that, despite these damning reports, no action was taken against Tucker and on his return to the United States in 1861 he joined the Confederate Army. The following year he was sent to Britain by the Confederacy to purchase commissary supplies. Keim was also critical of several other consuls in Britain, observing that: 'The consular business at Glasgow, for some time prior to the arrival of the present officer, Mr Jenkinson, who arrived in 1869, seems to have been conducted either without reference to an accountability to the Government, or else without much regard for honesty. [...] The consular books under Mr Duff[34] were entirely beyond comprehension.'[35] He also drew attention to a practice at Glasgow 'which displayed a peculiar flexibility of conscience.' Consuls had been adding sundry items, such as coats, hats, boots, etc., in vouchers of an entirely different nature. Sometimes a voucher for stationery or relief for a destitute seaman would cover expenditures on account of a new wardrobe for the official representative of the government. The new consul, Jenkinson, 'had been compelled to decline several overtures of this kind from enterprising stationers and boarding-house keepers.' Referring to the consulate at Leeds, he noted: 'The books of this consulate under the predecessor of Mr Richards, the present consul, were badly kept.'[36] And, in relation to Leith, he remarked: 'The business of this consulate under the former consuls seemed to have received but little attention. The books, upon the arrival of the present officer, were in bad condition.'[37] Finally, regarding the situation in Cardiff, he commented: 'I should judge from the lack of books and accounts during the time that a Mr Birch officiated here, that that individual had carried off the books and papers with him. Some reports which he had made out had not been sent, and were found among the rubbish which he had left for his successor.'[38] Keim had a particularly good knowledge of the consular service and its failings (as well as its successes), as he had visited the service's principal consulates in Asia, Africa and South America before embarking on similar inspections in the British Isles and Europe. This had taken him more than two years, a considerable feat when one considers the transport facilities at the time.

During a four-month period in 1886, Thomas M. Waller, the consul general in London, inspected all the United States consulates, commercial agencies and some of the principal consular agencies throughout the British Isles (which at that time included Ireland).[39] He was the senior American consular officer in the country and had overall

Figure 4.2 Nelson T. Johnson, consul general at large, 1925. In 1922, Johnson was sent to Britain to conduct a full investigation into the circumstances that eventually led to the closure of the Newcastle consulate. At that time, he was a consul general at large. In the photograph, dated 29 June 1925, he looks pleased with himself; and rightly so, because two days later he took up his post as chief of the Division of Far Eastern Affairs. He was uniquely qualified for this, having spent the bulk of his earlier career in China where he held interpreter and consular posts throughout the country. He returned to China in 1929 as minister, then ambassador, remaining until 1941 when he was appointed as minister to Australia. He retired from the Foreign Service in that post in 1945. [National Photo Company Collection, Library of Congress, Prints & Photographs Division, reproduction no. LC-DIG-npcc-27065.]

responsibility for all the offices. He reported to the State Department that the US consular corps in Britain and Ireland at the time consisted of 116 men – 34 Americans and 82 'Englishmen'.[40] He listed all the personnel and said that this showed:

> several facts so creditable to the service as to deserve special mention. Since the beginning of
> the present national administration only eleven removals of consuls and five of vice-consuls

Figure 4.3 Ralph J. Totten, consul general at large, 1914; later, envoy extraordinary and minister plenipotentiary to South Africa, 1930–1937. Totten entered the Consular Service in 1908 at Puerto Plato in the Dominican Republic and became a consul general at large in 1914. He subsequently held several appointments as a consul general, including stints as an inspector, ending his career on a high note as Envoy Extraordinary and Minister Plenipotentiary to South Africa, a post he held from 1930 until his retirement in 1937. The photo is undated. [Harris & Ewing Collection, Library of Congress, Prints & Photographs Division, reproduction no. LC-DIG-hec-16433.]

have occurred in this country. The consuls who have not been removed have been on an average ten and one-half years, and the vice-consuls who have not been removed nine years in their present or other places in the Consular service. The thirty-two consular agents, thirty-one of whom are Englishmen have held their appointments on an average for more than ten years, and some of the thirty non-commissioned consular clerks, twenty-nine of whom are Englishmen, have been in the employ of our Government from twenty to thirty years, and the average time of service of the members of this force is between six and seven years. The ability and faithfulness of the consular corps in this country which these facts tend to prove are, it is submitted, more clearly shown by this record of my official inspection.[41]

In a largely uncritical report, he drew attention only to the statute that limited the rent for consulates to one-fifth of a consul's salary, saying that it operated in some cases to the disadvantage of the consul, if not to the service. Also, the regulation which forbade the cost of heating and lighting in consulates being met from government funds meant that those necessary expenses had to be met by consuls personally. He also felt that some office furniture would benefit from replacement.

Robert Adams, Jr, former US minister to Brazil, was one of the early proponents of a consular inspection system. Writing in 1893, he said, presciently:

> A novel feature [...] to increase the efficiency of the consular service might be the institution of several superintendents, whose duty it would be to visit the various consulates and inform the Department in relation to their true state, such as the proper location of the office, the state of the records, the correctness of accounts, as well as to ferret out abuses and inquire into any charge of misconduct, all of which can only be done by personal inspection.[42]

The State Department was aware of the general inadequacies of the consular service but, other than the occasional ad hoc reports referred to previously, had no formal means of knowing whether individual consulates or consuls fell short of what might reasonably be expected of them. Often the Department's only information came from complaints or criticisms made by Americans who had used their services. Most of the previous so-called inspections were often 'pleasure trips at public expense [...] under the guise of official visits' given by presidents to their friends. By 1906, they were regarded as 'usually out-and-out junkets'.[43] There were, of course, exceptions such as Underwood, Keim and Waller mentioned earlier.

In an attempt to improve matters, the 1906 Consular Reorganization Act, which dealt mainly with the classification, grading and salaries of consuls, created a corps of five inspectors of consulates, designated and commissioned as consuls-general at large with an annual salary of $5,000 plus travel and subsistence expenses.[44] All were experienced consular officers, and their job was to inspect consulates at least once every two years and report on them to the secretary of state. In cases where the president believed that the business of a consulate general or consulate was not being properly conducted he could authorize any consul-general at large to suspend the consul general or consul and administer the office in his place for up to ninety days. Each consul-general at large had responsibility for a geographical area; Horace Lee Washington was given responsibility for Europe, which included the British Isles.[45] The number of consuls-general at large was increased to seven by the Act of March 4, 1919. Wilbur Carr, Chief of the Consular Bureau, was the guiding light behind establishing this new corps of inspectors and ensuring that their work was conducted on a standardized, uniform footing. The resultant inspection reports, which can be examined in the National Archives, show the systematic approach adopted by the consuls-general at large. Pre-printed forms were drawn up, containing detailed lists of questions that were to be answered, one part by the inspector, the other by the principal officer in charge of each consulate. Information was collected on a comprehensive and detailed variety of topics, such as the office address; names, nationality and pay of the principal officer (consul) and his subordinate staff; the principal officer's state of health, marital status (including his wife's nationality and whether she played a supporting role), his children (if any), standing in the community, his scale of living (extravagant, appropriate or shabby) and his efficiency rating (poor, fair, good, very good or excellent). Broadly similar information was collected relating to the staff. Information was also sought on the number of American residents in the consular district; whether the consular office was necessary and justified by the commercial, industrial or political importance of the city; the numbers of invoices certified, notarial services provided, applications for visas (issued and refused), income from fees, letters received and sent, value of exports from the district to the United States; running costs of the office (salaries, rent, heating, lighting, cleaning); an inventory of office furniture, equipment, seals, flags and so forth; and suggestions as to how the efficiency of the office may be improved. Occasionally there was a sketch map of the office accommodation and a photograph or picture postcard of the building; and an overall rating was given for the office (poor, fair, good, very good or excellent). Inspectors were encouraged to be frank in their appraisals and some of their remarks were of a personal nature; these can be seen in the consulate histories later in the book. However, to give a small example, in the 1919 inspection report on the Stoke on Trent consulate, the inspector, Ralph J. Totten, noted in respect of consul Robert S. S. Bergh, a naturalized American of Norwegian birth who had been in post since 1912:

> Because of his extensive knowledge of languages he would serve to the greatest advantage in a Continental post [...]. His attractive daughter, with great linguistic ability, would be of a great help to him in such a post. [...] He is very ill with rheumatism and asthma. He will die if left another year at Stoke with its smoke and ever-lasting dampness. His wife, who was an attractive American, died two years ago. He is a widower with three children, one son and two daughters. The Inspector has not met the son, a soldier in the American Army, but the daughters contribute most favorably to his standing.[46]

Bergh was reassigned that year (1919) to the French overseas department of Guadeloupe, but did not take up the post, and was reassigned to Stavanger, Norway, where he died in 1923.

Inspectors were conscientious but their recommendations were often ignored, possibly because of the limited power to dismiss. Of necessity, they spent considerable periods of time travelling and living away from home. A letter by Heaton W. Harris, one of these officials, gives a good idea of the pressures of living out of a suitcase. Writing from Leeds in July 1911 to Herbert C. Hengstler, who had taken over from Wilbur Carr as Chief of the Consular Bureau in Washington in 1907, he reported:

> I am Sundaying at Leeds. I took Bradford first as Mr Ingram was to start on vacation yesterday. [...] Mr Chase leaves for New York on Tuesday morning. I am well along with his office and will finish tomorrow without difficulty [...]. As it will appear in my report on Nottingham finished today, I think the office has one too many men [...]. I am to do Huddersfield from here and then go to Manchester and from there to Liverpool unless some change of plan should be ordered. [...] I went to London for the Fourth [of July] Dinner and back the next morning. Mr Griffith's speech was the gem of the evening as to choice, language, applause,

etc. He like Mr Washington, Mr Mason, Mr Thackera, Mr Skinner and some others have been a constant help in what is, as you fully realize, a rather hard job. Not being a married man you are not able to realize quite how much it means to have one's family scattered around as is my own. However, it has been a pleasant experience not easily to be forgotten.[47]

Inspectors were fairly intrepid individuals, making their way around a country on their own with no supporting staff. It could also be dangerous. Robert Frazer, Jr, who appears in several of the consulate histories later in the book, carried out inspections in Britain in 1924 when his territorial area of responsibility at that time was the whole of Western Europe.[48] However, in January 1921, when his territory was South America, Central America, the West Indies and Curaçao,[49] he had to inspect a group of small consular offices on the north coast of Honduras. In order to reach these he arranged a passage on a small unreliable schooner that had been chartered by two Englishman who were travelling to Nicaragua. The boat was caught in storms, the sails were shredded, the masts were broken and it struck bottom off the coast. Frazer and his companions had to swim ashore in their underclothes and pyjamas, fighting against the surf and a powerful undertow. The schooner eventually sank and they lost all their clothes and possessions. They were given a few clothes and some food by friendly natives, but Frazer's only protection against the elements was a sack across his shoulders. He and his companions trudged five miles to the small town of Omon where he reported the situation to the State Department a week or so later and seemed none the worse for the experience.[50] He received compensation 'of $195.75 ... [which represented] the value of reasonable and necessary personal property lost'.[51]

When the 1924 Rogers Act merged the separate Consular and Diplomatic Services into a unified Foreign Service, the powers and duties of consuls-general at large were made applicable to Foreign Service inspectors who would inspect the work of offices in both the consular and diplomatic branches.[52] Prior to this, the Diplomatic Service had not been subject to inspection. Foreign Service inspections have continued since then, under various administrative titles, with the creation of an inspector general in 1957. Little of import occurred between then and 1980 when the Foreign Service Act of that year, the last major legislative reform of the Foreign Service, required the inspector general to inspect and audit at least every five years the administration of activities and operations of each Foreign Service post as well as each of the Department's bureaus and operating units, although this requirement is routinely waived every year by Congress.[53] Nowadays, regular and systematic inspections are carried out by the Department's Office of Inspector General (OIG), which inspects regularly approximately 260 embassies, diplomatic posts and international broadcasting stations throughout the world.[54] Redacted versions of the reports are available online via the State Department website. The OIG carried out inspections of the London embassy and its constituent consulates in Belfast and Edinburgh in 1989, 1993, 1999 and 2009. Information about the findings are shown in the consulate histories for Belfast and Edinburgh and Leith. A more recent inspection was made in 2015, but the consulates were excluded on that occasion and the findings related only to serious shortcomings in the contract procedures for the new embassy building which opened on 16 January 2018.[55]

Consulate Accommodation

As we have seen, more than two hundred years have passed since the first United States consulates were established in Britain, and at times they formed a large and active nationwide network. With a few exceptions, they were usually located in commercial areas of towns and cities as these were where their clientele were to be found, especially in ports. They were never housed in prestigious accommodation, but were generally located within a bank, stock exchange, wool exchange, Baltic Exchange or insurance company building in which rooms were rented to other tenants. Two notable exceptions are the remaining consulates general in Edinburgh and Belfast, both of which are housed in attractive accommodation. Since 1951, the Edinburgh office has been in an elegant Georgian terraced house designed by William Henry Playfair in a much sought-after residential area of the city. An indication of its value can be gauged from the fact that a similar house a few doors along was on the market in May 2007 for offers over £2,225,000.[56] With a few exceptions, most of the other career consulates in Edinburgh are accommodated in more modest buildings; one exception is the Chinese consulate general, which is the only one accommodated in a purpose-built building. The Belfast consulate general was housed on the second floor of a leased city centre office building but moved in 2004 to new premises in Danesfort House, a Victorian mansion with extensive grounds in a highly desirable district of the city. The consul general's office has been described as 'easily the size of a good swimming pool', and 'Ardnavally House, his million pound-plus seven-bedroomed official residence, on up the road at Shaw's Bridge, boasts further opulence.'[57] Although now boasting 'opulence', Ardnavally House, which was built in 1925 and had been long identified with the US presence in Northern Ireland, had been neglected for many years and 'had been allowed to deteriorate to an unacceptable level'. It was unoccupied in 1999 and awaited 'overdue renovations, many of which were identified' in a maintenance survey team's report in 1991 carried out by the Department's Office of Foreign Buildings Operations.[58]

Consular Families and Long-Serving Consuls

Consular families are those whose members have served over a long period as consuls or agents, usually within companies of which they are owners or directors. In many instances, the consulships associated with these companies were handed down in a manner almost resembling apostolic succession. Of course, these arrangements suit both parties, and even today there are many such examples in Britain, although none of them American. Companies are allowed to display the countries' prestigious and colourful consular shields outside their premises, thus adding to the company's status within the local community and enabling them to become members of local consular corps. In the past, companies that were, say, merchants, shipping agents or brokers, were also able to take advantage of their consular position to steer business their own way. From the point of view of the countries represented, the ability to retain consulships within a company or family ensures continuity of local expertise, support staff and premises. It is therefore an inexpensive and cost-effective method of representation. There is a long tradition of consuls representing more than one country, a practice that began when the number of countries seeking consular representation in a town outstripped the number of suitable candidates located there. This was especially the case in the smaller ports where there might be only one or two suitable individuals. For those who were already consuls there were only marginal additional costs involved in taking on another country's consulate. Surprisingly, there is no evidence that conflicts of interest arose when an individual represented more than one country.

The best known of these consular families in Britain is the Fox family, which had a long association with the United States and is of interest on several counts. It is an old, established Quaker family based in Cornwall, principally in Falmouth although others served at Plymouth, and has the distinction of having the longest unbroken record for providing consuls in Britain during more than two hundred years, and in the same period it also represented the highest number of countries, 36. The firm of George Croker Fox & Company was founded in Fowey in 1754, moving to Falmouth in 1762 where it had interests in shipping, mining and tin smelting. The family's first consular appointment was held by George Croker Fox as vice consul for Portugal in 1790.[59] The list of heads of states who appointed members of the family as consuls reads like a roll call of history. For example: American Presidents Washington, Madison, Lincoln, and Grant; European monarchs Leopold I and II, Christian IX, Queen Wilhelmina, Gustav VI, and Kaiser Wilhelm; the Mexican Emperor Maximilian; and Führer and Reich Chancellor Adolf Hitler.[60] Many Fox family members had similar, sometimes identical, Christian names and their middle names are sometimes spelled Weare, Were, or Ware, which at times makes it difficult to keep track of them. The first member of the family to represent the United States was Robert Weare Fox who served as consul at Falmouth from 1794 to 1812 (with a break between 1812 and 1815 caused by the war between the United States and Britain) and from 1815 until his death in 1818. He is said to have been possibly the only consul to have used the familiar 'thou', favoured by Quakers, in his consular despatches to the secretary of state. For example, he and his brother Thomas Were Fox writing to Secretary of State James Madison in 1801 began their report: 'Esteemed Friend, I beg leave to inform thee […]', and signed it 'Thy assured Friends'.[61] Robert Were Fox, Jr, served from 1819 to 1854 when the consulate passed out of the family briefly until the following year when Alfred Fox was appointed, serving until his death in 1874. He was succeeded as consul by his son Howard who was very familiar with consular work, having been deputy consul since 1863, and served until the consulate was closed in December 1905. However, a few days later it was designated as a consular agency and he was appointed agent and held that position from 1 January 1906 until the agency closed on 20 November 1908.[62] The family continued to represent other countries, but their long consular tradition ended in 2001 when the last consul, Charles Lloyd Fox, decided for personal reasons to resign his six appointments (France, Germany, Greece, Netherlands, Norway and Spain).[63]

Another family, but about whom very little is known, is the Davy family. They were Americans, from Pennsylvania, but spent many years in Britain, acting as consuls in Hull from 1816 to 1842, and in Leeds from 1843 until 1862. The family businesses were variously merchants, drysalters and agents for fire insurance offices.[64]

Over the years there were also a large number of individual consuls with lengthy periods of service representing the United States. The longest was Thomas Aspinwall who served in London for 38 years, from 1815 to 1853. James Maury served at Liverpool for 36 years; it would have been 39 years but relations were broken off during the 1812–1814 war between the United States and Britain. Also serving for 36 years was Thomas Were Fox as consular agent at Plymouth from 1823 to 1859. Thomas Auldjo served as vice consul at Poole, then consul at Cowes for 32 years, from 1791 to 1823. Francis B. Ogden served a total of 28 years as, successively, consul in Liverpool, Bristol and Manchester. John Mason Guest Underhill served as consular agent at Birmingham for 25 years, from 1840 to 1865; Elias Vanderhorst and Rufus Fleming each served as consuls for 23 years at Bristol and Edinburgh, from 1792 to 1815 and 1897 to 1920, respectively. Freeman H. Morse served as consul, then consul general, at London for 20 years, between 1861 and 1881; George Knox served a similar length of time as consul at Hull from 1796 to 1816; and Thomas Wilson served as consul at Dublin for 21 years, from 1826 to 1847. There are many other long-serving consuls and consular agents. The one thing that they all have in common is that they served before the 1924 Rogers Act, which established a unified Foreign Service. After that time, consuls usually spent no more than about three years in a post before being reassigned. A curious feature of the early lengthy appointments is why so many did not fall victim to the custom of being replaced when a new administration took office. However, while there were considerable changes made when a new administration took office it was seldom that a completely clean sweep of appointees took place. Also, some consuls were British subjects who were businessmen and for whom the consular appointment was a sideline. As their consulate was run from within their existing office accommodation it made good economic sense to leave them in place for lengthy periods.

Other 'American' Consulates – the Texas and Hawaii Consular Services

Texas proclaimed its independence from Mexico on 2 March 1836. For nine years it was an independent republic before being annexed by and admitted to the United States under a joint resolution of Congress on 1 March 1845. It is not generally realized that during its relatively short life it established a fairly extensive consular service, with consulates in the United States and Europe. In Britain, in 1842 and 1843, it established consulates and vice consulates in London, Liverpool, Glasgow, Greenock, Falmouth, Plymouth, Kingston upon Hull, Newcastle upon Tyne and Dublin. There was a consulate general in London, headed by Lachlan Mackintosh Rate, which was under the overall control of the Texas legation in the city headed by chargé d'affaires Ashbel Smith. The consul in Liverpool was Francis Ogden, who held the post despite being also United States consul in Bristol from 1840 onwards. Unsurprisingly, this unusual dual appointment aroused the belief that he would vacate the Liverpool post and it led to several candidates applying for it. Writing from the Texas State Department, Smith informed Rate that there appeared 'to have been some misapprehension concerning the Consulate at Liverpool. Mr Ogden was appointed Consul some time since, and his conduct, so far as known, meets the approbation of this Government. It is not proper therefore to revoke his appointment.'[65] On annexation in 1845, Texan foreign representation ceased. The London consulate was located at 15 Bishopsgate Street; the legation was at 3 St James's Street and its location is marked by a plaque in Pickering Place.[66]

In May 1856, Manley Hopkins (1818–1897), father of the English Jesuit priest and poet Gerard Manley Hopkins (1844–1889), was appointed the first consul general of the Sandwich Islands in Britain. Eight additional consulates and vice consulates were established in September 1859.[67] It is unclear when the Sandwich Islands were definitively renamed the Hawaiian Islands, but by January 1872 the new name was used in the year book of the British Foreign Office.[68] The Republic of Hawaii was established in 1894 and was annexed by the United States in 1898. It became a United States territory in 1900, and was admitted as a state in 1959. Despite its annexation in 1898, Hawaii continued to have 16 consulates throughout Britain (including Ireland) as late as 1900, with Hopkins's son, Cyril, heading the London vice consulate.[69]

Wartime

American consuls as well as officers in the embassy or legation in London lived through or witnessed most of the historic and major wartime events that faced Britain in the last two hundred years. One of their duties was to report local military preparations or indications of war to the State Department and also to notify arrivals and departures of American merchants and ships. The nineteenth century was one that saw frequent conflicts between European powers. The first event of which the consuls would be aware during this time was the Battle of Trafalgar in 1805, when the Royal Navy defeated the larger, combined fleets of the French and Spanish navies. The Peninsular War, part of the Napoleonic Wars, was fought from 1808 to 1814, with combined British, Portuguese and Spanish forces defeating French forces. During this period consuls would be acutely aware of another war affecting them more directly, this time when the United States declared war against Britain from 1812 to 1814. They saw their appointments suspended although no actions took place on British soil, and no consul was imprisoned or detained as an enemy alien (some of them were, of course, British subjects). The war was ended by the signing of the Treaty of Ghent in 1814. As we have seen, Reuben G. Beasley, the consul in London, was given the additional appointment as Prisoner of War Agent dealing with the welfare and eventual repatriation of the large numbers of American prisoners of war. The following year saw forces led by the Duke of Wellington defeat Napoleon's army at Waterloo. But there was little time for respite before war broke out once more, from 1854 to 1856, when British and French forces fought Russia in the Crimean War. Upheaval in the United States led to the American Civil War, from 1861 to 1865, which was a period of intense activity for United States consuls in Britain trying to counter the activities of Confederate agents who had been sent there. This is covered extensively in Chapter 5. The last major conflict of the century was the Boer War, from 1899 to 1902.

The twentieth century saw the most momentous conflicts, namely the two world wars. During the First World War, Germany and a number of other countries at war asked the United States to represent their interests in enemy countries and responsibility for administering their relief funds was undertaken by the Consular Service.[70] For example, the Liverpool consulate distributed German relief funds each week. Wesley Frost, the consul at Queenstown (Cork), in Ireland reported the torpedoing and loss of the Lusitania on 7 May 1915 and was the first to supply the names of the survivors.[71] He also vouched for the innocence of two American citizens, Lindell T. Bates and Newton B. Knox, who were arrested on a charge of espionage while searching the shore off the coast of Kinsale for the body of Bates' brother, Lindon, who was believed to have gone down with the Lusitania. The two were accused of being officers from a U-Boat.[72] During this time the consuls in London and Nottingham were in constant danger from German air raids for many months.[73] In 1916, Wilbur Carr, at the time Director of the Consular Service, made the perilous transatlantic crossing through U-Boat infested waters to Britain, the first time he had been abroad. While on the voyage he used the time to ask various well-connected passengers for their views on the Consular Service and on individual consuls. One passenger spoke 'well of Van Sant at Dunfermline and McCunn of Glasgow'.[74] Carr was met at Liverpool by his friend Horace Lee Washington, the consul there, and later spent time in London with the consular staff.

However, the Second World War proved a more dangerous assignment for the consuls as the sustained blitzkrieg by the Luftwaffe targeted major ports and industrial centres, locations that generally had an American consulate or agency. The consulate general and embassy in London received regular, often daily, reports from consuls around the country about the effects of air raids in their districts. In Liverpool, consul general Philip Holland reported that there had been no air raid or alert for a week, but reporting on 2 December 1940, he said 'the lull was broken by the longest and most severe raid yet made on this part of the country, resulting in considerable loss of life and extensive and serious damage [...]. It is said that between three hundred and four hundred enemy planes took part in the attack, and high explosive and incendiary bombs and parachute land mines were used.'[75] A few days later, he reported that 264 people had been killed in the big raid at the end of November 1940, and there had also been considerable destruction.[76] Walton C. Ferris, consul in London, reported news he had received from a friend in Sheffield: 'Sheffield is in a state of chaos. It is supposed to be worse than Coventry and Birmingham put together. [...] The sights I have seen have made me feel literally ill.'[77] The consulate in Sheffield was slightly damaged in December 1940 and the decision was made to vacate it.[78] Southampton, with its important docks, was a particularly attractive target and sustained heavy casualties and damage. Consul General George K. Donald's reports described the harrowing effects. On 25 November 1940: 'Yesterday about 250 planes attacked harbour installations, docks and warehouses [...] dropping 250 tons of high explosive bombs and thousands of incendiaries.' His home was struck by four incendiary bombs and two of the consulate clerks had to abandon their homes due to unexploded bombs. There were four bomb craters in front of the consulate.[79] A few days later: 'Casualties amounted to at least 428, of which 113 were killed and 197 seriously injured.'[80] Less than a week later:

For six hours steadily last night practically with no intermission high explosives and incendiaries rained on Southampton. It was a most harrowing experience [...]. Time bombs are all over town and in front of my residence there are three. Three large high explosives fell in the grounds and missed the building by about ten feet, damaging it somewhat. We were putting out incendiaries all through the raid. [...] The staff are all safe.[81]

The next day: 'My residence had two more high explosives fall within a dozen feet of the building and the largest crater I have ever seen is just across the street [...] I have been putting out incendiaries most of the night. All the staff are safe.'[82] The following day he reported: 'As far as the consulate is concerned I propose keeping it open in the mornings only for the next few days so that those of the staff who want to leave town for a night's rest may do so.'[83] Roy W. Baker, consul in Bristol, after reporting the damage commented that 'in the centre of the town the invaders followed the streets that had apparently been selected for attack in a way that suggests to me, at least, that they must have some sort of help from the ground'. As a postscript, he added: 'Since writing the above regarding the accuracy of the raiders' fire, the clerk here, who is an auxiliary fireman, has told me that yesterday he learned from the police themselves that they were looking for Fifth Columnists in connection with the Sunday night raid. He says that the policeman [...] told him that the police authorities had a report that rockets had been sent up during the raid.'[84] Baker's residence was damaged by an incendiary bomb.[85] Consul James R. Wilkinson in Birmingham warned: 'If air raiding continues along present lines, on a basis of the law of probability, it is inevitable the building in which the Consulate is situated will be destroyed or seriously damaged in the near future. It is not my intention to move the Consulate unless I am specifically ordered to do so by superior authority.'[86] Reporting from Plymouth on 28 November 1940, Henry M. Wolcott said: 'This, the 207th raid, was the longest by one hour and the most intense since the beginning of air attacks on the Plymouth region five months ago.'[87] Eventually, the consulates at Plymouth, Bristol, Liverpool and Manchester were completely gutted by bombs and fire.[88] Ambassador Winant described reports he had received of the effects of bombing in Clydeside in April 1941, where 1,100 persons had been killed and 1,600 seriously injured.[89] In May 1941, the Belfast consulate had to move for three weeks into the Grand Central Hotel as an unexploded bomb was in the street outside the office.[90]

These are just a few of the reports submitted regularly throughout the war, not only about the effects of air raids in the consular districts but also on the mood of the local people. The reports were at times rather moving. One account by James R. Wilkinson, the consul in Birmingham, made two days after Christmas 1940, is typical. His reason for writing the report (which runs to four pages) was:

to put down something which will perhaps convey in a general way the effect that air raids are producing among working people in the Birmingham area, and I here hasten to add that all of the people I have picked up [in his car] have been working people. [...] In not one instance have I noted any spirit of disloyalty or defeatism among these people but to say that their mental health is not being undermined by bombing is to talk nonsense.[91]

He describes how in many cases their homes had been totally destroyed and gives accounts of their daily routines. 'It is true enough that working-class people in this area make a brave showing before the camera or to the eye of the official visitor. However, when the camera shutter has closed and the official eye has turned away, the picturesque scene vanishes and the smiling faces of those who figured in it assume a grimness born almost of despair.' He concludes by saying that many of the people hope that the United States will soon enter the war. Herschel V. Johnson, the Chargé d'affaires ad interim in London, to whom the report was sent, forwarded it to Secretary of State Cordell Hull, saying 'In my opinion this report merits particular attention.'[92] These consuls and their colleagues in London were brave individuals who endured the same dangers that the British population faced. Also, until the United States entered the war in December 1941 they could have been forgiven if they had asked to be recalled. Why face such risks when your own country was neutral? However, most Foreign Service personnel remained at their posts and performed their duties throughout the war.[93] Even after the war, consuls in Britain remained affected by measures introduced in wartime. Walter M. McClelland, vice consul in Liverpool from 1950 to 1952, recalled many years later that food, clothing and coal were still rationed when he and his wife arrived in the city. They had ration books and lived on British rations because his appointment was consular, not diplomatic.[94]

In more recent times consular staff in Belfast experienced the effects of what is euphemistically described as 'the troubles', the sectarian violence between nationalists and unionists in Northern Ireland. Differences had simmered beneath the surface ever since the south of the island had gained independence from Britain in 1922, later becoming the Republic of Ireland. But the period from the late 1960s to 1998 was a particularly bloody time that by the end saw more than thirty-six hundred people killed and at least thirty thousand injured in Northern Ireland and on the British mainland, mainly as a result of bombings by the Irish Republican Army (IRA) and actions by 'Loyalist' groups.[95] Throughout this time, the consulate general in Belfast played a pivotal role as American presidents, keenly aware of the political influence of the large Irish American lobby, became more involved in the events unrolling in Northern Ireland and demanded to be kept up to date on the situation.[96] Successive consuls general were required to report closely on the political events unfolding, and the office became more like a small embassy. The White House took a close interest, particularly the Reagan and Clinton administrations. In 1995, President Clinton made the first of several visits to Northern Ireland, both in and out of office. On each occasion the consulate general was closely involved and extra staff were drafted in. In addition, numerous visits by prominent senators and congressmen, such as Edward Kennedy, were made during 'the troubles', all of which put tremendous pressure on consuls general and their staffs. On several occasions the consulate general had to be evacuated because of bomb scares.[97] Staffs at the embassies in London and Dublin also came under increased pressure during these times, particularly when the ambassador in London, Raymond Seitz, the consular staff in Dublin, the State Department, the FBI, the CIA and the Justice Department all opposed granting Gerry Adams, president of Sinn Fein, the political wing of the Irish Republican Army (IRA), a visa to visit the United States. President Clinton ignored their advice and granted the visa. The ambassador in Dublin during this time was Jean Kennedy Smith, an influential member of the Kennedy family and a strong supporter of Adams.[98] This incident is described in detail in the history of the Belfast consulate. The 'troubles' ended with the signing of the so-called Good Friday Agreement on 10 April 1998. After this, the consulate was able to resume normal consular business.

From its early days in Britain the American consular presence has waxed and waned and today is found only in Edinburgh and Belfast and the large consular section in the embassy. Since those early days the activities of consuls and their families in Britain have provided a good picture of how the American consular function as a whole has evolved since the Consular Service was established and later became part of the Foreign Service. Britain was small enough geographically for all the new procedural changes to be introduced without much difficulty. Similarly, the consuls-general at large in their quest to root out inefficiency were able to make their way round the entire consular network in a relatively short time without having to cover vast distances. Standards were undoubtedly improved although, with surprisingly few exceptions, the calibre of candidates sent to Britain was generally higher than those sent elsewhere. Britain was also a good proving ground for consuls to expand their normal reporting function, as there were no language difficulties preventing them from engaging with their clientele and local officialdom. Britain was also one of the few countries to host two different 'American' consular services, those of Texas and Hawaii. Despite the frequency of staff changes in the early days, we have seen that a few staff managed to remain in the same posts for many years, some even choosing to settle in the country after retirement. Wartime brought out the best in the consuls, many of them enduring the same dangers as the rest of the population; Luftwaffe bombs did not discriminate. A much earlier period of hostilities that was closer to home for the consuls was the American Civil War, from 1861 to 1865. During those years, the American consuls in Britain played a key role in preventing the breakup of the United States, by setting up and running an extensive espionage network. How they carried out that role is described in the next chapter.

Chapter Five

IMPACT OF THE CIVIL WAR
AND THE ROLE OF AMERICAN
CONSULS IN BRITAIN

Independence did not prove to be the panacea that would cure the new American nation's ills. There were further major military battles to be fought. This time however they were not against a foreign power, but against fellow countrymen. The abolition of slavery had long been a vexatious topic: in broad terms, the southern states, and in particular their cotton plantation owners, favoured the retention of slavery whereas the northern states did not. Confederate President Jefferson Davis said that the 'northern majority was tyrannous because it actively opposed slavery, and so secession was practically justified as well as constitutionally proper'.[1] US President Abraham Lincoln, on the other hand, maintained that 'One-eighth of the whole population were colored slaves, not distributed generally over the Union, but localized in the southern part of it. These slaves constituted a peculiar and powerful interest. All knew that this interest was somehow the cause of the war.'[2] With such diametrically opposed stances there was no room for compromise. The southern states therefore decided to secede from the Union.

The ensuing Civil War pitted Americans against each other. The Union, or North, fought to prevent the break-up of the United States of America, while the Confederacy, or South, fought to establish a separate Confederate States of America. The first shots were fired in April 1861 when Confederate troops bombarded Fort Sumter, a US military post situated on an island within the harbour of Charleston, South Carolina. The engagement lasted only about 36 hours; there were no casualties and a surrender was quickly negotiated. Although the war began without casualties, by its end the losses were enormous. Estimates of the number who died range between 530,000 and 620,000, greater than the total number of Americans killed in both world wars.[3] To put this into a more modern perspective, 620,000 dead represented 2 per cent of the American population; in 2002, 2 percent would have been five million.[4]

Action was not confined to American soil, however, and Britain, the old enemy, found itself caught up in events. All southern US ports were blockaded by the US Navy and this had an unexpected and unintended consequence. Lincoln had regarded the actions of the Confederates as civil war, a purely internal matter within the United States; but in international law a blockade was regarded as the action of one sovereign state against another. As a result of this, the Confederacy received belligerent status and *de jure* recognition, although it was never recognized by any country as a sovereign state. Among other things, this gave it the right to purchase supplies in neutral countries and to contract loans. Under international and domestic law it also allowed countries to sell arms and equipment to both sides (which they did), but with one important proviso: ships could be sold only if they were unarmed. Britain proclaimed its neutral status on 14 May 1861 and remained neutral throughout the war, and other European countries followed suit. In the early stages of the war, British and French consuls in the southern states who had been accredited to the United States were permitted by the Confederacy to remain in place and to continue their roles. However, there were repeated calls within the Confederacy for them to obtain new exequaturs (formal approval of appointment) from President Jefferson Davies rather than to continue operating under those issued by Lincoln. After months of acrimonious exchanges of correspondence about their activities the Confederate government withdrew the British consuls' recognition in October 1863 and told them to leave.[5] French consuls, however, were permitted to remain.[6]

The United States, like many other countries, has a tradition of sending special diplomatic agents. Reasons for doing so include representing the country at coronations, weddings, funerals, special negotiations, international congresses, conferences and exhibitions. In the first year of the Civil War, Lincoln appointed eight special diplomatic agents for assignments at the American legation in London. They were Edward Everett (a former minister to Great Britain and, briefly, secretary of state), John Pendleton Kennedy (a former secretary of the US Navy), Robert Charles Winthrop (a former US senator), Archbishop John Hughes, Bishop Charles P. McIlvaine, Thurlow Weed, Henry Shelton Sanford (discussed later in the chapter) and Commander William M. Walker. In the event, Everett, Kennedy and Winthrop did not take up their appointments. The mission of Hughes (Roman Catholic archbishop of New York), McIlvaine (Episcopalian bishop of Ohio) and Weed (a New York politician, *eminence grise* and friend and political adviser of William Seward) was: 'To endeavour through social contacts to promote a better understanding of the Union cause throughout Europe.'[7] Walker's brief was: 'To obtain information about the outfitting of Confederate cruisers in European ports, especially in Great Britain, and about the shipment of arms and ammunitions to the Confederate States; to observe general Confederate activities in Europe and to report on them.'[8] All remained only during that year. Weed, in particular, seems to have made a favourable impression on Charles Francis Adams, the US minister in London. Adams received a letter from his son, Charles F. Adams, Jr., a cavalry officer serving in South Carolina, who remarked:

> Some things in your letters filled me with astonishment and laughter. First and foremost among them was the idea of your new intimacy with Thurlow Weed [...], Thurlow the unforgiving and corrupt. [...] Verily politics does give and take strange bed fellows, and to find you working heart and hand with Weed, advising with him, confiding in him and believing in him, is something I did not dream to see. I am glad of it. The devil is not indeed so black as he is painted.[9]

From an early date, Lincoln began building up a legal case against Confederate agents operating in Britain and France, using not only the considerable amount of evidence being gathered by the consuls in Britain and elsewhere but also by two further special diplomatic agents whom he sent to Britain in 1863. They were William Maxwell Evarts and William Whiting. Both were distinguished lawyers whose brief was: 'To prepare evidence for the Government in the matter of vessels fitted out in England and France for use of the Confederate States, and to consult with such British counsel as the American Minister in London may employ.'[10] Evarts would later be part of President Andrew Johnson's defence team during the latter's impeachment trial in 1868, US counsel at the Geneva Arbitration of the Alabama Claims in 1872 and finally secretary of state from 1877 to 1881. Whiting was the War Department's solicitor from 1862 to 1865.

The blockade of their ports was a major problem for the Confederates and as they had no navy they needed to look abroad to obtain ships, both blockade runners and warships. They looked principally to Great Britain (but also to France), and James Dunwoody Bulloch was the man they chose to organize and supervise this task. Bulloch was born in 1823 near Savannah, Georgia, and had served in the US Navy from 1839 until 1853, when he went into the merchant marine. When the war broke out in 1861 he joined the Confederate Navy but was not given command of a ship. Instead, he was sent to Britain to be the Confederacy's agent in Europe, with the job of buying ships and arming them for the embryonic navy. He based himself in Liverpool with its strong shipbuilding facilities, arriving there on 4 June 1861. He was also active in other parts of the country, notably Glasgow and Dumbarton, in Scotland. He dealt principally with the firm of Laird & Company in Birkenhead, just across the River Mersey from Liverpool. Lairds had been founded by William Laird, a Scottish engineer, and had a strong and deserved reputation for building fine ships. Bulloch wasted no time and within days of his arrival he placed an order with William C. Miller & Sons, Liverpool, for a screw steamer, initially named the *Oreto*, and then *Manassas*, but finally renamed the *Florida*. Less than two months later he signed a contract on 1 August with John Laird Sons & Company of Birkenhead for a wooden screw steamer known variously as *No. 290* (it was hull number 290 on the order books) and *Enrica*. However, it would become better known by its final name: the *Alabama*. The cost of this ship was £47,500, payable in five equal instalments of £9,500 as various stages were completed, the final one payable when it 'was satisfactorily tried, and delivered afloat uninjured in the River Mersey with the Builder's Certyficate [*sic*]'. Completion and delivery date was to be on or before 1 June 1862, or much sooner if possible. Lairds kept to this, and the contract shows that the *Enrica* was launched and docked in Number 4 Dock on 14 May 1862 and sailed on 29 July.[11] Both ships succeeded in entering service with the Confederate Navy. Bulloch was also active in France but his attempts to buy ships at Bordeaux and Nantes proved unsuccessful.

Secretary of the Confederate Navy Stephen R. Mallory was keen to acquire two ironclad rams (ships that had sharp underwater 'noses' projecting from the bows that could be used to inflict serious damage when ramming an enemy ship). Bulloch began looking into obtaining these in March 1862[12] and placed a contract for them with Lairds in June (orders no. 294 and 295).[13] In order to pre-empt allegations by the US government that the ships were intended for use by the Confederates, the British government, after protracted deliberation, seized them in October 1863 before they were completed.[14] It eventually bought them in May 1864 and put them into Royal Navy service as HMS

Scorpion and HMS *Wivern*.[15] While expressing an overwhelming regret at losing these ironclads, Bulloch remarked:

> I am bound to say that as soon as it was decided to get out of the difficulty by buying the ships, the Admiralty conducted the operation in a perfectly fair and straightforward way. The ships were valued with scrupulous regard to their intrinsic worth, and with due reference to the state of the shipbuilding trade at the time, and as a mere commercial transaction the sale was satisfactory, the aggregate amount agreed to be paid by the Government being about £30,000 in excess of the original contract price of the two ships.[16]

In 1863, Lincoln sent two hard-headed businessmen, John Murray Forbes of Boston and William Henry Aspinwall of New York, to Britain to see if they could pre-empt the Confederate's purchase of ships, especially the ironclad rams. They set off on 18 March, armed with credits of $10 million of bonds from the US Treasury to enable them to obtain a loan of £1 million sterling for their task, as well as letters of introduction to the consuls at Liverpool and London and to Baring Brothers, the United States' financial agents in London. In Liverpool, they met up with the consul Thomas Haines Dudley, who informed them about his 'espial' activities on the two Laird rams and they gave him additional funds for these activities.[17] In London, they obtained £500,000 from Barings as an initial loan and went on to meet Adams, the US minister. Adams, reminiscent of present-day ambassadors when meeting one of their country's 'spooks': 'wanted to know only what was absolutely necessary of our mission, so that he might not be mixed up with our operations, which we knew might not be exactly what a diplomat would care to indorse'.[18] Forbes and Aspinwall reported the consuls' opinions on the ironclads, which were that since the Confederates were able to give Laird at least part of the money for the contract 'it would be impossible to approach the builders of the ironclads with an offer with any chance of acceptance. We are of the same opinion.'[19] They therefore abandoned any attempts to buy them and sought other means to assist in the war effort. After examining the consuls' intelligence-gathering and surveillance operations they concluded that the system needed tightening up. They provided additional funds for this and divided the country into two zones, with Freeman Morse, the consul in London, supervising the south, and Dudley supervising the north (including Scotland).[20] On their voyage home in July 1863, Forbes and Aspinwall wrote an official account for Secretary of the Navy Gideon Welles, concluding that: 'While failing to accomplish any great object, we hope that we have done something to enlighten public opinion by our constant intercourse with leading public and literary men and others, and also by aiding and encouraging our consuls in their efforts to stop the outfit of pirates in what ought to be the friendly ports of Great Britain.'[21]

Among the other ships the Confederacy obtained in Britain were the *Alexandra* (built in the Liverpool yard of William C. Miller & Sons), the *Georgia* (built in Dumbarton, Scotland, in 1862 as the merchant ship *Japan*), the *Pampero* (built in the Glasgow yard of George Thomson), the *Rappahannock* (built originally on the Thames in 1857 as the Royal Navy's HMS *Victor*) and the *Shenandoah* (built in Alexander Stephen & Sons shipyard in Glasgow, under the name *Sea King*). Most of these played havoc with the blockade, sinking almost 150 Union ships and forcing others to re-register under foreign flags.[22] There was of course the important proviso about purchasing the ships: in order to comply with the law, none of them could be fitted out as warships. Although it was fairly obvious why he was purchasing ships, Bulloch was scrupulous in observing the letter of the law. He was advised throughout the war by Frederick Hull, a member of a leading firm of Liverpool solicitors, who also sought counsel's opinion on the matter.[23] So an elaborate game of bluff ensued. Of all the ships, it was the *Alabama* that caught the public imagination and it has remained the best known thanks largely to a combination of events: the scale of the damage it inflicted, attempts by US consuls in Liverpool (Dudley), London (Morse), Glasgow (Underwood), Dundee (Smith) and the ministers in London (Adams) and Brussels (Sanford) to prevent its sailing, and action by the British government. However, before looking at the activities and fate of the *Alabama* we should introduce Consul Dudley and his colleagues at this point.

Thomas Haines Dudley was born in Camden, New Jersey, in 1819 to a Quaker family and was a lawyer, admitted to the New Jersey Bar in 1845. A strong supporter of Lincoln's bid for the presidency, he was eventually rewarded by him. Dudley recalled the circumstances of his consular appointment in 1861.

> [Lincoln] looked at me and said, 'Mr Dudley there are but two places that are worthy of your acceptance that have not been already filled. One is the Consulship at Liverpool, the other Minister to Japan. If you desire it I will have a Commission made out for you as Minister to Japan.' I replied, 'Mr President, I am sick and stand in need of good medical advice, I could not get that at Japan but could at Liverpool, therefore I would rather take the subordinate position of Consul at Liverpool than Minister to Japan.' Lincoln was not happy about this, and remarked: 'I want the Consulship for my friend Gov.[ernor] Kroener of Illinois and would rather you would go to Japan.'[24]

However, after several further interviews Lincoln agreed to appoint Dudley to Liverpool.[25]

Dudley and his family set off from New York on the steamship *Africa* on 6 November 1861 and arrived at Liverpool 19 November and were taken to lodgings at Mrs Blodget's Boarding House, 153 Duke Street. Henry Wilding, the vice consul, called on Dudley there and told him that he was ready to hand over the consulate office and archives and asked if Dudley proposed to continue to employ him. After ascertaining from him the level of his salary, Dudley agreed to retain him. On the day before Dudley took possession of the consulate he was informed that members of the American Chamber of Commerce in Liverpool always formally called on the consul. The meeting was held in the boarding house; the delegation was headed by its president, William Rathbone, and secretary, George Melley.[26] After the usual friendly introductions had been completed, Melley 'criticised the action of the Government of the United States and strongly censured its actions in attempting to suppress the Rebellion'. Dudley was having none of this: 'The thought immediately came to me to be very decided in my reply.' And he gave a lengthy and spirited response, using phrases such as:

> the question involved was whether human slavery should be limited and confined to the territory it then occupied [...] or whether the then existing government should be destroyed and the slave empire embracing all or most parts of the Continent of America, erected on

the ruins'; [it is] 'the oppressors rebelling against liberty – it is a rebellion got up in favour of slavery against liberty, for the purpose of perpetuating human slavery'; […] 'it is to destroy the best, purest and finest government that the sun shines upon […] to build upon its ruins an immense slave empire.

He concluded his account by saying:

> I spoke with much animation and feeling, I felt that the time and occasion fully warranted it – indeed I regarded it occupying the position that I did and knowing the feelings and views of my people and Government as a duty. This terminated our interview and they withdrew – I saw by their manner that my remarks had not been what they expected and had not left a favourable impression upon them. They had not expected to hear remarks like these.[27]

Dudley wasted no time in seeking to thwart the efforts of Bulloch and the Confederates. He hired detectives, notably Matthew Maguire a retired Liverpool police superintendent with good contacts in the police, and built up a network of contacts around Britain to alert him to possible attempts by the Confederates to obtain merchant ships that could be converted to warships for use against the Union. One account states that he had a force of one hundred men working for him.[28] He toured England and Scotland in 1863 to check shipyards and to organize his network of agents and informers.[29] This is when he discovered that a vessel, known simply as *No. 290*, was being built in Laird's Birkenhead shipyard; as we have seen, this was later known as the *Enrica* and finally the *Alabama*. But others were watching Dudley and he received anonymous threats that 'unless he ceased his opposition to the extension of assistance to the Confederate government […] his life would be taken, and if found in certain designated spots he would be shot on sight'.[30] The consulate was frequently the object of attacks and its flag 'was often found with tin kettles tied to it as an object of contempt'.[31] Notwithstanding this, Dudley enjoyed Liverpool and remained in post there for 11 years.[32]

Freeman Harlow Morse was born in Bath, Maine, in 1807. His early career was as a carver of ships' figureheads, but at the age of 33 he went into local politics in the state legislature and advanced to the national level and served in Congress from 1843 to 1845 and 1857 to 1861. Between these dates he returned to local politics, as mayor of Bath and a member of the state legislature. In 1861, President Lincoln offered him the post of consul in London, where he worked closely with Dudley and Charles Francis Adams, the US minister there. In 1869 Morse was promoted consul general in London, but was replaced the following year by General Adam Badeau. He was not happy at being replaced and decided not to return to America, although his wife and their two daughters did so. He settled in England and died there on 6 February 1891; he is buried in the churchyard of St Mary's, Long Ditton, Surrey.[33]

Charles Francis Adams was a Bostonian, born in 1807. He was a lawyer and had served locally in the Massachusetts State Senate and nationally in the House of Representatives. He had a distinguished pedigree; on his paternal side being the son and grandson of former presidents of the United States John Quincy Adams and John Adams, respectively, both of whom had also served as US minister in London. On his maternal side, his grandfather was Joshua Johnson, who had served as the first US consul in London from 1790 to 1797.[34] In 1861, Lincoln appointed Adams as minister in London, a post in which most commentators agree he served with distinction during the next seven years, a particularly difficult period in Anglo-American relations. In 1871, he was appointed the US arbitrator at the Tribunal of Arbitration which met the following year in Geneva to settle the compensation to be awarded to the United States as a result of the depredation caused by the *Alabama* and other British-built ships.

Henry Shelton Sanford was born in Woodbury, Connecticut, in 1823, moving with his family to Derby, Connecticut, at the age of 13. When he was 17, his sight deteriorated and he had to abandon his studies and thereafter wore pince-nez spectacles. He was of medium build, with a beard that progressed as he grew older from a trim version to a bushy one that covered a good part of his upper chest. He began his diplomatic career in 1847 when he was made secretary of the American legation in St Petersburg and the following year moved to Germany where he was acting secretary of the legation at Frankfurt. While there, he found time to continue his studies and was awarded a Doctor of Laws degree by Heidelberg University. In 1849, he moved to Paris and remained there as secretary and later chargé d'affaires until 1854, when he resigned because the newly appointed minister John Y. Mason insisted on his 'donning a diplomatic uniform'.[35] This was at a time when American diplomats were ordered to wear plain civilian clothes, not the elaborate uniforms that other countries' diplomats wore. Ironically, Mason himself was reproached for having worn a type of uniform. Sanford returned to the United States where he undertook business work both there and in Central and Latin America. However, the diplomatic life beckoned once more and in 1861 he was appointed by Lincoln as minister to Belgium as well as US fiscal agent in Europe; he was also given responsibility for supervising the US Secret Service in Europe during the Civil War. His Secret Service appointment was listed as a special diplomatic agent in the London legation, with the brief 'To counteract by all proper means the efforts of Confederate agents in Europe to gain recognition of the Confederate States.'[36] However, Sanford's rash approach to his Secret Service role began to worry his superiors who feared it might produce yet another US–British crisis. So the Lincoln administration thanked him but told him to hand over his Secret Service activities to Consul Morse and concentrate on his diplomatic duties as US minister to Belgium.[37] In 1869, he finally left the diplomatic life and among his many pursuits founded a town in Florida, naming it Sanford. Along with the explorer Henry Morton Stanley he became closely involved with King Leopold II of Belgium's controversial slave labour regime in the Congo. He died in 1891.[38]

Throughout the Civil War, other US consuls in Britain and Ireland were on the lookout for Confederate operations and provided intelligence on suspicious shipping movements in ports such as Belfast, Bristol, Falmouth, Queenstown and Cardiff.[39] In 1861, Neil McLachlan, the consul at Leith reported that 'a number of Southerners were trying to purchase arms and munitions of war' locally.[40] In 1862, Hugh Smith, the consul in Dundee, discovered that Confederate agents (one of whom was Lieutenant George T. Sinclair, discussed later in the chapter) were living in Bridge of Allan within easy reach of the Clyde shipyards. Information from these consuls, and from those in other parts of the world, was sent to the State Department where it was collated and then sent to the Navy Department which forwarded it to the Atlantic Blockading Squadrons and other interested military units.[41] In June 1863, Charles Dexter Cleveland, the consul in Cardiff, received information about the cargo being loaded on the steamer *Lord Clyde* and suspected that it included arms and ammunition for Confederate forces. He arranged with the collector of customs to carry out a search. Hidden under flooring they found bales containing 'various soldiers clothing, blankets, &c., but no guns nor ammunition; and as she was going to Nassau, she could not be stopped, and went next morning. [...] My opinion is that she is to be converted into a light-armed steamer to prey on our commerce.'[42] In November of that year the consul in Glasgow, Warner L. Underwood, formally requested the detention of the ship known as *Canton*, which was being built in Thomson's shipyard in Glasgow on the design of the *Alabama*, and which became the *Pampero*. Lieutenant Sinclair had made an arrangement with the builders to acquire the ship,[43] but following Underwood's request the British government began legal action to prevent the sale; in the meantime, a Royal Navy ship was moored abreast of it. The court proceedings dragged out until after the war had ended.[44] Bulloch claimed that the ship was Thomson's property when it was seized by the British government and 'she never really became a Confederate vessel at all'.[45] Zebina Eastman, the consul at Bristol, remarked that:

> Quite a prominent part of my duties was to look after the fitting out of ships for running the blockade of the Confederate Coast. [...] Probably forty ships were fitted out or touched at my port, every one of which came to a bad end, sunk or captured – some of them, however, made several successful voyages. One of them, the 'Old Dominion' [...] was being fitted out in Bristol. Hearing about it I employed a photographer to plant his camera like a cannon in a vacant house on a convenient elevation opposite to it, and he took several good views. I sent them to the Department of State with explanations, together with the recital that the Captain had boasted that 'No damned Yankee was smart enough to capture this ship.' This was forwarded through proper channels to the commander of the blockading squadron and the ship was captured in her first attempt to break through![46]

It is worth reminding ourselves that transatlantic communications throughout the Civil War were slow, which meant that officials had to rely largely on their own initiative rather than receiving constant instructions and advice from their superiors in America. Although an Atlantic telegraph cable had been laid in 1858 it failed after less than three months and communications were not re-established until 1866. During that time communications between Britain and America were conveyed by ships. In 1861, typical travel time by sea between the two countries was 12 to 14 days.[47]

Dudley (as we have seen), Morse and Sanford employed British detectives to gather intelligence. However, Dudley was not particularly enamoured of their type. Writing to Secretary of State Seward in 1861 he said: 'it is necessary to employ one or two seasoned detectives and occasionally to pay money in way of travelling expenses to the men so employed. They are not as a general thing very estimable men but are the only persons we can get to engage in this business, which I am sure you will agree with me is not a very pleasant one.'[48] Morse hired Ignatius Pollaky, described as 'superintendent of a private inquiry-office', who established surveillance posts in London and elsewhere from which he received daily reports. Morse was cautious about appointing him, saying to Sanford: 'He is unknown to me except from what you and Field [a retired London police officer] have said and there may be some risk in dealing with him. But it is a "risky business" any way [*sic*] and I think we better engage him at once.' Pollaky wanted £100 for thirty or forty days work, with £25 advanced to him every ten days. Morse added, alert to the possibility that the Confederates might recruit him, 'I think it very important that we engage him fully so that he may be <u>wholly ours</u>, at once.'[49] Pollaky's operatives bribed postal workers to supply the names and addresses on correspondence sent and received by Confederate agents and also intercepted Confederate telegrams.[50] At one point, he had 17 Confederate 'conspirators' in London under surveillance. In a report to Sanford he described the routine:

> We are watching Bullock [*sic*], [Major] Anderson, [Captain Caleb] Muse [this should be Huse], [Lieutenant] Hughes & Co. but they do nothing else from morning till night than inspecting and buying Arms, Rifles, visit the different Manufactories, superintend their packing and loading. To watch their movements and Report them in detail is now super-fluous, as we have discovered the channels of their ultimate destination.[51]

And he mentioned the frustrations of surveillance: 'They know they are watched and Capt[ain] M[should refer to Huse] said that he cannot move a step without a detective on his heels.' Also, 'It is impossible my dear Sir to watch a house unfortunately so situated like B's [Bulloch's, at 58 Jermyn Street] for 3½ months without attracting some notice in such a neighbourhood.'[52] Bulloch, Anderson, Huse and Hughes were all staying at 58 Jermyn Street,[53] a lodging house owned by William Wyborn, which was a convenient base for dealing with Isaac, Campbell & Co., a major supplier of military equipment for the Confederacy, which was situated just a few doors along the same street.[54] However, this proximity of customer to supplier made it easier for Pollaky's men to keep an eye on both parties' movements and transactions, although as Pollaky noted, Bulloch and his colleagues were well aware that they were under surveillance. Morse also persuaded a young London mechanic to get a job with Lairds shipyard in Birkenhead, promising in return to recommend him for a position with a US shipbuilder. However, the infiltration never took place, as the youth's mother found out and threatened to expose Morse.[55] Bulloch's other suppliers included Firman & Sons of London, Robert Mole & Sons of Birmingham and James Westa of Sheffield.[56]

Bulloch was, of course, highly critical of the Union's spying activities, stating that: 'The spies of the United States are numerous, active, and unscrupulous. They invade the privacy of families, tamper with the confidential clerks of merchants, and have succeeded in converting a portion of the police of this country into secret agents of the United States.'[57] This was bad enough, but he complained that:

> The extent to which the system of bribery and spying has been and continues to be practised by agents of the United States in Europe is scarcely credible. The servants of gentlemen supposed to have Southern sympathies are tampered with, confidential clerks, and even the messengers from telegraph offices, are bribed to betray their trust, and I have lately been

informed that the English and French Post Offices, hitherto considered immaculate, are now scarcely safe modes of communication.[58]

He was particularly critical of Dudley, describing him as a person: 'who manifested a bitterness of temper, and practised a sharpness and asperity in language and correspondence, and a recklessness in his statements, which would have been appalling, but for the conviction that public sentiment in Europe would revolt against such pretentious extravagance'.[59] He also damned him with faint praise, saying:

> All who examine the records will admit that he manifested both zeal and ability, although he sometimes permitted the former to outrun his discretion. His own personal statements were doubtless made in good faith, but he often accepted the evidence of talebearers without duly testing the probability of the story or the character of the informer, and thus the evidence tendered by him failed when brought to the test of judicial inquiry; and appears to have been frequently discredited, or at least looked upon with suspicion, by the law officers of the Crown.[60]

This latter criticism did appear to have some validity. Dudley's enthusiasm appeared at times to run ahead of the facts. For example, in a letter to Adams he described the acts of the *Alabama* as piratical. Adams referred the letter to the British authorities who, in turn, sought the opinion of the Law Officers. They were not impressed, and reported: 'So far as relates to Mr Dudley's argument [...] that the *Alabama* is an English piratical craft, it might have been enough to say that Mr Dudley, while he enumerates everything which is immaterial, omits everything that is material, to constitute that character.'[61]

To strengthen his hand in Europe, President Jefferson Davis decided to replace the Confederate commissioners in London and Paris and sent James Murray Mason to London and John Slidell to Paris. Having evaded the Union blockade at Charleston in October 1861 they arrived in Cuba where they embarked on the *Trent*, a British mail packet. However, a US warship, the sloop *San Jacinto*, commanded by Captain Charles Wilkes, stopped the ship off Cuba and a boarding party removed Mason and Slidell and their two secretaries, all of whom ended up in prison in Boston. In Britain, the government and popular opinion were outraged by this incident, which was contrary to international law. (There was more than a whiff of hypocrisy in this as British warships had for long stopped American ships and removed any British sailors on board who were then impressed into the Royal Navy.) The British demanded the immediate release of the men and made it clear that failure to comply could lead to hostilities. Lincoln had enough to worry him and was anxious not to become embroiled in a limited military action or even a war with Britain, hence his oft-quoted remark: 'One war at a time.' Accordingly, a compromise solution was found. Mason and Slidell were released on 1 January 1862, allowed to continue on their way and Captain Wilkes was said to have acted without instructions. Writing a few weeks after this, Adams, the United States Minister in London, remarked:

> The disputed mock-heroes, who came so near creating a war between people vastly better than themselves, have arrived safe and sound in this city. The Trent affair has proved thus far somewhat in the nature of a sharp thunderstorm which has burst without doing any harm,

and the consequence has been a decided improvement of the state of the atmosphere. Our English friends are pleased with themselves and pleased with us for having given them the opportunity to be so. The natural effect is to reduce the apparent dimensions of all other causes of offense.[62]

Zebina Eastman, consul in Bristol, when recalling the fallout from what he described as the 'Deluge of the Trent' said: 'There was awful indignation, you may believe, with the John Bulls; they tore around as if they were already in our China shop. I felt as if I were the only one in a minority on that question. Yet I believed then and now [1872] that it was wrong and an unfortunate affair for us.'[63]

It is worth keeping in mind that the Southern cotton trade played such a pivotal role in the Confederacy's attempts to gain international recognition that the policy became known as king cotton diplomacy. Cotton was also important to Liverpool's commercial and mercantile development. In 1801 Liverpool had a population of about 77,000, which rose to 437,740 in 1861; in 1801 it had a merchant fleet of 459,719 tons, which by 1861 had risen to '4,977,272 tons, an increase of about 1000 percent. All this development was fundamentally due to the growth of the cotton industry.'[64] Britain also relied heavily on Southern imports. In 1858, Britain's total imports amounted to 931,847,056 tons, of which 732,403,840 tons came from the South.[65] With this in mind, the Confederacy had imposed an embargo on its cotton exportation in the belief that Britain (and France, equally dependent on the commodity) would support its cause, would force the North to raise the blockade of Southern ports, and bring about the recognition of the Confederate states. However, the tactic was unsuccessful. Thanks to unusually good crops in 1859 and 1860, Britain and France had been able to build up sufficient stores of surplus raw cotton to see them through the immediate impasse, although towards the end of 1862 their cotton industries began to experience serious difficulties. After the spring of 1862 the South relaxed, then scrapped, its self-imposed embargo since it was having difficulty obtaining supplies from abroad and cotton was 'the only medium of exchange left in the South which was acceptable abroad.'[66] A further factor was that, by then, Britain had significantly increased its importation of cotton from India and by the end of the war was getting 85 percent of its supply from that country.[67] Also, significant numbers of ships were successfully breaching the blockade, arriving with arms and gunpowder and general supplies and leaving with cotton.[68] For example, the US consul in Tampico, Mexico, told the State Department that British cotton buyers and New York cotton importers took on large cargoes of cotton at his port and shipped it direct to Liverpool or New York.[69]

Another of Bulloch's early actions was buying the screw steamship *Fingal*, which had been built in Greenock for use within Scotland. He had it loaded surreptitiously in Greenock with 15,000 rifles, other guns and ammunition. Flying the British flag and captained by a British officer, it sailed from Greenock on 11 October 1861 and four days later picked up Bulloch and a few others at Holyhead from where it headed off to run the blockade, arriving in Savannah Harbour, Georgia, on 12 November.[70] Pollaky, Morse's private detective, had been keeping the ship under surveillance. Although he had not prevented its departure he remained remarkably upbeat in the three-page report that he sent to Sanford on 11 October 1861, stating that: 'The Fingal is gone. We have a full descriptive Sketch of her which I gave this day to Mr M [Freeman Morse] who will send it off today by Despatch box or tomorrow by mail to the States. We have a start of [*sic*] her anyhow, and will capture her notwithstanding she is a fast screw.'[71]

Bulloch was not the only Confederate agent working to purchase ships and matériel in Britain. Lieutenant James H. North, Lieutenant George Terry Sinclair (previously described) and Commander Matthew Fontaine Maury were also active, the first two of them were interested in ships in Glasgow shipyards, but their efforts proved unsuccessful.[72] Another agent, but with another agenda, was Henry Hotze. Ostensibly a journalist, in modern parlance he is best described as a propagandist or spinmeister. He was an under-cover Confederate operative who wrote pro-Confederacy editorials which he gave to a small coterie of freelance leader writers; they, in turn, sold them on a non-attributable basis to leading newspapers and journals. He also founded a successful weekly review called *Index, A Weekly Journal of Politics, Literature, and News*, 'which appeared to be a British publication', and 'hired British journalists and syndicated their pro-Confederate articles to dozens of British and European publications'.[73] Other agents were Major Edward Anderson and Major (previously Captain, see preceding) Caleb Huse who purchased military supplies, the latter using credit supplied by Fraser, Trenholm & Co. of Liverpool, and Nathaniel Beverly Tucker who purchased commissary supplies. Tucker had been consul in Liverpool until 1861 and as we have seen was severely criticized by a US Treasury auditor for his financial probity while in charge of it.[74]

Let us return now to the *Alabama* and its activities. Dudley and his spies were keeping a close watch on the ship with a view to getting the British government to prevent its sailing. In the meantime, after its launch from Laird's shipyard on 14 May 1862 the ship set out on 29 July for what was supposed to be a test sail with Bulloch as well as guests and a band on board. After a successful test, Bulloch, the guests and band were taken off by the tug *Hercules* and sailed back to Birkenhead while the *Alabama* continued on and anchored off the Welsh coast. The following morning, Bulloch boarded the tug once more and rendezvoused with the *Alabama*, to which he transferred. It dropped him off near the north-west coast of Ireland and then headed for the Azores to meet up with the British merchant ship *Agrippina* which transferred arms and ammunition to it. The *Alabama* had managed to escape, but unknown to Bulloch the ship's paymaster, Clarence Yonge, was reporting back to Dudley.[75] Dudley's annoyance at the escape may, how-ever, have been tempered by his awareness that he could have done more to prevent it. Adams had asked him on 20 June [1862] to obtain the necessary witness statements affirming that the ship was intended for the Confederacy, with a view to using them in a possible legal action. But Dudley delayed doing this and decided to visit his friend William L. Dayton, the minister in Paris. When he returned to Liverpool on 7 July, he discovered that Adams had asked Henry Wilding, the vice consul, to give all the evi-dence about the ship to the local customs collector. Dudley then did so, but it was not in a legally acceptable form and of course the Board of Customs' legal advisers rejected it as inadmissible. Adams told Dudley to re-submit the documents but this time to engage a solicitor to ensure that they were in proper form. These were presented once more to the local customs collector. Consideration of the evidence then became the subject of protracted deliberation by some of the most senior government legal authorities in

England. However, due to a succession of errors, including, bizarrely, the papers being passed to the Queen's Advocate Sir John Harding who had been formally committed as a lunatic and had taken the papers with him to the asylum, the decision was taken on 30 July that the *Alabama* should be prevented from sailing. But this was too late, the ship had sailed the previous day. If Dudley had carried out Adams' initial instruction a few weeks would have been saved and this might have speeded up the final decision.[76]

Such was the extent of the damage inflicted by the *Alabama* on US shipping that the State Department decided to establish a consulate on St Helena, in the south Atlantic. This was because: 'Many destitute seamen have been landed [on St Helena], taken from burning vessels destroyed by the Alabama, and the presence of a consul there to receive and afford relief to our seamen, and to communicate intelligence to our naval officers, and masters of American whalers and merchantmen touching at this port, to and from India and China, is imperatively required.'[77] Confederate cruisers were estimated to have captured or sunk more than one hundred and fifty US merchant ships and caused such widespread fear that many US ships transferred to the flag of other countries.[78] On 11 June 1864 the *Alabama* put into Cherbourg for refitting, word of this got out to the North and the USS *Kearsage* was positioned outside the harbour. Almost in the manner of a duel between gentlemen, the two captains (Winslow and Semmes, respectively) agreed that the *Alabama* would be allowed to leave the harbour and their ships would fight seven miles beyond it. In the ensuing short engagement on 19 June, the *Alabama* was sunk. Zebina Eastman, the consul at Bristol, was in chapel on that day and recalled the clergyman's remarks:

My pastor, Rev. Hebditch, who from indifference became a fast friend of our country – always prayed for us in our calamity – that day he prayed most earnestly, that the right might triumph. Just as he had said the words, as one of his parishioners the next day computed the time, the [cannon]ball of the Kearsage struck the Alabama in the hull. Our minister was noted for his efficacy in prayer, and this cause of right made a good hit.[79]

Attitudes in Britain towards the Civil War

It is difficult to give a clear-cut description of British attitudes towards the warring parties during the Civil War. North and South were both highly critical of Britain's decision to remain neutral, feeling that the decision weakened their respective causes. On the other hand, Britain regarded the North's blockade of Southern ports as a particularly unfriendly move as it seriously affected the important cotton trade between the countries. Generally speaking, however, although there were notable exceptions in all classes, the sympathies of the British upper and middle classes were with the South (the plantation landowners) while those of the working class were with the North (the abolitionists). A leading English economist, the curiously named Nassau William Senior, summed up the feelings of many in Britain at the time. He complained to his old friend John Murray Forbes (who, as we have seen, had been sent to Britain with Aspinwall):

One thing has tended to embitter us, your different treatment of France and of us. The conduct of the two governments has been identical [both had proclaimed their neutrality in the conflict], but you have been as civil to France as you have been rude to us. Now I happen to know that the French feeling is with the South. They say that the New Orleans people are their brethren. They are all friends of slavery, and I have peculiar reasons for believing that Louis Napoleon proposed to our government to join him in breaking the blockade.[80]

Although under considerable pressure, Adams, the American minister in London, tried to adopt a light-hearted tone. Writing to his son Charles Francis Adams Jr. (an army officer), he remarked: 'In the meanwhile the [British] newspapers indulge their respective fancies as freely as ever. Their abuse is not very pleasant, but I am always consoled for it, when I reflect that Lord Lyons [the British Minister in Washington] is likely to get about as much on his side.'[81] A notable exception was the weekly conservative magazine *The Spectator* which has claimed that it 'was the only publication in Britain to offer unequivocal support to the North over the slave-owning South'.[82] For much of the time, however, there was a great deal of gloom among the American diplomatic and consular representatives about British attitudes towards the war. Dudley, in Liverpool, reported to Secretary of State Seward: 'The current is against us and is strong: and threatens to carry everything with it. I do not think we have any thing to depend upon in this country or Europe. They are all against us and would rejoice in our downfall.'[83] In London, Adams lamented: 'Every effort to run the blockade is made under British protection. Every manifestation of sympathy with the rebel success springs from British sources. This feeling is not the popular feeling, but it is that of the governing classes. With many honourable exceptions the aristocracy entertain it as well as the commercial interest.'[84] Even the mood of his younger son, Henry, who was his father's unofficial and unpaid private secretary in the legation, reflected this:

> As for this country, the simple fact is that it is unanimously against us and becomes more firmly set every day. From hesitation and neutrality, people here are now fairly decided. It is acknowledged that our army is magnificent and that we have been successful and may be still more so, but the feeling is universal against us. If we succeed, it will still be the same. It is a sort of dogged English prejudice, and there is no dealing with it.[85]

British official support for the South appeared to be strengthened when William Ewart Gladstone, the Chancellor of the Exchequer, gave a speech in Newcastle upon Tyne on 7 October 1862 in which he stated that the South had made an army and navy and 'they have made a nation'. And he added his belief that: 'We may anticipate with certainty the success of the Southern States so far as regards their separation from the North. I cannot but believe that that event is as certain as any event yet future and contingent can be.'[86] Two weeks later, on 23 October, Adams had a meeting with Lord John Russell, the Foreign Secretary, who informed him that Gladstone's speech had been regretted by the Prime Minister (Lord Palmerston) and other members of the cabinet, and that government policy remained one of strict neutrality although 'he could not tell what a month would bring forth'.[87]

Despatches between an ambassador and a secretary of state are generally kept from the public gaze, at least for a few years. But towards the end of 1862 Secretary of State Seward decided to publish the despatches he had been receiving from Adams. Adams was surprised and irritated by this but remarked, resignedly: 'I have said merely what everybody knows. The great body of the aristocracy and the wealthy commercial classes are anxious to see the United States go to pieces. On the other hand the middle and lower class sympathize with us, more and more as they better comprehend the true nature of the struggle.'[88] A succession of early Southern victories suggested that a Confederate States of America would indeed be established, and it was only after the North's victory in the Battle of Gettysburg in July 1863 that the tide turned irretrievably in favour of the United States. But more than two months later Adams remained gloomy:

> The aristocracy are very much against us, but they do little or nothing to sustain the rebellion beyond the mere force of opinion. The commercial and moneyed people go a step farther and furnish more or less of material aid. On the other hand we have the sympathy of the majority of the inferior class, whose strength consists merely in opinion. The balance of political influence is therefore adverse.[89]

As late as April 1864, Adams's son Henry was equally despondent: 'As for politics, there has been scarcely any time when our hopes stood so low in the opinion of persons in this country. The current is dead against us, and the atmosphere so uncongenial that the idea of the possibility of our success is not admitted.'[90] There was considerable support for the Confederacy in Liverpool, which was the port of arrival for most of the cotton for the Lancashire cotton mills. Fraser, Trenholm and Company was an important merchant house in the city with offices also in Charleston, South Carolina. It acted effectively as the Confederate government's bankers in Britain. Its partner in Charleston, George A. Trenholm, became secretary to the Confederate states' Treasury in 1864. Charles Kuhn Prioleau, partner in the Liverpool office, had been born in Charleston. The company was therefore wholly committed to the Confederate cause and provided the essential financial backing for the purchase of armaments. However, its motives were not entirely patriotic. The partners were also pragmatic businessmen and the financial backing was given in return for cotton. Of course, once again, all this complied with the letter if not the spirit of the law, since none of these armaments was supplied to any of the ships being built for the Confederacy in Britain. Instead, they were transported on British merchant ships, which then met up with the British-built ships in international waters where transfers took place.

Despite the dispiritedness of Adams and his son, and Gladstone's injudicious remarks, the Civil War ended in victory for the North on 9 April 1865 when General Robert E. Lee surrendered the Army of Northern Virginia to General Ulysses S. Grant at Appomattox. Lincoln was assassinated a few days later, on 14 April.[91] President Davis was captured the following month and imprisoned on treason charges until May 1867, when he was released on bail pending trial. No trial was held and he finally benefited from an amnesty in February 1869.[92] The Union was secure. Feelings in Britain continued to be strained, however, as the United States pursued with vigour its claims against the British government over the depredations allegedly caused by the latter's unwillingness or inability to prevent the building of warships for use by the Confederacy, particularly the *Alabama*. The question would not be finally resolved until 1872.

The United States sought compensation for the damage caused by Confederate cruisers, claiming that Britain had allowed them to be built in British shipyards knowing that they would end up in the Confederate Navy, and permitted them to be armed, albeit subsequently on the high seas, by British companies. The amount of compensation sought was huge. Some US politicians even wanted Britain to hand over Canada (known then as British North America) as part of the reparation. All claims were rejected by the British. However, after protracted negotiations both sides agreed to submit the claims to a joint high commission, which met in Washington for the first time on 27 February 1871. Under the terms of the subsequent Treaty of Washington, signed on 8 May 1871, both countries agreed to submit all claims to a tribunal of arbitration. The tribunal met in Geneva and was composed of five arbitrators from the United States, Britain, Italy, Brazil and Switzerland. Its findings, issued in September 1872, were that Britain should pay the United States $15.5 million in gold.[93] US consuls were instructed to try to recover Confederate property from individuals or organizations. In particular, legal action was taken against Fraser, Trenholm & Co. Bulloch alleged that the: 'unhappy firm was pursued with relentless zeal, and was so persistently involved by their persecutors in Chancery and other proceedings, that it was hardly possible for the partners to give due attention to their private business, and finally their financial credit was affected, and they were reduced to commercial ruin'.[94] Several presidential proclamations of amnesty and pardon were issued with a view to reconstructing the nation. However, they excluded certain categories of persons, such as Confederate officers and agents and persons who had been or were absentees from the United States for the purpose of aiding the rebellion. Bulloch fell into both categories. He saw that his future lay outside the United States and on 14 January 1869 applied for British naturalization, supported by four local merchants who 'solemnly and sincerely declared' that he was 'a man of great respectability and loyally disposed towards her Majesty Queen Victoria'. His application was granted on 21 January.[95] The last act of President Andrew Johnson, who as Vice President had assumed office after Lincoln's assassination, was to issue an unconditional amnesty on Christmas Day, 1868. Of course, by that time Bulloch was well on the road to becoming a British citizen and one wonders if he might have returned to America had the unconditional amnesty come earlier. However, for the rest of his life he was a merchant in Liverpool and became Director of the Liverpool Nautical College.[96] His nephew, future president Theodore Roosevelt, visited him there on several occasions. Bulloch died in Liverpool on 7 January 1901 and is buried in Toxteth Cemetery, in the city's Smithdown Road. A stone was erected on his tomb in 1968 by the United Daughters of the Confederacy, and they also placed dedicated grave markers on it in January 2001.

William H. Seward was secretary of state throughout the Civil War. An austere figure, described as an Anglophobe,[97] he was vigorous and relentless in his determination to thwart Confederate ship-purchasing activities in Britain. However, his criticism of the actions of the British authorities that had permitted the *Alabama*'s escape softened following a visit he made to the Foreign Office after the war, on 15 September 1871. He commented that administration procedures in Britain:

> had been contrived to secure caution and deliberation at the expense of time; while in the United States the more simple constitution of the departments gives greater promptness and dispatch, at the risk, perhaps, of precipitancy. We no longer wonder at the blunder of the

British Government in failing to stop the Alabama, when we see that no secretary could move on that question until he had the studied opinion of the 'law advisers of the crown.' The Government of the United States has one legal adviser, the Attorney General, who sits in the Cabinet, and advises, like other heads of departments, without having questions specially referred to him, except on extraordinary occasions.[98]

The Civil War had been a challenging time for the Consular Service. Established for just over seventy years it had to change from its role of protecting US citizens and shipping, and monitoring and protecting American commercial interests, to conducting clandestine activities against individuals who only a few short years previously they regarded as fellow countrymen. But they rose to the challenge and played a significant role in thwarting the Confederacy's attempts to acquire ships and matériel. After the war, the immediate task for the United States was the difficult process of reuniting the divided country. And for the Consular Service, at least in Britain, it was time to resume its normal role, one that did not involve espionage and counter-espionage duties. So, what was its normal role? The preceding chapters have given numerous examples of consul functions and duties. However, in the following chapters we look in detail at a representative sample of 15 consulates in all the regions of Britain and how they conducted their business over the years. This includes the dates on which the offices were operational, short biographies of the staffs who served in them, and an indication of their routine activities, including a few incidents or highlights.

Part 3

Chapter Six

CONSULAR POSTS AND CONSULAR AGENCIES IN MAJOR CITIES

An idea of the variety and extent of the United States consular presence in Britain, and Ireland up to independence in 1922, may be gained from the lists shown in the Appendix. The first offices were established in 1790 and over the years there was scarcely a city or town that did not have an American consular presence of some description, whether a consulate general, consulate, vice consulate, consular agency, or commercial agency. It would be difficult to provide a history of all of the offices. However, the 15 shown in Chapters 7 to 21 – Belfast, Birmingham, Bradford, Bristol, Cardiff, Dublin, Dundee, Dunfermline, Edinburgh and Leith, Falmouth, Liverpool, London, Newcastle upon Tyne, Southampton and Stoke on Trent – have been selected to give a representative sample from all the regions of the United Kingdom, plus Ireland up to 1922. The accounts in each of these micro-histories describe the individuals who staffed the offices, the nature of the business transacted, the office accommodation, mundane as well as important incidents, accommodation, routines, health, dangers faced during wartime, and closures (with the exception of the consulates in Edinburgh and Belfast, both of which have been established for more than two hundred years). All of which will, it is hoped, give a better understanding of this relatively unrecognized, but important, area of foreign relations. One feature that soon becomes noticeable in all of the accounts is the wide variety of previous occupations held by the early consuls who joined the original Consular Service – for example, lawyer, blacksmith, ship's figurehead carver, newspaper editor, army officer, politician, clergyman, rancher, pharmacist, worker in a reindeer enterprise, worker in paving and road construction. Such an interesting and diverse mix of backgrounds inevitably produced many 'characters' in the early Consular Service so that there was no stereotypical model of an American consul in those early days. Unlike, for example, in the British Consular Service and its offshoots – the China Consular Service and the Levant Consular Service – whose entrants were drawn largely from similar backgrounds and education and for the most part without the influence of political patronage. This may also have been true of members of the consular services of other European countries at the time. However, there is no denying that the histories of the consulates in these chapters make fascinating reading.

Chapter Seven

BELFAST

Ireland was part of Great Britain until 1922 when it became the Irish Free State, a dominion within the British Commonwealth. The United States opened its first consulate in Ireland in Dublin in 1790 and six years later it opened another in the north of the island, in Belfast. While the Dublin consul was an American, the Belfast one was British – James Holmes, a local merchant who served for almost twenty years until 1815 when he was succeeded by James Luke, another local businessman. It was not until 1830 that an American, Thomas W. Gilpin of Philadelphia, was appointed. He served until 1842 and had a second appointment from 1845 until 1847. Also in 1830, the first consular office in Londonderry was opened, headed by Thomas Davenport as vice consul. Between then and 1920 the Belfast and Londonderry offices were variously consulates, vice consulates and consular agencies. There were also other consular offices between 1842 and 1908 in Newry, Ballymena, Sligo and Lurgan, which were subordinate to Belfast and Londonderry. In the southern part of the island there were consular offices at various times, sometimes for only short periods, in Athlone, Ballina, Cobh, Cork, Crookhaven, Dundalk, Galway, Kingstown, Limerick, Waterford and Wexford.

Belfast was a busy consulate and the total value of goods exported to America from its district during 1871 and the first quarter of 1872 exceeded £2.5 million, or almost $11 million, and the consulate earned almost $16,000 in fees from certifying these goods. The goods were not shipped direct to America but via Liverpool. The consulate had only one subordinate agency, at Ballymena.[1] In 1881 the consulate moved premises to 5 Donegal Square, and the following year it established an additional agency at Lurgan.[2] In 1885 George Washington Savage, born in New York, was appointed, and nominated his son John Marbacher Savage as his vice consul. Both would later serve in Dundee. Savage was succeeded by Samuel Ruby (1889–1893) and James B. Taney (1893–1896). In 1896, Taney appointed Malcolm T. Brice as his vice and deputy consul. Brice was also an American citizen, a native of West Virginia, who after graduation at the Linsly Military Academy in 1893 had gone to Belfast to attend art school in 1894 and then entered the consulate as clerk the following year.[3] He remained until 1901 when he returned to the United States. Taney was succeeded in July 1897 by William W. Touvelle, a native of Ohio, who had qualified as a lawyer and had practised mainly as a public prosecutor in the state until being appointed to Belfast. The consulate was housed in two rooms of the Scottish Provident Building at the corner of Wellington Place and Donegal Square. Touvelle was succeeded by Samuel S. Knabenshue and Henry B. Miller.

The early part of the twentieth century in Ireland was a period of intense internal political struggles and conflicts. A protracted campaign for Home Rule (that is, devolving government of the entire island, but remaining part of the United Kingdom) was followed by the Irish War of Independence from 1919 to 1921. This led to the Anglo–Irish Treaty of 1921 which created the Irish Free State the following year. The Free State was a self-governing dominion within the British Empire, similar to the status of Australia and Canada at the time. It was composed of the majority of the island, with 26 counties, while the remaining 6 counties formed Northern Ireland which became an integral part of the United Kingdom.[4] The massive upheavals of the First World War also took place within this period. Hunter Sharp served as consul throughout the time, from 1911 until 1920 when he was succeeded by William Kent and transferred to Edinburgh. The consulate was upgraded to a consulate general in 1924 and successive consuls general from then until the start of the Second World War were Henry Starrett, Thomas Bowman, Lucien Memminger and Ernest Ives. During the war, Northern Ireland saw considerable military activity and suffered great losses as a result of German air raids on its important shipbuilding and aircraft industries. Casualty rates were high. Consuls who served at this time were John Randolph, Parker Buhrman and Quincy Roberts.

One of the aftermaths of the Second World War was the large number of women marrying American servicemen who had been based in the United Kingdom. One estimate suggests that 1,800 women from Northern Ireland did so. In 1946, a group of about a hundred of these wives occupied the consulate demanding transportation to America to join their husbands. The consul general, Quincy Roberts, met the leaders and assured them he was doing everything he could to arrange transportation, saying 'Your husbands want you and you want your husbands, and, believe me, we don't want to detain you here one moment longer than necessary.' Roberts himself went on to marry a local woman.[5] Appointments continued regularly every few years and there were nine between Roberts's transfer at the beginning of 1948 and 1971.

In 1972, Lawrence H. Hydle arrived in Belfast from Vietnam as vice consul for political affairs. 'I was there, kind of like in Da Nang [...] and I basically did political reporting.' The consul general at the time was Grover Penberthy (1971–1974). Hydle recalls that one of the things that struck him soon after arriving in Belfast:

> was that actually there were a very significant number of Irish Catholics who did not want to be part of the Irish republic; [they] wanted to be part of the UK but they wanted to be treated fairly. They were not separatists. They were civil rights guys basically. Whereas I found that most Irish American politicians and their constituents have ideas about Northern Ireland that were formed maybe back in 1920, frozen in time.

He also recalled escorting a congressman whose 'idea of a moderate politician was Jerry [sic] Adams who was then clearly an IRA guy.'[6] During his stint in Belfast, Hydle was sent back to Vietnam on a temporary duty assignment of a few months to assist with monitoring the success of the 1973 peace agreement there. He returned to Belfast, finally leaving in 1974. Penberthy, the consul general, also left in 1974 and was posted to Liberia; he was succeeded by Peter Spicer who had transferred from Swaziland. He remained in Belfast until 1977. Much of his three successors' time was taken up with reporting on the continuing political unrest in Northern Ireland.[7]

Robert P. Myers Jr., served as consul general from August 1986 and was in the course of leaving when the post was inspected in the summer of 1989; his deputy, consul Francis Scanlon, was in charge during inspection. The report noted that although it had been recommended that the consulate general, together with the one in Edinburgh, should be closed, the inspectors disagreed. They said that it should remain 'at the same size and with the same functions as at present, for policy, political, and consular reasons', but added that 'Careful consideration should be given [...] to the security risks and benefits of [its] location.' Moreover, the post had 'screened out some likely terrorists who would probably not have been detected by the more mechanized visa screening.' However the clincher in ensuring the continuance of the post was summed up thus: 'Finally, and perhaps most importantly, to close the post in the face of terrorist activities designed to disrupt the efforts of the United Kingdom and a great majority of both sectarian communities to promote economic and political progress would give an undesirable political signal. It would assist the terrorists' aims and would be resented strongly by British allies.' The question of relocating the offices had been under consideration since the early 1970s because of the security situation. However, the inspectors concluded that 'While the danger of the current location is real [...] no place in Belfast is secure from a terrorist bomb attack.'[8] The 'Compliance Followup Review' to the inspection noted that the inspectors' recommendation in respect of equipping an 'armored sedan' had been implemented.[9]

Douglas B. Archard took over in July 1989 and was in charge when the next inspection took place in 1993. Security aspects featured prominently throughout the report. It notes that Archard had 'performed impressively in strengthening the US image among all legitimate elements in Northern Ireland society'.[10] The post's: 'reporting on terrorist activities and significant political developments is prompt, adequate in coverage, and usually contains a brief, pertinent comment. However, there is almost no classified analytical reporting, which should be corrected in the next post reporting plan.'[11] It noted that the 'post's familiarity with the sensitive security situation has been the key argument against consolidating consular functions in [the] Embassy'.[12] The inspectors continued to believe that the office should remain in its current building.[13] The report concluded that: 'Over the past four years [...] Belfast has performed impressively in strengthening the US image among the contending elements in Northern Ireland and pursuing the US goal of a peaceful, negotiated settlement.'[14] Archard's successor was Valentino Martinez who remained until 1995 (see following paragraph regarding one of his assignments while there).

Kathleen Stephens arrived in July 1995, the first woman to be appointed consul general, although women had held junior consular posts.[15] She was succeeded by another woman, Jane Fort, who took over in July 1998. During her time, the embassy and the consulates general in Belfast and Edinburgh were inspected in 1999. The report placed greater emphasis on the role of the Belfast consulate general in the peace process in Northern Ireland, stressing that this required careful coordination between the embassies in London and Dublin. The inspectors recommended that 'although subordinate to Embassy London, the location of the Consulate General and the cross-border nature of many US programs and activities supporting the peace process place a premium on the role of the Consulate General'.[16] In a masterly understatement the inspectors noted: 'Fortunately, policy differences that previously characterized the dialogue between London and Dublin have given way to a more collaborative relationship.'[17] These 20 words mask what were at one time serious disagreements between the ambassadors in London and Dublin. Raymond Seitz, the ambassador in London, was a career diplomat and the first (and still, the only) non-political appointee to hold the London post in its long history. Jean Kennedy Smith, the ambassador in Dublin, was a political shoo-in, a sister of President Kennedy and Senator Edward Kennedy. She had her own agenda in respect of Irish reunification and was 'an ardent IRA apologist'.[18] Gerry Adams, the president of Sinn Fein, the political wing of the Irish Republican Army (IRA), had consistently been refused a visa to enter the United States when he had applied at the consulate general in Belfast. Seitz in London, career members of the Dublin Embassy staff and, within the Clinton administration in Washington, the State Department, the Justice Department, the FBI and the CIA were all opposed to granting him a visa.[19] However, Smith was in favour of it and was able to exert considerable influence through her strong family connections. Adams made a further application and in January 1994 was interviewed in Belfast by consul general Valentino Martinez (1993–1995) who was given a list of questions by Washington to be answered by Adams. These included being asked whether he was prepared to state publicly that 'you personally renounce violence'. Based on his replies, both Martinez and Seitz felt that Adams had not met the requirements that had been laid down for granting the visa.[20] Nevertheless, bowing to the strong Irish American lobby, President Clinton personally authorized it. Smith did not take kindly to the fact that several of her staff had sent a cable of dissent to the State Department registering their opposition to her recommendation and life was made difficult for two of them, particularly the consul general James P. Callahan. They complained to the Department and this led to an investigation by the Office of Inspector General. As a result of its findings, Smith was formally reprimanded in a letter from Secretary of State Warren Christopher in early 1996.[21] In May 1994, Seitz was succeeded as ambassador in London by Admiral William J. Crowe, a political appointee. Crowe later described the situation in which he found himself when dealing with the Irish problem. Speaking during an interview in 1998, after he had retired from the post, he said:

'On Irish matters, I did not deal with the State Department. I dealt with the National Security Council. State Department literally opted out.' *Interviewer:* 'It just didn't want to get in on this?' *Crowe:* 'They wanted to and they tried, but they discovered early in the game that Lake wasn't going to let them in it.' *Interviewer:* 'This is Tony Lake, the National Security Advisor.' *Crowe:* 'And Nancy Soderburg, his deputy. They were going to handle Ireland problems.'

He was asked about the role of the ambassador during this time.

Crowe: 'Northern Ireland was part of Great Britain and we have a Consul there now, which we probably wouldn't have had except for this problem. We would have eliminated it. It was essentially the lead-in to North Ireland politics. The Sein Finn [*sic*] was very wary, however. They much preferred to deal with the Ambassador down in Dublin because she was very sympathetic to them.' *Interviewer:* 'Who was this?' *Crowe:* 'Jean Kennedy Smith'.[22]

The consulate was heavily involved in the peace agreement process throughout 'the troubles' and at times operated more like an embassy, receiving numerous high-level visitors, including several visits by President Clinton. One of its many routine functions was submitting 'relevant biographic data on persons charged with, or suspected of, terrorist activities'. This is known as the 'visa viper program', which screens such persons against a watchlist should they apply for visas or seek to enter the United States.[23] The 1999 inspection report noted that the consulate general 'continues to lead consular posts worldwide in the submission of such data to the Department'.[24] Barbara J. Stephenson was consul general from 2001 until 2004.[25]

In 2004, the consulate general moved from its city centre offices in Queen Street to Danesfort House, a large house in its own grounds in the south of the city. Dean Pittman arrived later that year, from Baghdad, and was succeeded in September 2007 by Susan M. Elliott. Elliott's assignment lasted until June 2009, when she was transferred to Moscow as minister counselor for political affairs.[26] Her successor, Kamala S. Lakhdhir, arrived in August from the State Department where she had been Director of the Office of Maritime Southeast Asia in the Bureau of East Asian and Pacific Affairs. She left Belfast for Washington in November 2011 to take up appointment as executive assistant to the under secretary for political affairs. Kevin Roland, who had been deputy consul general since 2009, became acting consul general. His appointment in Belfast seems curious, given that he was a Middle East specialist and an Arabic speaker, but is an example of the varied career of a Foreign Service officer. He left in April 2012 and was replaced for a few months by Sandra Kaiser, a former diplomat. She held the fort until June, when the new consul general Gregory S. Burton arrived from Afghanistan where he had been senior deputy coordinating director for development and economic affairs at the embassy in Kabul. He was succeeded in July 2015 by Daniel J. Lawton who arrived from Washington where he had been deputy director of the State Department's Office of Southern European Affairs.[27] He is still in post at the time of writing. It can be seen from this long roll call that the State Department has frequently sent some of its most experienced officers to serve in Belfast.

Chapter Eight

BIRMINGHAM

Birmingham is a large important city in the midlands. American consular representation there began in 1836 when Alfred Burrish, a local businessman, was appointed consular agent. He was succeeded in 1840 by another local businessman, John Mason Guest Underhill, who served until 1865, but it was not until 1865 that the first American citizen was appointed agent; he was Elihu Burritt of Connecticut. A philanthropist, he was nicknamed 'the learned blacksmith' because that had been his earlier career; before taking up his appointment he was heavily involved in world peace movements and other causes.[1] He served until 1869, when another American, J. B. Gould of Maine, was appointed consul. Gould had previously been nominated as consul in Cork but for some reason the appointment had not been taken up. By the time of his appointment to Birmingham there were consular agencies in Leicester, Wolverhampton, Kidderminster and Redditch that reported directly to him.

Birmingham was one of the busiest consulates in Britain. In the year ended 30 September 1871 the value of goods exported to the United States and verified by the consulate and its agencies was almost $8 million. The fee income from certifying the invoices for exported goods earned the consulate and agencies more than $12,000 for the year ended 30 June 1872.[2] In 1878, Eugene Schuyler, a high flier in the Consular Service, arrived in place of Sevellon A. Brown, Chief Clerk of the State Department, who had been nominated but had declined the appointment.[3] Schuyler was an expert on Russia and Central Asia and during the previous 11 years had held posts in Moscow, Reval (renamed Tallinn, Estonia), St Petersburg and Constantinople. Given his background it was obvious that he would not remain long in Birmingham and, indeed, he left the following year.[4] However, during his short time in Birmingham he occupied himself by finishing his translation of Tolstoy's novel *The Cossacks*.[5] Later in his career he wrote *American Diplomacy*, which became a standard work on US foreign affairs.[6] In 1879, Wilson King, of Pennsylvania, consul at Bremen, was appointed. He said years later:

> I had never heard anything pleasant about Birmingham when I first went there, and I was more than agreeably surprised to find a very modern town, governed by a body of capable, go-ahead, modern men. Everything was improving. Parks, libraries, picture galleries, baths were being started, slums were being torn down and rebuilt into better buildings, schools were being improved.[7]

King reminisced in 1923 about being in the Consular Service when consuls were replaced without any reason being given. After handing over the consulate to his successor in 1885: 'he received an official despatch in 1886 informing him that his accounts had been

Figure 8.1 Elihu Burritt, consular agent, Birmingham, 1865–1869. Burritt was born in New Britain, Connecticut, in 1810. He began working life as a blacksmith but was a passionate auto-didact, with an aptitude for learning difficult and archaic languages. He was deeply involved in the nineteenth-century pacifist movement and travelled widely lecturing on his anti-war beliefs in both the United States and Britain. In an unusual departure from this he was appointed consular agent in Birmingham where he served from 1865, the end of the Civil War, until 1869. [Author's collection.]

found to be correct, and that since then he has heard nothing. He says, "As I was never dismissed and did not resign, I must still be in the Service." '8

He returned home to Pittsburgh but in 1890: 'having arrived at the really romantic age, he married an English lady and settled down in Birmingham … [where he] was for two years a writer of weekly letters for a Boston paper and was also the Birmingham weekly correspondent for Pittsburgh papers for seventeen years'.9 King died in Birmingham on 21 January 1930, at the age of 83.[10] His successor in 1885 was Joseph B. Hughes.[11] Successive consuls appointed to the end of the nineteenth century were Adam Everly, John Jarrett, George F. Parker and Marshal Halstead. Halstead was appointed in 1897. During his term of office members of the local legal profession were disproportionately represented in the operation of the consulate and its agencies. The vice consul and the four consular agents were all practising lawyers.[12] Halstead resigned in 1906 to return home to Cincinnati to look after his ailing father, Murat Halstead, a former newspaper editor. Tragically, Marshal died early in 1908, some six months before his father and shortly after his own marriage. He was succeeded as consul in Birmingham in 1906 by his brother, Albert, at a salary of $4,500. After a career spent mainly in Europe, Albert's final appointment was to London from where he retired in 1932.[13] The agency at Leicester had closed by then.

In 1908, when the consulate received its first inspection under the 1906 Act, the inspector, Horace Lee Washington, noted that the offices at Newton Chambers, 43 Cannon Street, were rented from the vice consul Arthur V. Blakemore, appointed in 1907, who was a solicitor, as was his predecessor, and rented six offices, three of them to the consulate. In addition to the vice consul there were three other members of staff, all of them British. Washington remarked that: 'A door communicates with the solicitor's office of vice consul from the General Office. This door bears his sign as a Solicitor, which is unusual and noticeable.' It was certainly an unusual, though not unheard of, arrangement but it prompted an unnamed official in the Department to write a memo saying: 'Mr Johnson. Write Birmingham that Dept. would like to put an Amer. in his office as V & D & prin clerk [Vice and Deputy Consul and Principal Clerk] & ask if he cannot arrange his force as that this could be done & an Amer paid about 800 [dollars] per yr. Say that it is very desirable that the subordinate wherever possible be Amer & also that the prin clerk be also V & D.' It would be 1919 before this wish was implemented. Fee income for the year was $7,500. The overall rating for the consulate was 'good'.[14]

The next inspection was carried out in 1909 by Heaton W. Harris. As an aside to confirming that none of the staff was engaged in any other business he added:

'although Miss [Ethel] Webb [the stenographer] [...] sings frequently in the evening at professional entertainments. This, of course, does not interfere with her consular work.' Halstead gets glowing reports. He is:

exceptionally diligent in the matters of trade reports. It is a field in which he is exceptionally at home [...] his social and official standing in the community is good; [...] he and his family live in a good house [...] the consul owns his own home which includes about two acres of land [...]; [...] He is one of the very efficient men in this regard [writing reports] in the service; [...] this office is exceptionally strong in the attention given by the consul to trade reports and to the answering of commercial enquiries. The office has perhaps but few equals in the United Kingdom, if any, in this respect.

After reading these remarks it comes as something of a surprise to read at the end of the report: 'The inspector regrets not to be able to rate the consulate of this really brilliant and personally attractive man at least good. It should be rated as but Fair.'

He sums up his reasons:

> There will be no scandal attached to this office while under its present management. There
> is not the slightest suggestion of laziness or inactivity in the conduct of the office. The defects
> are chiefly those of routine […], [the consul] is sure his methods are best, the practice of
> other consulates is no concern to him. Some one has told him that he is the most efficient
> consul in the United Kingdom. He has not the slightest doubt this is true and would readily
> agree that he is the most efficient in the world. […] The inspector regrets to have to say this
> of a brilliant man from whom he received courteous treatment and who has many splendid
> qualifications.[15]

Harris also carried out the next inspection in 1911. Things had improved dramatically
in the interim. Halstead's personal rating changed to: 'Excellent. He has improved in
the conduct of his office very materially since the former inspection. His splendid work
in connection with the commercial side of his office, his vigor, energy and industry and
his degree of intelligence and conscientiousness fully make up for a little excess of self
esteem that in a weak man would detract from his standing.' Fee income had increased
to more than $12,000, almost nineteen hundred letters had been received and almost
two thousand one hundred sent. It was also noted that the sign on Blakemore's (the vice
consul) door denoting that he was a solicitor had been removed. The office's overall
rating was 'good'.[16] The next inspection was carried out in 1914, by Ralph J. Totten,
more than two months after the outbreak of the First World War. It was noted that as
Halstead had a private income 'his scale of living is perhaps on a more extravagant scale
than the salary of his office [$4,500 per year] would permit'. However, 'his home and
entertainments are a credit to the service'. His rating continued as 'excellent'. More than
four thousand invoices were certified and more than five hundred other certificates were
issued, all of this generating a fee income of more than $11,000. Seventeen hundred
letters were received and two thousand five hundred issued. The report concluded: 'After
carefully considering everything connected with this Office, the clean American tone
and the business-like treatment of visitors, the care with all the routine work and the
generally good impression made upon the stranger makes it possible to rate this office
EXCELLENT.'[17] Truly an amazing transformation from the inspection undertaken
in 1909.

Albert Halstead remained until 1915 when he was promoted to consul general and
assigned to Vienna.[18] His replacement was Samuel M. Taylor who was succeeded in
1917 by E. Haldeman Dennison who had served in Dundee from 1911 to 1915 and
arrived at Birmingham from his post as consul general in Christiana (Oslo). The first
inspection after the war was in 1919 when Dennison was already under orders to go
to Québec and his successor, Wilbur T. Gracey, had been appointed. Ralph J. Totten,
the inspector, commented that Dennison's: 'service spirit is but low because of his frequent transfers and the fact that he seems to never be satisfied with a post. He is in all
other ways, except physical, a good officer!' Totten explained his remark about 'physical'.
Dennison 'is very lame, probably locomotor ataxia. The move to Quebec would probably suit him as his wife was Canadian.'[19] Dennison was partly paralysed and walked

with the aid of two sticks. However, his move to Québec had tragic consequences. He served there until March 1931 when he overbalanced and fell into a bathtub of boiling water in his apartment and was severely scalded before his wife could pull him out. He died two days later.[20] Totten continued:

> He was inspected by the present Inspector at Dundee, 1914, Christiana, 1916 and Birmingham 1919. In Christiana he seems to have gotten worse but at present he is no worse and possibly better than at either of the other inspections. He drags both legs but can walk considerable distances. His general health is good. He always conducts a good office and has been rated excellent by the present Inspector at Dundee and Christiana, but at Birmingham there was little to do as the office was already in excellent condition.

The fee income had fallen to slightly less than $7,000. The vice consul, Albert Hilliard, was an American, the first to be appointed, and had recently arrived from Edinburgh where he had held a similar post. He was not, however, an asset; his: 'appearance and intelligence, poor [...] not the slightest interest in the work, not at all alert and no service spirit. [...] This young man [twenty-six years old] frankly admits that he only took the post of vice consul to get a foreign wedding trip and that he has no intention of remaining in the service. [...] He is incompetent and useless in the office. He may be rated POOR.' Fortunately, the other two staff, both young British women, were rated as 'EXCELLENT' and 'GOOD'. The remaining agencies at Kidderminster and Redditch had closed. The office was rated 'EXCELLENT, from every standpoint'.[21]

The consulate moved to new accommodation at 111 New Street in April 1920 and was inspected the following year, once again by Ralph Totten. The vice consul, Herbert C. Biar of Chicago, was temporarily in charge of the office and had transferred from Glasgow seven months prior to the inspection.[22] Invoice and visa business had increased considerably and had generated more than $33,000 for the year. Although business was just as brisk by the time of the next inspection, by Robert Frazer, Jr, in 1924, the fee income had fallen to almost $14,000. This was probably due to increased staff costs: in addition to the consul, John Franklin Jewell, who had been appointed in 1922, there were now six members of staff, two of them American, all of whom were under the age of thirty and were rated between 'good' and 'very good'.[23] The next inspection was conducted by Louis G. Dreyfus, Jr, in 1926. Business had once again increased, and after deducting staff and other expenditure the consulate was able to remit more than $18,000 to the Treasury.[24]

Harry Campbell was appointed in 1928, serving there until 1930. His successor, George A. Makinson, who had been in post since 1930, was coming to the end of his tour of duty when the consulate was inspected in March 1934 by Homer M. Byington. Fee income continued to show strong levels, and for the years 1932 and 1933 was $23,000 and $20,000, respectively. Byington drew attention to requests to consulates from the embassy for political reporting. The consulate prepared regular monthly political reports and:

> it may not be amiss to add that Birmingham was among the posts mentioned by the Embassy as having furnished helpful material during the past year. [...] Political reporting is handled

exclusively by the principal officer [Makinson]. Newspaper editorials, contacts with local officials and casual conservations [*sic*] with American visitors and local business men and bankers, supply the background for these reports.[25]

Makinson was succeeded by William W. Heard in 1934. When the post was next inspected, at the end of 1938 by John G. Erhardt, it was headed by James R. Wilkinson who had been there since 1936. It was now accommodated in Neville House, in Waterloo Street. The inspector noted that in the period from March 1934 until November 1938 the consulate had remitted more than $122,000 to the Treasury.[26] Wilkinson remained in post throughout most of the Second World War. His wartime reports are described in Chapter 4.

Post-war appointees included Samuel Sokobin (1945), Phil H. Hubbard (1948) and Walter W. Hoffmann (1954, previously in Bradford). Hoffmann had worked in the export business and as purser and agent for a steamship company for 11 years before joining the Service in Port Limon, Costa Rica, as a clerk in 1931.[27] By the 1950s, the consulate was located at 14 Waterloo Street. William D. Morgan arrived from Paris in 1958 as vice consul, taking over from David Ortman. The consul at that time was Harold Pease who retired shortly afterwards and was replaced by Kenneth B. Atkinson in September 1959. The highlight of Morgan's posting was being given complete responsibility for building a new consulate.

So I got out the Foreign Service Manual to find out how you build a new Consulate. I really started from scratch. The Department said, 'Go ahead and arrange for it. You'll find instructions in Section So and So of the [...] Manual.' And there the instructions were – pages and pages of them. I followed the instructions, with no real direction from anyone but with the encouragement of the Administrative Counselor in the Embassy in London. There was a new building under construction in Birmingham – still on the drawing board. The builder said that he would love to have the American Consulate in his new building. He said that he would give us this and that free.[28]

Although his functional position was vice consul, Morgan was promoted to the personal rank of consul during his time in Birmingham. He and his wife and their two children shared a large house with the Thai honorary consul and his family, from whom they rented it. He recalls an example of the left and right hands of the Department not knowing what the other was doing. Two years after he had arrived he received two letters in the same diplomatic pouch from officials at under secretary and director level: one said that he had been promoted and chosen to be consul general in Edinburgh. 'This was definitely a step up.' The other said that he had been chosen for Russian language training and eventual posting to Moscow. After discussing with his wife he decided on the Russian language training because they both felt that it would lead to faster promotion.[29]

Dr Alice T. Curran was the last officer in charge of Birmingham. This was a particularly apt appointment as her mother had been born in the city. Both parents were British and had emigrated to the United States where Alice had been born. Widowed relatively recently, she arrived in Birmingham in 1963 from Manchester where she had been consul from 1959. In 1964 she was promoted to consul general. An experienced officer whose career had included postings in Rome, Paris, Cairo, Baghdad and Beirut she was described as possessing a 'combination of shrewdness, energy and efficiency'. She was also 'blunt, and at times alarmingly outspoken' and 'never a woman to mince her words or to suffer fools gladly'. This manner did not endear her with colleagues in Birmingham where only the United States and France had career consuls; 25 other countries were represented by businessmen acting as honorary consuls. Her 'emphatic manner in making it perfectly plain that she does not regard them as professionals has led to a few hurt feelings'.[30] That is probably an understatement.

The consulate closed on 31 October 1965.

Chapter Nine

BRADFORD

When the United States opened its commercial agency there in 1863, Bradford, a Yorkshire town, was a major centre of the British woollen industry and exported its goods principally to the United States. The offices occupied two large rooms in the Bradford Exchange building at a quarterly rent of £21. The agency came under the oversight of George J. Abbott who was appointed consul at both Sheffield and Bradford in September 1864.[1] The first commercial agent appointed in 1863 was J. Emory McClintock, a native of Carlisle, Pennsylvania. It was a responsible post for someone who was only twenty-three years of age and completely inexperienced. He had come from Paris where his father was pastor of the American Chapel. McClintock was not paid a salary but derived his income from fees and was not allowed to trade. Expenses such as clerk hire, office rent, stationery and so forth were deducted from the fees and the balance was retained as his income. He left Bradford in 1866 and in later years became a distinguished actuary and mathematician.[2]

McClintock was replaced by E. D. Webster, of Nebraska, who also was not paid a salary, deriving his income from fees but, unlike McClintock, was allowed to trade. The value of goods exported to the United States through the district for the quarter ending 31 December 1866 was more than two and a half million dollars, with the majority of the goods being 'stuffs [dress materials and linings], carpets, and machinery'. The fees charged for that quarter were just under $3,000.[3] Webster remained less than a year, resigning in March 1867. He left in charge James L. Raymond, the vice commercial agent and an American citizen, and recommended him as a suitable replacement. The value of exports to the United States from the district remained high, and during the year ending 30 September 1867 was almost eleven and a half million dollars. Much of the agency business was of a routine nature, although there was a complaint by a prominent Bradford firm engaged in the export trade about the high tariff charged on goods entering the United States. Although Raymond ably deputized for the next 17 months, he was replaced by George Makepeace Towle, of Washington, DC. Towle was consul in Nantes and while there received notification of his transfer to Bradford in July 1868. He regarded this as a promotion, writing to Assistant Secretary of State Frederick Seward, 'I take this as a mark that you judge me worthy, after a trial, to take a more responsible position than that I have hitherto occupied.'[4] Raymond handed over formal responsibility to Towle on 22 August 1868, forwarded the customary inventory to the Department, and declared that he would 'set sail for the United States immediately'.[5] He had no doubt expected to have been given the post, and his parting remark sounds as though he could not wait to quit Bradford.

Within two weeks of assuming control, Towle sent Seward suggestions for improving the organization of the agency. In particular, in addition to the existing clerk he had appointed on a temporary basis an individual named N. C. Towle, presumably his son, as deputy agent. The appointment was refused by the Department and N. C. Towle was appointed to the more junior post of clerk. Two months later, George Towle returned to the charge of reorganization. He felt that one of the office's two large rooms would be sufficient for the agency's business and that relinquishing the other would reduce the rental. This must have been music to the Department's ears and he received approval for it, reducing the quarterly rent by almost a third, but he later found it necessary to pay for the cost of erecting a partition to divide the remaining room into two areas.[6] He forwarded to the Department a petition he had received from the principal merchants in Halifax calling for the re-establishment of a consular agency in the city. Under the existing arrangements they or their staffs had to travel to the commercial agency in Bradford on most days to have their invoices verified, a journey of seven miles. Towle supported the petition and recommended the appointment of H. H. Rankin, a Halifax lawyer who had previously held the post of agent. The appointment was approved.[7] Towle was also a lawyer and an author and during his time in Bradford was commissioned by a firm of London publishers to write a book about the institutions and resources of the United States. His object in doing so, he said, was 'to try to impart to English readers a better knowledge of the country, to correct many prevalent errors and ignorances, and to promote as far as I can, that international acquaintance which is the best of guarantees for peace and mutual prosperity'.[8] Towle was replaced by W. Yates Selleck of New York State in November 1869.[9] The customary handover inventory was agreed between them and was unusually detailed. For example, it included: 'Wash bowl – basin and water holder. Soap bag. Letter bag attached to door.'[10] Despite Towle's zeal for reorganizing the agency Selleck was singularly unimpressed by what he found. Bypassing the assistant secretary of state, he notified Secretary of State Hamilton Fish (1869–1877) that the agency's affairs were: 'in a very slovenly and incomplete condition. Letters instead of being properly entered and filed away have been carelessly scattered about; the Books have not been indexed; 2382 entries have been left out of the Fee Book that should have been entered therein.' He was keen to point the finger for this at Towle, remarking: 'I cannot see any reason for such neglect for my predecessor employed enough persons to enable him with proper attention to keep the Books and Papers of the Office in a proper condition and at the same time attend to its current business.' All was not lost, however, since he reported rather ingratiatingly that he had 'employed [his] time day and night with [Towle's] clerks [...] to put the affairs of the office in a decent and proper condition'.[11] Robert Richardson, a local solicitor, was appointed vice consul in 1870 and remained in office until his death in 1882.[12]

In 1872, a Treasury inspector, the grandly named De Benneville Randolph Keim, visited various consulates in Britain and Europe. He reported that the Bradford agency had dealt with more than eleven thousand invoices in the year ended 30 June 1872, generating an income of more than $19,000. The agent received a fixed salary and fees. Keim expressed his objections to 'the class of officer known as commercial agent' and recommended its discontinuance at Bradford and the creation of a consulate headed by a consul. He also drew attention to the recently established consular agency at Halifax, which was subordinate to the commercial agency at Bradford.[13] Selleck left in 1873. Keim's recommendation was implemented and William W. Douglas, of Virginia, who had been appointed commercial agent in April 1873, was regraded as consul in June 1874. His compensation was changed to a salary of $3,000.[14] Colonel Charles Otis Shepard arrived in 1877; he had previously been consul in Kanagawa, Japan, from which he had resigned in November 1873. He remained at Bradford until the arrival of William F. Grinnell in 1882. In 1886, Thomas M. Waller, the consul general in London, carried out an inspection of all the consulates in Britain (for which he had overall responsibility). He reported that Bradford was headed by consul Grinnell, an American, appointed in 1882[15] and that there was a support staff of four British nationals: T. L. Renton, vice consul (appointed 1884), and three clerks (appointed 1882, 1884, 1886); the office included five rooms in Market Street, occupied since 1882. Business had been brisk in the previous year, with almost seventy-three hundred invoices certified; this was the third largest number dealt with by a consulate after London and Liverpool.[16] It was common for consuls to give reports on social conditions in their districts as well as on commercial matters. A good example of this was given by Grinnell in March 1886:

> As to the general conditions of the working classes, I have before said it is exceptionally good in the Bradford consular district. Strikes are rare, and when recently the workmen of London, Birmingham, and almost all the larger towns of England began a series of riots, those of Bradford remained quiet and showed little or no sympathy for their fellow-workmen. The prosperous condition of the people here is largely due to the charity of the better classes in Bradford, who do much to alleviate the conditions of such working men and women as are unemployed or disabled. Great good has been accomplished in founding coffee taverns, which have rapidly increased in favor, and have done more than anything to counteract the evil effects of gin and beer saloons. These taverns, besides selling milk, coffee, tea, and choc-olate, provide simple lunches and dinners at very low prices.

However, after this glowing report he continued:

> In closing I may say that the British workingman is very different and very inferior to the American of the same class. He is indifferent, stolid, dull of comprehension, and unambi-tious. He follows in the footsteps of his father and grandfather, content if he can earn enough to support himself and family, and happy if the surplus will allow of some coarse form of recreation or dissipation. He seems to find no possibility of bettering himself and no desire to see his children better educated and more capable of succeeding in the higher walks of life, but works on in dull apathy, without hope or ambition.[17]

The comparison between British and American working men is a sweeping generaliza-tion based only on Grinnell's observations in Bradford. Also, the stereotypical American counterpart he has in mind is likely to be a recent immigrant who, like all immigrants, is keen to better himself in his new country.

   Major John Arnold Tibbits arrived in 1889. He was obviously ambitious and had sought the post of consul general in London, the most senior post in Britain. When that went to John C. New he turned his sights on the Manchester consulate, but that had been set aside for a friend of Vice President Morton. The Bradford appointment was worth about $8,000 a year, while the Manchester one was at least $20,000. He accepted the Bradford appointment 'as the best within his reach, but he is by no means satisfied'.[18] On the eve of his departure for Bradford a newspaper account of him said 'His whole political career has been that of a spoilsman, and he will go abroad as a beneficiary of the spoils system.'[19] His previous appointments had included membership of the Connecticut House of Representatives, of which he had been Speaker in 1886–1887. He suffered from ill health, and writing in April 1893 mentioned that 'he had been laid up in the house with no immediate prospect of being able to get out'.[20] He died in New London, Connecticut, from Bright's disease three months later, in July 1893, at the young age of 49.[21] He was replaced by Claude Meeker of Ohio, who was appointed in 1893 at a salary of $3,000.[22] Meeker was a journalist and writer and as a keen Brontë enthusiast was in his element in Yorkshire, visiting the Brontë home in Haworth. He wrote a book – *Hawarth, the Home of the Brontes* – which was published by the Bronte Society.[23] His appointment in Bradford was described as the happiest years of his life, where he spent the earliest years of his marriage and where all three of his children were born.[24]

Erastus Sheldon Day, a Connecticut lawyer, was appointed consul in April 1897 at a salary of $3,500. Like Tibbits, he had previously been a member of the Connecticut House of Representatives, and had also been an unsuccessful candidate for the post of consul general in London in 1889. Some of his Republican colleagues had arranged for him to be offered a consulship in Argentina. However, as: 'along with the office goes an excellent chance of catching the yellow fever [...] [he] concluded that his Republican friends have been endeavoring to send him away from the State in the hope that his absence might be made permanent'.[25] The consulate staff now consisted of two British nationals, the vice consul (who continued to work as sole partner in his family's woollen merchant business) and the 'deputy and clerk' who had been appointed in 1893. The offices were composed of three rooms in a block of buildings known as Swan Arcade. The value of goods exported to the United States from the district was almost ten million dollars in 1900 and more than five million dollars in 1901.[26] Day served until 1909 when he was replaced by Augustus Eugenio Ingram, an experienced officer who had served in Paris, Antwerp, Stockholm and Berlin, including a year in Nottingham as vice consul from 1904 to 1905. He remained in Bradford throughout the First World War until 1920, when he was replaced by Wallace J. Young who arrived from Prague. Unfortunately, Young died in 1923 at the young age of 43. Frank C. Lee then took over the consulship; earlier in his career he had been vice consul in Petrograd during the Russian Revolution.

Lee was replaced in 1925 by Alfred Ray Thomson of Maryland. He had begun his career as an assistant observer in the US Weather Bureau, serving there from 1907 until 1911. Like Lee, he had served in Russia during the Revolution at posts in Moscow, Odessa and Irkutsk. He remained in Bradford from July 1925 until December 1929 when he transferred to Manchester. During his time in Bradford he completed a course at the Technical College; the college's records are now held by the University of Bradford's Library but, unfortunately, they do not give any clue to the nature of the course.[27] Many of the consular staff over the years had made special studies of the wool industry with the aid of the technical colleges in both Bradford and Leeds.[28] Thomson's successor

Figure 9.1 Staff of the Bradford consulate in 1930. The office began as a commercial agency in 1863, headed by J. Emory McClintock, a native of Carlisle, Pennsylvania. It was reclassified as a consulate in 1874. The photograph shows the staff in 1930. The three men seated in the front row are American consular staff, with the consul Robert B. Macatee in the middle. All the other members are British staff. [Reproduced with permission of the American Foreign Service Association.]

was Robert B. Macatee, a Virginian, who arrived at the end of 1929 from London, where he had been one of the team of consuls since 1923. However, he did not remain long in Bradford and returned to London in September 1930, remaining there until being posted to Belgrade in 1935. Clement S. Edwards, who arrived in 1930, had had an extensive career with appointments in Mexico, the Dominican Republic, France, Lithuania and Spain. He had nearly lost his life during the Mexican Civil War when he was held as a prisoner on a Mexican troopship.[29] Ernest Edwin Evans of Rochester, New York, took over in 1933, arriving from Naples. In 1936 the total of exports to the United States from Bradford was the highest for many years; at just under three million pounds it was an increase of more than a million pounds over the previous year.[30] Evans remained until May 1941, when he transferred to Matamoros, Mexico, and was succeeded by Joseph G. Groeninger of Baltimore who arrived in October of that year. Groeninger was a veteran officer who had been a member of the former Consular Service. During his wide-ranging career he had served in Denmark, Germany, Estonia, Holland, Indonesia, Pakistan, Afghanistan and New Zealand. Bradford was his final appointment and he served there throughout the Second World War, after which he retired. Nathaniel Lancaster of Virginia arrived from Bangkok in 1947 but remained only a year before being succeeded by Frederick C. Johnson.[31] Johnson had been born in 1885 in Nova Scotia of American parents and entered the former Consular Service in 1918 at Paspebiac, Québec. He had served at Fredericton, Canada, since 1921 before moving to Bradford, which would be his last post.[32]

Bradford gradually ceased to be an important export centre to the United States and the consulate was closed in May 1953 on the grounds of economy.[33] The last consul, Walter W. Hoffmann, had arrived in 1951 from Barranquilla, Colombia. In his farewell address to the Bradford Soroptimists Club he said that after having spent a long career in several countries he and his family 'should not find it difficult to settle down in another place'. I wonder if he was aware at the time that his next move would not be to another country but to Birmingham, only some one hundred and thirty miles away.[34]

Chapter Ten

BRISTOL

The city of Bristol in south-west England was an important port, particularly for the shipping of tobacco and port wine, and for the slave trade. The first United States consulate in the city was opened in 1792, headed by Elias Vanderhorst. Contrary to the claim on the official plaque on a house at 37 Queen Square, Bristol was not the location of the first US consulate in Britain.[1] As is shown in the history of the Liverpool consulate, that honour goes to Liverpool in 1790. Vanderhorst was a South Carolinian who in his mid-thirties had moved with his wife and family to Bristol in 1774, continuing as a merchant the business that he had pursued in America. Some eighteen years later he was appointed consul by President George Washington. His commission of appointment, signed by Washington and co-signed by Secretary of State Thomas Jefferson, dated 4 May 1792, is in the archives of the Bristol Record Office.[2] His exequatur was signed by King George III on 10 February 1793.[3] Vanderhorst declined renewal of his appointment on 2 October 1815 due to infirm health, informing John Quincy Adams, the American minister in London of this, and died seven months later in May 1816.[4]

Harman Visger, of New York, who succeeded Vanderhorst in 1816, was already living in Bristol and was 'a rich merchant, an American [...] [with] a family of seven children'.[5] The consulate was now located at 6 Brunswick Square.[6] Visger died in office, in Ilfracombe, on 4 June 1833, and was succeeded temporarily by his son Harman Visger, Jr,[7] until 1834, when Thomas Dennison, of Pennsylvania, who had served in the consulate at Liverpool from 1833 until 1834, took over. He remained until 1841 when Francis Barber Ogden, of New Jersey, was appointed. Up to that time Ogden had been consul in Liverpool from 1829. Throughout his time as consul he was a pioneer in the use of nautical steam engines. In addition to his Bristol appointment he was consul for the Republic of Texas in Liverpool (see the item on the Texas Consular Service in Chapter 4). In 1852, he was appointed consul in Manchester but retained his Bristol connection. He died there in office on 4 July 1857 and was buried in Arnos Vale Cemetery, Brislington. Like Visger, he was succeeded by his son, but on a permanent basis. Francis B. Ogden, Jr, served as deputy consul from 1853 until 1858.

In 1858 Colonel Samuel Ward of New York was appointed consul by President Buchanan and remained until 1861. Zebina Eastman, his successor in December of that year, gave a witty description of him on their handover meeting.

> I was ushered into [...] the august presence of the consul [...]. He received me with dignified formality [...]. He evidently wanted to impress me with his importance. [...] After some preliminary skirmishing on general politics against which I did not care to put in a dissent [...] he condescendingly volunteered to me considerable useful information and advice. [...]

He rose from his seat, and planting himself in front of the fire, his back to the mantle and spreading his coat tails like a pair of shears, to the exhilarating effects of the warmth in the rear uttered great swelling words of ponderous wisdom, interpolated with greater oaths, several sometimes in a single sentence.[8]

Eastman, of Chicago, had a background in printing and publishing and was a leading abolitionist and had sought a government position when Lincoln was elected. Lincoln wrote to Secretary of State William Seward asking that something be found for Eastman as: '[He] is one of the earliest and most efficient of our free soil laborers. If a position with even moderate pay could be found for him in England, he is just the man to reach the sympathies of the English people to the extent that he can come in contact with them. He is more than a common man in his sphere; and I shall be very glad if you can find out [...] some such place as I have indicated.'[9] Eastman remained until 1869, and summed up his time in Bristol as follows: 'Although on my landing a gloomy impression was produced, it was not so during my eight years in the consulate. It was a time of recuperation. I had been wearied by years of toil in connection with the press, in the thankless task of turning the drift of public sentiment, and the consumation [sic] of all my hopes in reform had been realized in the establishment of equal civil rights in the country.'[10]

Edgar Stanton of Illinois arrived in 1870 and served for five years before being transferred to Barmen in Germany (not Bremen, as some records show), later becoming consul general in St Petersburg. In 1872 the Bristol consulate had subordinate consular agencies at Brixham, Gloucester and Worcester. That same year Keim, the Treasury agent who was carrying out inspections of consulates, recommended the closure of Bristol and its agencies 'and, if the service should demand, the establishment, in its place, of an agency subject to the jurisdiction of the consul at Cardiff'.[11] The recommendation was not implemented. Stanton's successor was Theodore Canisius who had been born in Germany but had become a naturalized US citizen. He had served previously at Vienna and Gustemunde (Germany). Prior to joining the Consular Service he had edited the *Illinois Staats-Anzeiger*, a German language newspaper that was owned by Abraham Lincoln, though that fact was not generally known.[12] In 1861, in the early days of the Civil War, Lincoln had sought the services of Giuseppe Garibaldi, a leader of the Italian independence movement, holding out for him the prospect of a command in the Union army with the rank of major general. Canisius was at this time consul in Vienna and without obtaining permission wrote to Garibaldi asking if he would join the Union's military struggle against the Confederates. Canisius's approach caused a great deal of embarrassment in American government circles and in October 1862 he was dismissed from his consular appointment, but was later reinstated.[13] He remained in Bristol until 1881 when he was transferred to the Samoan Islands from where he returned in delicate health in 1885 and died soon afterwards in Chicago.[14]

Colonel John Farrell succeeded Canisius. In addition to his army career he had been a merchant in New York for 40 years. He was also described as a 'prominent Irish Republican'.[15] As evidence of his commercial acumen, he announced when setting sail from New York to Bristol that he intended to stock the consulate with: 'all the commercial and trade papers of the Union as also maps, facts, figures, and annual reports from the Agricultural Department, Post Office, Land Office, and Statistical Bureau at Washington'.[16] This seemed hardly worth the effort as he held the post for just over a year, and in 1882 was succeeded by Lorin Andrews Lathrop of Ohio. Before coming to Bristol, Lathrop had been employed in the US Mint at San Francisco for three years. The consulate was then located at Queen Square once again, but this time at number 51. Lathrop retired in 1889 but was reappointed in 1891, at a salary of $2,000 and remained at Bristol until 1907 when he transferred to Cardiff, where he continued throughout the First World War until 1919. He was posted to Nassau, staying there until 1924.[17] He died in Paris in 1929.

Lathrop's successor in 1907 was Dr James Perry Worden. Like so many appointees he had no previous consular service experience. He was professor of modern languages at Kalamazoo College, Michigan, a Germanophile, and a frequent contributor of articles to the *New York Times*. In his youth he had cycled around Europe, and while in Edinburgh had stayed as the guest of Wallace Bruce, the American Consul.[18] He did not remain long at Bristol, announcing at the end of 1908, after learning of his father's death, that he had decided to leave the consular service to devote himself to a literary career in Berlin for two or three years.[19] He never returned to consular work and died in Pasadena, California, in 1945. Homer Morrison Byington of Connecticut arrived in 1909 from Rome, where he had been vice and deputy consul. He held the same rank on arrival at Bristol but was soon promoted to consul, at a salary of $2,000. After four years he transferred to Leeds in 1913. Roger Culver Tredwell was appointed that year as consul. His previous posts had been as vice consul in Yokohama, Burslem, Dresden and a temporary detachment to Stoke on Trent from 1911 to 1912.[20] Bristol proved to be another short assignment and he transferred to Amsterdam after only a year. His replacement, John Samuel Armstrong of North Carolina, arrived in 1914 from Salonika and remained in Bristol for most of the First World War before transferring to Venice. Robertson Honey was appointed in 1918, followed by Samuel Reid Thompson in 1924 and Digby A. Willson in 1927. All were experienced consular officers. Roy William Baker of Buffalo, New York, was appointed in 1931, having served during the previous two years as a vice consul in London. He had begun his career as a vice consul in Edinburgh in 1919. He served in Bristol throughout most of the Second World War until 1943, when he retired, and died in Buffalo in November 1945.[21]

The final consuls included Winfield Harrison Scott in 1944 and Paul H. Pearson in 1947. The consulate was closed on 30 November 1948.

Chapter Eleven

CARDIFF

Cardiff, the capital city of Wales, was once the world's largest coal-exporting port with ships arriving via the Bristol Channel and the Severn Estuary. The first US consular presence in the city opened in 1830 and was an agency, headed by Edward Priest Richards, a local alderman and town clerk.[1] Consular agencies were similar to honorary consulates and were headed by local businessmen and other professionals. Richards was succeeded in 1836 by Richard Jones Todd, a clerk in the customs house, who remained until 1842. During the next twenty years, the agents included Henry H. Parry (a partner in Parry, Brown & Co., who were also vice consuls for Denmark, Germany, the Netherlands and Russia), David Brown and Sidney D. Jenkins (a naturalized American citizen).[2]

The first consulate was established in 1861, with Charles Dexter Cleveland of Pennsylvania in charge. He was 59 years of age and had been a leading classicist, having held the chair of Latin at New York University; he was also an abolitionist and a writer of textbooks and poetry.[3] He remained at Cardiff until 1864 when Charles E. Burch, also of Pennsylvania, was appointed. Burch was allowed to trade in addition to his consular duties.[4] It seems that he may have given more attention to the former than the latter because when the consulate was inspected in 1872, three years after he had left, the inspector was not impressed by his record-keeping. He noted: 'I should judge from the lack of books and accounts during the time that a Mr Birch [sic] officiated here, that that individual had carried off the books and papers with him. Some reports he had made out had not been sent, and were found among the rubbish which he had left for his successor.' More in sorrow than in anger, the inspector added: 'This consulate has been subjected to the vicissitudes of good and bad officers to an extent no less notorious than I discovered at many other places.'[5] Harry H. Davis, another Pennsylvanian, arrived in 1869. The inspector's report on him was a mixed one: 'Under the present consul at Cardiff the affairs of the office are well attended to as far as books and accounts are concerned.' However, he added: 'I may say that all the business of the consulate is transacted by the deputy and vice consul. The consul, who resides some miles out of the city, visits his consulate two or three times a week.' This is hardly a ringing endorsement, and he concluded: 'It is not for me to determine whether this fully answers the expectations of the Government.' One cannot help feeling, however, that if it were for him to determine, the consul would have received an admonition.[6] Davis remained until 1874 when he was transferred to Valencia. His successor was William H. Shortt, nominally another Pennsylvanian, although he had been born in Scotland but had become a naturalized American citizen. By this time, the consulate had subordinate agencies at Llanelly (opened in 1839), Milford Haven (opened in 1798), Newport (opened in

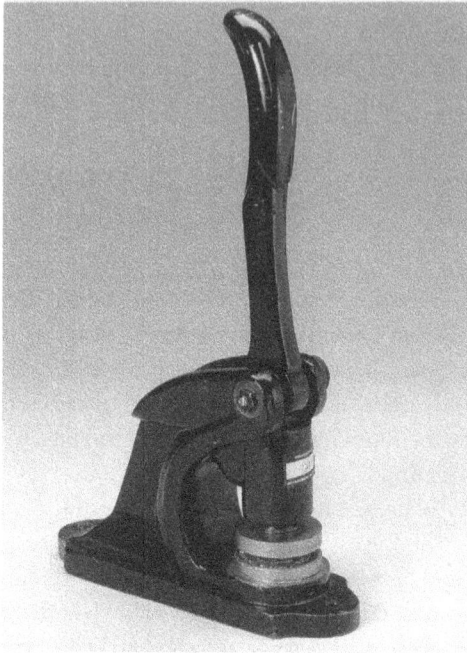

Figure 11.1 Embossing seal press used in the Cardiff consulate. The majority of consular documents had to be authenticated when they were issued. For the more frequent and numerous ones this was done by stamping them with rubber stamps. For those of a more legal nature a wafer seal was affixed and then impressed with the consulate's official seal. This bore the name of the consulate and the Great Seal of the United States. The photograph shows the consular seal press used in the Cardiff consulate. [US Diplomacy Center, US Department of State.]

1835) and Swansea (opened in 1862).[7] Swansea later became a commercial agency (and therefore no longer subordinate to the Cardiff consulate), then a consulate, before closing in 1928.[8] During the year ended 30 June 1872, the amount of fee income at Cardiff generated from the certification of invoices, from ships, and miscellaneous sources was almost thirty-six hundred dollars; the value of exports to the United States during the same period was almost five and a half million dollars. The agencies generated $400 in fees.[9] Shortt departed in 1876.

William Wirt Sikes arrived that year. An American journalist who visited the consulate and interviewed Sikes reported:

It is a faded eagle that guards the portal of the American Consulate at Cardiff; a worn, weather-beaten bird, the most venerable thing in the busy Bute road leading to the busy Bute docks. 'Why do you not renovate the majestic king of the air?' I asked Mr Wirt Sikes, the representative of the United States, who met me at the door. 'I found it here almost as dirty and time-stained as you see it,' he said, looking up admiringly at the sign, 'and I would not have it cleaned on any account; they like old things in England [did he not know that Cardiff is in Wales?], old institutions, relics, antiquities'.[10]

Sikes married Olive Logan, an American actress and author, in 1872; it was the second marriage for both of them, and lasted until Sikes's death in 1883 in London. He is buried in Brookwood Cemetery, also known as the London Necropolis. She returned to America, remarried in 1892, but fell on hard times and became a recluse. Hearing of this, an American friend in England, Lady Cook, sent money and arranged to bring her to stay with her in England.[11] This seemed not to have worked out and Olive ended up in a 'lunatic asylum' in Banstead, London, where she died in April 1909. A newspaper announcement of her death said that 'unless claim is made within a few days for her body it will be buried in a pauper's grave.'[12] It is not known whether anyone came forward.

In 1884, Major Evan Rowland Jones of Wisconsin was transferred from Newcastle where he had been consul since 1869.[13] He was a veteran of the Civil War. Born in Wales in 1846, he had gone to America at the age of 15 and enlisted in the 5th Wisconsin Infantry, in which he later attained the rank of major. He was at one time editor of *The London Globe*. When he arrived the consulate offices were in 50 Mount Stuart Square. Consulate business had begun to slow down, and by 1886 there was not a great deal of business transacted. During that year, the consulate certified fewer invoices (38) than three of its four subordinate agencies (Llanelly, 41; Newport, 85; and Swansea, 473. Milford Haven had none). The excess expenditure that Jones had to pay out of his earnings to meet the amount not covered by official allowances was the third highest in Britain after the Liverpool and London consulates.[14] In 1892, he resigned his consulship in order to stand for Parliament and was elected as the Liberal Party member for the Carmarthen Boroughs.[15] He died in 1920.

Walter Eugene Howard, of Vermont, arrived in 1893 but remained only a few months, returning to Vermont to become state school commissioner. Prior to the Cardiff appointment he had had a varied career as a school principal, lawyer, a member of the Vermont State Senate, consul in Toronto from 1883 to 1885 and professor of political science and history.[16] He was replaced as consul in June 1893 by Anthony Howell, who had been born in Wales but had emigrated to New York state. By 1895, there were three subordinate consular agencies at Llanelly, Milford Haven and Newport; Swansea became an independent commercial agency that year. Howell was succeeded in 1897 by Daniel Thomas Phillips of Illinois, another Welsh-born consul who had moved to America and acquired American citizenship. Before moving there he had worked in Cardiff as a merchant's clerk and in the borough treasurer's office. He then changed career and was ordained as a Baptist minister at Llantwit Major, a small town near Cardiff, and served as pastor there and in Swansea and Bristol. After this, he moved to America, serving as a pastor in Philadelphia, Baltimore and Chicago for over twenty years. Like many of his compatriots who had become American citizens, he sought retirement as a consul in the land of his birth. His vice and deputy consul in 1899 was Ernest L. Phillips, possibly his son.[17] The value of exports from the consular district to the United States during the year ended 30 June 1901 had fallen to just over one hundred and fifty thousand dollars; the value of American goods imported during the same year, on the other hand, was a staggering three million dollars.[18] Although he had been ill for some time Daniel Phillips died suddenly in 1905 when a gas explosion wrecked part of his house; however, it was thought that this had hastened rather than caused his death.[19]

In 1905, Daniel Webster Williams of Ohio arrived. For 30 years he had been editor of the *Standard Journal*, a weekly newspaper in Jackson, Ohio. By this date, only one agency, Newport, remained. He was replaced in 1907 by Lorin Andrews Lathrop, also of Ohio, who prior to joining the Consular Service had worked in the US Mint at San Francisco. His first appointment was consul at Bristol in 1882 where he had served, except for a break of 16 months, until being appointed to Cardiff where he received an increased salary of $2,500.[20] His wife, Annie Wakeman Lathrop, arrived in 1883 'as the correspondent of the Boston Herald, and later contributed to The Chicago Tribune, Philadelphia Record and the San Francisco Chronicle.'[21] She died in Britain in 1911. Lathrop remained in Cardiff throughout the First World War until 1919 when he was transferred to Nassau.[22] He later wrote a six-part account of his life in the *Saturday Evening Post* in 1925 entitled 'The Recollections of a Consul', and died in Paris in 1929. William F. Doty arrived in 1919 from Nassau and remained for less than a year before being transferred to Stoke on Trent. For more about this colourful character see the histories of the Newcastle upon Tyne (Chapter 19) and Stoke on Trent (Chapter 21) consulates. During his time in Cardiff, his wife was reported as being one of several Americans held prisoner by 'the Bolshevist Government' in Moscow.[23] Quite why she was in Moscow is a topic for further research. Doty's vice consul was Edward B. Cipriani, another with a varied career; he had been born in Port of Spain, Trinidad, become a naturalized American citizen, practised law in New Jersey and was a newspaper editor in Trinidad. He became vice consul in Trinidad in 1912, followed by similar appointments in Venezuela and Jamaica before coming to Cardiff.[24] He left Cardiff in 1920, the same year as Doty, moving to Leeds and then Glasgow.[25] Charles Emery Asbury of Indiana arrived that year. Following a career in teaching and working in the office of the prosecuting attorney in Manila he had joined the Consular Service and served in Nova Scotia, Honduras, Montreal and Jamaica.[26]

In the 1920s, consuls included John Robins Bradley (1921–1923), Edgar C. Soule (1923–1926) and Ralph C. Busser (1926–1930). In 1930, Alfred Tyrrell Nester arrived from Naples but remained just over a year before being transferred to Tunis.[27] He was replaced by Stillman W. Eells, who relocated from Colombo, Ceylon, having served earlier in Leeds. Prior to joining the Consular Service he had been a manufacturer of fireproof wood in New York City. He remained at Cardiff until 1934 when he was transferred to Valencia, Spain, from where he retired a few months later.[28] His successor, Samuel R. Thompson of Illinois, arrived from Valencia and stayed longer than usual, from 1934 until the early years of the Second World War, 1941.[29] Richard S. Huestis and Sheridan Talbott served through the remainder of the war and Winfield Scott held office throughout the rest of the 1940s.

Samuel Gale Ebling of Ohio arrived in 1950, after having served just over a year as consul at Southampton. He had worked as a stenographer, as a clerk in the Department of Agriculture, and the War Trade Board and had served in the US Army before joining the State Department as a clerk in 1919.[30] He remained at Cardiff until 1954 when he was succeeded by Chester Earl Beaman. Beaman had been employed by the US High Commission for Germany (HICOG) before joining the Foreign Service. His first assignment was to London in 1951 where he remained until September 1954 before being posted to Cardiff as consul. For a number of reasons he regarded Cardiff as one of his best posts: his son was born there, he was his own boss and he had to drive the official car himself. He threw himself into the work:

> Not belittling, but the norm of previous consuls had been to clip items out of the newspaper, put them in a report, and send them to London. I started visiting people. I visited workers' institutes in the coal mine areas. I even went down into the coal mine. […]. I would just jump in the car and go up in the valleys or go over to Swansea and go through a steel mill. I had a grand time. I did a lot of speaking and visiting. […]. I was trying to project a good image of the United States. Those were the days when Dulles was Secretary. Unfortunately, the State Department would put out very dull booklets of very dull speeches that he made and would send those to the consulate. I put them out on the consulate's counter or I would distribute them to officials. But this wasn't the way to do it. That is why I made a lot of speeches. I tried to interpret U.S. policy or what was going on to the people.[31]

As far as visas and passports were concerned: 'I had a vice consul [James O. Belden] who just loved to sign and process papers. I left most of that to him. I would sign when it was expected.' He also made many friends in Cardiff, particularly George Thomas, one of the local Labour Members of Parliament, who became Speaker of the House of Commons and later Viscount Tonypandy. Their friendship lasted for more than forty years until Thomas's death in 1997. Beaman and his family left Cardiff at the end of 1955 on home leave and were due to return there, but while in America he was assigned to Arabic language training in Washington, DC, and Beirut and was then posted to Cairo.[32] He eventually retired in 1972 and died in 2007 at the age of 91.[33]

Neil Marshall Ruge arrived in 1956 from a posting as consul in London. Like his predecessor, he was very active, and his German-born wife Helga recalled that: 'He traveled widely in his district, visited factories, made speeches to organizations, such as the Rotarians.' Helga was equally active and did her 'share of entertaining, opening bazaars, making speeches to women's clubs, presenting diplomas'. The consul's rented residence was on Cyncoed Road and when the Ruges arrived there they found the ground floor flooded; the house had stood empty and unheated for three months since Beaman had left and the water pipes had burst in the cold weather.

> It was unsatisfactory as an official residence, no adequate heating system, primitive kitchen, etc. My husband was able to find a residence that the State Department found suitable for the principal officer in Cardiff and bought it. We stayed one year in each. […] Neil had one American vice consul and an American secretary and some local staff, no driver, but he had an office car for official use, a British model. We had a Mercedes for private use.[34]

During his time in Cardiff he had inaugurated a new consulate office in a brand new building in the city, taken an active role in promoting the United States in other parts of his consular district such as Bristol, Swansea and Bath, and had hosted an official visit by Ambassador John Hay Whitney. In 1958, he transferred to a post in the State Department. After subsequent postings to Munich and Guatemala City, he retired in

1968, and the following year became a professor of general contract law at California State University, Chico. He died in 2000, at age 86.[35]

Ruge was succeeded by Walter G. Walcavich in 1958 and Stanley P. Harris in 1961. The final appointee, Magdalen G. H. Flexner, arrived from Paris in 1963 and the consulate closed that year. However, in November 2000 the State Department established the Welsh Affairs Office, known as the Cardiff Virtual Presence Post (VPP). It is staffed by a junior diplomat, a political officer based in the London Embassy who bears the title of Welsh Affairs Officer and travels to Cardiff for several days a month. When the officer is in London, phone enquiries and correspondence are automatically forwarded to his or her desk and there is a VPP webpage on the embassy's website. It is a very cost-effective method of providing an official American presence in Wales. The office is located at Temple Court, Cathedral Road. Although this is the first and only Virtual Presence Post in the United Kingdom, there are others in, for example, France, New Zealand, Russia, Sweden and Turkey.

Chapter Twelve

DUBLIN

Dublin, together with Liverpool, was among the first consulates established in Britain by the new US republic in 1790, and at that time Ireland was still part of Britain. William Knox of New York was appointed consul and arrived on 24 November, thereby just missing by a few months the distinction of being the first American consul in Britain, as James Maury began his appointment at Liverpool in September.[1] As an example of the ill-preparedness of the new Consular Service, one of Knox's first purchases a week or two after arrival was commissioning a local engraver to manufacture a consular seal in brass.[2] This should already have been issued to him on appointment.

Knox's performance seems to have been somewhat erratic. Writing from Cork less than a year after taking up his appointment, he informed Secretary of State Thomas Jefferson that: 'Business of an indispensable but private nature having required me to be England [sic] for some time past has been the cause of your not receiving in due course the return directed in the Instructions I had the honor to receive from you.' However, he promised that as soon as he returned to Dublin he would send a report on the arrivals of American ships during 1791. He also hoped that the government would make provision for payments to their consuls, as was the custom of other countries: 'for my own part were my private resources such as to admit of it, I should with great cheerfulness serve our country without any pecuniary consideration'.[3] Two months later, he sent a long letter to President Washington informing him of how friendly Ireland was towards the United States and of the many contacts he had made. He continued at length about his financial difficulties (which was probably the main reason for the letter).

> Not being possessed of a fortune I was only capable of taking with me [to Ireland] a temporary supply of the means for my support, trusting that Congress during the last session would have passed a Consular Act, which would have embraced a provision for their consuls; but I find I have calculated erroneously, and that error (although I hope not criminal) has involved me in much anxiety for my support in this country.

He ends by hoping that he has not caused offence by writing in those terms but feels that 'the Government of America suffers their Consul in Ireland to be without the means of existing, when three or four hundred pounds sterling per annum would support him with some decency in that character'.[4] Knox's few reports deal with topics such as movements of cargoes, the impressment and seizure of American crews and ships at Belfast, and unrest among the Catholic population as 'the penal laws still exclude them from citizenship'.[5] He mentions that he may have to return to America 'at least for a few months',[6] and indeed shortly afterwards, in the last document on the microfilm of his despatches, writing from Philadelphia, he says that he left Dublin in July 1792.

Knox came from a family of 10 sons, only 4 of whom reached adulthood. When he was younger, he was fairly active and at the age of 19 assisted his older brother Henry, an artillery colonel (later general), in his famous trek in the middle of a severe winter to bring much-needed cannons from Fort Ticonderoga, New York, to Boston during the Revolutionary War.[7] However, he seems to have been unsuited to the work of a consul from the outset. He: 'was a well-bred gentleman, extremely well educated, but possessed of feelings too sensitive for his future happiness on earth. He had been American consul at Dublin, and became deeply enamored of a lady there who did not reciprocate his love. It was a wound that neither time nor absence could cure.'[8] This 'sensitivity', coupled with the constant anxiety about his financial situation, would ultimately lead to his early death. Following his return to America in 1794 he worked for a few months as a clerk in the employ of his brother Henry who, by that time, was Secretary of War. At least seven years before being appointed consul he had suffered from 'occasional fits of derangement' and after his return to America it seems that he suffered what would nowadays be termed a complete nervous breakdown; one account states that 'he died insane'.[9] A contemporary account of his condition was given by Samuel Breck, a Philadelphian merchant and politician who was visiting the Pennsylvania Hospital. He had just finished speaking to one of the patients (who was chained to a block) when he heard his name being shouted loudly by another patient. 'On looking round I saw a sick person in bed, and to my sorrow and astonishment found William Knox in it. The occurrence was unexpected and melancholy. The poor fellow did not detain me after begging a cent to buy snuff. [...] [he] was soon relieved by death [...] dying [...] a month or two after.'[10] Knox had been admitted on 14 January 1795 not long after his return from Dublin, with security posted by his brother, Henry, and died on 30 December of that year at age 39. The cause of death was noted simply as 'an infection', although some romantic accounts said that he had died of a broken heart.[11]

Joseph Wilson was appointed consul in 1794. Although born in Scotland, he had moved to America and had become a naturalized citizen. He took part in the Revolutionary War, and served under George Washington who was a personal acquaintance and had nominated him to the post.[12] He remained until 1809 when he was replaced by Thomas English of Pennsylvania. English got off to a shaky start; writing from Philadelphia to Secretary of State Robert Smith (1809–1811) in July 1809 acknowledging the appointment, he added: 'I find it will require some short time to close my affairs here and make the necessary arrangements for the embarkation of my family.' He then 'proposed to appoint' his brother, John, 'who intends to sail for Dublin almost immediately' to run the consulate in his stead.[13] Surprisingly, the State Department did not object to this private arrangement. A year went by and Thomas had still not arrived in Dublin. John informed Smith that Thomas had been detained in America much longer than he had anticipated and had authorized him to perform the duties of consul. John then submitted various consular reports.[14] He was still doing so more than a year later and signing himself vice consul. The first report submitted by Thomas was in early 1812; there is no indication of the date of his arrival in Dublin, but it was almost two and a half years after his official appointment. John continued to act as vice consul and Thomas returned again to America in 1814 for several months, leading to confusion about his intention to continue with the consulship. Thomas Wilson, son of Joseph Wilson the previous consul, wrote to Secretary of State James Monroe (1811–1817) in August of that year and applied for the post. However, to his surprise, Thomas changed his mind and returned to Dublin. Wilson informed Monroe of this, adding: 'though I must candidly acknowledge that I am a little hurt at the conduct of Mr English, yet I feel for his situation (as he has lately been unfortunate in business) which may in some measure account for the uncertainty which has appeared in his determinations.' Wilson hoped that he might nevertheless be considered whenever a vacancy took place, and which he thought would not be too long in coming 'as Mr English seems to be still undetermined whether to remain here, to settle in England, or return to America.' He enclosed a letter from English in which he explains that he had intended resigning in the previous summer, and had mentioned this to his friend Wilson who informed him that he had then applied for the post. The purpose of the letter was 'in order to remove from your mind any unpleasant impression respecting the conduct of Mr Wilson on the occasion.'[15] English was reappointed in 1816 and continued in post until his death at the beginning of 1825. The amount of time he spent on his duties is questionable, however, because his brother, Isaac, when giving official notification of his death took the opportunity of applying for the vacant post, adding that: 'my pretentions [sic] are grounded on having principally performed the duties of the office for thirteen years past, and altogether for the last five years, during which latter period my brother was generally absent and had delagated [sic] his signature to me'.[16] There is nothing on the file to indicate that the State Department was aware of this situation. Isaac was allowed to continue as 'consul pro tem' until April 1827 when Thomas Wilson, doubtless to his relief, was at last appointed consul. He was active for the next twenty years, submitting regular shipping reports, returns indicating the low level of fees generated at the post (ranging from $23 to $162 per half year) and offering suggestions about consular salaries. He particularly drew attention to the disastrous failures of the potato crop. In the first half of 1847 he reported: 'an unusually large number of vessels arriving at this Port has been caused by the failure of the Potato Crop of this country. They all brought Provisions and went away with Passengers or in ballast. There did not any of them take goods.'[17] Wilson served until 1847 when he was informed that he had been replaced by Hugh Keenan, and that the change was not caused by any complaint about the way in which he had discharged his duties but was due to a regulation that stated, wherever practicable, consular posts should be held by American citizens.[18]

Keenan arrived in 1847. He had been born in Ireland but had moved to America where he had attained citizenship and had a career as an attorney. Giving a clear indication of the arrangements then in force for obtaining consulships, he wrote to Secretary of State James Buchanan (1845–1849) thanking him for 'the promptness with which you acceded to the application of my friends, in appointing me to the situation of consul'.[19] He also described the situation which happened all too often throughout the Consular Service when a transfer of consulship took place. He informed Buchanan that he had called on Wilson but received from him only the American flag and coat of arms, since Wilson's view was that the:

> Official Seal, books and papers [...] were purchased and paid for by himself and were not the property of the United States Government, and would not be handed over. [...] As I have not any books or materials from which to compile a return as directed on the first of January I shall probably have nothing to report until the next time, say in June. I am now having a Consular Seal engraved and will procure books and the other requisites for the fulfillment [sic] of my duties.[20]

Several of Keenan's reports began with 'I have no special information to transmit' and 'I have nothing special to report.' However, he warned that emigration from neighbouring ports to the United States was likely to be 'very large', and reported that the British Government was 'sending into this country immense bodies of troops, and carrying their coercive measures by military force. The inhabitants are in most wretched conditions.'[21] He also drew attention to his fears that: 'during the recent excitement in this country some letters addressed to me through the Post Office had the appearance of having been broken open previous to delivery'.[22] He sought reappointment on the change of administration but was allowed to serve only for a further 20 months before being replaced in September 1850 by James Foy of Pennsylvania.[23] However, he was appointed consul at Cork and served there from 1854 until 1859. The Dublin consulate addresses changed according to the business premises of the consul. At various times it was located in 20 Upper Dominick Street, 27 Palmerston Place, 2 Lower Buckingham Street and 3 Portland Place.

Foy was recalled in 1853 and replaced temporarily by Michael Lynch who was appointed consular agent but resigned the following year. Robert Loughead, consul in Londonderry from 1845, was transferred to Dublin in 1854 but died the following year. Keenan was drafted back as acting consul until handing over to James Arrott of Pennsylvania. Arrott served until 1858 and during that year also took over temporary control of the Belfast consulate. At various times during his appointment in Dublin the consulate was run temporarily by Michael Lynch and an individual named Murphy, both of whom were described as acting consuls.[24] Samuel W. Talbot of New York was appointed in 1859, transferring from Galway where he had been consul from 1856. He remained at Dublin until 1861 when he was succeeded by Henry B. Hammond of Massachusetts, a lawyer and president of the Indiana and Illinois Central Railroad. He resigned in 1863 and was replaced by James Cantwell of Pennsylvania who served until 1867. During Cantwell's term of office the vice consul was William B. West who had been born in Ireland but had moved to America where he acquired citizenship. In 1861 he was appointed consul at Cork and served there until 1867, while also holding the vice consulship at Dublin. In 1867 his position was put on a more usual footing when he was appointed consul at Dublin and gave up his Cork post.[25] After he left office in 1869 he applied through the House of Representatives for 'relief' [repayment] of 'a good deal of extra expense' he claimed to have incurred as consul. His claim amounted to more than $5,000 and included such items as $2,400 for extra clerk-hire and vice consul,

$150 for copying correspondence, $25 for postage, and $2,000 'for personal services and attention, during a period over three years'.[26] The Committee on Foreign Affairs rejected the claim, setting out its reasons in 'an adverse report in writing'. These included:

> The consul, when he accepts the position, undertakes to discharge faithfully and to the best of his ability the duties incumbent on him. For this his fees or salary is regarded by the Government as a full equivalent [...]. The charges [...] are all of an exceptional character, and are mainly of a personal nature, unaccompanied even by vouchers [...]. The Government claims the entire time and services of the consul, and takes no account of his charities, hotel-bills, railway-fares, or physicians' bills.[27]

West was succeeded at Dublin by the Reverend Edward D. Neill of Minnesota. He was born in 1823 and was an ordained Presbyterian minister and chancellor of the University of Minnesota. He cut his political teeth when he was appointed in 1864 as Lincoln's Secretary to Sign Land Patents and he continued in this post under Andrew Johnson after Lincoln's assassination. He was nominated for the Dublin consulship by President Ulysses S. Grant and served until resigning in 1870. Returning to America in 1871, he established Macalester College in St Paul, Minnesota, serving as its president and teaching history and political science there until his death in 1893.[28] Wilson King of Pennsylvania arrived in 1872 for his first assignment. He described his time there as delightful. 'I spent four of the pleasantest years of my life there, meeting many famous, interesting and agreeable people and making some lifelong friends.'[29] Fees generated during the year ended 30 June 1872 amounted to more than $2,000. There was no direct shipping with America; all invoiced goods were sent across the Irish Sea to Liverpool and shipped from there.[30] Following an inspection of the consulate in 1872, the inspector suggested that the amount of business transacted justified its upgrading to a Class III consulate which meant that the consul was allowed to keep the fees, up to $2,500 in any one year, and was entitled to certain allowances. This placed him:

> in a better position than most of the full and principal officers receiving fixed salaries. This is one of the eccentricities of our system. [...] Dublin is a place of considerable importance, in [sic] a commercial point of view, with the United States. The officer here should, therefore, be placed in a position of complete responsibility to the Government. [...] If not made a full consulate, Dublin should, for the sake of responsibility, be made an agency under Belfast. My suggestion, however, is that it be placed in Class III.[31]

King was posted to Bremen in 1876, and to Birmingham in 1879, and was succeeded in Dublin by Benjamin H. Barrows. He had previously been surveyor of the Port of Omaha, Nebraska.[32] By this time there were subordinate agencies at Limerick and Sligo. Barrows was succeeded in 1885 by James L. McCaskill. During his time the consulate occupied two rooms at 204 Great Brunswick Street and when inspected in 1887 the condition of the office furniture was described as 'poor'.[33] Alexander J. Reid of Wisconsin took up his appointment in 1889; a journalist by profession, he had also seen military service in the Philippines.[34] There was now also an agency at Athlone.

John James Piatt was appointed in 1893. He had been consul at Cork from 1882 to 1893 and was well-known as a poet. In a varied career his previous positions had included employment as a clerk in the US Treasury, working on the staff of the *Cincinnati Chronicle*, literary editor and correspondent of the *Cincinnati Commercial* and Assistant Clerk and then Librarian of the United States House of Representatives.[35] He had been considered for a consulship 17 years earlier, in 1865. Abraham Lincoln, when president, had sent a memo to Secretary of State William H. Seward, saying: 'I have some wish that [...] John J. Piatt [...] should have [one of] those moderate size consulates which facilitate artists a little [in] their profession. Please watch for chances.'[36] Nothing came of this. Piatt had also actively sought a consulship in 1881 and had sent a petition for a post to the president, signed by many famous men, among them the poet Henry Wadsworth Longfellow.[37] The Cork appointment was the successful outcome of this. Piatt's wife, Sarah, was equally well known as a poet. They had six children, one of whom, Louis, drowned in an accident in Cork Harbour in 1884 at age nine.[38] Piatt seems to have given two of his sons a taste of the consular life: Arthur Donn Piatt (born 1867) was appointed vice consul in Dublin in 1893 and Frederick Piatt (born 1865), who was a clerk in the Cork consulate, transferred to Edinburgh the following year as vice consul.[39] There is more about Frederick in the Edinburgh consulate history (Chapter 15). John James Piatt remained only six months in Dublin, returning to America to devote himself to literary work. His son, Arthur, remained as vice consul until his death in 1914.[40] John James Piatt was replaced in 1893 by Newton Benisha Ashby of Des Moines, Iowa, who was in turn replaced in February 1898 by Joshua Wilbour of Rhode Island.[41] He was connected with several banking and financial institutions. In the year ended 30 June 1901 exports to the United States from the district were valued at just under one hundred thousand dollars.[42] By 1902 there were agencies at Athlone, Ballina, Galway and Limerick. Wilbour's appointment was cut short by ill health and after undergoing surgery for cancer in Dublin at the end of 1901 returned with his wife to America where he died on 12 March 1902.[43]

When Alfred Keane Moe of Buffalo, New York, arrived in 1904 the salary for the post was $4,000 and the consulate was located at 9 Leinster Street in premises rented from The New York Life Insurance Co. Like many consuls, Moe was a lawyer and his previous assignment was in Honduras, where he had been consul at Tegucigalpa for two years.[44] The consulate received its first inspection under the new 1906 Act arrangements in May 1908, and was conducted by Consul General at Large Horace Lee Washington. Moe mentioned to him some of the problems emanating from the burgeoning Irish home rule movements.

> American exporters to Ireland must also reckon with a systematic hostility on the part of the party which flaunts its banner "Ireland for the Irish." This party is very numerous and buys extensively, but wherever Irish goods can be bought, no foreign article of a similar nature will be accepted. So strong is this spirit becoming that a boycott of foreign goods is already abroad, and American goods share a worse fate it would seem than other foreign varieties. I am sure, however, that judicious advertising, and actual display and demonstration will overcome such prejudice as now exists.[45]

The value of goods exported to the United States from the district during 1907 was $1,400,000, and fee income generated during the same year amounted to more than $3,000. The inspector was impressed by Arthur Donn Piatt, the vice and deputy consul, remarking: 'he has full knowledge of the routine business of the office, and its conduct appears to be largely left to him [...]. He is a valuable subordinate and employee in this office, but is undoubtedly capable of performing more responsible consular work.'[46] The inspector was less enamoured of Moe, noting:

> He seems best suited to a quiet post with little or no change in his routine, and for that reason is fitted for this post, or one with similar volume and character of work. He appears to be disposed to live in a retired manner, socially, so that a post with the requirements of an American colony would not be suitable. He evinced a lack of tact in criticising certain of his colleagues severely, when inspector first met him as an entire stranger.

The inspector's comments were taken up when his report was received in the State Department, and Wilbur J. Carr, Chief Clerk, wrote to Moe about these.

> It has come to the Department's attention that the current business of your office is conducted largely by the Vice Consul and that you give little attention to the routine work. Numerous suggestions were made to you for the proper conduct of your office by Consul General at Large Horace Lee Washington, at the time of his inspection of the Consulate. These suggestions should be carefully followed. You should be thoroughly familiar with the details of your work and should take an active interest in carrying it on. A consular officer can properly represent the business interests of this country only when he is thoroughly interested in the work and has a wide and influential acquaintance with the people of his district.[47]

Moe had already left Dublin and Carr's letter was sent to him at an address in New Jersey; three months later, in March 1909, he took up the post of consul in Bordeaux. Hardly a 'quiet post' for someone 'disposed to live in a retired manner, socially'. He served there until 1914.

When Edward Le Grand Adams of New York arrived from Stockholm in July 1909 only the Galway agency remained, as the Limerick agency had become subordinate to the Cork consulate. Adams was a late entrant to the Consular Service having had a varied career before joining in 1902. For the previous 29 years he had been a journalist, an oil producer, a deputy collector in the US Internal Revenue and a New York state tax commissioner. The office was inspected again in 1909, this time by Heaton W. Harris. He had little to say about Adams, who had arrived only the month before the inspection, but noted: 'The consul is married and has two children with him, a girl of 23 and a boy in his teens. [...] The daughter was in a country village ill and the other members of the family [were] temporarily with her. [...] [The consul] is a newspaper man and will doubtless give this part of his work adequate attention.'[48] Harris was critical of Piatt, believing:

> that he has fallen into somewhat easy-going and lax methods of work. He has spent practically his entire life in Ireland where business starts at 10 in the morning or later and he does not

realize that some of the methods in vogue around him are not adapted to a consular office, as such office is now conducted. He feels that he is much underpaid and ought to have a consulate, while the fact is that he is better paid [at $1,000 a year] than most men in the United States, with the same ability and for the same amount of work.

The report continued:

The situation in this office is doubtless well understood at the Department. The father of the one subordinate was himself a consul, writer of books and [sic] literary man, with whom this son was associated as clerk. [The son] married at Dublin and is probably quite as much Irish as he is American. He is easy-going, slip-shod in his methods, inclined to be quick tempered, absolutely sure that he understands all about the service, and feels that he is abundantly able to conduct a difficult consulate. He laments that he would have to be examined [i.e., sit a competitive examination] before he would be eligible to appointment. What the office needs most, perhaps, is to have it brought clearly to Mr Piatt's mind that the methods of his father's day are out of date, and that to retain a place in the service, American clerks should keep abreast with the changes that the service has undergone. The inspector hopes that Consul Adams will be able to improve the efficiency of this office. The inspector does not think that Mr Piatt fully appreciates his own limitations as a public servant.[49]

Some of these remarks about Piatt would be echoed when Harris inspected the Edinburgh consulate the same year, in 1911, and reported on his brother, Frederick, who had served there from 1894. Harris gave the Dublin consulate an overall rating of 'fair', just one grade above 'poor'.

When he carried out the next inspection in 1911, Harris noted that the value of exports to the United States was $1,400,000 and the amount of fees collected was more than $3,500.[50] Adams' salary was $4,000 and Piatt's $1,200. There was a considerable amount of notarial work (almost seven hundred and seventy transactions) due to the district being large 'and many persons living in it have relatives in the United States leaving in some cases property or other matters'. The office had 'no special weak points'. However,

The consul has the training of a newspaper office and of the editorial part of such office. He cannot bear to destroy an old newspaper or clipping lest he may need it and has not quite sufficient of the faculty of order to lead him to arrange for scrap books or other media for keeping clippings, etc., so tables, windows, etc., have more than their legitimate share of literary decoration of various kind. The consul knows his weakness in this regard and talks about it pleasantly without quite the force to clean up.

Harris concludes, rather generously: 'There are other offices in the service with the same weakness, and in quite as serious a degree as this one. It is training – newspaper training which has given this service so many of its conspicuous men that the inspector looks with some forbearance upon this particular form of weakness.'[51]

Harris's hopes that Adams would be able to improve the office's efficiency unfortunately proved to be misplaced. When the consulate was next inspected, in 1914, by Ralph J. Totten the situation had changed dramatically. Piatt had died that year, work on preparing many of the various routine returns had not been started and Adams's physical condition was described as 'very poor'. Totten noted that Adams:

> seemed to be on the edge of a nervous breakdown. He claimed that he could neither eat nor sleep and several times began to cry when questioned by the Inspector. He was totally unable to answer the simplest question in regards to the routine work of the office. He frankly admitted that he had always depended on subordinates for the clerical and routine work and that he knew nothing about either. The Vice and Deputy Consul [John F Claffey] had been in the office for about two months and had the advantage of the instruction of Mr Tracy Lay, Consular Assistant, for less than one month. He was very frankly ignorant concerning the greater part of the office work. The accounts for the quarter ended June 30, 1914 had not been commenced on July 25. The Inspector was able to get the accounts started and to coach the Vice Consul to a limited degree in this and other rudimentary work. The books were in a bad condition and the office needs the assistance of a trained man to get it in good condition.

He concluded his report by saying: 'It is earnestly recommended that, if at all possible, one of the experienced Consular Assistants be sent to Dublin so that Mr Adams can take a much needed rest. Even if Mr Claffey was able to carry on all the branches of the work it is too busy and important an office for one man to successfully handle.'[52] The inspection file does not record whether this recommendation was carried out. Claffey remained at Dublin until 1921 when he transferred to a similar post in London.[53] Adams recovered and remained in Dublin throughout the First World War until being transferred to the consulate at Sherbrooke, Québec, in 1919, from where he retired in 1924.[54]

Frederick Theodore F. Dumont of Lancaster, Pennsylvania, was appointed in 1919. He had been a construction engineer with the Pennsylvania Railroad for 12 years until joining the Consular Service in 1911 in Guadeloupe, after which he served in Madrid (1912–1914) and Florence (1914–1919). Business at Dublin had increased by then and there were now four vice consuls,[55] although only the Galway agency remained. Dumont left in 1922 and his subsequent posts included Frankfort and Havana. Dr Charles Montgomery Hathaway, Jr, of New York state replaced Dumont. He was educated at Yale where he obtained a PhD in 1902. Before joining the Consular Service in 1911, he had worked in estate agency and insurance businesses and taught English in New York at Adelphi College and Columbia University and was an instructor in English and law at the United States Naval Academy. A very experienced consul, he arrived from Bombay where he had served for a year; he had previously been consul in Puerto Plata (Dominican Republic, 1911–1913), Hull (1913–1917), Cork (1917–1919) and Budapest (1919–1920).[56] The next inspection took place in 1924 and was conducted by Robert Frazer Jr. By that time, Ireland was no longer a constituent part of Britain but in 1922 had become the Irish Free State, with dominion status (similar to, for example, Canada and Australia) although still under the British Crown. The office was located at 14 and 15 Lower O'Connell Street. Hathaway was still in charge as consul, but things were changing rapidly, reflecting Ireland's new status. Including himself, there was now a staff of 10, 4 of whom were Americans, and business had increased considerably. Fee income was at an all-time record of more than $72,000, the chief source of which was $66,000 for more than 6,600 visas issued to people seeking to travel, and probably emigrate, to the

United States. Correspondence also increased, with 9,000 letters received and a similar number sent. Even after paying salaries and wages (almost $15,000) and other operational costs, the consulate was able to remit more than $51,000 to the Treasury. The inspector concluded his report with the prescient recommendation:

> It is believed that the office at Dublin should be raised to the status of a Consulate-General. The Irish Free State is now as completely a separate political entity as Canada; our office at its capital is as important a one in itself as some of our existing Consulates-General; several important nations have established Consulates-General at it; and unquestionably the Government would immensely appreciate our establishing an office of that grade in the Free State. Southern Ireland is highly important politically, we shall probably always have to have an officer of high grade at Dublin, and no reason is known why his office should remain under the supervision of our Consulate-General at London rather than be an independent Consulate General itself.[57]

This recommendation was put to Herbert C. Hengstler, Chief of the Consular Bureau, and was approved.[58]

The consulate became a consulate general in 1924, headed by newly promoted Hathaway, and was to all intents and purposes an embassy-in-waiting. By the time of the next inspection, in 1926, staff numbers had increased to 24; the inspector, Louis G. Dreyfus, Jr, commented: 'This is one of the largest visa agencies in the world.'[59] In 1927 it moved to 15 Merrion Square and was upgraded to a legation headed by an envoy extraordinary and minister plenipotentiary, Frederick A. Sterling, a career Foreign Service officer. In 1950 the mission was finally elevated to an embassy. Apart from Sterling, all subsequent chiefs of mission have been political appointees.[60] Hathaway therefore has the unique distinction of being the last consul at Dublin when Ireland was part of Britain, and the first consul and then consul general there in the new Irish Free State. He left Dublin in 1927 and transferred to Munich, from where he retired in 1939. He died in Santa Barbara in 1954.

Chapter Thirteen

DUNDEE

The city of Dundee is situated on the north shore of the Firth of Tay in Scotland. Originally internationally famous for the three 'Js' of its main industries: jam, jute and journalism, only the latter now remains.

The first United States consular officer was Edward Baxter, a Scot, whose earliest despatch was sent in December 1833 in which he describes himself as vice consul.[1] He was nominated by President Andrew Jackson in March 1834 to be upgraded to consul and confirmation of this was announced in July.[2] He served until 1845 when he was replaced by Stewart Steel of Pennsylvania, an attorney and businessman, who had been born in Ireland but had become an American citizen. James McDowell of Ohio succeeded him in 1850; in the remainder of the 1850s the consuls were Thomas Steere of Rhode Island (1853–1858) and Joseph B. Holderby of North Carolina (1858–1861). The salary in 1853 was $500 with the right to carry on trade, however this was increased in 1856 to $2,000 but the consuls were no longer permitted to engage in trade.

In 1861, Lincoln appointed Hugh Smith of Kentucky, the son of his old friend the Reverend James Smith. The appointment was short-lived, however, for after a year Hugh turned over the appointment to his father due to ill health and returned to America.[3] Reverend Smith, who took over formally in 1863, had been born in Scotland but had become a naturalized American citizen. Lincoln asked Secretary of State Seward in January 1863 to 'send me a nomination for Rev. James Smith […] an intimate personal friend of mine'.[4] Smith had been pastor at the First Presbyterian Church in Springfield, Illinois, and in 1850 had conducted the funeral service for Lincoln's three-year-old son, Edward. Lincoln had become so interested in a book written by Smith in the 1840s entitled *Christian's Defense* that he asked him for a copy so that he could finish reading it. The two struck up a close acquaintanceship. Two years later, Lincoln gave a lecture on the Bible in Smith's church 'which was said by ministers to be the ablest defense of the Bible ever heard in that pulpit'.[5] Smith served in Dundee until his death in 1871; his funeral was held in public and was attended by the provost and magistrates of the city, a detachment of troops, sailors, police and 'upward of 200 of the principal merchants'.[6]

Matthew McDougall of New York was appointed in 1871 at a salary of $2,000. Trade between Dundee and the United States was brisk and consisted chiefly of jute and linen goods and during the year ending December 1871 the total value of exports was $6 million which generated $7,000 in consular fees. The jute was 'manufactured into grain bags and shipped in enormous quantities', some twelve million of which were imported by San Francisco merchants alone in 1871. An indication of the rapid increase in this trade may be gained from observing that only two years previously the number of bags imported by these same merchants was four million.[7] The vice consul, William Reid, a Scot, was appointed in the same year as McDougall but three years later left for the United States where he became a leading figure in the railroad, finance, banking and flour milling industry in Oregon.[8] A consular agency at Aberdeen, headed by William White, dated from 1830.[9] Trade to the United States from the Dundee district consisted chiefly of woollen goods and granite.[10]

McDougall was replaced by John F. Winter of Illinois in 1881, but he remained for only a year and was succeeded by Willard B. Wells. At this time the consulate occupied three rooms at 81 Murraygate. Wells left in 1885 when Arthur Wood was appointed. Although there was a clerk hire allowance, in salaried consulates such as Dundee any amount paid to a clerk over the official allowance had to be paid by the consul out of his income. In many cases, the allowance was insufficient to meet the actual salary of a clerk and the excess amounts paid by consuls in Britain ranged from nil to $2,750 in 1885. In the case of Dundee, Wood had to pay his clerk $560 on top of his allowance.[11] The Aberdeen consular agent was Andrew Murray, a local advocate and notary, who had been appointed in 1890 with offices at 214 Union Street.[12] George Washington Savage of New York was appointed in 1893 but died the following year at age 73. He had transferred from the Belfast consulate and before that had been a judge in New Jersey. One of his sons, John Marbacher Savage, had been vice consul in Belfast during his father's tenure and had moved with him to Dundee and become vice consul. He succeeded his father as consul there in 1894.[13] The consulate was still located at 81 Murraygate and Savage's new vice consul was Allan Baxter, a 43-year-old local solicitor.[14] Savage's mother, whose maiden surname was Marbacher, resided with him and his wife in Dundee and died there in 1897, the same year that he left the Consular Service and went into business in Belfast and New York. He rejoined the Service in 1914 and was appointed consul in Sheffield and then in Southampton in 1919, where he remained until retiring in 1929.[15]

John C. Higgins of Delaware arrived in 1897. His previous career had included many years in manufacturing businesses and a term in the Delaware State Legislature. The value of exports to the United States from the consular district during the year ended 30 June 1901 was more than $7.5 million, showing an increase over the previous year of $300,000. During the same year the consulate certified almost three thousand invoices, and about one hundred inquiries from American businessmen were received each year. The only American ships calling regularly at Dundee were those of the Arrow Line which called at New York; all other shipping to the United States was via Glasgow. The annual office rental was $315, and vice consul Baxter's salary was $800.[16] In 1906, the consul's salary was increased to $4,000 and in the same year William P. Quann, a naturalized American citizen of Irish birth, was appointed agent in Aberdeen.[17]

The consulate was inspected in 1908 by Horace Lee Washington and was rated as 'fair'. The income from fees was approximately $8,000. Washington felt that Baxter's long tenure as vice consul had made: 'the tone of the office [...] become local. With a new consul this would probable [sic] be more radically changed than by placing an American subordinate with present Consul.' His chief criticism, however, was that Higgins: 'fears being obtrusive if active in trade matters [...] and is reluctant to get involved in this. […] He feels that it would endanger his standing to be energetic in trade matters.' The inspector suggested that 'some other officer might be more effective here'. The Department followed up his report and wrote to Higgins drawing attention to a few weaknesses, such as record keeping. The main thrust of the letter, however, was set out in the following two sentences:

> Finally, the Department desires to emphasize to you the fact that among the most important duties a consular officer can perform is that of reporting on commercial matters in his district and particularly of pointing out opportunities for the extension of American trade. While you have undoubtedly striven to do good work along other lines the Department trusts that you will hereafter devote more attention to this particular branch of your work.[18]

The consulate was inspected again the following year by Heaton W. Harris who repeated the previous inspector's conclusions:

> There is an evident tendency at this consulate, as at some others where similar conditions exist, to over-load the clerk by assigning duties to him that ought to be performed by the consul himself. It was made plain at this office that, if information was needed on a trade matter, the clerk is sent to get it. It is Mr Baxter this and Mr Baxter that, to such an extent that he does an amount of work perhaps in excess of his compensation. Some of it is, however, work which a younger and more vigorous consul would do himself, and which he ought to do himself. The more capable consuls all agree that investigations of trade matters can not as a rule be delegated to clerks, and especially clerks of a foreign citizenship, who are not received by manufacturers and others in person, as is the consul.

Harris noted that 'the consul is about to retire from the Service at the age of 71 and more'. He tempered his criticisms by adding that he had:

> met no other consul more courteous and kindly disposed than this one, and probably but few who stand better in the community in which they live than does this consul. He had reached an age when he came into the Service when it was difficult to take up the routine work of an office and conduct it with vigor. Neither he nor his well-meaning clerk have quite realized that the Service had advanced during the past ten years, and have not fully adjusted themselves to the conditions as they are.

Having said this, he felt that 'Under all the circumstances, the office should be rated Fair.'[19] Higgins retired from the Consular Service that year and died in 1924.[20]

William Stanley Hollis of Massachusetts arrived in 1909 from Lourenço Marques in Mozambique. When that post had been inspected earlier that year Hollis was described as a broken man. He was in debt, and had had to send his ill wife home. He said he would take 'anything to get out of this place, which is a penitentiary to me in my present condition'.[21] He remained in Dundee for just over a year before being transferred to Beirut as consul general.[22] The status of the Aberdeen agency was questioned in 1909 during the inspection of the Dunfermline consulate that year. The inspector gave his views on closing Dunfermline or of reducing it to an agency, and raising Aberdeen to a full consulate.[23] Hollis's replacement was Edwin Haldeman Dennison of Ohio, who arrived in

1911 from the consulship at Bombay. One of Dennison's reports dealt with the popu-
larity of cinemas.

> The present popularity of the cinematograph theatre in Scotland is remarkable. [...] The
> rise of the picture palace in Dundee has been extraordinary. A few years ago there were only
> two or three of these; today there are twenty-five licenses [*sic*] issued for buildings used for
> cinematograph entertainments. [...] There is now under construction here a building with a
> seating capacity of 1,500, which is to be used as a picture palace. In Aberdeen every motion
> picture theatre reports phenomenal patronage, and three new ones are to be opened there
> shortly.[24]

Harris inspected the consulate again in 1911. It was now located at 31 Albert Square, and
by this time there was an assistant clerk (paid $250) to lighten the overburdened Baxter's
workload. The total value of exports from the district to the United States during the
fiscal year was $7.6 million which generated a fee income of $11,700. The office was
rated as 'good', 'Its only defects are those of having a foreign substitute officer, and being
not quite in accord with the best offices of this class in commercial correspondence.'
Harris remarked that Dennison 'is at present suffering from extreme lameness which
he believes will ultimately leave him'. It was noted that Dennison's predecessor, Hollis,
had: 'inaugurated the practice of binding correspondence much more expensively and
elegantly than is necessary or proper. No other consulate in the European District uses
binding approaching the cost or elegance in use at the Dundee office. This is wholly
unnecessary. [...] Hollis bound the correspondence as if it was to have a permanent
place in some splendid library.'[25] On 5 May 1912, a consular agency was established in
Kirkwall, in the Orkney Islands, headed by James Flett. He was a member of Macrae
& Robertson, solicitors, and the agency operated from their offices at Commercial Bank
Buildings, 8 Albert Street. This was the most northerly US consular presence in Britain.[26]

The next inspection took place in 1914 and was undertaken by Ralph J. Totten.
Under Dennison's charge a marked improvement in the running of the consulate had
taken place. He was given a personal rating of 'excellent', as was the office, and Baxter
was rated as 'good'. Totten observed that Dennison 'maintains the sort of office it is a
pleasure to see. [...] [it] has a distinctly American tone. This is one of the best arranged
offices the Inspector has seen.' He also noted that Dennison 'is fond of music and is a
good singer'. His physical condition, however, was now noted as 'fair'. The value of
exports to the United States in the year ending 31 December 1913 was $11 million; fee
income during the fiscal year 1913–1914 was more than $13,000, and after deducting
the running costs of the consulate a credit balance of more than $7,000 was remitted
to Speyer Brothers, merchant bankers, who were agents in Britain for the US government. As an example of Dennison's thoroughness the inventory included 17 samples of
impressions made by the rubber stamps used in the office. Also mentioned in the inventory was: 'Photographs, framed of former consuls, 8'. It would be interesting to know
what became of these photographs.[27] Dennison served in Dundee until 1915 when he
was appointed consul general in Christiana, Norway, remaining there until 1917 when he
transferred to Birmingham. His story is also taken up in the account of the Birmingham
consulate in Chapter 8.

Figure 13.1 William S. Hollis, consul, Dundee, 1909–1910; consul general, London, 1918–1920. After Dundee he transferred to Beirut as consul general. Despite his short time in Dundee his fastidious nature was evidenced by his practice of having the consulate records elegantly bound. When an inspection of the consulate took place after his departure the inspector noted that Hollis 'bound his correspondence as if it was to have a permanent place in some splendid library'. Dundee must have made an impact on Hollis because in 1918 when he was consul general in London he returned briefly to Dundee to marry a local nurse. [Harris & Ewing Collection, Library of Congress, Prints & Photographs Division, Reproduction Number LC-DIG-hec-16661.]

Like his two immediate predecessors, Charles Louis Latham of North Carolina, who took up appointment in 1915, must have been keenly aware of the Dundee climate, having transferred from Punta Arenas, Chile. In the same year, George McClellan Wells replaced Quann in the Aberdeen agency. Wells had an unusual background; born in New Jersey he had spent 16 years 'in providing musical entertainment' throughout the United States. He moved to Scotland where he was business manager of the American Roller Rink Company Ltd from 1908–1912, and of the Rothesay Pavilion Ltd, Glasgow, from 1912–1914. He moved to Aberdeen and was general manager of the Aberdeen Winter Recreation Institute from 1914–1915 before being appointed consular agent that year with his offices at 34 Bridge Street.[28] The Aberdeen Winter Recreation Institute, a huge ice skating rink known also as the Glacierium, had opened in 1912 in the building previously housing the American Roller Rink. Towards the end of the First World War it was acquired by the Scottish Aircraft Factory; the last aircraft built there was an Avro biplane in January 1919.[29] Baxter, although retained in Dundee, was replaced as vice consul by Edward Roland Pottle of Georgia in 1917. Pottle wrote an interesting report that year that highlighted the importance of Dundee's jam industry during the First World War. In his view, by organizing itself to meet:

> the enormous requirements of the British Army and Navy [...] [it] is one of the commissary triumphs of the war. [...] Having installed modernized and standardized machinery at the outset of the war in 1914, they are now producing jam on a scale hitherto unequalled, and it has been estimated that were the weekly output of tins of one Dundee manufacturer stood end to end, they would reach up forty miles into the heavens. It is said to be no unusual thing for this firm to deal with 100,000,000 oranges.[30]

Latham's term of office ended in 1917 and he was transferred to Kingston, Jamaica; Pottle transferred to Bilbao as vice consul in 1919.

Henry Albert Johnson of Washington, DC, took over in 1917, arriving from Ghent where he had been consul for six years.[31] He had been a naval officer before joining the Consular Service in 1886 as consul in Venice. The consulate was inspected in 1919 by Ralph J. Totten who rated Johnson as 'good', Baxter as 'very good' and the office as 'excellent'. Johnson was married and had nine children, four of whom were living with him and his Italian-born wife. The value of exports to the United States was more than $8 million and the fee income was $3,900. However, for the first time, the consulate's expenditure exceeded its income and showed a loss of more than $4,000. The Kirkwall agency was closed in June 1919 and the Dundee inventory includes taking possession of a typewriter withdrawn from there.[32]

Totten inspected the consulate again in 1921. By this time ratings for consuls were no longer set out in the reports, only those for subordinate staff. Baxter was rated as 'excellent' and the two clerks were rated as 'excellent' and 'good'. On the other hand, William Anderson Poindexter, an American who had been appointed vice consul and clerk in October 1919, was proving to be a problem and was rated as 'poor', the lowest possible rating. He had served in the Spanish American War and was described as 47, married, with three children, with: 'Habits, good except for his being in debt. Lacks in courtesy, neatness and interest in his work. Not alert and no service spirit.' [He] 'is a brother of Senator Poindexter. He owes some $1,500 in Dundee and apparently makes no effort to pay. He has had several judgements against him but as his Government salary cannot be attached and he has no other resources there has been no result.'[33] Totten said that he had written a separate report regarding Poindexter and would forward it to the Department. It is not on the file. Exports to the United States were valued at more than $20 million and there was a huge increase in the fee income during the 1920–1921 fiscal year. Including fees from offices in Aberdeen and Dunfermline it amounted to more than $42,000, of which more than $27,000 came from applications for visas for foreign passports – an indication of the number of local people seeking to leave for the United States. After the running costs of the consulate were met it was possible to remit a balance of more than $31,000 to the Treasury.[34] The Aberdeen agency closed in the early 1920s.

Robert Frazer, Jr, inspected the consulate in June 1924, two days before Johnson's retirement 'having passed the age of 65'. Baxter died almost two months later; Poindexter was no longer there and had been replaced by Bernard Franklin Hale, an American career officer who had arrived in August of the previous year. There was now an American clerk (rated as 'fair') and three local female clerks (one rated as 'excellent', two as 'very good'). However, the effects of Poindexter's presence were still being felt. Herbert C. Hengstler, Chief of the Consular Bureau, asked Frazer when inspecting the consulate to investigate allegations made by Poindexter that Johnson had 'profited personally prior to July 1, 1921, in the accounts and expenditures of his office on account of the exchange situation.'[35] Frazer carried out a careful examination of the accounts and concluded that 'Mr Poindexter's allegations were unfounded and false in every particular.' He described Poindexter as 'unquestionably immoral, unscrupulous, and unworthy of credence; he was also a heavy drinker and often intoxicated'. Frazer added that Johnson had informed him that Poindexter: 'had a habit […] of buying expensive furniture and other things that he would keep and use until hard pressed for payment by suppliers, when he would return them and feel that he was freed of all obligation. On one occasion he took an expensive article on credit and a few days later – without having paid for it – put it up [at] an auction for sale!'. He continued:

> Miss Low, a clerk of seven years' experience in the Consulate and a very fine type of woman, confirmed to the Inspector personally Mr Johnson's statement that Mr Poindexter had been so drunk in the office one day that he had to be carried out and sent home in a cab; also Mr Johnson's statement that one day, when Mr Johnson was out for lunch, Poindexter had called the three girl clerks into his private office in succession and made indecent advances to and almost assaulted them. The following day he apologized before the whole staff and sought to condone his action by saying frankly that he had been drunk.[36]

Wilbur Carr, the Director of the Consular Service, wrote personally to Johnson: 'I deeply regret that you should have been annoyed and embarrassed and that the Service should have suffered in the way that it has from the appointment of Mr Poindexter.' There is no indication of what action, if any, was taken against Poindexter. He returned to the United States where he joined the Veterans Administration until retirement in 1942. He died in Florida in January 1968 at age 93 and is buried in Arlington National Cemetery.[37] Consulate business continued to increase, with income in excess of $55,000, the bulk coming once more from visa applications ($44,000), and after running costs were met it was possible to remit $45,000.[38]

Johnson was succeeded by Maxwell Kennedy Moorhead of Pennsylvania, a widely experienced consular officer, who arrived from the consulship at Stuttgart. Hale, the vice consul and clerk, had transferred to Edinburgh and was replaced by William A. Hickey. The consulate received a further inspection in 1926, by Louis G. Dreyfus Jr. Although showing a healthy total of $41,000, income had gone down from the time of the previous inspection. For some unexplained reason, however, there were now eight clerks in addition to the vice consul and consequently the salary and wage bill had increased substantially to $15,500, compared to $5,800 at the previous inspection. The credit balance of income over expenditure was therefore reduced to $20,000. Unsurprisingly Dreyfus found the office 'considerably overstaffed', even 'shamefully overstaffed', particularly when compared with the Edinburgh and Birmingham consulates which had a similar volume of business. He recommended a reduction of up to three staff. Revealing an unusual sensitivity for an inspector, he asked the Department to say when implementing the reduction that it was 'made after careful analysis of the Summary of Business rather than as a result of my recommendations'.[39] Moorhead remained in Dundee until 1928 when he transferred to Johannesburg. He was succeeded by John J. C. Watson of Kentucky who arrived from Swansea. He had been a lawyer for 14 years before joining the Consular Service in 1914.[40] Unfortunately his tenure in Dundee was cut short by his death there in September 1932 at age 54.[41]

Maurice Pratt Dunlap of Minnesota arrived in 1932 from Stockholm. For 11 years he had had a varied career as a journalist, as an employee in the Philippines Civil Service and the US Department of Agriculture before joining the Consular Service in 1915 in Stavanger.[42] The consulate was inspected at the end of 1933 by Homer M. Byington who noted that the issuing of immigration visas in Scotland had been centralized at the Glasgow consulate, thus eliminating that work in Dundee and the other consular offices. The previous inspector's staffing reduction recommendations had been followed and apart from the vice consul, Julian Kemble Smedberg, an American appointed in 1931, there were now only two local clerks. Smedberg's background was unusual; before joining the consular service in 1920 he had worked as a clerk in Buenos Aires for 12 years, then pursued a career as a professional singer in several countries for nine years.[43] Byington noted that there were 158 American citizens living in the consular district, of whom 101 were students taking medical courses at St Andrews (including University College, Dundee) and Aberdeen Universities. Dunlap left Dundee in 1937 and transferred to Bergen.

Phil Henry Hubbard of Vermont, whose previous assignments had included Manchester and Liverpool, arrived in 1937 and remained until 1940 when he transferred to Milan.[44] Smedberg transferred to Edinburgh as vice consul in 1938 and the consulate closed in February 1940.[45]

Chapter Fourteen

DUNFERMLINE

Situated some three miles inland from the Firth of Forth, Dunfermline was for several hundred years the capital of Scotland. The town is also the birthplace of Andrew Carnegie, the famous industrialist and philanthropist.

Manufacturers in Dunfermline had to travel to the Edinburgh consulate to have their invoices certified before they could export their goods to the United States. As is explained in the Edinburgh and Leith consulate history (Chapter 15), a group of Dunfermline manufacturers wrote to Colonel John Robeson, the Edinburgh consul, in February 1871 asking him to have a consular agency established in Dunfermline with John Burn Doig as agent. This would save them making the twice-weekly, 34-mile journey to Edinburgh. (The Forth Railway Bridge, which eventually would considerably shorten their journey, did not open until almost twenty years later.) Robeson wrote to the Department that month supporting the request, adding that more than eight hundred of the previous year's two thousand invoices verified at his consulate had come from Dunfermline.[1] The Department agreed to the proposal and 20-year-old Doig was appointed on 24 March.[2] In 1872, the business of verifying invoices was described by a government inspector as 'quite large', and for the three quarters ended 31 March 1872 generated fee income of $1,740.[3] Doig remained as consular agent until 1877 when he was replaced by George H. Scidmore of Ohio who was appointed as vice consul.[4] The following year a further agency was opened in nearby Kirkcaldy headed by Andrew Innes, a local solicitor and notary public.[5]

Dunfermline became a commercial agency in 1881, rather than a consular agency, and was headed by Henry Ray Myers, with James Penman as vice commercial agent. Myers had been born in Germany but had become a naturalized American citizen.[6] From 1881, the offices occupied one room in St Margaret's Hall, St Margaret Street.[7] The agency's normal routine was shattered in March 1883 when W. H. Josts, a wealthy New Yorker, committed suicide by shooting in Myers's residence. Newspaper reports suggested that he did so because of an unsuccessful divorce suit.[8] Scidmore left in 1884;[9] Myers left the following year and was replaced by Lucien J. Walker. During the year ending 31 December 1885, the commercial agency authenticated 1,131 invoices, and collected more than $3,000 in fees, but Walker had to pay an excess of $72 for clerk hire to meet the difference between the actual amount paid to the clerk and the official allowance allocated. At the Kirkcaldy consular agency more than three hundred invoices were authenticated during the same year.[10] He retired in December 1889 but was appointed consul at Cork from 1893 to 1897.[11] In 1889, James Douglas Reid arrived in Dunfermline as commercial agent. He was born in Edinburgh in 1819, moving to

Canada with his parents at the age of 15, and three years later to the United States where he became a clerk in the Rochester [New York] Post Office, and began a long successful career in the telegraph industry, eventually holding the most senior positions in leading companies such as Western Union. It was he who gave 14-year-old Andrew Carnegie a start in life by employing him as a messenger in the Pittsburgh office of the telegraph company of which he was then superintendent. Reid and Carnegie remained lifelong friends and it was Carnegie who secured the Dunfermline commercial agent post for him. Before setting off for Dunfermline, Reid was honoured at a dinner given by the various telegraph companies for which he had worked over a period of almost fifty years. During the dinner, at which Carnegie was one of the speakers, Reid reminisced about his long career and said that his proudest achievement was being the first to appoint a woman to duty in a telegraph office.[12] He served at Dunfermline until 1897 and returned to America where he died four years later at the age of 82. Penman was his deputy throughout his time in Dunfermline.

The office's status was then changed from a commercial agency to a consulate. Reid's successor was John Niven McCunn, also Scottish-born, who became a naturalized American citizen only some six months before being appointed consul in 1897. Before joining the Consular Service he had been engaged in farming and teaching in Wisconsin and was proprietor of the Green Bay Business College there from 1888 until 1900 (three years after he had become consul).[13] Penman was replaced as vice consul in May 1899 by Charles Drysdale, a local man who, in addition to his consular post, was a retail dealer of books and stationery.[14] During the year ending 30 June 1901, exports to the United States from the district were $1.3 million, the bulk of which was linens; 804 invoices were certified. The office still occupied a room in St Margaret's Hall, St Margaret Street, for which the amount paid for rent, including heat, light, and janitor service for the year ending 30 June 1901 was $146. The room was obviously fairly small because the inventory showed only 'principal articles of furniture are a writing desk, a writing table, a bookcase, 6 chairs, a carpet, and window shades'.[15] During the same year, the Kirkcaldy agency dealt with 476 invoices. In 1902, Andrew Innes was still agent there, despite being 83 years old.[16] On his death the following year, he was succeeded by his son, J. Lockhart Innes.[17] The agency's days were numbered, however, and it was closed in 1907.[18] During that year, the value of linen goods to the United States from the consulate district was £337,265 and of cotton goods £29,576. Compared with 1906, these figures showed decreases of £25,595 and £2,001, respectively.[19]

In early 1908, McCunn was transferred to Glasgow, the city of his birth. He had been replaced in Dunfermline at the end of the previous year by Maxwell Blake of Missouri who had joined the Consular Service in 1906 as consul at Funchal on the island of Madeira. Before joining the Service he had been engaged in ranching, real estate and bonding businesses. The consulate was inspected in 1908 by Horace Lee Washington, by which time the office had relocated to 4 Abbey Park Place. His report stated that Blake was married, had no children and was 'a young man, active and ambitious, and is, also, adapted to a post where there is a certain social demand'. Blake had told Washington that 'in his opinion a Consulate was not justified at this post' and Washington suggested that 'by reason of its proximity, and for the advantage of concentration, Edinburgh is the right place to best serve the interests of this neighborhood'. Drysdale, the vice consul, was paid $500 and 'out of office hours conducts a small stationery business […]. An outside business interest of necessity occupies his thought and attention more than consular matters.' Washington discovered that the consulate was closed for two days a week, and he noted against Drysdale: 'It is entirely possible that the closing of the consulate two days a week may have been prompted by his private business demands.' Washington thought that the salary was sufficient to employ a full-time clerk rather than Drysdale. Income from certifying 863 invoices and other documents during 1907 generated $1,700.[20] Following the inspection, the Department wrote to Blake expressing surprise: 'to learn that it has been the practice for the consulate to be closed from Friday afternoon to Tuesday morning, and you are accordingly instructed that it must open daily during the ordinary hours of banking and official business'.[21]

Possibly because of the Department's concerns, the consulate was inspected again the following year, this time by Heaton W. Harris. Blake complained that he had practically nothing to do and was keen to get a post where there was more work. While accepting this, Harris believed that Blake:

underestimates somewhat the opportunities afforded by his little district and by the North of Scotland, of which his district is a part and on the trade conditions as a whole and in some detail he might properly comment more than he does without encroaching upon his consular neighbors. [He] overestimates […] his abilities and training as a consular officer. He feels that he should now be a consul general and would be, except for some circumstances over which he did not have control.[22]

These 'circumstances' are not spelled out but there is a suggestion that Blake felt that other officers were permitted to bring political aid to their careers, yet he was not. It was quite clear that there was not a great deal of business conducted at this consulate and it was remarked that even many agencies, which of course were subordinate to consulates, dealt with a greater volume of business. Harris gave a detailed account of Blake's typical day. He lived 'in a good hotel' in Edinburgh, arrived by train at Dunfermline at '10.39 am. Within 5 or 6 minutes thereafter he is at his office. He usually returns [to Edinburgh] on a train leaving Dunfermline at 3.47 pm.' Surprisingly, Harris thought that these hours were sufficient, but they would not be in the average consulate, and that while residence outside of one's district would normally be objectionable it was not so in this case.[23] He recommended that Blake should be transferred to another post at the same grade but with plenty of work. He also raised the possibility of reducing the consulate to an agency or of closing it altogether.[24] In 1910 Blake was transferred to Bogotá, Colombia, and later had a distinguished career in Morocco.[25]

The grandly named Howard de la Coeur Van Sant, of New Jersey, was appointed in 1910 at a salary of $3,000. His previous post was consul at Kingston, Ontario. Prior to joining the Consular Service in 1905 he had worked in the real estate business and conveyancing and been heavily involved in New Jersey local politics, concluding with six years as mayor of Island Heights.[26] His first wife had deserted him, and in 1902 he had obtained a divorce on the grounds of her desertion.[27] He had remarried and his wife and their two-year-old daughter were with him when he arrived in Dunfermline. The consulate was inspected again by Harris in 1911. He was struck immediately by Van Sant's physical condition.

> He has a serious physical disability which makes it practically impossible for him to walk even with assistance beyond a short distance. He goes from place to place in a tricycle which he propels by levers using his hands and is able to go to and from his office and do a considerable travel in and about the city. He goes from his office to the street where he leaves his tricycle by the aid of a cane but with considerable difficulty as it would seem.

As further evidence of the disability Harris 'regretted', in relation to the section of the report that had to be prepared by consuls in advance of an inspection: 'to forward these sheets with the answers so poorly written as to penmanship. The Consul's physical infirmities and the illness of his wife seem to warrant passing what would otherwise not deserve passing.' His wife's physician warned that 'she cannot endure the Scotch winter [...] and the plan now is for her to return to the United States for the ensuing winter'. However, despite his infirmities Van Sant was: 'of more than ordinary alertness and ability. He is conscientious, industrious, and pleasant and agreeable in a marked degree. He has great anxiety to do his work satisfactorily and to earn advancement in the Service.' He was rated as 'good', as was the overall running of the office. At the risk of stating the obvious, Harris pointed out that Dunfermline was: 'unsuited to the consul in that it is built on uneven ground with portions of the business part where the consul cannot go with his tricycle on account of the hills. He believes that he should be transferred to some post where the streets do not present this difficulty.'[28] It is ironic that one of the many reports that Van Sant sent to the Department during his time in Dunfermline highlighted a pressing need for a low-priced 'small motor or motor tricar' for the many disabled officers and soldiers returning from the war, as well as for thousands of invalids and crippled civilians. 'It should be a good hill climber for Scotland.' He had received several enquiries asking whether such cars were made in America and whether catalogues were available.[29] This type of vehicle, if available, would have been a boon for him in the hilly streets of Dunfermline. Although there was not a great amount of business transacted, the consulate nevertheless operated at a small profit ($340 in the year ending 31 December 1910). Harris still felt that it could be either downgraded to an agency or closed altogether.[30]

The next inspection was by Ralph J. Totten in 1914. Van Sant, now aged 49, was still in post, with his physical condition described as 'very poor'. Drysdale, the vice consul, had been replaced the previous year by James Whitelaw, a young man who had served previously as a messenger and clerk in the Edinburgh consulate and was paid $600. Totten rated him as 'excellent'. However, he drew attention to an anomaly about his appointment.

> A peculiar situation is found in Dunfermline regarding the post of Vice Consul and Clerk. The present Clerk, who is a very capable young man, is not yet of legal age [he was 20] and so cannot be appointed Vice Consul. There are eleven applicants for the combined post of Vice Consul and Clerk, the majority of whom intend to engage in outside business as well. [...] The Consul has allowed outsiders to advise him through too much good nature and a

certain lack of firmness and decision until practically the whole town seems to be interested in the matter as the backer of some one or other of the applicants. The main fight seems to be between the Carnegie Trust people [...] and the Anti-Trust faction. [...] The whole situation is ridiculous and undignified.

In the event, Whitelaw was appointed vice consul on 3 March 1915.[31] The number of invoices certified in 1914 was 1,349, down slightly from the number at the previous inspection, while exports to the United States remained much the same as before at just over £2 million. The consulate continued to operate at a small profit, but Totten reported that 'the continued maintenance of this office is in no way justified'.[32]

In 1920 the consulate was inspected once more by Totten. Van Sant was still in post and 'feels very strongly the Department's refusal to consider his request for a transfer to a less hilly city, but not to the extent of disloyalty'. He was now a widower 'with one daughter of about fourteen years, who is of great assistance to him'. His house at 47 McLean Place also doubled as the consulate. The vice consul was an American, Albert W. Scott and was given a mixed report by the inspector: '25 yrs old and good health, appearance poor, intelligence fair, other points, excellent. [...] Paid $1,200 p.a. [...] may be rated good. This young man is of poor appearance and personality but is faithful, reliable and industrious. He should be given a chance to develop in some more important post.' The remarks about his appearance seem at odds with his previous career as a corporal in the US Marine Corps. He transferred to Hull the following year and was replaced by Warren C. Stewart. Scott must have improved himself because later in his career he held senior appointments as consul in Jerusalem and Cairo.[33] Van Sant's physical condition remained unchanged. Totten made a further plea for a transfer: 'The tremendously hilly city of Dunfermline is one of the worst possible places for this officer. [...] For the sake of the Service, at least until we have some system for retirement, it is strongly recommended that he be transferred to a city that is level, preferably in Canada.' Business had fallen dramatically and for the first time the consulate was operating at a loss of more than $2,200. It seemed that its future was sealed; Totten recommended its closure, or its removal to Kirkcaldy but as a vice consulate if the Department wanted to have a presence between the consulates at Edinburgh and Dundee.[34] During the inspection of the Dundee consulate the following year, Totten once more recommended Dunfermline's closure.[35]

Incredibly, despite all that was said in the 1920 inspection, both the consulate and Van Sant were still there when the next and final inspection took place in 1924 conducted by Robert Frazer Jr. There had been an extraordinary number of foreign passports visaed during the previous year which generated more than $14,000 in fees and enabled the consulate to remit almost $13,000 to the Treasury. This was a high point financially for the consulate, but nevertheless Frazer once again recommended its closure and Van Sant was finally replaced at the end of the year by Bernard Franklin Hale, of Vermont, who had been vice consul at Dundee.[36] Hale remained only a few months before transferring to Marseille and was replaced in August 1925 by Milton Stover Eisenhower, a vice consul on a temporary attachment from Edinburgh, and younger brother of future President Dwight D. Eisenhower.[37] Howard Van Sant continued to reside in Dunfermline and died there a year after being replaced, on 1 September 1925, at age 60. The consulate office and residence were at McLean House, 57 Buffies Brae, and it was there that his funeral service was conducted. His remains were sent to his former home in Toms River, New Jersey, where the funeral took place on 5 October.[38] The consulate was finally closed on 19 October.[39]

From a present-day perspective it is difficult to understand why the Department ignored so many requests from inspectors and from Van Sant himself to transfer him to some more suitable post. Such a move might have made his daily life more bearable, and possibly prolonged his life.[40] Instead, he was forced to soldier on in Dunfermline for almost fifteen years and joined the list of American consuls in Britain who suffered from ill health or had a disability of some kind. For example, Robert Bergh (Stoke on Trent), Edwin Dennison (Dundee and Birmingham), William Doty (Stoke on Trent), Rufus Fleming (Edinburgh), David Gould (Leith), Hugh Smith (Dundee), John Tibbits (Bradford) and Francis Underwood (Edinburgh).

Chapter Fifteen

EDINBURGH AND LEITH

Leith was at one time an independent burgh, with its own provost and town council. However, it was always regarded as Edinburgh's port, and in 1920 was incorporated into the City of Edinburgh.

Initially, therefore, the consulate was located in Leith but it moved several times between Leith and Edinburgh before settling permanently in Edinburgh's city centre, some two miles away, in 1883. The first consul was Harry Grant, a South Carolinian, who was appointed in October 1798. One of his earliest comments was to complain about the cost of obtaining his exequatur, saying 'ten guineas is a great deal [sic] money to pay.'[1] He seems not to have regarded his appointment as warranting his full-time presence since during 1800 and 1801 he spent almost eight months in Paris on business, although he informed Rufus King, the American minister in London, rather magnanimously, that while there he would be on the lookout for and report on French 'sentiments regarding our country'.[2]

His successor, Joel Hart, a physician from New York, is probably best known for having been absent from his post for 16 years, the Department being unaware that he had left.[3] He was appointed in February 1817 but did not assume nominal charge until 1818 whereupon he immediately appointed Robert Grieve, a Leith businessman and Justice of the Peace (magistrate), as vice consul to run the office. Grieve explained to Secretary of State Louis McLane (1833–1834) 'the reason why you have not heard from that Gentleman [Hart]' is because 'he had never resided' in Edinburgh but had chosen to live in London, leaving Grieve in complete charge. As far as he was aware, Hart had returned to the United States round about 1823. As well as acquainting McLane of the situation, Grieve made the case for upgrading the Leith office to be headed by a full-time consul and put himself forward for the position. He had had long experience in representing American interests. In 1806, William Lyman, consul in London, had appointed him agent for American seamen at Leith, although it transpired that he had no authority to make such an appointment and William Pinkney, minister in London, informed Grieve of this in 1810. Pinkney, however, was favourably disposed to Grieve being appointed deputy consul. Grieve had also been appointed as vice consul by successive consuls in Glasgow in 1824, 1831, and 1833. His request to be appointed consul in Leith was successful and he became consul in October 1833.[4] His financial situation was affected by the decision in 1834 to upgrade the subsidiary vice consulate at Dundee to a full consulate, thus depriving him of a share of its fees.[5] Added to this was the fact that he was out of pocket because of unpaid loans he had made to his predecessor Joel Hart (twenty pounds) and to a Dr Telfair (five pounds), a visiting American

Figure 15.1 Edinburgh Consulate General. The Edinburgh consular office was established in 1798 in the city's port of Leith and moved to the city centre in 1883. After a few changes of premises it finally moved into its present accommodation in 1951. The property is in an exclusive residential part of central Edinburgh. Together with the consulate general in Belfast, it is the only US consular presence in Britain outside of the consular section of the embassy. The photograph shows the US flag flying and the coat of arms above the door. [Author's collection.]

who had falsely purported to be secretary of the legation in London. He tried to recover these sums by requesting the intervention of the legation and Secretary of State John Forsyth (1834–1841). The files do not show whether he was successful, although it would be unlikely as the debts would have been regarded as private transactions between Grieve and the two individuals.[6] The fees he received during the two years ended 30 June 1837 amounted to only $224. In 1837, in his 76th year, he drew Forsyth's attention to an article criticizing the United States for not paying salaries to its consuls in Britain and elsewhere in Europe. The writer of the article maintained that: 'It is clear that there is no want of funds to be alleged by the American authorities, for the government is universally represented to be even embarrassed with an accumulation of surplus revenue. Why not devote a portion of these superfluous means to the proper and respectable remuneration of these consuls?' Grieve added that he had suffered severe financial losses in recent years 'which has rendered it more than ever desirable that a salary were annexed to the office, as the fees at the consulate are very limited'.[7] However, his request fell on deaf ears and the fee system for the consulate continued until 1874 when an annual salary of $2,000 was introduced.[8] Grieve remained until 1852, by which time he was almost ninety years of age and probably the oldest consul in the country.

James McDowell of Ohio took over in 1853 with John Broadfoot, a Leith shipbroker who was involved in shipping emigrants to Australia, as his deputy. Broadfoot died suddenly in 1860 and was replaced by McDowell's son, also named James.[9] McDowell junior reported in July 1861 that his father had been severely indisposed for the previous four months.[10] As he was unable to continue, the Department replaced him with Neil McLachlan, a Scot who had lived in America for 14 years and had become a naturalized American citizen. He took over in July 1861 and from the start complained to Abraham Lincoln, no less, in a series of appallingly badly spelled letters, that he could not 'remane [sic] at this port' unless he could receive a salary 'with or without the fees which at this time do not amount much to suport [sic] a family'. Fees collected during the previous 70 days had amounted to only 22 dollars.[11] He returned to America with his family for four months without informing the Department, leaving his clerk, William Black, in charge but returned without his family and appointed Black as vice consul. Fees began to increase considerably, for the year ending 31 December 1865 they were $2,500, which made life easier for him and enabled him within two years to give up his business activities.[12] At that time, the consulate was located at 94 Constitution Street, Leith. David Gould, of Massachusetts, succeeded him in July 1866 and within a few months appointed his cousin William Gould, of Connecticut, as vice consul, who served only three months before resigning.[13] David Gould soon found the Leith climate challenging, and sought two months' leave of absence because 'the prevailing East Winds [...] have been unusually severe [and] have affected my health unfavourably'. He appointed James Galloway to act as vice consul in his absence. The Department's letter approving the leave of absence 'found me completely prostrated by inflammatory action'. Sadly, he died four weeks later, on 22 July 1867.[14] Galloway continued as vice consul but two weeks after Gould's death wrote to Secretary of State William H. Seward (1861–1869) seeking promotion to consul. However, unknown to him, the Department was already lining up a successor: John Safford Fiske of New York was appointed at a salary of $2,500 with permission to trade as a merchant, and arrived at Leith in November to take up his duties. Galloway's service ceased but, as we shall see, he later achieved his wish to become consul, albeit temporarily.[15]

Things appeared to be going well. Fiske was efficient, submitted regular accounts and interesting reports and income from fees continued to increase. But Nemesis was awaiting him. He had unwisely fallen in with a louche group of upper-class men from London who had visited Edinburgh and he had become attracted to one of them, Ernest Boulton, and had written several indiscreet letters to him. Boulton and his friend Frederick Park were theatrical types and were given to cross-dressing in public. They were arrested in London and Fiske's letters were discovered. At age 32, he was arrested in Edinburgh on 9 June 1870 and taken to London where along with Boulton and Park and another individual, Louis Hurt, he eventually went on trial at the Central Criminal Court (The Old Bailey) in May 1871. All four were charged with 'frequenting theatres and other places of public resort in women's clothes'.[16] It was clear that Fiske was not involved in any of these activities, his only link with the others was his letters to Boulton. All the defendants were found not guilty. In the case of Fiske and Hurt, the judge, the Lord Chief Justice, criticized the actions of the London police who had gone to Edinburgh and: 'without any authority, searched their lodgings, and then arrested them, and put them on trial here [London] along with Park and Boulton, without taking them before a magistrate at all, and thus they are tried with the two other defendants for an alleged offence having no connexion whatever with their conduct'. He added that they 'should have been tried in Scotland, if at all'.[17] There is an almost palpable sense of decency and disbelief in the resignation letter that Fiske sent to Secretary of State Hamilton Fish (1869–1877) two weeks after his arrest.

> I have had the honor to hold the position of United States Consul at Leith since the sixth of November 1867. During this time I have endeavored to discharge the duties of my office in all faithfulness and integrity. I believe I may confidently refer to my despatches and accounts as showing that I have not altogether failed in my attempt. Lately, however, a charge has been preferred against me in a criminal court. I may say that I am utterly innocent of the offence imputed to me. But I am unwilling that my office should bear any part of the misfortune which has befallen me. I therefore beg, unsolicited, to offer you my resignation of my position as Consul of the United States at this place.[18]

John Lothrop Motley, the US minister in London, had prevailed upon him to send the letter from his Edinburgh address rather than from his address while detained in Newgate Prison, London.[19] Reading through his many despatches one gets the impression that Fiske had formed an unfortunate, if brief, friendship with some outré individuals outside of his usual milieu, finding them amusing and superficially attractive.

Galloway finally achieved his ambition and on 1 July 1870 was appointed consul until a replacement for Fiske was found.[20] Earlier that month J. C. Bancroft Davis, assistant secretary of state, wrote to Colonel John T. Robeson, consul in Tangier, Morocco, appointing him to the Leith post.[21] Robeson, a native of Tennessee, took up his appointment on 1 November 1870 but had to relinquish it to Galloway until 1 January 1871 as his completed bond had not been received in the Department, nor had his exequatur been issued.[22] Within a month of assuming his duties Robeson replaced Galloway as vice consul with George Smith, a Leith businessman, although the files give no reason for this. In February 1871, a group of manufacturers in nearby Dunfermline wrote to Robeson asking him to have a consular agency established in the town, with John Burn Doig as agent, which would save them making the twice-weekly 34-mile journey to the consulate to have their invoices verified. (The Forth Railway Bridge, which eventually would considerably shorten their journey, did not open until almost 20 years later.) Robeson wrote to the Department supporting the request, adding that more than eight hundred of the previous year's two thousand invoices verified at the consulate had come from Dunfermline.[23] The Department agreed to the proposal on 24 March.[24] In September 1871, Robeson wrote a 12-page letter to the Department, and also enclosed several newspaper extracts, in defence of his predecessor, Fiske. He claimed that Fiske had been badly treated by the English (but not the Scottish) legal authorities and was still held in high regard in Leith and Edinburgh. During a visit to the Department 'a Robeson left the letter with a clerk to be shown to Fiske if he should call. But Fiske did not call, unsurprisingly, at least not by March 1872, so it is not clear if he ever saw the correspondence, although he did return briefly to the United States in 1873 before spending his remaining years in Europe, mainly in Italy where he died in 1907.

In July 1872, as part of his audit of American consulates in Europe and the British Isles, Treasury inspector De B. Randolph Keim recommended that the Leith consulate should be renamed 'Consulate of the United States for Edinburgh and Leith'.[25] Robeson was succeeded by Joseph Alexander Leonard, an American physician and lawyer, who served from 1881 until 1883 when he was appointed consul general at Calcutta.[26] Oscar Malmros, a German who had become a naturalized American citizen, arrived in 1884 from the consulship in Winnipeg. He remained until 1887 when he transferred to Cognac and was replaced by Willoughby Walling.[27] Events moved on and in 1889 Wallace Bruce, a well-known American poet, took over as consul. The Dunfermline agency had been raised to a consulate by then and he had only one consular agency reporting to him, established in Galashiels in 1882. Bruce is best remembered for his role in having a statue of Abraham Lincoln erected in the Old Calton Burial Ground in Edinburgh to commemorate Scots who had fought in the Civil War and was instrumental in raising the funds for it on both sides of the Atlantic. A month before the unveiling ceremony was due to take place on 21 August 1893, performed by his daughter, Bruce wrote to Josiah Quincy, assistant secretary of state, requesting two large flags to use at the ceremony, as the consulate ones were worn and frayed, and asked if he could keep one of them as a 'memorial of the ceremony'.[28] He reported on the success of the ceremony, saying that among those present were the Lord Provost and Town Council of Edinburgh, Lieutenant General Fremantle – the General Officer Commanding the Army in Scotland – attended by his staff and 250 soldiers of the Argyll and Sutherland Highlanders, and many prominent and representative American citizens.[29] One of Bruce's final official duties was notifying the Department of the suicide of an American businessman in one of the city hotels.[30]

Bruce's successor, Francis Henry Underwood of Massachusetts, took up his appointment on 5 September 1893 after the customary handover of the consulate's archives, records and seals.[31] He had previously been consul in Glasgow from 1885 until October 1889, after which he had resided there until 1892 when he had returned to Massachusetts.[32] A contemporary account describes him as: 'a brilliant man of letters' and 'for thirty-four years [...] a neighbour of Longfellow and Emerson at Concord, and [...] the intimate associate of the leading American poets, novelists, and essayists of his time'.[33] The year after his appointment in Edinburgh he had an acrimonious falling-out with Richard Lees, the consular agent in Galashiels, and informed the Department that he had asked Lees to resign from his post. The reason given, which was not unreasonable, was that since Lees had so many other occupations – including a solicitor's practice in both Galashiels and Edinburgh, Town Clerk of Galashiels, agent for the British Linen Bank, local Secretary of the Board of Trade and so on – it was impossible for him to discharge properly his duties as consular agent. The Department approved Underwood's decision[34] but Lees refused to resign and wrote a lengthy letter to Secretary of State Walter Q. Gresham (1893–1895). He said he had met with Underwood and:

> there and then determined that should I eventually be superseded in the office (for I shall on no account voluntarily resign it, or indeed resign it at all) I would be careful that every Manufacturer with whom I have done business, and the public to whom I am known, should have very advantageous opportunities of acquainting themselves with all that was passing and would pass between myself on the one hand and the Government and its Representatives on the other.[35]

This seems a remarkably unusual and unwise tactic to adopt, almost a threat of blackmail, especially as Lees was a solicitor. Underwood proposed to replace him with another local solicitor, John Stalker. Lees did not hand over to Stalker until 31 July, and even then continued to hinder the agency's work by refusing to surrender government property until the end of September.[36]

Underwood informed the Department of the sudden death of Hugh C. Peacock, the vice and deputy consul, on 15 June 1894. Peacock had served for 15 years with 'probity, discretion, fidelity and tact'. Underwood nominated as his replacement Frederick Piatt, a 25-year-old American who was currently clerk in the Cork consulate at Queenstown and was the son of a former consul there, John James Piatt.[37] The appointment was approved and Piatt took up his duties the following month. Within days, his first official act was to notify the Department that Underwood had 'been for some time seriously ill', and two weeks later, on 7 August 1894, he cabled the Department 'Consul Underwood died today'. He followed this with a letter the same day describing reaction in Scotland to the death and saying he would begin preparations for the funeral immediately with the family. The American flag would fly at half mast and the consular coat of arms and the front of the consulate building 'would be draped with mourning'.[38] Underwood had died from septicaemia following a minor operation.[39] The Department offered to meet the cost of 'the preparation of the remains […] and their transportation to the United States', but Underwood's widow, who was from Glasgow, wished the funeral to take place in Glasgow.[40] Messages of regret were received from all American consuls in Britain, as well as from members of the local consular corps. The funeral was held on 10 August, with a short service taking place in Underwood's residence in Mansion House Road attended by, among others, the Lord Provost, Piatt, and the American consuls from Dundee and Dunfermline. A company of a hundred soldiers from the Black Watch regiment was drawn up outside and accompanied the cortege through the streets to the Waverley Railway Station where a large crowd had gathered. From there it was conveyed to Glasgow where a further large crowd had gathered, which included civic representatives, the American consul in Glasgow and other members of the city's consular corps. The burial took place in the Glasgow Necropolis.[41]

On 28 August 1894, Robert J. MacBride, a Wisconsin attorney, was appointed consul and he took up his duties on 23 October.[42] The consulate had by then been finally transferred from Leith to Edinburgh for the past 11 years and was located in York Buildings, 8 Queen Street. Although on the first floor, (in US terms, the second floor) it had its own entrance from the street, with the consular arms displayed above the door. The office consisted of three large rooms (one each for the consul, the vice consul, and the waiting room) with five windows looking on to Queen Street, and was rented at $450 per annum from a local lawyer. The other tenants were insurance companies, lawyers and businessmen.[43] MacBride noticed that the flag was in poor condition and requested replacements because the ambassador, Thomas F. Bayard (who had been secretary of state a few years earlier), was due to visit Edinburgh – although MacBride left for America on leave a month before the visit to accompany his wife home, as she was in ill health.[44]

Three American citizens, a man and two women, and a Scot who had served in the US Army during the Civil War, died in Edinburgh during MacBride's tenure and the consulate was involved in the funeral arrangements. The American man was age 22: his burial was paid for by the consulate, the women were aged 26 and 'seventies'. The latter was a wealthy widow and was accompanied on her visit to Edinburgh by a representative of her Pittsburgh attorney's office. Piatt, the vice and deputy consul, was called to the lady's hotel to assist in preparing an inventory of her effects. This revealed a considerable amount of money, share certificates and jewellery. All of this was sealed and put in the consulate safe to await instructions from her executors. The former soldier, Alexander Smith, was aged 76 and had served latterly as a sergeant in Company G, 66th Regiment of the New York Volunteers, and was in receipt of a pension from the US government, having been wounded in action. He left property valued at £734, the equivalent of approximately £76,000 in 2016.[45] His service included not only action in the Civil War but also in the war against Mexico and the Black Hawk War. He was buried in the Old Calton Burial Ground in the plot donated by the City Council for Scottish/American veterans of the Civil War and was the first person to be buried there, beside the memorial raised by Consul Bruce.[46] The consulate was also involved in December 1895 with the affairs of another wealthy American, Rutherford Stuyvesant, who had purchased a newly built steel steam yacht from a Leith shipbuilder. It cost £18,000, the equivalent of approximately £1.9 million in 2016, and Stuyvesant wanted the consulate to certify the bill of sale.[47]

In October 1897, Rufus Fleming of Ohio, managing editor of the *Cincinnati Times-Star*, was appointed consul and took up his duties on 1 December at a salary of $3,500[48] and would prove to be the longest-serving consul in Edinburgh, serving until his death in 1920. Perhaps reflecting his previous journalistic background he ordered the consulate's first typewriter, operated by Piatt, which the Department purchased via the Navy Department. After this, there were no further manuscript despatches from the consulate.[49] In July 1903, shortly before he was due to return to America on leave, Fleming found himself deeply involved in the aftermath of the death of a prominent American colleague. He sent a cable to Secretary of State John M. Hay (1898–1905) on 29 July informing him that John G. Long, American consul general and diplomatic agent in Cairo, had died in an accident in Dunbar, near Edinburgh. Long, who was age 56, had been spending a few days there visiting his friend Major General Sir Francis Wingate, who was home on leave from his post as Sirdar, or Commander-in-Chief, of the Egyptian Army and Governor General of Sudan. Long was due to return to America in August but late one evening, returning on foot from Wingate's nearby home, he found the 'common entrance' to the hotel in darkness. He was unaware that the area to the right of the entrance steps overlooked an open basement which was unguarded except for a six-inch coping stone. Fleming enclosed a sketch of the entrance and reported that 'after examining the place, one can readily believe that Mr Long mistook this coping stone for the first step, and thus fell into the area below'. He fell eight feet, landing on his head and fracturing his skull, and died two or three hours later. Although Fleming was not involved in the actual funeral arrangements, which were undertaken by the brother-in-law of Mr Long's ward (a young lady who had been staying with the Wingates), he had to affix the consular seal to the casket for shipment to America, and he paid the accounts of the two doctors and the funeral director.[50]

Over the next few years, the business of the consulate returned to its normal routine. This included Fleming requesting a new enamel coat of arms for placing over the street door, presenting bravery awards on behalf of the president to the captain and crew of a Leith steamer who had rescued American seamen, and performing two marriages in the consulate.[51] In July 1908, following the introduction of consulate inspections in the 1906 Act, the consulate received its first inspection. This was carried out by Consul General at Large Horace Lee Washington. His report described the business of the consulate, its personnel, and two agencies in Galashiels and Kirkcaldy. During Fleming's 10 years in office his wife 'had been much of the time [...] in America'. As to Fleming himself, 'He appears suited to the post, and if any undue partiality for the community and its interests has grown upon him during his ten years residence it is not manifested in his archives, or apparent attitude.' In other words, he had not developed 'localitis'. Overall, the consulate was rated as 'good', one grade below 'excellent'.[52]

In the inspections of 1909 and 1911 the inspector, Consul General at Large Heaton W. Harris, reported that the total value of exports to the United States from the consular district in 1908 exceeded one million dollars, the largest single item being whisky, followed by commercial fertilizers and wool. He also drew attention to the high cost of living in the city. The Kirkcaldy and Galashiels agencies had closed in 1907 and 1909, respectively.[53] Harris also gave his views on Fleming and Piatt, the vice and deputy consul. Fleming, he remarked, 'is not keeping house but lives at a hotel, his family being in the United States. [...] The consul is understood to be a man of somewhat quiet and retired habits but of good standing in all respects. [He] is a reader and probably lives a somewhat quiet and domestic life when not at the office. He spends long days at his work [...]. In golf season [he] takes much interest in golf.' Piatt comes in for a lengthy report, which, confirmed by the author's reading of the despatches, captures the nature of the man accurately.

His intellectual operation can be illustrated by one incident that probably will not occur at any other office in the entire service. It was genuinely Piatt. The office hours at this office begin at 10 am. At the close of the first day the inspector said he believed, that if it made no difference, he would be in the office the next morning at 9.30 (the consul was away on leave). The Vice said very courteously 'That will be all right, the office will be open. You can make yourself at home until I come. I will be here at ten.' This is Frederick P Piatt.[54]

He added that Piatt:

is a methodical clerk, painstaking in his work, keeps admirable records, takes much interest in his work, and is fairly suitable for the place he fills. He is entirely loyal to his chief whom he regards as without a superior in the service. [...] [He] is somewhat odd in manner. He is an ultra believer in the absolute equality of all men and in each being entitled at his office counter to precisely the same consideration. The inspector is not quite sure that were he engaged with an office messenger in some invoice matter he would stop were he to see a Supreme Court Justice or other distinguished American in line.[55]

Harris also drew attention to the grade of the office, believing:

that the present grade [...] is below what it should be. It is conceivable that the Consul at Dundee or Dunfermline be merely business man [sic] with out [sic] attemp[t] to move in society and this service not be seriously discredited. This cannot be said of the office at Edinburgh. There are social and other functions at this post which the Consul and his family, if he has one, must take part in or they and this service be discredited.[56]

Consulate expenditure exceeded income for the year by $211. The consulate's overall ratings for 1909 and 1911 continued to be 'good'.[57] Fleming had been instructed to obtain new offices for the consulate, as the last two inspectors had both been 'of the opinion that the interior arrangement and appearance of the office are not very creditable'. Wilbur Carr, the Consular Bureau Chief, wrote to Fleming in early 1915 reminding him of this.[58] Following an inspection in 1914, Consul General at Large Ralph J. Totten noted: 'As this is the only post ever held by this officer [Fleming] a change of environment might be of advantage to him and the service.'[59] In May 1915, the consulate moved to new accommodation at 71 George Street, leased initially for five years.

The next inspection, also carried out by Totten, was in 1919 and noted that Fleming was still in post. '[He] possesses considerable natural ability but has only had the one post (22 years) and lacks variety of experience and service spirit. He does not seem to realize the strides the service has made.' As to whether he could serve more effectively elsewhere, Totten commented: 'After 22 years in Edinburgh it is doubtful if he could adapt himself to a change, although he should have been transferred years ago.' However, the question proved academic as Fleming died less than a year later on 3 April 1920, having been in ill health for six months. The local press noted that: 'Although he did not come very prominently before the public in Edinburgh he was known to a large circle as a man of unusual capacity, quick and accurate judgment, and strong and decisive character.'[60] The report shows that the consulate now had three staff in addition to the consul. Piatt had died in 1918, at age 48, and been replaced by another American, and there was also a British stenographer and a clerk. The stenographer obviously made a good impression on Totten because she was rated as 'excellent', the first such rating at the consulate since inspections began. The office's rating continued as 'good'. Totten concluded his report by saying that in his opinion there should be a consul general in Scotland located at either Edinburgh or Glasgow.[61]

The 1921 inspection by Ralph J. Totten showed a new consul in charge, Hunter A. Sharp, who had been consul in Belfast from 1910 until 1920. Office receipts exceeded expenditure and the consulate was able to remit $24,600 to the Treasury. Work undertaken included processing almost 1,700 invoices, 1,750 'alien visas', more than 1,600 letters were received and almost 1,800 sent.[62] In 1924, Wilbert L. Bonney arrived from Rosario, Argentina, to take over from Sharp who had died a few months earlier in 1923 after a long illness. During his 1924 inspection, Consul General at Large Robert Frazer Jr., was not over-impressed by the office's accommodation and felt 'we should pay two or three hundred dollars more rent, or four hundred more, if necessary, and secure really creditable quarters as soon as possible'. Wilbur Carr wrote to Bonney in September 1924 suggesting he made a search for new quarters.[63] However, in the next inspection, in 1926, the first under the new unified Foreign Service, the inspector, Louis G. Dreyfus, Jr, took an opposing view on the accommodation. 'The present location is excellent. Although Consul General Frazer recommended a change of quarters as advisable, I disagree with his opinion as I find the quarters better than any of the 5 other cities, outside of London, that I have visited thus far in the British Isles.'[64] Business increased, with almost 3,700 invoices and 1,900 visa applications being processed; 3,800 letters were received and 5,000 sent. The consulate continued to remit a healthy balance to the Treasury.[65] Bonney, like all consuls, often spoke at local professional and business organizations and in 1927 he gave a talk on *Famous Scottish Americans* at the Edinburgh Rotary Club. After giving a roll call of the great and the good he concluded by saying: 'As to the Bonney family, it is a little embarrassing to speak of them, as he had discovered one to be a pirate and another to be a whisky smuggler.'[66]

When the next inspection took place in 1933, by Foreign Service Inspector Homer M. Byington, the consul, Robert D. Longyear, had arrived only two weeks previously from the Munich consulate. His predecessor in Edinburgh, Austin C. Brady, had moved to Nice. Staffing levels remained unchanged despite immigrant visa work for Scotland having been centralized at the Glasgow consulate.[67] Charles Roy Nasmith, appointed in 1935, remained in Edinburgh until 1941 when he undertook temporary detached duty in Newcastle upon Tyne and Liverpool, returning to Edinburgh in 1944. In November 1942, he was appointed the first dean of the newly established Edinburgh and Leith Consular Corps.[68] Earlier in his career, also at Newcastle, he had featured in the 1920s episode when relations between the United States and the United Kingdom became strained over what is best described as the Newcastle incident, and which led to the closure of the consulate in that city for two years until being reopened by Nasmith. The events are described in the history of the Newcastle consulate (Chapter 19). Nasmith retired from the Foreign Service in Edinburgh in 1946 but had grown 'so attached' to the city that he remained there until his death on 5 December 1954. Another factor may have been that his wife was 'descended from an old Scottish family'. He and his wife are buried in Liberton Cemetery, Edinburgh.[69] He was succeeded in Edinburgh by Henry B. Day and Robert L. Buell in 1946 and 1949, respectively.[70]

In 1951, the consulate moved from George Street to its current accommodation in Regent Terrace. Charles H. Derry was consul from 1952 when Edward L. Killham, a junior officer, was sent there from London for four months to fill a vacancy caused by a vice consul having been moved during the McCarthy era upheavals. Killham describes his short time there as: 'one of the most stimulating periods that I spent in the Foreign Service. I was brand new in the Service and the feeling of active involvement in representing the US in a small post was quite different from my early experience in London, which consisted mostly of signing consular invoices.' At the end of his Edinburgh assignment he was accepted for Russian language training and went on to become a distinguished Soviet specialist in the State Department.[71] In 1953, Robert Bruce Houston arrived from Vienna to take up the number two post. He also enjoyed the posting, saying that Edinburgh 'was a delightful place to be. I had Scottish ancestry. My names are Robert Bruce and they treated me like one of them.' He was not enamoured of the cold weather, which seems odd considering that he had come from Vienna. The heating in their house was inadequate:

We had fireplaces in every other room, which had been converted to electric fires. The first time the guy came to read the meter, he said that we must have been using electricity all the time. The next time, he found the meter did not have enough capacity to keep track of all the electricity we were using to keep warm. [...] We learned about chilblains. [...] A Scottish dog bit me, but the National Health Service fixed it for free. Our children got free orange juice.[72]

His stay was brief, and the following year he was posted to Bangkok. However, while on home transit leave in Kansas City his orders were changed: he went on Polish language training and the following year was posted to Warsaw.[73]

Consuls in the 1950s and 1960s included Eldred D. Kuppinger, Vaughn R. De Long, and Elias A. McQuaid. In 1961, the Department's Bureau of Security and Consular Affairs suggested that the Edinburgh, Manchester or Liverpool and Southampton consulates might be considered for closure.[74] Edinburgh was reprieved, but Manchester closed in 1963 and Southampton in 1965. Liverpool eventually closed in 1976. Paul DuVivier arrived in August 1965 from Nice. In addition to him there were two vice consuls and about ten clerks. The post was inspected in 1967 by Robert McClintock who at that time had been ambassador to three countries. DuVivier recounts that McClintock told him he would recommend that the post should be elevated to a consulate general 'but only if I could show him the Loch Ness monster'. By chance, a BBC crew were attempting to film the monster and DuVivier arranged for McClintock to accompany them on a steamer plying up and down the Loch. The 'westerly cross wind aroused a series of ripples' on the water and: 'everyone shouted "There she is."' This was 'photographed and copiously toasted in Glen Livet single malt whiskey [*sic*]' and the next day McClintock 'pronounced my management "simply superb" and the office was reclassified with suitable publicity, new stationery seals and several well merited promotions.'[75] The office was formally elevated to consulate general on 18 August 1967.[76] Joseph Godson took over the following year.[77]

Consuls in the 1970s included Richard Funkhouser (1974–1976), Theodore B. Dobbs and Carl E. Bartch, and in the 1980s Leonard F. Willems, Norman A. Singer, Douglas Jones and Donald K. Holm. Funkhouser, an oil expert and former ambassador to Gabon, often used humour in his telegrams. Complaining to the embassy about its slowness in forwarding official mail to Edinburgh he headed the telegram: 'Limp Pony Express', saying that it was 'A gentle reminder to those who thoughtfully think of keeping us informed here in the tundra.'[78] When asking the embassy for guidance on dealing with a journalist who wished to interview him, he added: 'He is now asking for photographs of me at work (tough shot to capture).'[79] But he could also be critical. On retiring from the Foreign Service and the consulate he sent a stinging valedictory telegram to the US ambassador at the United Nations, his friend Daniel P. Moynihan, criticizing US policy in the Middle East. 'Ten of my years have been in the Middle East, but I have not before seen anything like the danger to our country as it appears today. Despite the lessons and cost of extracting ourselves from Vietnam [where he had also served], we seem to be becoming entangled tighter and tighter in the centuries-old civil and religious war between two Semitic families.' And he went on to lambaste powerful political interest groups for their roles in the conflict.[80] In later life he and his wife, whom he had married in 1944, lived in a retirement home in Washington, DC. By this time, her health had seriously deteriorated and she had dementia. He had cared for her devotedly for years but it seems that the stress of doing so had become too much and in what was described as 'an act of love' he shot her and then turned the gun on himself. He was 90; she was 84.[81]

A few days before Christmas 1988 a terrorist bombing of Pan American Airways Flight 103, occurred over Lockerbie, in south-west Scotland. As well as the unspeakable heartbreak this caused for the families and friends of the victims it also created a huge burden of work for consul general Douglas Jones and his staff. He was alerted to the disaster by Edward Kreuser, the consul general in London, after returning to Edinburgh from the US Naval Station at Edzell, in Angus, where he picked up his diplomatic pouches twice a month. The consulate was under particular pressure at this time because the month before the bombing 'a budget cut had eliminated sixty percent of the consulate staff positions'. Jones's team was augmented by a number of consular officers sent from London. The detailed and harrowing work continued for several months. Jones highlighted the work undertaken by the vice consul, Elizabeth Leighton. The consulate inspection undertaken in 1989 praised all the staff: 'Edinburgh deserves special commendation for its outstanding performance in the aftermath of the Lockerbie tragedy.'[82] The inspection report also mentioned that although the Edinburgh and Belfast consulates general had been recommended for closure the inspectors disagreed with this. In the case of Edinburgh, they said the city:

> is the center of the United Kingdom's important petroleum industry and has greater economic importance than Belfast. It has a larger consular district population than Belfast in a more important self-governing area. [...] Edinburgh's recent personnel cuts were too severe

in light of its responsibilities and the inspectors are recommending that the Department restore some Foreign Service National positions.[83]

In August 1992, Bobette Orr, the first woman to do so, took over as consul and from that date to at least 2018 all the consuls have been women. Is this a deliberate policy on the part of the State Department? The inspection carried out in 1993 recommended selling the property adjoining the consulate, while retaining the other government-owned residence in another part of the city.[84] In July 1995, the consulate general's future was once again thrown into doubt when the Department announced its intention to close 19 posts throughout the world, one of them Edinburgh, in the following year as part of its Strategic Management Initiative. This was expected to make annual savings of about $12 million. However, thanks to a vigorous campaign, both local and international, and which included the support of Presidents George H. W. Bush and Jimmy Carter, the office won a reprieve a few days before its planned closure.[85] The 1993 inspection criticized the Department and the Embassy, saying they had 'not adequately addressed the appropriate presence needed to represent US interests in Scotland' and recommended that the Embassy should conduct a management review to determine this.[86] One of the consulate's more unusual tasks in 1999 was assisting in the return of a ghost shirt to the Sioux tribe of South Dakota. Believed to have been taken from a fallen warrior at the Battle of Wounded Knee in South Dakota, it had originally been presented to Glasgow by a member of Buffalo Bill's Wild West Show in 1891.[87]

Julie Moyes and Cathy L. Hurst were successive consuls in the 1990s. Liane Dorsey was appointed at the turn of the millennium and was succeeded in 2003 by Cécile Shea who arrived from Tel Aviv. In 2004 the consulate lost its visa-processing function and all such work for Scotland is now handled by the embassy. Ironically, the Belfast consulate continues to deal with this work despite having a considerably smaller consular district than that of Edinburgh. In theory, the Belfast consulate is in the same position but in practice the recent involvement of US presidents in Northern Ireland and the strong Irish American lobby in the United States will ensure its continued existence. In September 2006, Lisa Vickers arrived from Merida, Mexico, to take up her appointment, Cécile Shea having left for an assignment as deputy political counsellor in the embassy in Islamabad. Lisa Vickers's tour finished in 2009 and she was assigned to a one-year fellowship at Tufts University, Boston; she returned briefly to Edinburgh in 2010, though not in an official capacity but in order to marry her British fiancé. At the time of writing she is Consul at the Consulate General in Alexandria, Egypt. Her successor in Edinburgh, Dana M. Linnet, was the founder and CEO of a Boston-based international consulting firm before joining the Foreign Service in 2000. An accomplished linguist, her Foreign Service career includes assignments in Italy and Estonia and in the State Department.[88] She transferred to a post in the Department in July 2012 and was succeeded the following month by Zoja D. Bazarnic, whose previous post was a one-year assignment advising Senator Susan M. Collins of Maine on foreign policy and assistance issues as a Pearson Fellow.[89]

Much of Bazarnic's appointment was taken up with a major political event that had the potential to alter the future of the United Kingdom. On 18 September 2014 a referendum was held in Scotland to decide whether it should become an independent nation or remain part of the United Kingdom. Declassified documents made available to the author by the State Department under the Freedom of Information Act (FOIA) reveal that the embassy and consulate were very much aware of the significance and consequences of a 'yes' vote and were closely monitoring the situation during the two years' run up to the referendum and also in the immediate aftermath. Reports were routinely copied to other embassies and consulates with an interest, such as Canada because of the close-run 1995 referendum there to establish whether Québec should become an independent state. Copies were also sent to a number of federal agencies such as the CIA, National Security Council, and the Department of Defense. In a previously secret briefing paper for Secretary of State John Kerry the embassy said: 'We have not taken a public position on the question of Scottish independence: when asked, we say we regard it as an internal matter.'[90] They maintained this line throughout the campaign. The consulate's Emergency Action Committee (EAC) also reviewed its security procedures in relation to the referendum and concluded that they were satisfactory, although it was arranged that the responsible Assistant Regional Security Officer based in the embassy would spend a few days at the consulate during the period of the referendum. After the EAC's decision had been taken it was learned that a march would take place in central Edinburgh by '10–12,000 members of the Orange Order, a sectarian Protestant group', which was opposed to Scotland becoming independent. Although the police and the pro-independence 'Yes Scotland' campaign group were confident that there would be no unrest the consulate took the opportunity to confirm that the local police had up to date records of the locations of the consulate and the consul's residence.[91] In the event, there was no unrest. In the course of the FOIA request, the State Department identified a three-page document which it referred to the Defense Intelligence Agency (DIA) for review. After a very long delay the DIA informed the author that 'Upon review, it has been determined that all substantive portions of the document (3 pages) must be withheld in full from disclosure.'[92] Might the document have referred to Trident, the UK's submarine-based nuclear deterrent, which is located at Faslane in the West of Scotland? The ruling party at the time in the Scottish Government was the Scottish National Party whose policy is to scrap Trident.

All countries with consulates in Scotland would also have been monitoring the referendum debate because if the vote had favoured independence they would have had to establish diplomatic relations with the new state. Similarly, the new Scottish state would have had to establish diplomatic relations with other states. Countries such as the United States with career consulates in Scotland would have had the choice of upgrading them to embassies headed by a resident ambassador, or continuing them but with their ambassadors resident in London, or in another state, having dual accreditation. Countries with only an honorary consular presence would have had their nearest ambassador obtain dual accreditation and delegated their consular affairs in Scotland to the embassy of another country that was based there. This is a common practice in the diplomatic world. For example, Luxembourg's ambassador to the United States is also a non-resident ambassador to Canada, where it has no embassy but five honorary consulates, and to Mexico, where it has no embassy but two honorary consulates. Its consular affairs in both countries are handled by the Belgian Embassy.[93] Such speculation remains academic, however, as the result of the referendum on 18 September 2014 was 55 per cent in favour of remaining part of the United Kingdom. Nevertheless, debate on independence has continued unabated and has intensified following the referendum held on 23 June 2016 on whether the United Kingdom should leave the European Union. The outcome was 52 per cent voted to leave, the so-called Brexit. However, within that figure, 62 per cent of those who voted in Scotland voted to remain. This has led to the Scottish Government and its First Minister, Nicola Sturgeon, continuously raising the question of holding a further referendum on Scottish independence.[94] On the other hand, even if this were held it is by no means certain that the result of the 2014 referendum would be significantly different.

Zoja Bazarnic left Edinburgh in July 2015 for an assignment in the State Department as Director of International Narcotics and Law Enforcement Affairs and was succeeded the following month by Susan A. Wilson who arrived from the US consulate in Adana, Turkey.[95] She is in post at the time of writing.

Chapter Sixteen

FALMOUTH

Falmouth is a small maritime town in Cornwall, in the south-west of England. The story of the American consular presence there is unusual in two respects: with only one exception, during a presence of more than a hundred years not only were all the consuls members of the same Quaker family but they were also British nationals. Additionally, the same family, by the name of Fox, provided American consular representation in nearby Plymouth for almost seventy-five years. Indeed, the family had a remarkable record of being consuls for a number of countries well into the end of the twentieth century. For example, between 1859 and 1965 they represented 36 different countries at Falmouth, Plymouth, Southampton and Totland Bay.[1]

Edward Long Fox was nominated as the port's first American consul by George Washington on 19 February 1793 and the appointment was confirmed by the Senate the following day.[2] He had trained at Edinburgh University and was a busy physician, and very active in the new field of establishing 'lunatic asylums'. However it is doubtful if he actually took up the appointment because just over a year later Washington rescinded it, saying: 'It now appears that the name of the person intended to be nominated is Robert Weare Fox. I therefore nominate [him].' The appointment was approved the following day.[3] Robert Weare Fox, the elder, was a mine owner, merchant and shipping agent in Cornwall and principal partner in the family firm of G. C. Fox & Co.[4] The consulate was operated from the company premises at Arwenack Street, Falmouth. He served until his death in 1818, apart from a break of two years due to the war between the United States and Britain from 1812 to 1814. When the war was declared he 'took down the American coat of arms, stored away the American flag, and waited for the war to run its course. At its conclusion, up went the coat of arms and the American flag, and Mr Fox resumed his duties.'[5] He was succeeded by his son Robert Were Fox (the spelling of their middle names was different), a distinguished geologist and physicist who was also a supporter of religious emancipation and the abolition of slavery.[6] He gave long service as consul until 1854 when he was succeeded by the first, and only, American citizen, Augustus W. Scharit of Missouri. Scharit was a political appointee, but soon became homesick and returned to Missouri the following year.[7]

The consulate reverted to the Fox family in 1855 when Alfred Fox, brother of Robert Were Fox, took over. He had been vice consul during the incumbencies of his brother and Scharit. James Buchanan, the US minister in London, appointed him 'to act temporarily as Consul […] in place of A. W. Scharit, resigned, until the pleasure of the President shall be made known to him'.[8] However, he was denied permanent appointment but nevertheless continued as vice consul for eight years, frequently petitioning the Department to be appointed consul. Of course, the refusal to upgrade him was to the Department's advantage, as the consul's salary in 1853 was $1,000, while that of the vice consul was considerably less.[9] Finally, in recognition of the useful information he had provided about Confederate shipping during the Civil War the Department relented and Abraham Lincoln appointed him consul in 1863.[10] By then, he was 69 years of age. In 1862, a consular agency, subordinate to Falmouth, was established on the Scilly Isles headed by Thomas J. Bruton.[11] In 1872, a Treasury inspector reported that 'There being no necessity for a consular officer at Falmouth, I should suggest the abolition of the office, and the establishment in its place of an agency subject to the consul at Cardiff.'[12] However, nothing came of this.

Alfred Fox died in 1874 and was succeeded by his son Howard, who had been deputy consul since 1863 and senior partner in the family shipping agency and merchants business.[13] He would be the last member of the family to represent the United States at Falmouth.[14] In 1876, John Banfield was appointed agent on the Scilly Isles. A State Department 1902 report noted that: 'The business of this agency is practically nil, as there are no American residents on the islands, and no American vessels have put into port for some time.' As no fees were received the agent was not compensated.[15] Another of Alfred's sons, George Henry Fox, was appointed vice consul in 1875.[16]

There was very little business in 1885, with only thirty-four invoices certified and only five American ships calling.[17] Despite this, personnel in the following year consisted of Alfred, George Henry and clerks Henry Pollard (who had been employed since 1856) and W. H. Daniell.[18] In view of the lack of consular business they would have been occupied on other work within the family business. In 1900, Robert Barclay Fox, great-grandson of Robert Were Fox, was appointed vice and deputy consul in place of George Henry who had resigned that year.[19] In 1900 the Scilly Isles agency passed to Banfield's son, also named John. Business at Falmouth picked up in 1901, when 309 invoices were certified and about forty enquiries were received from American businessmen. The chief export to the United States was china clay, some 45,000 tons of which were invoiced through the consulate.[20] However, the continuance of the consulate was no longer a viable proposition and it was downgraded to an agency in December 1905. Howard was appointed as agent on 28 December, remaining in charge until the agency, in turn, was closed on 20 November 1908 when Joseph G. Stephens, the consul at Plymouth, called on him that day and notified him of the closure decision.[21] The consular seal, archives and official books were sent to Plymouth, which then assumed responsibility for the Scilly Isles agency.[22] Howard Fox had served the United States for 45 years, as vice consul, consul and consular agent.

While that marked the end of the Fox family's unique service to the United States it is interesting to wonder why during such a lengthy period only one American was appointed and why he remained only a year or so. The answer may be found during a Senate debate in 1868 about whether only American citizens or naturalized American citizens should be permitted to hold consular appointments. Republican Senator Charles Sumner remarked: 'There were many important places abroad which American citizens would not think it worth while to take. For example, the Consulate at Falmouth, England, had been held by a Quaker family of the name of Fox, he believed, since the revolution, several Americans having declined to take it when it was offered to them, on the ground it was too small.'[23] Yet, it was claimed in 1901 that: 'For more than a century there has been continuous pressure from outsiders to get the Consulship away from the Fox family, and there have been many applicants for the place.'[24] There may well have been 'many applicants', but they probably withdrew their candidatures when they discovered that Falmouth did not offer lucrative pickings. Whatever the truth, it is likely that the Fox family retained the Falmouth post for so long because no one else wanted it. As for representing other countries, the family's long consular tradition ended in 2001 when Charles Lloyd Fox, the last member of his family to hold consular posts, decided for personal reasons to resign his six appointments as consul for France, Germany, Greece, the Netherlands, Norway and Spain.[25]

Chapter Seventeen

LIVERPOOL

Liverpool, in the north-west of England, was the country's premier port and had extensive shipping links with the United States. So it was a natural choice of location for one of the first two consulates established in Britain by the fledgling US republic in 1790.

In view of his important place in consular history in Britain James Maury, the first consul, merits a brief biography in this chapter. He was born on 3 February 1746 near Charlottesville, Virginia, the son of the Reverend James Maury.[1] The latter, who was born in Dublin, had a small one-room school in Albemarle County, near Charlottesville, in which he taught classical languages, mathematics and literature. Young James attended his father's school and his fellow pupils included a unique coterie of future presidents: James Madison, James Monroe and Thomas Jefferson, all of whom remained his lifelong friends.[2] He was married twice; first in 1782 to Catherine Armistead of Virginia (she died in Liverpool in 1794 without issue, and is buried in Fredericksburg, Virginia) and second in 1796 to Margaret Rutson an Englishwoman (she died in Liverpool in 1830 and is buried there). He had four sons and one daughter, all of whom were born in Liverpool: James (1797), William (1799), Matthew (1800), Ann (1803) and Rutson (1805).[3]

For several years, Maury had occupied himself as a merchant in Fredericksburg, Virginia. However, after the Revolution he decided to seek pastures new in England and intended to move to Bristol but was dissuaded from going there by Thomas Jefferson who said that Liverpool offered greater business prospects. Maury took this advice and he and Catherine arrived in Liverpool in August 1786. He had been keen for some time to obtain a consular post and within a few weeks of arriving in Liverpool wrote to Jefferson, who was by then American minister to France, on 17 September 1786:

> Almost ever since you left America have I been waiting for the Consular arrangement to take place, til at length I became quite tired of remaining in Suspense and came out. My friends in Congress, however, still assure me I am continued on the list of Candidates. [...]. If in the Course of your Correspondence it occur, you'll much oblige me by putting our friends in Mind of me. London is my first object, and if this cannot be had, it would be a secondary one to be appointed for this place. [...] This is now become the second port in Britain for Trade in General or with America in particular.[4]

Jefferson became secretary of state in March 1790 and in discussions the following month with President George Washington about possible candidates for consular appointments he suggested Maury's name for the Liverpool post.[5] Washington agreed with this and signed a commission on 7 June appointing Maury as consul, and King George III gave the formal British approval on 6 November.[6]

Figure 17.1 James Maury, consul, Liverpool, 1790–1829. Maury was born in Charlottesville, Virginia, in 1746. He became a merchant and moved to England in anticipation of improving his business prospects and also with an eye on getting a consulship. He was successful in both aspirations; he was nominated as consul in Liverpool on 4 June 1790 and began work in September before any of the other nominees that year. He therefore holds the distinction of being the first operational US consul in Britain and, apart from a short break of two years from 1812 when the United States declared war on Britain, he held the post until 1829 when by then he was 83. The photograph is of an oil painting by Gilbert Stuart Newton completed circa 1825 which today hangs in Liverpool Town Hall. [Courtesy of Pamela Raman, the Lord Mayor's Office, Liverpool Town Hall.]

Maury had the same nomination date, 4 June 1790, as William Knox of New York, who was selected as consul at Dublin – at that time part of Britain – and Thomas Auldjo, a British subject, who was selected as vice consul at Cowes. However, the honour of being the first operational consul in Britain falls to Maury, who began his appointment at Liverpool in September, while Knox did not arrive in Dublin until 24 November.[7] As we have seen, Auldjo's appointment was postponed because the Senate was initially doubtful about appointing foreign citizens as consular officers, but it was confirmed a week later.

The appointment was delayed even further because the British government refused to recognize it on the grounds that there had never before been a foreign consul at Cowes. As a compromise, they offered to recognize him at Poole, while turning a blind eye to his residing in Cowes. The United States accepted this arrangement and the Senate agreed the appointment on 24 February 1791.[8] These appointments were also at a time of a break in diplomatic, but not consular, relations between the two countries from 1788 to 1792.[9] As an indication of the importance of the Liverpool post, it was two months after Maury's appointment before the United States made its first consular appointment in London, the country's capital. Joshua Johnson of Maryland was appointed consul there in August,[10] and his first official correspondence was a letter dated 1 November to Maury.[11]

As the post of consul was unpaid at that time Maury was allowed to combine it with his business activities. Here I must dispel a popular local belief, namely, that the premises occupied by the Eagle public house in Paradise Street were the site of the consulate. In 1790, when he was appointed, Maury's business and the consulate were located at 30 Old Dock, not Paradise Street.[12] By 1796 he had moved to 22 Paradise Street, followed by further moves to numbers 26 and 33 in that street by 1800 and 1805, respectively.[13] By 1807 he had moved to 3 Exchange Buildings, Town Hall.[14] As far as I have been able to ascertain he never moved back to Paradise Street. The Eagle appears only to have been at 81 Paradise Street and over the years the occupiers of the building included a pawnbroker, coffee rooms, a boarding house and victualler.[15] For example, in 1824, the occupier was Robert Mair, a muslin manufacturer and retailer.[16] One reason that may have given rise to the local belief about the building's consular antecedents could be that for many years its façade sported a magnificent gilded American bald eagle, similar to but smaller than the one that graces the embassy in London. Hence, in Victorian times the pub was called The American Eagle.[17] Both the eagle and the building fell into severe disrepair over the years; the eagle was removed in 2003 to the Museum of Liverpool and underwent conservation, and the building made way for the Liverpool ONE retail redevelopment in 2008. A replica of the eagle now adorns the building. It is unfortunate that in early 2009, the American chargé d'affaires ad interim, Richard LeBaron, was shown the Eagle building by a local journalist in the unwitting belief that it was the location of Maury's consulate. In May 2014 the museum announced that the original eagle had been fully restored and now graced the entrance to one of its galleries. The press handout wrongly described the eagle as having 'adorned the world's first US consulate on Paradise Street' and that the United States had chosen Liverpool 'as the site for its first ever consulate'.[18] We have seen in Chapter 3 that the first consular appointment made by the newly independent United States was not to Liverpool but to Canton (now Guangzhou) and was the reappointment there of Samuel Shaw on 10 February 1790.[19] Shaw and Thomas Randall had been consul and vice consul, respectively, there since February 1786.[20]

Maury was in partnership with Arthur Latham as Maury, Latham & Company, commission merchants and forwarding agents. His main residence was in Rodney Street and his addresses there are given over the years as at numbers 4, 37, 38 and 44; a cast iron plaque has been placed on number 4 by the Liverpool civic authorities.[21]

From 1801 to 1802 he was a founder member and first president of the newly formed American Chamber of Commerce in Liverpool.[22] Writing to Secretary of State Thomas Jefferson acknowledging receipt of his consular commission, Maury, echoing a plea common to the early consuls, added: 'But as the powers appertaining to the Consuls of the United States have not been particularly defined to me, I request such further information thereon as may be needful.'[23] It took almost a year before he felt satisfied that he had received sufficient information to enable him to perform his duties with confidence. Although his duties were not full-time they appeared to tire him. Writing to their son William, Margaret said: 'Father seems to have great fatigue in his Consular office, with little profit […] he did not come home to dinner today until long after five.'[24] He continued at Liverpool until the United States declared war on Britain in 1812, but after the war was recommissioned in the post by President Madison on 3 March 1815.[25]

During August 1827 Maury travelled extensively throughout Scotland, accompanied by his daughter, Ann.[26] In 1829, President Andrew Jackson decided to replace him as consul with Francis B. Ogden. Although Maury had been in the post more or less continuously for almost forty years and was by this time 83 he seemed somewhat piqued at losing the appointment. Writing to his son James on 8 September of that year he remarked:

> It is somewhat of a singular coincidence that my functions ceased 31 Ulto, which was the same day of the same month Mrs Maury & myself landed here from Virginia in 1786 – each a memorable day in my life. I have treated Mr. Ogden, I hope, with that respect due from a Consul of the U.S. to his successor. As to myself, I do feel rather out of joint, and I suppose I am to feel so for a time, but such things wear off and probably it will be so with me.[27]

Maury was obviously well-regarded by the authorities in Liverpool because on his retirement he was given a dinner by 'the merchants and gentlemen of Liverpool' at which he was presented with 'a handsome silver service'.[28] Within a few weeks of retirement, the Maurys moved to Seacombe, a small seaside resort on the Wirral Peninsula, a short ferry trip from Liverpool across the River Mersey. It proved a short stay, however, as Margaret died suddenly four months later on 27 January 1830. Maury decided that it was time for him to return to the United States and in April of the following year, accompanied by Ann, he set sail from Liverpool to New York on the packet ship *Caledonia*, a voyage that took 24 days. In New York he was given a testimonial dinner by a number of prominent local citizens on 4 May. Over the next 10 years he and Ann visited old and new friends in New York, Philadelphia, Washington and Virginia. He died on 23 February 1840 at age 94 and is buried in New York.

Francis Barber Ogden of New Jersey assumed the consulship in autumn 1829 and was assisted for a year, from 1833 until 1834, by Thomas Dennison of Pennsylvania who then transferred to Bristol as consul. In 1837, Ogden married Louisa Pownall, a native of Liverpool.[29] As well as his consular duties he continued his lifelong interest in designing marine steam engines and also acted as consul for the Republic of Texas before it became part of the United States. In 1840, he transferred to Bristol where he remained until 1852

before transferring to Manchester. He retained his Bristol connections, however, and died
there in 1857. Philip Schuyler,[30] a member of a wealthy New York family who lived in
the aptly named town of Schuylerville founded by the family, succeeded Ogden in 1840,
but remained only two years.[31] His successor was James Hagarty, of New York, who
died in post in 1844. The quick turnover of consuls continued when Joel Wales White
of Connecticut learned after having commenced his duties that the Senate had refused
to confirm his nomination. He was therefore obliged to relinquish the appointment after
only a few months, despite its having received royal approval.[32] Obviously he should
not have taken up his post until all the formalities had been completed. Years later he
was appointed consul at Lyons. Things got back to normal with the appointment of
General Robert Armstrong of Tennessee in 1845 who remained until 1849 when he was
succeeded by another former soldier, Colonel Thomas Leonidas Crittenden. Crittenden
came from a distinguished Kentucky family and was a lawyer who, during his military
career, had fought in the Mexican War. He remained at Liverpool until 1853, when he
returned to Kentucky where he resumed his legal career. During the Civil War he joined
the Union army, ending up as a major general.[33]

In 1853, the author Nathaniel Hawthorne of Massachusetts was appointed consul,
becoming one of the best known holders of that office. The consulate was then located
on the first floor of the appropriately named Washington Building in Brunswick Street.[34]
The writer Henry David Thoreau reflected disparagingly about Hawthorne's forth-
coming appointment: 'Better for me to go cranberrying this afternoon [...] to get but a
pocketful and learn its peculiar flavor [...] than to go consul to Liverpool and get I don't
know how many thousand dollars for it, with no such flavor.'[35] Hawthorne was not
enamoured of his office accommodation, declaring afterwards that 'he hated the very
sight of it "from first to last." '[36] On the other hand, he was impressed by the standards
of his local staff, James Pearce, the vice consul, and Henry J. Wilding, the chief clerk.
They were 'as faithful, upright, and competent subordinates [...] as ever a man was
fortunate enough to meet with, in a line of work altogether new and strange to him'.
Pearce 'carried his reminiscences back to the epoch of Consul Maury [...] and has
acquired almost the grandeur of a mythical personage in the annals of the Consulate'.
Wilding was 'a man of English integrity [...] combined with American acuteness of
intellect, quick-wittedness, and diversity of talent'. These talents were wasted there,
Hawthorne felt, and 'had it been his luck to be born on our side of the water, his bright
faculties and clear probity would have ensured him eminent success in whatever path
he might adopt'.[37] There was also another clerk and a messenger. Hawthorne was cyn-
ical about the oath-taking requirements he had to administer to his 'clients', remarking
that there was a 'consular copy of the New Testament, bound in black morocco, and
greasy, I fear, with a daily succession of perjured kisses.'[38] While consul, his circle of
acquaintances included Robert Browning and Elizabeth Barrett Browning, and visitors
to the consulate included the author Herman Melville and Commodore Matthew
Perry, 'just returned from the voyage to Japan where he had signed a commercial treaty
between the United States and Japan'.[39] Throughout his time in Liverpool Hawthorne
had concerns about the health of his wife, Sophia, and on one occasion he arranged
for her to spend the winter in Portugal. Hawthorne's appointment ended in October

Figure 17.2 Colonel Thomas Leonidas Crittenden, consul, Liverpool, 1849–1853. Crittenden came from a distinguished Kentucky family. He was a lawyer who had previously fought in the Mexican War from 1846 to 1848. The following year he was appointed as consul in Liverpool where he served until 1853. Returning to Kentucky, he resumed his legal career and during the Civil War (1861–1865) he joined the Union Army where he ended up as a major general. The photograph shows him in civilian clothes. [Brady-Handy Collection, Library of Congress, Prints & Photographs Division, Reproduction Number LC-Dig-cwpbh-04815.]

1857, and he and the family returned to the United States where he died six years later. Sophia and their two daughters, Una and Rose, and son Julian moved to Germany and then to England. She and Una died in England, in 1871 and 1877 respectively, and were buried in Kensal Green Cemetery, London, but reinterred beside Nathaniel in 2006. Rose, after an unhappy marriage, converted to Catholicism and founded an order of Dominican nuns that cares for cancer victims.[40] Julian became an author and journalist, and died in 1934.

Figure 17.3 Nathaniel Hawthorne, consul, Liverpool, 1853–1857. Hawthorne is best known for his literary works, especially *The Scarlet Letter*. However, when already well established as an author, he had agreed to write a campaign biography for his old friend Franklin Pierce, the Democrat candidate in the 1852 presidential election. The biography played an important part in the successful campaign. Hawthorne had been keen for some time to obtain a lucrative consular post, preferably Liverpool. Pierce offered him the Liverpool post and Hawthorne served there from 1853 to 1857. [Brady-Handy Collection, Library of Congress, Prints & Photographs Division, Reproduction Number LC-Dig-cwpbh-03440.]

Hawthorne's successor was another Nathaniel, Nathaniel Beverley Tucker, a journalist from Virginia. This would prove to be an unwise appointment, however, and his stewardship of the post soon became the subject of the most severe criticism. It is ironic, although he did not realize it at the time, that Hawthorne when writing on 7 June 1855 to President Pierce about financial and other matters cautioned: 'to my office, when I quit it, you must appoint either a rich man or a rogue – no poor, honest, and capable man, will think of holding it'.[41] The chief criticisms of Tucker's performance were made by

Treasury auditors John C. Underwood and De B. Randolph Keim. Underwood reported in 1861 that although consuls were required to submit quarterly reports Tucker's last one was 31 March 1858.

> Since then he had strangely been permitted to hold on without reporting, spending all the funds he could reach, neglecting the payment of claims for food, clothing, and medical attendance of our sick and destitute seamen, and by a course of plunder and profligacy unequaled [sic] in our consular history, contracting public and private debts, which I am informed by a neighboring consul probably exceed $200,000. It is perhaps some consolation to know that this plunderer no longer disgraces the Government abroad.[42]

Keim, inspecting the consulate in 1872, reported: 'Accountability to the Government was evidently the last consideration which entered his mind, and with a degree of extravagance perfectly astounding he squandered not only large sums of the public money, but contracted debts, both public and private, which must long remain a disgrace to the consular service for being capable of harboring such a person for so long a time.' During two quarters in 1858 Keim found that: 'out of $13,888.88 received [...] $13,690.04 were drawn out on various accounts almost wholly personal. [...] There is no trace that this person ever attended personally to business, except to consume the funds of the consulate.' The *New York Times* reported that Tucker had: 'plundered the Consulate of a large amount of its receipts [...] his prodigality has been immense and his stealing on a scale almost equal to Floyd's'.[43] It is astonishing that nothing was done about Tucker's misappropriation of funds and defalcations at the time. However, he was probably saved by the fact that when he left in 1861 the Civil War had begun and he immediately joined the Confederate Army. He was later accused of complicity in the plot to murder Lincoln, although the charges were subsequently dropped.[44]

Thomas Haines Dudley of New Jersey replaced Tucker in 1861. He was not, however, first choice for the post; three other persons were nominated before him.[45] During the summer of 1861, Lincoln noted: 'It is said that Mr Dudley is acting as Vice-Consul at Paris, & would like to remain awhile. Let us remember this whenever we think of appointing a Consul to Paris.'[46] Dudley's commission of appointment to Liverpool was dated October and he arrived there to take up his duties on 19 November.[47] We have seen the pivotal role that he and the Liverpool consulate played during the Civil War. In 1863, the consulate office was in Tower Building South, 22 Water Street, and by 1865 there was a subordinate consular agency at Bank Chambers, Hardshaw Street, St Helens, with John Hammill in charge. From 1871 to 1872 Dudley's son Edward acted as vice consul, before returning to the United States to take up employment as a partner in his father's law firm in New Jersey.[48] Henry Wilding was still vice consul in 1872.[49] Dudley remained in Liverpool for almost eleven years, leaving in 1872. Writing of him at the time, Keim said: 'The Government has now at Liverpool the services of an officer in every respect equal to the dignity and trust of the office. It is true his fidelity to the interests of the Government has brought him many accusers. It is what might have been expected, after a previous season of unbridled corruption.'[50] Dudley returned to his legal practice in New Jersey, where he died in 1893. In a largely fulsome obituary which appeared in *The Times* (London) the comment about 'accusers' was repeated: 'While his vigorous and aggressive conduct during the war times made him many enemies on this side of the Atlantic, his failure to prevent the sailing of many privateers rendered him unpopular at home.'[51]

General Lucius Fairchild of Wisconsin was appointed in October 1872 at a salary of $7,500. During his military career he lost his left arm at the battle of Gettysburg in 1863 but it is a tribute to the skills of the army surgeons and of his will to survive that he went on to lead a high-profile public career. After Gettysburg, he served several terms as governor of Wisconsin. His clerk in Liverpool was Charles D. Atwood, also of Wisconsin, who was regraded as deputy consul three months after Fairchild took charge.[52] In 1877

Figure 17.4 Thomas H. Dudley, born in Camden, New Jersey, in 1819, was a lawyer and member of the New Jersey Bar. He was a strong supporter of Lincoln who appointed him consul at Liverpool in 1861. This was an important appointment at an important time because he was there during the entire period of the Civil War and played a pivotal role in thwarting the Confederacy's attempts to obtain ships and matériel. He remained in post for the relatively long period of 11 years, leaving in 1872. [Proceedings of the American Philosophy Society 1895, Vol. 34, No. 147, Plate V, p.103.]

Fairchild accompanied Civil War veterans Ulysses S. Grant, former US general and US president, and General Adam Badeau, consul general in London, on a visit to Newcastle that was headed at the time by another Civil War veteran, Major Evan R. Jones. The following year Fairchild transferred to Paris as consul general, remaining there for two years before being appointed US minister to Spain.

In 1878, Colonel Stephen B. Packard a former governor of Louisiana was appointed. Trade with the United States at that time continued at record levels. During 1881, American imports amounting to almost $303 million arrived at Liverpool; although including an enormous variety of commodities, the principal ones were cotton, grain, bacon and ham and cheese.[53] The following year, almost 189,000 passengers sailed from the port to the United States in 522 vessels.[54] By now, there were consular agencies at St Helens and Holyhead. Packard remained until 1885 when he was replaced by Charles T. Russell of Connecticut. His nomination and appointment did not meet with universal

Figure 17.5 During the Civil War (1861–1865) Lucius Fairchild of Wisconsin fought at the Battle of Gettysburg in 1863 where he lost his left arm. He attained the rank of brigadier general. After Gettysburg he served several terms as governor of Wisconsin. In 1872, he was appointed consul in Liverpool where he served until 1878, transferring to Paris as consul general. From there, he was appointed as minister to Spain in 1880. As can be seen, his left sleeve is empty. [Library of Congress, Prints & Photographs Division, Reproduction Number LC-DIG-cwpb-05336.]

approval back in Connecticut, where he was relatively unknown, having lived and worked in Liverpool for a number of years although retaining his residence and voting in Connecticut. A Democrat senator complained that: 'It's a little rough to have so good a consulate go to a man almost unknown even in his own State.'[55] There was a considerable increase in the consulate staff and in 1886, in addition to Russell and the two agents at Holyhead and St Helens, this included vice consul Harold Marsh Sewall, a US citizen, a consular clerk, four clerks, two sanitary inspectors (British doctors) and a rag inspector. Russell paid almost $3,000 excess over the allowances he received for clerk hire and office rent.[56] While in Liverpool, Sewall wrote to a friend: 'It is no plan of mine to remain in this service all my life. I hope I am fitted for something better; but now that I am in it, I do not want to retire until I am promoted.'[57] He did not have to wait long for promotion and in 1887 he was transferred to Samoa as consul general. Later, he was appointed US minister to Hawaii and received the transfer of the islands to the United States in 1898.[58]

Russell's successor in 1889 was Thomas H. Sherman, a former War Department telegrapher and later confidential secretary to James G. Blaine, a senator and secretary of state (1881 and 1889–1892). Sherman was replaced in 1893 by Colonel James E. Neal of Ohio who served until 1897 when James Boyle took over that year. Boyle was a journalist, who had been born in England in 1853 and had accompanied his parents to the United States where he had become a naturalized citizen. He had been private secretary to William McKinley during his two terms as governor of Ohio. The consulate offices were now in Richmond Buildings, 26 Chapel Street.[59] Boyle reported that in 1898 Liverpool led all other foreign ports in the world in clearances of goods for the United States.[60] Exports to the United States through Liverpool during the year ended 30 June 1901 exceeded $17 million, and during the previous year more than eighty-two thousand emigrants sailed to the United States on 228 ships. Business at the consulate was brisk during the year ended 30 June 1901, with almost seven thousand invoices certified, almost a thousand bills of health issued as well as a similar number of debentures or landing certificates. There was a continual stream of persons claiming to be destitute American seamen whose claims had to be checked to determine whether they were entitled to assistance under the law.[61] By 1905 only the Holyhead agency remained, St Helens having been transferred to the superintendence of the consulate at Manchester.[62]

John L. Griffiths replaced Boyle in 1905 at a salary of $8,000. The main staff consisted of two British nationals: William J. Sulis, the vice consul, had been appointed in 1887 and William Pierce, the deputy consul, had been appointed in 1894. By 1907 there were two agencies once again: Holyhead, headed by Richard D. Roberts a ship and insurance agent, appointed in 1896, and St Helens headed by John Hamill II, appointed in 1888. The fees collected by both agencies were minimal: during the year ended 30 June 1906 Holyhead collected only $6, while St Helens collected $861.[63] In 1909, Griffiths transferred to London as consul general and served there until his death in 1914. There is more about him in the London consulate history (Chapter 18).

Horace Lee Washington of Washington, DC, arrived in 1909 from Marseilles where he had been consul general. He was one of the new breed of career consuls, having also served in Egypt, Syria, Spain, Switzerland and South Africa. He had also been one of the

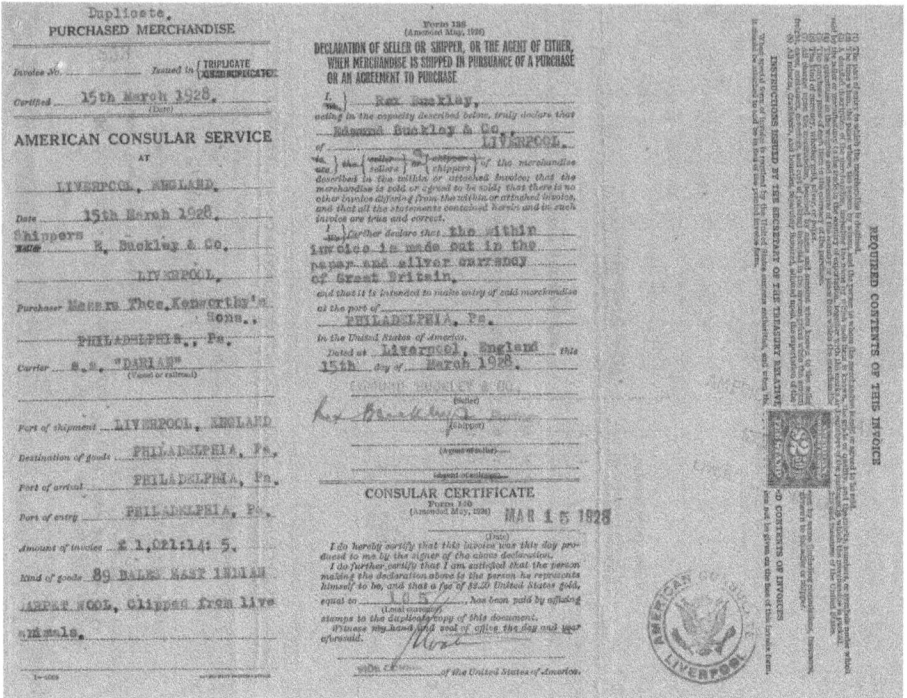

Figure 17.6 Consular invoice, certificate and fee stamp issued by the Liverpool consulate in 1928. Invoices covering goods exported to the United States that were over a certain value and subject to customs duty were required to have their value certified by local consuls. In the early days, the fees from this were an important part of a consul's income. There were abuses, however, with some consuls charging whatever fees they could get away with. A standardized tariff was eventually brought in, and in 1906 consular stamps were also introduced. These had to be affixed to invoices and were accountable to the State Department. They were used up to 1955 when they were discontinued. The photograph shows a 1928 invoice in respect of wool being shipped from Liverpool to Philadelphia. It is signed by the exporter, certifying that all the entries and values are correct, and countersigned by Hugh Watson, vice consul at Liverpool. The fee was $2.50, or ten shillings and five pence in local currency, and the fee stamp is affixed on the right, above the consulate seal. Fees had to be paid in advance before the stamps were cancelled. [Author's collection.]

first consuls general at large tasked with implementing the formal scheme of conducting consulate inspections that had been introduced under the 1906 Consular Reorganization Act. Liverpool, where his salary was $8,000, was his longest assignment; he served throughout the First World War and was promoted to consul general in 1923. For the most part, his vice consuls were also American career officers. One of them, William Force Stead, had an unusual career path. He had previously served at the consulate in Nottingham before arriving at Liverpool in 1913. He left the Consular Service in 1915 and was ordained as an Anglican priest. When the United States entered the First World War in April 1917 he did not meet the US Army's physical standards but nevertheless wanted to serve his country, so he rejoined the Service and returned to Liverpool. After the war he left the Service finally and resumed his career in the church, serving variously in Florence, then as chaplain to Worcester College, Oxford. He was a poet and man of letters and had many famous literary figures among his circle of friends; people such as T. S. Eliot, W. B. Yeats, C. S. Lewis and Monsignor Ronald Knox. He later was received into the Roman Catholic Church. His younger son, Peter, followed in his footsteps and became a Benedictine monk.[64] By 1916, only the St Helens agency remained and by 1922 there were no agencies. In 1924 Washington was transferred to London as consul general, serving there until 1928 and retiring the following year.[65]

Leo John Keena of Michigan replaced Washington in 1924. Before joining the Consular Service in Chihuahua, Mexico, in 1909 he had had a varied career, first as a seaman in the US Navy, then employment in mining, lumbering and office equipment businesses. His appointment in Liverpool was as consul, and he served in that capacity until 1927 when he was transferred to Havana as consul general.[66] His successor, Philip Holland of Tennessee, arrived from Guatemala and took charge as consul general. The consulate was still at 211 Tower Building, Water Street. Holland served in Liverpool until 1942 and therefore experienced wartime conditions at first-hand. Towards the end of his posting he wrote a classified memorandum in which he severely criticized the wartime work ethic of the local workforce. It makes uncomfortable reading today.

> That a vast number of the industrial workers are not pulling their weight is obvious. [...] They are happier and more contented than they have been in the past twenty-five years. They are drawing good wages while loafing in their jobs. They absent themselves from their work when they like, without let or hindrance. [...] A railroad official told me recently that 'sickness' reduces the numbers of the railroad workmen an average of twenty-five percent. When I asked him what he meant by 'sickness' he said, 'absenteeism.' [...] I was informed by a responsible employee of Vickers-Armstrong Limited a few days ago that the average daily absentees from that plant are more than three hundred. Wherever I inquired I found the same condition. Moreover, when this class are at work they do the minimum and manage to get in overtime whenever possible. Another man said to me, 'We always have full forces of laborers on Sundays, because there is time-and-a-half for Sunday work.' This is true among the munitions, shipbuilding, docks, and railroad workers, and everywhere.[67]

Charles J. Pisar took over as consul general at the beginning of 1943. He was familiar with Liverpool having served there twice as consul, in 1937 and 1941. However, his latest assignment was short-lived as he had to retire because of ill health after only a few months.[68] His replacement was Clark Porter Kuykendall of Pennsylvania whose long consular career had been spent almost entirely in Europe. His replacement in 1950 was John F. Huddleston. The offices were now in the Cunard Building, and other staff at the time included consul Philip Ernst, and vice consuls Maynard B. Lundgren, John F. Rogers and Walter M. McClelland. McClelland recalled that austerity conditions still existed when he and his wife and their two sons were there.

When we first arrived in Liverpool, food, clothing, and coal were still rationed. We had to have ration books and live on British rations because we were Consular and not Diplomatic. Franna and I have often joked that in our entire Foreign Service career, our greatest 'hardship post' was Liverpool rather than any Middle East post! Liverpool was damp and chilly most of the time, and electricity was cut off some time most days, usually late afternoon. We did not have any gas heat, but we managed with our one coal fire and woolen underwear. Nevertheless, we enjoyed Liverpool. The Brits we knew were very hospitable and they invited us to be part of their clubs and social groups. We were invited to many dances and parties and came to feel very much a part of the community.[69]

Sheldon Thomas replaced Huddleston in 1955. The other American staff included three consuls and three vice consuls. Stanley D. Schiff, one of the vice consuls, who served from 1953 to 1954, echoed McClelland's memory of conditions at the time. They were:

Tough. Some food items were still being rationed. Living quarters were hard to find. One of my more amusing experiences was in looking for a place to live. By that time, we had three children. We ended up staying in a hotel in a small village outside Liverpool for close to three months, which is the maximum that we were allowed. I had advertised in one of the Liverpool papers for a house in a nice neighborhood. First of all, I learned what the definition of 'nice neighborhood' was and how elastic that could be. Then I got one call from a guy on the Isle of Man, asking me if I wouldn't really like to rent a house that he had there. How was I supposed to get there? 'Well, you can fly.' This was one unrich American who couldn't fly. That was tough.[70]

Ed Williams, another vice consul, recalled a temporary detachment to Liverpool from London in 1956. He went several times on a date with a member of the local consular staff to a jazz club named The Cavern. One of the groups playing there was named The Quarrymen. Many years later when he saw newspaper photographs he realized that the group's leader was John Lennon.[71]

Thomas was replaced by John F. Stone of Pennsylvania in 1957. One of his consuls was John (Jack) Stewart Service. Service was a noted Sinophile whose views on the future direction that Communist China might take, and his numerous contacts with journalists from the *Amerasia* magazine to whom he passed government documents, led to accusations about his loyalty. He was arrested in 1945, but acquitted. In the early 1950s he was questioned on several occasions by Loyalty Security Boards and once again was cleared of all charges. However, he then fell foul of the infamous Senator Joseph McCarthy who was obsessed with the notion that there were Communist sympathizers, or 'Pinkos', in the State Department, and in other areas of American public life. Service's loyalty was further considered by a Loyalty Review Board. Once again, no charges were proved but this time the Board felt that there were reasonable doubts about his loyalty and he was dismissed in December 1951. In order to survive financially he embarked on a career in steam pipe engineering. However, he was not prepared to accept that his dismissal from the Foreign Service had been fair, and he successfully challenged the decision all the way to the Supreme Court and was reinstated in 1957. After a short stint in the Department, where he was given a mundane assignment reorganizing the Department's system for dealing with the personal and household effects of personnel moving between foreign postings, he was transferred to the Liverpool consulate in 1959. While there, he had a temporary assignment in London as supervising consul general for the United Kingdom. Sensing, probably correctly, that his future career prospects were limited he retired from Liverpool and the Foreign Service in 1962 and pursued an academic career.[72] He died in February 1999 at age 89.[73]

In 1961, the Department considered closing several British consulates, one of which was Liverpool.[74] Stone remained until 1961 and after he left the post was run by consuls, one of whom, George H. Steuart, was appointed consul general in 1964. This began a series of fairly short-term appointments, with Steuart being replaced later that year by Weldon Litsey of Wyoming who was replaced by Roy L. Wade just over a year later in 1966, who in turn was replaced by William L. S. Williams at the end of that year. Williams was reappointed in 1970 and served for two years until the final appointee, Normand W. Redden, arrived in 1972. The consulate general's future had been in the balance for some time and the embassy notified the Foreign and Commonwealth Office on 25 February 1976 that the State Department intended to close the office on 29 (later changed to 28) May.[75] By that time, it had been reduced to a two-man operation. The official State Department announcement was short and to the point, despite Liverpool having been the United States' first consulate in the United Kingdom. After announcing the date of closure it said: 'The American Government greatly values its long association with the city of Liverpool but the Department of State regretfully has concluded that the post must be closed for reasons of economy.'[76] Ambassador Ann Armstrong notified the Department of the predictable strong local commercial and political reaction to the closure but this did not alter the decision. Normand Redden transferred to Rome as Narcotics Coordinator in February then to London as consul general, from where he retired in September 1979. He and his wife then decided to settle in London; coincidentally, they were long-time friends of Jack Service and his wife, whom they had first met when serving in Wellington, New Zealand.[77]

Chapter Eighteen

LONDON

Although London is the capital city of the United Kingdom it was not the first British city to have an operational American consulate. As we have seen, that honour goes to Liverpool. However, the new US republic had its first diplomatic, as opposed to consular, presence in London and established its legation there in 1785, headed by John Adams of Massachusetts as minister plenipotentiary. In 1893, the legation was upgraded to an embassy and was headed by Thomas F. Bayard of Delaware as ambassador extraordinary and plenipotentiary.

The first consul in London was Joshua Johnson, a merchant. A native of Maryland, he had moved to London in 1771 as resident partner of the Annapolis merchant firm of Wallace, Davidson, and Johnson. He terminated the partnership in 1774 and he and his family moved to Nantes, in France, where he continued as a merchant from 1778 to 1783. In 1781, he formed a new partnership under the name of Wallace, Johnson, and Muir then returned to London with his family in 1783 and continued with the partnership until January 1790. In August of that year he was appointed consul in London, with offices at 8 Cowper's [or Cooper's] Row, Crutched Friars, Tower Hill.[1] Secretary of State Thomas Jefferson reminded Johnson of the importance of the appointment, since the United States had 'no diplomatic character at that court' at that time.[2] Accordingly, Johnson was expected to undertake more than the usual consular functions involving commerce and navigation. Jefferson informed him that 'in your position we must desire something more'. And the 'something more' was 'Political intelligence from that country is interesting to us in a high degree. We must therefore ask you to furnish us with this as far as you shall be able.'[3] Although agreeing to do so, Johnson said that as Jefferson would know from personal experience of living in France that it was difficult to obtain reliable information without spending considerable amounts of money. This would be 'inconsistent with my pursuits and not justifiable to my Family'. He returned to the question of finance, noting that Congress was considering a bill to define the duties of consuls and their fees but it had been defeated by the Senate. He hoped it would be reconsidered in the following session, trusting that 'Congress will not be too confined and that their liberality will be such as to enable me to continue the execution of the Office, the acceptance of which has involved me into a considerable expence [sic].' Also, being the representative of his country '(until a superior appointment takes place) [...] brings down on me an expence which I hope will not escape your consideration'.[4] He returned to the question of finance frequently in his despatches and also discussed it with Maury in Liverpool and Knox in Dublin. His despatches are lengthy and detailed and staff in the Department must have groaned whenever they received them.[5] This preoccupation with finance reflected the difficulties he was experiencing in his business, which eventually failed in 1797. However, on a family level, 1797 was a momentous year for the Johnsons: one of their daughters, Louisa, married John Quincy Adams in London. Adams became sixth president of the United States in 1825. At the end of 1797, Johnson returned to Maryland where he was appointed Superintendent of Stamps and spent some time unsuccessfully pursuing claims against his former partners until his death in 1802.[6]

Johnson was replaced in 1797 by Samuel Williams of Massachusetts who transferred from the consulship at Hamburg and opened his London consulate offices in Finsbury Square.[7] However, his tenure in London was not a success and he was eventually relieved of his post. Informing him of this decision on 29 June 1801, Secretary of State James Madison (1801–1809) reminded him that when he had been appointed he was:

> particularly instructed to be punctual in your correspondence with this Department and to transmit your accounts quarterly on the first days of January, April, July, and October annually. Notwithstanding the manifest propriety of frequent transmissions of accounts and the sanction of this authority, it is found that not a single statement has been received since your appointment. The surprise is the greater as the accounts of Messrs Bird, Savage and Bird show that you have previously to the 1st of July last had advances from them amounting to upwards of 88,000 dollars.[8] It appears even that not a line from you on any subject has been received by this Department since the 29th of November last, nor for some time previously, with any degree of frequency.

He was instructed to wind up his affairs, settle all his 'pecuniary transactions', and hand over all consulate papers and documents to his successor.[9] Williams appears to have been quite unfazed by this criticism and replied that he would close his public trusts with a full statement of financial transactions and send the amounts to the Treasury, and pay Rufus King, the minister in London, the balance of public money. He added, rather cheekily, that he hoped his successor would 'serve the United States and the claimants as faithfully as I have served them.'[10] His successor was George William Erving of Massachusetts. He was another who favoured very lengthy despatches, particularly recording his dislike of Rufus King, the minister. Erving remained until 1804 when he transferred to the legation in Madrid as secretary, later in his career becoming minister there.

General William Lyman of Massachusetts succeeded him. After a military career he entered politics at both the state and national level. He died in office as consul in 1811 while in Cheltenham, Gloucestershire, and is buried in Gloucester Cathedral.[11]

The post remained unfilled during the 1812 War between the United States and Britain. After the War, in 1815, Thomas Aspinwall was appointed. He was another former military officer, also from Massachusetts, and a lawyer, who had entered military service during the war, in the course of which he lost his left arm. This might have seemed an insensitive appointment given the circumstances in which he had lost his arm, however there were no ill-feelings either on his part in accepting the post or on that of the British government in recognizing him. Indeed, he was held in the highest regard in Britain and he retired from the consulship in 1853 after almost thirty-eight years, a tenure exceeding that of James Maury in Liverpool. On the occasion of his retirement a group of leading bankers, such as Baring Brothers and N. M. Rothschild, and other firms presented him with a silver service. In their covering letter they said 'You have administered the arduous duties of your office with dignity, ability, and integrity unimpeached.'[12] During his time, the consulate was located at Bishopsgate Church Yard, and when he retired the post attracted a salary of $2,000 and fees.[13]

George Nicholas Saunders of New York succeeded Aspinwall but served for less than a year. He had been appointed during a recess of the Senate and when the appointment came up for formal consideration he was rejected. Later, during the Civil War, he was Confederate commissioner to Europe. Robert Blair Campbell, appointed from Texas, arrived in 1854. He had had a varied political career, having been a state senator and congressman in South Carolina, and a member of the Alabama State House of Representatives. He then entered the Consular Service in 1842 and served as consul in Havana for eight years. His London appointment lasted until March 1861, when he was recalled. However, he did not return to the United States but moved to Ealing, in London, where he died the following year and is buried in the crypt of Kensington Church.[14] Freeman Harlow Morse of Maine took over in 1861. He had begun his working life as a carver of ships' figureheads but had become interested and involved in politics at both the local and national level. As we have seen in Chapter 5, he served in London throughout the Civil War and took an active part in trying to thwart the Confederates' attempts to purchase guns and equipment. For example, he was closely involved in setting up the US spy network in London and engaging agents such as Ignatius Pollaky.[15] By 1866, his salary was $7,500 and in 1869 he was promoted to consul general[16] but was replaced the following year, a decision that he resented bitterly. Indeed, such was the intensity of his bitterness that he refused to return to the United States and even obtained British nationality. His wife and daughters, on the other hand, returned to America. Morse lived for many years in Surbiton, near London, and died there on 6 February 1891, at age 83.[17]

In April 1869, General Adam Badeau of New York was appointed assistant secretary of the London legation, but he resigned the post a few months later in order to become consul general in 1870.[18] The result of the consulate inspection in 1872 revealed that during the year ended 30 June 1872, almost twenty thousand invoices were certified, generating a fee income of almost $50,000; in addition, more than $5,000 was generated from shipping and other sources; and exports to the United States during the same period totalled almost $45 million. The inspector drew attention to this large volume of work and criticized the Department for not allowing the appointment of a consular clerk, pointing out that other less busy consulates were better provided for in this regard. In his opinion, London ought to have two clerks. This was addressed later; see for example, the situation in 1885–1886, described later in the chapter. He also recommended transferring the residence of the consul general to Liverpool, 'where the authority of a superior officer is most needed to exercise a supervisory control over the consulates in the British Isles'. This emphasizes once more the importance of Liverpool. If this recommendation had been accepted, the London officer's salary would have been reduced to $4,000. The inspector noted that there were consular agencies at Dover, Ramsgate, Margate and Deal.[19] In 1874, Badeau's salary was $6,000, and by 1879 the offices were at 53A Old Broad Street.[20] During the Civil War Badeau had been on General Ulysses S. Grant's staff, and while consul general was given leave

Figure 18.1 Freeman H. Morse, consul, then consul general, London, 1861–1870. He held the post throughout the American Civil War (1861–1865). He was replaced in 1870, a decision which he bitterly resented, to the extent that he remained in Britain and obtained British nationality, dying in Surbiton, Surrey, in 1891. [Library of Congress, Prints & Photographs Division, reproduction no. LC-USZ6-589.]

of absence by the State Department from 1877 to 1878 to accompany Grant, who was then ex-president, on his world tour. Also while in London, Badeau was nominated for the posts of minister in Brussels and Copenhagen, but declined both and remained in London until 1881 when he was transferred to Havana as consul general.[21] Although he was no longer serving in London, questions began to be raised about the nature of the business he had conducted there and the income he had derived from it. In 1886, he successfully defended a case brought against him by the United States government seeking to recover more than $10,000 relating to fees he had received when consul general. However, he maintained that the fees were unofficial and therefore belonged to him personally. The court found in his favour, ruling that the fees were: 'for services done for private individuals in private business, and not under the authority of the United States government, and that all were for use in the individual states of the

Union, and under the state laws.'[22] This decision is a useful reminder of the division of legislative powers between individual states and the federal government. However, such a case would not arise nowadays as all Foreign Service officers work exclusively for the US government.

Edwin Atkins Merritt of New York took over in 1881. Trained as a civil engineer and surveyor, his varied career had included membership of the New York state assembly, army officer, naval officer and surveyor and collector for the port of New York.[23] The London appointment offered him a $6,000 salary, $1,200 for house rent and $2,000 for clerk hire. When fee income was added to this, it was reported that 'the income of the London Consulate-General is about $50,000 a year'.[24] Another report stated: 'it is

Figure 18.2 General Adam Badeau, consul general, London, 1870–1881. Badeau, of New York, served during the Civil War (1861–1865) on the staff of General Thomas Sherman and General Ulysses S. Grant. When he eventually resigned from the army in 1869 he was awarded the rank of brevet brigadier general. Initially appointed to the legation in London, he resigned from that post and was appointed to the more lucrative post of consul general in 1870. He was nominated as minister to Belgium in 1871 and to Denmark in 1881 but declined both appointments and continued in London until 1881 when he transferred to Havana as consul. [Brady-Handy Collection, Library of Congress, Prints & Photographs Division, reproduction no. LC-Dig-cwpbh-00094.]

estimated that the Consul Generalship at London, which paid $6,000 a year and fees, brought in to its fortunate officer in charge as much as $75,000 in a peak year'.[25] Merritt's son, Edwin Albert, accompanied him to London and for a while was one of two deputy consuls general.[26] In 1885, Thomas McDonald Waller of Connecticut replaced Merritt. His previous appointments included Connecticut secretary of state (1870–1871), mayor of New London (1873), speaker of the Connecticut general assembly (1876) and governor of Connecticut (1883–1885). By 1886, London had a consular clerk, chief clerk and four clerks, so the Department had acted upon the criticisms made by Keim, the inspector, in 1872. The offices had moved to 12 St Helen's Place, Bishopsgate Street, in 1885. More than twenty thousand invoices were certified during the year ending 31 December 1885. Waller paid almost $3,000 in excess expenditure for clerk hire and rent over the allowance he received. Only the Dover agency remained, headed by F. W. Prescott. In 1886, Waller, as superintending consul general, inspected all the consulates in the British Isles.[27] His son, Martin, was for part of the time vice consul general.[28] The farewell banquet given for Waller when he left in 1889 was described as 'the most notable Anglo-American dinner that London has ever seen' and 'involved the presentation of a silver loving cup costing $600'. Scores of applicants for places were turned away 'after the list of over two hundred was filled, although the price of tickets was placed unprecedently high'.[29]

Waller's replacement was John Chalfant New of Indiana, whose background was in law, banking, publishing and as an Indiana state senator. He was also Treasurer of the United States from 1875–1876 and assistant secretary of the Treasury from 1882 to 1884. In his capacity as Treasurer, he had the distinction of signing US currency.[30] When he left the London consulship in 1893 he was presented with an album containing photographs of all the consular officers in Britain and Ireland.[31] His replacement was Patrick Andrew Collins of Massachusetts. Born in Fermoy, Ireland, he had acquired American citizenship and like many Irishmen of his time he found his niche in Boston trade union, legal and political circles, and became a lawyer, member of the Massachusetts House of Representatives and Senate and US representative from Massachusetts. His salary on appointment to London was $5,000.[32] He, too, as was common, employed his son as vice and deputy consul general.[33] He left the post in 1897 and returned to Boston where he became mayor from 1902 until his death in 1905. Collins was succeeded by William McKinley Osborne. He was born in Ohio and practised law there, but later in his career moved to Massachusetts where in addition to practising law he became a state politician. He was appointed to the London post in 1897 by his maternal cousin, President William McKinley, and served until his death in Wimbledon, London, on 29 April 1902. He had never been completely well since taking up the post and for the final six months had been confined to his residence.[34]

The London consulate general was always a busy office. For example, in 1902 it was said to 'embrace the performance of almost every act known to the consular service in civilized countries'. Its office hours at that time were: 'from 10 to 4, except Saturdays, when the office closes at 2, but the officials and clerks are obliged to remain much later in order to keep up with the work. On account of the pressure of invoices on Tuesdays and Thursdays, work is not finished until 6 or 7 pm, and on Fridays until

7, 8, or 9 pm.' As if that were not bad enough: 'On some Fridays they have had to
remain until 10 pm.'[35] The offices were still at 12 St Helen's Place, Bishopsgate Street,
and consisted of three rooms: a central room where the public entered and where most
of the clerks sat, a rear room occupied by the vice and deputy and the deputy consul
general, and a front room occupied by the consul general. Such was the volume of
business, however, that the consul general's room was 'frequently occupied by people
who have no other place to sit or stand in while transacting their business.' The government allowed only $1,000 for office rent despite the fact that the sum actually paid
for the offices 'largely exceeded' this. During 1900, the total office expenses, including
stationery (which included the cost of invoice forms supplied to the consulates and
agencies throughout the country), postage, cleaning, lighting, heating, rent and
repairs – but excluding salaries – amounted to more than $4,000. Thanks to the
healthy income generated from fees, the consulate general was able to remit a surplus
of almost $46,000 to the government.[36] Henry Clay Evans was appointed in 1902, the
first holder of the post from Pennsylvania, although most of his working life, as a businessman and congressman, had been spent in Tennessee. He was US commissioner
of pensions before resigning to take up the London post[37] where he served until 1905
when he was succeeded by Robert John Wynne of New York. Wynne's immediately
preceding post was US Postmaster General. He was the first London consul general
to be subject to the provisions of the Act of 5 April 1906 which increased the salary to
$12,000, but with no fee income. Also, holders of the post were now prohibited from
transacting any business, whether as merchants or lawyers.[38] Up till then, consuls who
were members of these professions had derived considerable fees from such activities.
The consuls general in both London and Paris now received salaries of $12,000, the
highest in the Consular Service.

During his time in London Wynne became the focus of attention of the local
American community, which felt that he was being snubbed by members of the embassy
at social functions. It was reported that:

> as every well-informed American in London very well knows [...]. There is an established
> protocol in Europe which fixes a Consul General's social status as clearly as his duties are
> fixed by the regulations of the State Department. He ranks next to an Ambassador or Acting
> Chargé d'Affaires. The American Embassy is the only one in London which ignores this
> protocol [...]. The trouble did not originate with Mr Wynne. It is so ancient it has become a
> tradition. While the Consuls General of other countries have always been seated at table on
> state occasions immediately below their Ambassadors, the official representatives of American
> trade interests have been relegated to far down the line, after Second and Third Secretaries
> and Naval Attachés. The Consuls General of other countries, as well as prominent members
> of the American colony in London, have repeatedly discussed this practice, which has tended
> to bring the post of American Consul General here into ridicule.

Wynne said he had no grievance and that he and his wife had been treated most hospit-
ably by Ambassador Whitelaw Reid.[39] An attempt appears to have been made to improve
matters and it was noted with pleasure that at a Thanksgiving dinner several months later
Wynne and his wife had been seated at the table of honour together with Ambassador

Reid and his wife.[40] However, Emily Bax, who was employed as a secretary, and was the only British woman in the embassy at the time, maintained that:

> there had been more or less friction between the two Services [the Diplomatic Service and the Consular Service] in London for years. The Consuls in England resented their minor status and the fact that, not being accredited to the Court, they were left out of many Court functions [...]. The Consuls were always touchy about their social status, with which actually the Embassy had nothing to do. I dare say the Embassy might have been a bit more tactful, and the Ambassador could just as well have signed the letters to them if anyone had thought of it, instead of their receiving instructions through 'young puppies at the Embassy'. But the Consular Service seemed to suffer badly from inferiority complex, and the Rogers Act, passed after the War making the two Services interchangeable, was probably at least in part inspired by disgruntled Consuls who wanted their share of the limelight.[41]

A throwaway remark by her showed the gulf between the embassy and the consulate general: 'There was also, of course, the Consulate-General in the City of London, in charge of American commercial interests, with whom our relations were official and more or less friendly.'[42] Few people reading that sentence would have realized that the two establishments being described were both official overseas posts of the same government in the same city.

Wynne was not at all impressed by many of the Americans living at that time in England and three years after leaving the consul general post wrote a swingeing attack on them.

> I know there is a class of Americans in London who are ashamed of everything American, and yet who remain Americans abroad to avoid having their pasts too closely inquired into [...]. In London from 4,000 to 5,000 Americans live at various periods of the year – some all the year round. About 2,000 of them, according to a directory published when I was Consul General, represent legitimate American business and professional interests. The rest are, in every sense of the word, from an American standpoint, undesirables. They live in England and on the Continent because they can afford to, and their greatest delight is in attracting the notice of or basking in the company of some one connected with the nobility. They are almost invariably imitation Englishmen in every company except American, and are Americans only on the Fourth of July and Thanksgiving Day, for the purpose of identifying themselves with the colony and the flag. In other words they are 'professional Americans'.[43]

It is strange when writing about the early 1900s that he uses the term 'colony' to describe the United States. One of the Americans living in London during Wynne's appointment, though arguably 'legitimate', was the writer Henry James. Apart from a one year gap when he moved to Paris he lived in London from 1876 until his death there on 28 February 1916. The year before his death he became a British subject.

John Lewis Griffiths of Indiana arrived in 1909. His previous post was consul in Liverpool, but prior to that he had been a lawyer and a member of the Indiana House of Representatives. The year after he arrived in London, the consulate offices moved from 12 St Helen's Place, Bishopsgate, to Orient House, New Road, described as 'a fine suite of offices on the ground floor of a new building in one of the principal thoroughfares of the town'.[44] Griffiths was popular in London, and had a great reputation as an after-dinner speaker and wit. A good example of this is shown in the following account of an incident at the consulate general.

> Several years ago, when the racing season was on in England, and London had many of the racing folk from America, an over-dressed blonde breezed into the Consulate General in London and addressed Mr Griffiths as 'Mr Council' to a chewing-gum accompaniment and made a rather insistent request that the Consul General furnish her with transportation to the United States. Consul General Griffiths politely explained to her that the United States Government provides no fund for the transportation of its citizens, and lacking any appropriation on which he could draw for expenses to be incurred for such purpose, he kindly informed her that rather than see her stranded, he would provide her with transportation expenses to Liverpool at his own expense. The blonde young lady was requested to return to the Consulate General in the afternoon to obtain the railroad ticket. She called again at the appointed hour and was handed the railroad ticket. Upon examining it, she noticed that it was a 'third-class' ticket. Whereupon, she turned to Mr Griffiths, and in a way of showing her gratification for his kindness, said [in a strong New York accent?]: 'How dare you give me a third-class ticket! What kind of a guy do you think I is. Why! Say! I aint never rode thoid class in my young life! I pray God no other loidy ever asks a favor of you as long as you live!' Mr Griffiths merely replied 'Madam, I shall pray that your prayer may be answered.'[45]

Griffiths died unexpectedly in his London home on 17 May 1914. His remains were repatriated to the United States via Liverpool, and while in the city his body lay in state in the Town Hall. At that time, the only other foreigner to have been accorded that honour was William J. Gaynor, mayor of New York.[46] When the ship bearing his remains docked in New York a week later its flags were at half mast and the captain and officers lined up on deck in their dress uniforms as the coffin, covered with the Stars and Stripes, was carried off. Much to everyone's surprise, however, it was not put into a hearse but was loaded onto an express wagon, an open flat wagon with low retaining sides used for carrying freight. Passers-by turned to gaze at the unusual spectacle as the horse-drawn wagon made its slow passage through the streets accompanied by two of the pallbearers walking on the adjacent pavement. 'Some thought it might contain the body of a soldier or sailor, who had been killed, or died in Mexico.' When asked why the coffin was being conveyed on a freight wagon the undertakers said that it 'was too wide to fit into any hearses in New York. [...] And its width? Thirty inches.'[47] This does not seem particularly wide but perhaps New Yorkers at the turn of the twentieth century were slimmer than their contemporaries in the twenty-first century.

Robert Peet Skinner of Ohio took over in 1914. Originally a newspaper editor, he entered the Consular Service in 1897 at Marseille and prior to coming to London was consul general in Berlin. At one point, it seemed as though his London appointment might be short-lived. It was reported that he had been recalled to Washington and that there was British government displeasure at trade reports he had sent to the State Department. These said that 'although the British Government was detaining American cargoes destined for neutral ports on the Continent of Europe, it was shipping similar

Figure 18.3 John L. Griffiths, consul, Liverpool, 1905–1909; consul general, London, 1909–1914. Griffiths was born in New York City, although the family moved to Iowa where he later had a career as a lawyer and as a member of the state legislature. In 1905 he was appointed consul in Liverpool, where he served until 1909 before transferring to London as consul general. A very popular figure in both cities, he died unexpectedly in London on 17 May 1914 at age 58. His remains were transported to New York where his funeral was held on 1 June. The photograph shows his coffin being borne from First Presbyterian Church, New York, after the funeral service. The mourners on the right of the photograph, reading from right to left are: unknown; Sir Courtenay W. Bennett, British consul general in New York; George McAneny, journalist and New York City politician; George T. Wilson, second vice-president, Equitable Life Assurance Society of the United States; and James B. Curtis, a New York attorney. On the left is possibly Judge Alton B. Parker. Sir Arthur Conan Doyle was one of several honorary pall bearers (but not in the photograph). [George Grantham Bain Collection, Library of Congress, Prints & Photographs Division, Reproduction Number LC-DIG-ggbain-16186.]

British-made goods to the same ports.' The reports were confidential reports and their publication in the Department of Commerce's daily Commerce Reports was thought to have been caused by 'an inadvertence'. Skinner denied that he had been recalled and after his consultations in Washington he returned to London.[48] When Wilbur Carr, the Director of the Consular Service, visited the consulate in 1916 it was situated in New Broad Street where its male staff 'made a brave show in their top hats and long-tailed coats, which were still customarily worn each day by all of them, but the quarters were dingy and inadequate.'[49] Skinner served there throughout the First World War and in 1924 transferred to Paris as consul general. He later went on to ambassadorial posts in

Greece, Estonia, Latvia, Lithuania and Turkey.[50] During most of his time in London, the consulate general was located at 18 Cavendish Square.[51] William Stanley Hollis of Massachusetts, who had been consul in Dundee from 1909 until 1910, also served as consul general for part of the time during Skinner's tenure before being transferred to Lisbon in 1920.[52] Russell Rhodes, one of the vice consuls, described a little-known but important part of a consul's duties: sealing the coffins of American citizens who had died in the London consular district.

> It was the sad and gruesome part of my job. My first experience, strangely enough, was in sending back to America [in 1922] the body of my superior officer, Richard Westacott, to whose consular desk I succeeded after three years' service in the London consulate. [...] It was part of his duty to seal down caskets and I recall him telling me when he was in his last illness how it should be done properly. Little did I then think that I should have to perform the melancholy duty for him.[53]

Westacott, who had been born in Boston, Massachusetts, was a familiar and well-respected member of the consulate general, having served there for 23 years as a vice consul. It was unsurprising, therefore, that his funeral service was attended by representatives of the embassy, the entire personnel of the consulate general, representatives of Anglo-American organizations, representatives of London official and social life and numerous friends.[54]

In capital cities such as London, one of the changes introduced by the Rogers Act of 1924, which created a unified Foreign Service, was bringing the separate consulate general and embassy offices under one roof. Also, Foreign Service staff could then be commissioned as diplomatic or consular officers, or both, and depending on their roles would hold the titles of counselor and consul general, first secretary and consul, or third secretary and vice consul. The first part of the title denoted their diplomatic rank, the second their consular rank.[55] In 1925, Horace Lee Washington of Washington, DC, arrived from Liverpool where he had been consul general. As a former consul general at large appointed under the 1906 Act he had undertaken inspections of the consulates in Britain so was very familiar with the network. He remained in London until 1928 and was succeeded by John Ker Davis of Ohio. Davis had been born in China and had spent all his previous service there, amounting to almost eighteen years, starting as an interpreter and then undertaking a series of consular assignments, ending up as first secretary at the legation in Peking.[56] Given that background, he must have found his transfer to London a bewildering experience. Perhaps its purpose was to give him, and his wife and two sons, a respite from the arduous conditions of living and working in China. On the other hand, when in 1920 Edwin S. Cunningham, the consul general at Shanghai, dropped in to the London consulate he 'remarked encouragingly, as he looked out into the fog, that nothing could induce him to exchange the Orient for the Occident'.[57] It looks as though Davis was not expected to undertake the full range of duties in London because all the time he was there was another consul general, Albert Halstead, was in post and Davis eventually moved on to Seoul as consul general in 1930.[58] Halstead arrived in London the same year as Davis. Before joining the Consular Service he had been a colonel in the US Army and a newspaper editor and had also served as consul in Birmingham, where he had succeeded his brother. He remained in London until 1932 when he retired and returned to America.[59]

Robert Frazer of Philadelphia arrived in 1932. Before joining the Consular Service he had worked in Puerto Rico as a bank teller and a sugar cane planter. Like Horace Lee Washington, he had been a consul general at large (from 1919 to 1924) and had been a Foreign Service inspector from 1925 to 1927, and had inspected consulates in Britain. Prior to coming to London he had been consul general in Mexico City. He remained in London until 1937.[60] There is more information about his career in Chapter 4. Frazer's successor in London was Douglas Jenkins of South Carolina. He had been a member of the South Carolina Bar and had practised as an attorney for several years before joining the Consular Service in Halifax, Nova Scotia, in 1908. He had had extensive service in China and Hong Kong, and prior to his London assignment had been consul general in Berlin. He remained in London until 1939 when he was appointed minister to Bolivia.[61] It seems that he received this appointment despite earlier misgivings by Under Secretary of State Sumner Welles. Writing to President Roosevelt in 1937, Wells said: 'He [Jenkins] has had no service on this [American] continent and consequently, would not in my judgment be available as Minister to any one of the American Republics. I think, however, that he would be well qualified to serve as Minister, should a suitable opening occur, in one of the smaller European capitals or in the Far East.'[62] Jenkins' successor in London was John George Erhardt of Brooklyn, who arrived in 1939. He too had had a short legal career before joining the Consular Service at Athens in 1919, and had been a Foreign Service inspector prior to his London assignment. He remained only until 1941 before being reassigned to the Department.[63] There appears to have been no consul general as such during the Second World War, no doubt because there was no call for consular duties. There was, of course, a very large complement of Foreign Service staff at the embassy throughout the war.

The first post-war consul general was George Tait, of Virginia, who arrived in 1946 from Berne. Before his first Consular Service post in Rio de Janeiro in 1923 he had been a member of the Virginia Bar and had practised law for a short while. During his consular service he had been a lecturer on consular practice at Georgetown School of Foreign Service in Washington, DC, from 1931 to 1933. The year following his arrival in London he married there a British lady whom he had met while he was serving in Manchester from 1937 to 1941. He remained at London until 1949, when he transferred to Algiers as consul general and then to Antwerp. However, he died unexpectedly in a London hospital in 1952 after surgery.[64] In 1949, John William Bailey, Jr, of Texas, took charge of the consulate general. Before joining the Consular Service as a clerk in Geneva in 1924 he had had a variety of occupations, including working in the oil industry, ranching and real estate – all in Mexico. Because the Foreign Service and the State Department were separate entities at the time, and would not fully merge until 1957, he had resigned from the Service on 31 March 1935 and been appointed the following day as Assistant Chief, Director of Foreign Service Personnel in the Department.[65] He had resumed consular duties in 1943 as consul general in Santiago and prior to coming to London had been consul general in Geneva.[66] Kenneth Carl

Figure 18.4 Robert Frazer Jr., consul general, London, 1932–1937. Frazer had a distinguished career in the consular field, including two assignments as an inspector in the Consular Service and the Foreign Service. He was consul general in London from 1932 until 1937 when he was appointed minister to El Salvador, a post he held until his retirement in 1943. [Harris & Ewing Collection, Library of Congress, Prints & Photographs Division, reproduction no. LC-DIG-hec-20215.]

Krentz of Colorado, who succeeded Bailey in 1953, was another relatively late entrant to the Service and had worked for electricity and telephone companies before being appointed as a clerk in the consulate general in Hong Kong in 1926, and since then had spent most of his career in the Far East. He remained in London until 1957[67] when he was replaced by Donald W. Smith of Washington, DC, whose early career had been spent with the Department of Commerce, again in the Far East.[68] Round about this time, the title of the London consul general changed to counselor for consular affairs.

Thomas Eliot Weil of Chicago, who took over in 1962, had started his working life as a teacher, but eventually joined the Foreign Service in 1935 in Marseille where he remained for only a year. Like many other officers of his generation, he had spent a considerable amount of his career in China and South East Asia, and London was his first substantive European posting. He remained for two years and was replaced by Leon LeRoy Cowles of Utah in 1964. Before joining the Foreign Service in 1938 at Ciudad Juarez, Mexico, he had been secretary of the Latter Day Saints' Mission in France and a teacher of French and Spanish in California.[69] He was replaced in 1968 by Jack A. Herfurt of Ohio, whose previous occupations had included working with the Federal Security Agency, military service with the US Army and then a spell as an analyst with the Navy Department.[70] His subsequent postings were in the economic/commercial area. He remained in London until 1974 when he became Director General of the American Chamber of Commerce (UK).[71]

As well as having heavy workloads, consular sections with large numbers of staff often have personnel problems foisted on them by the Department. Retired Consul General Charles Stuart Kennedy said: 'I noticed when I was doing consular work in the late 60s, every once in a while we would realize, it would be pointed out to us, that we were taking people with personality problems and sending them to London. Because we figured it was a big post, and London could take it. Well, pretty soon, we found a consular section loaded with problems.'[72] Former ambassador Mary Ryan, to whom these remarks were addressed, agreed, adding: 'We had that in Montreal. We had that in the consular section, something like 11 people, and seven of them had serious problems of one sort or another. So four people were doing the work of 11, who were soon going to develop their own problems because of overwork.'[73] David L. Hobbs, a former member of the London consular staff, describing his time there from 1973 to 1976, recalled that personnel issues were a constant problem: 'Many of them [staff] came from other types of foreign service work. I used to get the impression that they were fleeing that other work for some reason or another and they weren't so interested in consular work but just wanted to get away from something else.' But he tempered this, adding:

> Now, of course, there were exceptions among the other group. In the old days there were people who were fantastic too, but there were a number of people who just didn't want to be there. In London we would get junior officers who were planning to do something else in the world, but also wanted to do a good job while in consular work. And that was great. However, we also got a big chunk of people who just really didn't want to be there. We always knew that the Department felt London could always absorb one more, but if you keep absorbing just one more, after awhile you have so many wounded people on your staff that it becomes very hard to deal with.[74]

Unrest in the consular section at this time was matched by serious concerns in the political section – not with the quality of the staff but with the Department's practice of leaving the embassy out of the loop on policy exchanges with the British embassy in Washington and even with the Foreign Secretary in London. In his confidential valedictory telegram to the president and the secretary of state summing up the current state of US/UK relations, Ambassador Walter H. Annenberg noted:

> To my chagrin, I have observed this mission become a bystander. Repeatedly we learn of significant statements of US policy in conversations with the British embassy or British officials visiting Washington, but we are all too infrequently advised of such exchanges, especially

those at high level. Like our colleagues in Paris we find that our host government is often better informed about US policy than we are. We lack the sense and reality of participation in the conduct of US policy toward the United Kingdom which is vital if we are to carry on the kind of dialogue and make the vigorous representation of US interests which are expected of us. [...] British officials have expressed dismay at this situation. The authority and standing of this embassy have been downgraded in British eyes. I need not point out how demoralizing this is for the professional members of my staff.[75]

He was echoing similar comments made the previous week by the ambassador in Paris, John N. Irwin II, in his valedictory telegram.[76] Nowadays, when it has become routine for heads of state and foreign ministers to make frequent direct and personal contact with their foreign counterparts it is even more essential that the relevant missions are kept fully in the picture.

John Robert Diggins of Massachusetts took over from Jack Herfurt in 1974 as counselor for consular affairs. He, too, had had a varied career before joining the Foreign Service in 1947 as a clerk in Puerto la Cruz, Venezuela. He had been a clerk for mercantile firms, served an apprenticeship in the Navy Department, served in the US Navy, worked as an adjudicator in the Veterans Administration and been a field auditor in the Department of Agriculture.[77] A colleague who had worked with him in London recalled: 'I remember once trying to talk him into doing some changes and he looked at me and said, "Look, I tell you what, you go ahead and do it. If it works, I will take the credit, if it doesn't work, I will get your ass." I thought that was fair enough, an interesting way to motivate people.'[78] Normand W. Redden arrived in August 1977. His previous substantive post was consul general in Liverpool, where he was in charge when the post closed in May 1976. One of the events he recalled during his time in London was the Fastnet yacht race in 1979 in which 15 competitors died. Several of them were Americans and the consular section was closely involved dealing with the necessary follow-up procedures. The section at that time occupied all of the embassy ground floor, except for the reception area and the commercial library. Redden retired from the Service in 1979 and he and his wife took up residence in London.[79]

Alan A. Gise, who took over, had served previously in London when he had been regarded as 'a tremendous motivator and got a lot out of what he had'.[80] Consular business during his time increased enormously. It was reported that:

The surge of applicants has made the embassy in London the busiest US visa office in the world. Lines of 100 or more British and other, primarily Third World, nationals spill down the steps and onto the sidewalk outside the embassy building on Grosvenor Square. Inside, 60 employees process as many as 6,000 applications a day. At any moment, some 60,000 to 80,000 British passports are in the embassy's hands. Boxes and baskets overflow with applications. Harried staff give hurried glances before rubber-stamping approval. Applicants, once thronged inside, now wait mainly outside. [...].U.S. Consul General Alan Gise attributes the upsurge to the 'Laker legacy' of cheap, no-frills flights, to exchange rates that until recently were favorable, to relatively low U.S. prices for food and hotels, and to the British worker's growing infatuation with Miami Beach.[81]

This picture of London at that time was confirmed by Diane Dillard, one of the consular section's branch chiefs.

> You had a waiting room that was hot and crowded and noisy. You had a situation where at the end of the day, you might have 800 people outside waiting to collect their passports. They would get unhappy if we'd have a hot day, which was unusual, or if we'd have a rainy day, and we just could not let them in the building. We had to hand them the passports through the door; there was no other way to handle it. Some days I'd have to go outside and get them to line up and convince them this was going to work, or we'd go out with baskets in the morning to collect their passports. It was a mill. It was incredible. Then they redesigned the consular section, which meant at one point we were 30 people in an area far too small for ten. That was a very hard period. That nearly drove us all mad, but we survived that. When you have that many people, it really becomes a management problem. We ended up, at one point, deluged with passports. We received 30,000 passports for visas one day [...]. Because of a mail strike.[82]

Alan Gise was succeeded by Robert William (Bill) Maule in 1981. He had served in troubled parts of the world, such as Beirut and Port au Prince, and welcomed the posting to a relatively tranquil London. Nevertheless, he recalled the incident in December 1983 when the IRA planted bombs inside and outside Harrods department store in London that killed six people, one of them an American citizen. Maule represented the ambassador at the memorial service in Westminster Abbey. 'As senior American present, I was ushered to the seat of honor on one side of the choir stalls. Despite the huge discrepancy in rank, the equivalent seat on the other side was occupied by a somber Maggie Thatcher.'[83] When he arrived in London, the large consular section was undergoing a complete renovation. For him, the downside of being in charge of such a large section was that it: 'removes one from the day to day human interest incidents that were the joys and frustrations of my staff. With some 34 American officers and sometimes over 85 locally hired staff, administration management became almost all-consuming.' Outside events also took up time, such as:

> speaking at ceremonies at US Armed Forces cemeteries; the annual [Door of Unity] ceremony at Plymouth commemorating pro-American activities there during the 1812 war; the estate in the southwest of Scotland [Culzean Castle] where a room had been dedicated for the use of General Eisenhower [...] membership of the Board of the American School in London, representing the Ambassador at formal balls and dinners, and accompanying the new Ambassador to Buckingham Palace to present his credentials [...] visiting the Consulates General in Edinburgh and Belfast.[84]

Maule recalled one visa incident that required his personal attention.

> I read in the press that Peter Pears [the singer] was quite angry that he had been refused a visa to perform in the United States, despite the fact that he had received many such visas in past years. I investigated and, as I had suspected, the problem involved Department of State records that had recently been augmented by those of many other agencies. A newly available record indicated that Mr Pears had joined the England-Soviet Friendship Society immediately after World War II. As this was considered a communist dominated organization, the

visa had been refused, but without full awareness of the exemptions available in the law. In an interview with Mr Pears I learned that he had joined simply because Russia had been our valiant ally in the war. After a meeting or two he discovered he did not like the organization and dropped out. Thus he should not have been refused a visa because his membership had not been meaningful. What amused me was that Mr Pears was not so much angry about the refusal, as by the fact that my ignorant visa officer did not know who he was and, even worse, had never heard of Benjamin Britten! That must have seemed unforgivable.[85]

An amusing footnote to that episode is that Maule:

> was aware that Mr Pears appeared to have a painful limp when on stage, so I arranged to avoid steps […] by meeting him for tea on the ground floor of my residence. My wife [who was an enthusiastic member of the St Martin Singers] was furious with me for not conferring with her, as she had a commitment and could not be home to meet this great singer. She was appeased, however, when I received a gracious thank you letter, enclosing two tickets for a wonderful concert at the Maltings where she was able to meet and chat with Mr Pears after the performance.[86]

As we have seen, for a number of years the chief of the embassy consular section, in other words the consul general, had held the title of counselor for consular affairs, but by the late 1980s this was changed to minister-counselor for consular affairs. Maule was succeeded by Edward Kreuser, who was the first to be shown in the London diplomatic list with the new title.[87] The background to this change is illuminating. In a spat reminiscent of the old distinctions between members of the former Diplomatic and Consular Services, the London Embassy objected to a 1988 ruling that senior Foreign Commercial Service (FCS) and Foreign Agricultural Service (FAS) officers, members of the Departments of Commerce and Agriculture respectively, at designated posts be accorded the diplomatic title of minister-counselor. The embassy's objection was: 'on the grounds that it is unnecessary and that it would place the senior FCS and FAS officers in protocol rank and precedence above other officers with broader and more senior responsibilities who had been of equal or higher rank on the diplomatic list. An officer's position on the diplomatic list is significant because it is often a determining factor in the officer's access to senior British officials.' In order to get round this but still comply with the law and maintain the desired hierarchy on the diplomatic list: 'the Embassy sought, and received, the Department's approval to upgrade diplomatic titles of its senior administrative, consular, political, and public affairs officers from counselor to minister-counselor.'[88] At the time of writing, the embassy had six officers of this rank.[89]

Norbert J. Krieg took over from Kreuser in July 1989. In 1991, the consulate section was staffed by 32 Americans and 89 Foreign Service National employees and was organized into three main functions – non-immigrant visas (NIV), immigrant visas (IV) and American citizen services – plus an anti-fraud unit and a front office. The volume of work was immense; in the financial year 1990, there were 314,577 non-immigrant and immigrant visas; 300,000 NIV/IV telephone calls, letters, and telegrams dealt with; 16,486 passports issued; and 4,037 reports of birth.[90] The embassy was inspected in 1993 when the inspectors reported that it: 'competently executes consular responsibilities to one of the largest, and almost certainly the most diverse and complex clientele of any American post. It has long set the standard to which well-managed consular sections aspire.' However, they noted that:

> NIV operations are the weakest link in the consular section operations. Despite dramatically declining work load under the visa waiver program, the NIV branch has struggled to keep up, extending to weeks the turnaround for applications by mail. Managers have passed on the stress to junior officers and FSN employees, resulting in poor morale and adversarial relations that impair productivity.[91]

Krieg remained until 1993.

The following year, Elizabeth Ann Swift became the first woman to head up the London consular section. Her initial attempt to join the Foreign Service had been less than promising. She recalled that after she had finished the oral examination, the chairman of the interview board had called her back into the interview room and said:

> 'Miss Swift, we're very sorry to tell you that you haven't passed.' And I knew it already so that didn't bother me. And he said, 'But we really liked you.' And I thought that was an odd comment, and 'we'd really like to have you in the Foreign Service so why don't you marry a Foreign Service officer and you can become part of the Foreign Service that way'. [...] I was so angry I walked out of the front door of the State Department and swore I would never ever come back.[92]

But she did come back and re-sat and passed the examinations. Earlier in her career she had been one of only two women to have been held hostage when the embassy in Tehran was seized by militant Islamic students in November 1979. She and the other hostages were finally released on 20 January 1981 after 444 days of captivity. In 1994 she married while serving in London and retired from the Foreign Service the following year. She died in a riding accident in 2004.[93] Max Newton Robinson was appointed in 1995 and remained until 1998 when he was succeeded by Wayne G. Griffith whose previous post was consular officer in Tokyo. He was an expert on consular affairs and immigration problems and before Tokyo had been principal deputy assistant secretary of state for consular affairs.

An indication of the volume of work dealt with by London in 1999 was given by Ambassador Philip Lader.

> We issue 25,000-plus passports each year. With 250,000 American citizens resident in the United Kingdom and 3.9 million annual American visitors to Britain, replacing passports is an everyday task. [...] Each year, we respond to deaths in the UK of, on average, 400 American citizens. We deal regularly with law enforcement officials regarding the 40-or-so Americans arrested every month, for everything from shoplifting to drugs offenses to murder. We annually arrange for the arrest and extradition of about 100 criminal fugitives wanted in the United States, and we are currently tracking 750 international child-custody cases. Year-in and year-out, our Consular Section receives nearly one million public inquiries about citizenship and passports, absentee voter registration, and visas. [In 1999], we processed 166,000

non-immigrant visa applications from individuals representing 185 nationalities. We register as citizens about 3,600 babies each year.[94]

Ambassador Lader's remarks were borne out by the inspection carried out in 1999 which acknowledged that: 'The consular operation is one of the busiest in the world with a widely varied and complex workload. It is also one of the most innovative […]. The post is now the "poster child" for the Department's increased efforts to improve customer service.' Additionally, 'London has one of the best anti-fraud units in the business.'[95]

Griffith left in 2002 and transferred to Washington where he became deputy assistant secretary for visa services. He was succeeded by Thomas Patrick Furey who prior to coming to London had been consul general at the embassy in Riyadh, Saudi Arabia, from 2000, and responsible for the management of all consular functions in the country, which included the consulate general at Jeddah. His Riyadh assignment had been a difficult one. Fifteen of the 9/11 hijackers had obtained their visas in Saudi Arabia, either at the consulate general in Jeddah or the embassy in Riyadh. The 9/11 Commission into the circumstances of the attack reported:

> Our investigation has determined that some of the criticism leveled against the State Department was warranted. State officials did approve incomplete visa applications and did expedite the issuance of visas, requiring few interviews of Saudi and Emirati applicants during a time of rising extremism in Saudi Arabia and, during the summer of 2001, heightened threat reporting in the Middle East generally.[96]

While he was serving in London, Furey was interviewed by the Commission. He stated that when he had first arrived in Saudi Arabia 'the Riyadh visa operation was "chaotic" and "dysfunctional". Morale was low.' He described the measures that he had taken to improve things, and insisted that: 'Had he been told Saudis were a security risk – something he said he learned on September 11, 2001 – he would not have established the Visa Express Program'. This program aimed at reducing the number of non-immigrant visa applicants turning up at the consulate by requiring them to apply at officially approved travel agents. Although it did lead to a reduction in numbers arriving at the consulate, it also meant a reduction in the numbers who were interviewed by consular staff. Several of the hijackers obtained their visas this way. However, the Commission concluded: 'As will become clear, the opinions of consular officers [at Jeddah] who were concerned about Saudi citizens as terrorists did not reach Furey's ears before the 9/11 attacks.'[97] During his assignment in London the consular section was once more described as: 'one of the busiest in the world, issuing about 175,000 non-immigrant visas a year to travellers from 188 different countries. It also issues 25,000 passports a year, mostly to United States citizens whose passports have been lost or stolen.'[98] Furey remained in London until the end of 2004 when he transferred to Abuja, Nigeria, as deputy chief of mission.

Furey's successor was John Patrick Caulfield who arrived in London in July 2005 from serving as deputy chief of mission in Lima. Much of his career had been spent in Latin American countries and the pattern continued when in September 2008 he was posted to Venezuela where he was appointed chargé d'affaires ad interim. This appointment arose as a result of uneasy relations between the United States and the government of President Hugo Chavez, which had led to the ambassador Patrick Duddy being expelled that month. Derwood K. Staeben arrived in September 2008 from serving as special adviser in the Department's Office of Passport Services, within the Bureau of Consular Affairs. The following month, Ambassador Robert Tuttle announced that the State Department planned to sell the embassy building, build a new one in Wandsworth, South London, and launch a design competition for the new building. 'The eventual move will cause a major upheaval for all sections of the embassy, but perhaps more so for the consular section which deals with such large numbers of the public.'[99] In November 2009, the State Department signed a contract with the Qatari Diar Real Estate Investment Company for the sale of the existing embassy building.[100] The design competition attracted considerable interest from architectural firms and in the first round, 37 submitted proposals, which was reduced to nine in the second round, and then four for the final phase. The winning design was announced in February 2010, the ground-breaking took place in 2013 and the move-in took place on 16 January 2018.[101] In 2011, Staeben was succeeded by David C. Stewart who had held the same appointment in the Berlin Embassy a year or two previously. He was succeeded in 2014 by Debra Heien whose previous post was in Kabul. She remained until 2017 when she was succeeded by Karen Ogle, who arrived from a similar appointment at the consulate general in Hermosilo, Mexico.

By way of a postscript, it is well known that the London Embassy has two constituent posts in the United Kingdom, the consulates general in Edinburgh and Belfast. Less well known, however, is that it has another one, but not in the United Kingdom. For historical reasons, the consulate general in Hamilton, Bermuda, has been a constituent post of London for many years, despite a recommendation in 2006 that responsibility for it should be transferred to the Department's Bureau of Western Hemisphere Affairs, and possibly to the Bureau's Fort Lauderdale Regional Centre.[102] The consulate general in Hamilton is also unique in being the only consulate that is occasionally headed by a political appointee. The breakdown of appointees from 1994 until 2016 is: Robert Farmer, 1994–1999 (political); Lawrence Owen, 1999–2000 (political); Denis Coleman, 2002–2004 (political); Gregory Slayton, 2005–2009 (political); Grace Shelton, 2009–2012 (career); Robert Settje, 2012–2015 (career); and Mary Ellen Koenig, 2015– (career).[103]

Chapter Nineteen

NEWCASTLE UPON TYNE

Newcastle upon Tyne is the principal city and port of the north-east of England and was formerly famous for its major shipbuilding industry, coal exports, engineering and other heavy industries. Nowadays, it is a vibrant commercial city with two world-class universities.

By 1824 the United States had established its first consular presence in the city in an agency headed by Matthew Plummer, a local ship and insurance broker with offices on the Quayside.[1] The extant records do not show when he was appointed, but his company traces its existence to at least 1811.[2] The agency reported to the consul at Hull. A consular agency is the equivalent of an honorary consulate, but Plummer often seemed uncertain of his status, describing himself variously as consul, vice consul and consular agent.[3] His consular income was derived from the fees that he charged which, throughout the 1830s, averaged just over $120 every six months. In 1831 and 1832 a serious outbreak of cholera occurred in the consular district, starting in nearby Sunderland and spreading rapidly throughout the country.[4] There was much consular activity, preparing reports for the consul at Hull, who forwarded them to the State Department. In Newcastle and Gateshead during December 1831 and early January 1832, 345 new cases were notified, 91 deaths occurred and 220 victims made recoveries.[5] It is not clear when Plummer relinquished his appointment, although it was probably in 1855. He died on 25 December 1856.[6]

In 1855, Albert Davy, the consul in Leeds (to where he had relocated from Hull, while retaining a vice consul there) appointed his son Herbert as vice consul at Newcastle.[7] The post remained unsalaried, with Herbert deriving his income from fees, which were fairly generous considering the largely routine nature of the duties. For example, during the quarter ended 30 June 1857 they amounted to $232. This was worth almost £5,000 in 2016.[8] One of Herbert Davy's early tasks was dealing with deserters from American ships arriving in Newcastle, reporting that: 'The extent to which desertion … is now so great that at one time not fewer than 108 men deserted from American vessels in the Tyne without any just cause.' He drew up a document authorizing the River Tyne police to apprehend the deserters and return them to their ships. However, the mayor and magistrates of the borough of Tynemouth ruled that as there was no treaty between Britain and America on the question of seamen deserting their ships the River Tyne police could not be so authorized.[9]

In 1862, Joseph Henry McChesney of Ohio was the first consul appointed by the president, as distinct from vice consuls appointed by the Hull consul, and at a salary of $1,500. His previous employment had included a spell as a state geologist in Illinois. In

1863 he established a consular agency at Carlisle. While in Newcastle he showed that he was keen to obtain a more prestigious consular appointment and on 13 January 1865 wrote to John G. Nicolay, Lincoln's secretary, seeking to upgrade his position in the consular world and asking Nicolay to put in a good word for him with Lincoln.[10] However, his timing was bad (Lincoln was assassinated that year) and he remained in Newcastle until 1869 when he was succeeded by Major Evan Rowland Jones of Wisconsin. Jones was a naturalized American citizen who had been born at Penylan Farm, Monmouthshire, Wales, and had emigrated to America at the age of 15. When the Civil War began he had joined the 5th Wisconsin Infantry, although under age, and eventually attained the rank of major.[11] He was later editor and proprietor of *The Shipping World*. When Ulysses S. Grant, former US president and veteran of the Civil War, was visiting Britain in 1877 he was persuaded by Jones to visit Newcastle where he received a rapturous welcome. The visit must have seemed like a Civil War reunion because in addition to Jones, Grant was accompanied by two other Civil War veterans, General Lucius Fairchild, the consul at Liverpool, and General Adam Badeau, the consul general in London. The consulate was accommodated in three rooms in 6 Grey Street and during most of Jones's tenure Herbert Davy continued as his vice consul; there were also subordinate consular agencies at Carlisle, Old Hartlepool, West Hartlepool and Sunderland.[12] Jones transferred in 1884 and was appointed consul in Cardiff. This was a familiar pattern for naturalized Americans who wished to retire to the country of their birth. He resigned the Cardiff consulship in 1892 in order to stand for Parliament and was elected as Liberal Member for the Carmarthen Boroughs.

In March 1884, 28-year-old Robinson Locke of Ohio was appointed. He was a frequent traveller in Europe and enjoyed the Newcastle appointment. Writing to his mother he said, 'since I have been here I have found that there were a great many applicants for the place and that some pretty hard work was done by some of them to get it. Newcastle is one of the best consulates in England and the other consuls cast longing eyes at it.'[13] While there, he met Jones, now at Cardiff, and 'saw a great deal of him during the three days he was here [for the annual dinner of the local Welsh Society in March 1884] and like him very much.'[14] He told his father that:

> One of the pleasantest evenings I have spent in Newcastle was at the residence of Mr Charles Mitchell, of the great shipbuilding firm of Sir William Armstrong, Mitchell, & Co. He has a magnificent residence on the outskirts of the city. [...] There were 26 at table, including the Japanese Consul-General from London and a number of his staff; the Italian and Spanish Consuls and a number of prominent business men. The dinner was superb.[15]

While in Newcastle he received mixed messages about his future from his father, David Ross Locke, who was the prosperous owner and editor of *The Blade* newspaper in Toledo, Ohio. On the one hand he exhorted his son:

> Blaine will be elected, sure. Then there will be no trouble in getting a promotion for you, to a second class mission, Switzerland or Denmark or Sweden, or at least a consul-generalship at Paris or Berlin, or some of those big ones. The moral to this, is – you want to keep pegging

away at languages […]. Let wine and beer alone severely, and keep yourself in shape to take a higher place after next March. There is a mission for you or a consul-generalship. Fit yourself for it.[16]

Then a week later, when describing the expansion of the business and the beautiful new private residence that he had built:

I wish you were at home, with a nice wife to occupy one side of the hall. […] But all the same I want you to keep at your languages. Blaine's election is certain, and I am going to move heaven and earth to get you a mission, either Switzerland, Sweden, Denmark, or Portugal. Even if you resign it and come home the week after you are appointed. I want you to have the honor of it anyhow. […] I want next year unless something very big turns up on the other side, for you to come home, sit down in Lane's office and learn his business thoroughly. […] I am getting tired, I assure you. I want you to come back this time with less pounds on you than you did from Germany.[17]

Many of Locke's reports described the high unemployment and destitution caused by the decline of the shipbuilding and shipping industries, both of which were major local employers. For example, in 1884 there were 118 fewer ships built compared to the previous year, 15,000 men were unemployed and 137 ocean-going ships were laid up in port.[18] Public appeals for funds to help the unemployed during the harsh winter 'were right heartily responded to, no less than $20,000 in cash having been paid in to the Relief Fund Committee'.[19] And during 1884, the Boiler Makers Society and the Iron Shipbuilders Society, the second largest trade union in Britain, had 'expended the enormous sum of £171,881 or $836,459' on benefits to members, 'the largest outlay in the history of the Society'.[20]

Locke had been appointed by Republican President Chester Alan Arthur in 1884, but there was a change of administration the following year when Grover Cleveland, a Democrat, became president. This spelled the end of Robinson's consular career and he was asked by the new Secretary of State Thomas F. Bayard (1885–1889) to resign to make way for a Democrat appointee. This was normal practice at the time. However, Locke sought the advice of his predecessor Evan Jones, whom he greatly admired, about the best date on which to resign.[21] He did so with effect from 8 August 1885, and began immersing himself in the family business and getting married the following year. His father died in 1888. The consulate and its agencies were fairly busy during Locke's short occupancy, with more than seven hundred and fifty invoices being certified. Nevertheless, the excess that he had to meet from his pocket to cover clerk hire and office rent was $600, because at that time the official allowances for these costs were woefully inadequate.[22] Nowadays, Locke is probably best remembered for his huge collection of scrapbooks containing press cuttings and other items relating to the American theatre which was acquired by the New York Public Library for the Performing Arts at the Lincoln Center.

On 14 September 1885, Locke was succeeded by Jasper Smith of New York, who had been US commercial agent at Nottingham since 1878. He arrived in Newcastle on 3 November at the office in 6 Grey Street. It was described as:

three stories high, but the offices are not self contained. The first flat is occupied by a Solicitor; the second flat also of three rooms, is devoted solely to the business of the Consulate, while the third flat also of three rooms is occupied by the Caretaker. [...] The rent per quarter is £15 or $73. [...] The furniture is not included on the Inventory as it is the personal property of the Consul.[23]

Questions about this furniture, for which Smith was being asked to stump up funds, and the absence of an allowance for clerk hire exercised Smith for some time, and he frequently requested grants for these. He eventually did receive assistance, and greatly enjoyed his time in the city. 'Aside from the inadequate compensation of the consul and the harsh climate I find Newcastle very pleasant. Our social relations are most agreeable.'[24]

At the beginning of 1889 Smith asked for a leave of absence because his doctors had advised him to leave Newcastle during the latter part of the winter. 'They advise me that my health and perhaps my life may depend on such change. My wife's health is also very unsatisfactory and the doctors advise a change for her.' Leave was granted, but instead of travelling to warmer climes as might have been expected he went to the west coast of England 'where the climate is much milder than it is here.'[25] Herbert Davy, the vice consul, died on 11 June 1889 and had been involved with the consulate since 1855.[26] Smith did not return from his leave of absence and Horace C. Pugh, a lawyer from Terre Haute, Indiana, was appointed in July 1889, although he did not arrive until 6 November; he was there only a year and a half, when he was appointed consul at Palermo. He recalled his time in Newcastle 'as a most delightful period in his life, having been fortunate in being received socially by the best families in the locality'.[27] His successor in 1890 was Horace W. Metcalf of Maine; his previous experience was in shipping, commission and coal businesses in Philadelphia. He retired as consul in 1893 and returned to America to conduct a business agency in New York.[28] William Shand Campbell of New York took over in 1893; salary continued at $1,500 and the fee income generated by the three agencies that year amounted to almost $1,400.[29] Campbell was 'an old-time Democrat' and served as consul in Rotterdam from 1843 until 1861 and in Dresden from 1862 until 1869, when he retired.[30] He had obviously hankered for a return to the consular life, and served in Newcastle until 1897 when he returned to America. Metcalf's business venture in New York had apparently failed to satisfy him because he applied for and was reappointed to the consulship in Newcastle in 1897. In 1902, the incumbents of the consular agencies were: Carlisle, Thomas Slack Strong, solicitor, Bank Street, appointed 25 October 1898; Sunderland, Thomas A. Horan, 45 West Sunniside, appointed 1891 upon retirement of his father James Horan; West Hartlepool, Hans C. Nielsen, 76 Church Street, appointed 15 May 1899.[31] By 1907, the consul's salary had been increased to $3,000.[32]

In 1908, the consulate received its first inspection under the arrangements introduced by the 1906 Act and was conducted by Horace Lee Washington, consul general at large. Metcalf's vice and deputy consul was a local man named Hetherington Nixon who had worked at the consulate since 1892. The offices were still at 6 Grey Street and were rented from Lamb & Edge, Collingwood Street, at an annual rent of $244, or £50. Washington noted that the rent was 'extremely reasonable' and that 'rents, generally, are very high here'. The three rooms were 'lighted by gas', the condition of the furniture was good, but 'a new seal and a coat of arms suitable for placing outside the premises were required'. The chief American import in the district was wheat; there was no longer a direct steamship line between the city and New York and importations were via London, Liverpool, Glasgow and Hull. Metcalf and his wife and daughter lived in 'a residential hotel'. Nixon obviously impressed Washington who described him as 'one of the most energetic subordinates of British nationality met at any post in this country [...] and shows a real interest, and not a perfunctory one, in his work'. Metcalf, on the other hand, 'does not appear to be of an energetic disposition', (he was, after all, 'about seventy-six years of age') and 'leaves the direction of his agents too much to his vice consul'. Because of this, the office's overall rating was 'fair'.[33] Ratings were graded excellent, good, fair or poor.

The consulate was inspected once more the following year by Heaton W. Harris, consul general at large. He took a more critical view of both Metcalf and Nixon, feeling that neither had 'quite kept abreast with the advancement the service has made the past few years'. It was Harris's custom with inspections to arrive both unannounced and anonymously and to be there at the beginning of office hours. He invariably found this to be revealing. On arriving at Newcastle he found Nixon on his own, who told him that the consul would be in at 10.30 a.m. as 'he was living at the seashore this summer and came to town at that time, but that he was the vice consul and if there was anything he could attend to it'. The 'anonymous inspector' said he would prefer to see the consul and would wait. Nixon, 'with some show of impatience said this would not be convenient as he was going to be absent from the office and wished to close the office for a little while and attend to some matter outside'. The 'anonymous inspector' reminded him that according to the office hours at the doors, the consulate was now open and that he, as an American citizen, wished to wait in the office until the consul arrived. 'All this was not in an ugly spirit, but indicated a lack of that sort of tact which is desirable at a consulate.' Nixon attempted to extricate himself later in the day, saying 'he thought the inspector was an agent with something to sell'.[34] A likely story! Harris was obviously unaware that Nixon also ran an outside business, and that this was probably the reason for his wanting to close the consulate for a little while. See the later remarks made by Consul General Nelson T. Johnson about Nixon following his inquiry in 1922.

Harris carried out a further inspection in 1911. Metcalf this time was said to be 78 and Nixon 52, being paid $3,000 and $800 a year, respectively; there was also a 16-year-old youth who had been appointed assistant clerk at $125 a year. Harris reported favourably on Metcalf's personal qualities; for example: 'The Consul has been a man of more than ordinary intelligence, official tact, probity and diligence. [...] The Consul is youthful for his years, is active in movements and much of his work is well done. [...] The inspector has never met a man of the Consul's age of more pleasant personality and kinder heart.' On the other hand: 'He is well advanced in years, and has scarcely felt able physically and otherwise to bring his office up to present standards of excellence. It is not a weak and indifferent administration, but has some of the marks that would be expected of a man of this age.' Nixon was 'a pleasant man [...] inclined to nervousness, old-fashioned in his office methods, runs the office on old lines but is a fair clerk.' Fred

Duke, the clerk, was an 'attractive bright boy, runs the type-writer, assists with the invoice book and with general clerical work [...] will make a satisfactory clerk'.[35]

Harris believed that it would be beneficial to have an American citizen as vice consul and recommended that when a new consul was appointed Nixon should be retained for only a year or so then replaced by an American. The consulate was a busy one, and in the year ended 31 December 1910 dealt with 1,146 invoices, 218 notarial services, 307 bills of health and 2,307 letters, and collected almost $4,500 in fees. He gave the consulate a 'fair' rating, but added that this 'reflects not in the least in the personal qualities of the Consul who is a most conscientious and worthy man. He lacks a year and a half of being eighty years of age. Much is to be made for an officer with this burden of years, which in his case is not so noticeable as in most men of the same age.' He summed up his report: 'It is an old office of fifteen years ago – no worse than many probably were at that time – but not fitted to modern ideas. Fortunately it is the last office of the type in the United Kingdom. Two years ago Leeds was far worse. Belfast was but little better. Burslem was of this type, Dundee was as bad or worse. None are left now but Newcastle.'[36] By 1910, only the West Hartlepool agency remained. Metcalf finally resigned on 12 January 1912, at age 78[37] and asked the Department if he could take with him the old coat of arms that had been replaced by two new ones, as recommended by the inspector in 1908, but this was refused.[38] The Department had a strict policy on this type of request. For example, several years earlier it had refused a request by Wallace Bruce, the consul in Edinburgh, who had asked if he could keep a worn and frayed flag that had flown at his consulate and had been replaced.

Walter C. Hamm of Pennsylvania took over on 16 April 1912 having been consul at Hull since 1903. Before joining the Service that year he had been a literary man and editorial writer in Philadelphia.[39] On 1 February 1913, the consulate moved from its premises in 6 Grey Street, which it had occupied since 1877, to 44 Grey Street, in two rooms rented from the London Joint Stock Bank Ltd at $292, or £60, per quarter. The consulate was inspected in 1914 by Ralph J. Totten, consul general at large. In his view, Hamm: 'possesses considerable ability but his almost total deafness reduces his efficiency to a marked degree' and he rated him as 'fair'. Nixon was still in post, and he too was rated as 'fair'. A young woman, Alice Mitchinson, had been appointed by Hamm the previous year as a clerk and stenographer. She 'is intelligent, reliable, courteous, neat and takes an interest in the work'. She was rated as 'good'. Despite the remarks about Hamm and Nixon, Totten rated the office as 'good'. This must have been due to Miss Mitchinson's contribution.[40] In March 1919, no doubt with a view to his pension, Hamm sent a despatch to the Department suggesting that: 'in view of the importance of Newcastle, the fact that the American Navy Department has created a permanent Naval Port Office there, staffed by a Lt Cmdr and 3 Lts, the Consulate should be raised to Fourth grade and the consul's salary be $4,500'. The Department merely noted the suggestion.[41] The next inspection took place after the First World War, in May 1919, and was again undertaken by Totten. Hamm was still in post, aged 72. Staff numbers had increased and there was a vice consul (Ellison, absent through illness at the time of the inspection), an American clerk (Robert Franklin Freer), Alice Mitchinson (the stenographer) and a clerkess (Barbara Young). Totten was scathing in his report on Hamm, and some of his comments would not be regarded as politically correct nowadays. 'He is neither very courteous nor obliging, being given to too great frankness and abruptness as is frequently the case with very old and deaf people. He is a man of 72 but at the time of the inspection he looked 80. He is stone deaf and can only hear at all when he is at his desk where he has a Dictaphone arrangement. He has just had pneumonia and is still very weak and ill.' And ominously, 'He will not live through another British winter.' Freer received a salary of $1,700; he was formerly vice consul at Bristol where he had married a local woman who turned out to be already married. The inspector regarded him as 'more sinned against than himself at fault, although his common sense and knowledge of the world were shown to be negligible'. Nevertheless, despite this unfortunate blip in his personal life, he impressed Totten with his standard of work and was rated 'excellent'. Miss Mitchinson was said to be 'responsible for all that is good in this office'. She was also rated as 'excellent' and Totten recommended that her salary be raised from $300 to $500 a year. It was the first time that any of the personnel had received the highest rating. The clerkess, who had only recently joined, was rated as 'fair, and improving.'[42] Hamm retired in August 1919.[43]

Totten carried out his third inspection in 1921, and had by then acquired a good overall knowledge of the working of the consulate. The consul was Fred C. Slater, who had been appointed in September 1919. He had been born in Germany in 1864 but had become a naturalized American citizen as a child when his parents had moved to America. He was brought up in Topeka, Kansas, and practised law there for 17 years before joining the Service and being appointed consul in Sarnia, Ontario, in 1909, where he had served until coming to Newcastle.[44] He was absent during the inspection, leaving Russell Mott Brooks, the vice consul, in charge. Brooks had arrived in June 1921, only two months before the inspection, and had joined the Service in 1919 as vice consul in Rotterdam. Previous employment had included paving and road construction in California, working for the Oregon State Fair, practising law, service in the Oregon National Guard and as a sergeant in the US Army.[45] There were no longer any agencies. The rating system had now been extended to five grades: excellent, very good, good, fair or poor. Brooks and the local staff received ratings ranging from 'very good' to 'fair'. Totten expressed concerns about over-staffing and accommodation, noting that numbers had increased to seven, including the consul, yet the consulate occupied only two rooms. The office was 'too crowded' and 'should have at least three rooms, possibly four'. He also felt that Newcastle was 'a little overstaffed as compared with similar offices in this section'.[46] The consulate transacted a considerable amount of business during the fiscal year ended 30 June 1921: 1,707 passports were visaed, 91 passports were refused, fees collected amounted to $22,560, 3,438 letters were received and 3,027 were sent; exports from the consular district to the United States were valued at $3.7 million. Brooks informed Totten that:

There appears to be an increasing bitter feeling against the United States in this District, which has manifested itself in the press and by anonymous communications addressed to the press. This feeling, at first directed against American automobiles, has grown until it is made the subject of editorials in the local press. The chief cause of complaint is the attitude of the United States on the Irish question and the proposed new tariff law levying a heavy duty on steel and steel products. Reprisals by the United Kingdom are urged against the United States.[47]

Totten's concerns about the size of the office were acted on fairly quickly and on 28 May 1922 the consulate moved into improved accommodation at 20 Saville Row.

Brooks seems to have been unaware that a 'bitter feeling against the United States in this District' was also being expressed in other quarters. In June 1922, the North Atlantic Passenger Conference (NAPC) contacted the Board of Trade and reported allegations that Slater and Brooks were making it difficult for applicants to obtain visas to travel to the United States unless they agreed to book passages with American shipping lines. This was strenuously denied by Slater and Brooks. The NAPC was a group, one might say a cartel, of shipping lines on the transatlantic route which agreed among its members such things as common tariffs, classes of passage, and the accreditation of approved travel agents. The Board of Trade forwarded details of the allegations to the Foreign Office (FO) in June and July, together with statements from several individuals who allegedly had experienced difficulties.[48] On 14 July, a Foreign Office official suggested warning the US government, via the British Embassy in Washington, of the tendency of some consuls, without naming them, to press persons going to America to do so on American ships.[49] This low-key course of action would have nipped things in the bud. However, Rowland Sperling, head of the American and African Department in the FO, minuted:

> It is hard to imagine a grosser abuse of the visa system, nor one which would be more hotly resented in the United States if the positions were reversed. [...] To ensure a circular warning it might be advisable to request a reprimand in this case and add that if any more come to our notice we shall be reluctantly compelled to withdraw the exequatur of the Consular officer concerned. We have had another complaint about the US Consul at Newcastle. He was alleged to have delayed clearance of a British ship because he wanted to go to the local races. It is perhaps hardly worth mentioning to the USG [United States Government], though it is evidence of his frame of mind. (The 'Consul' is referred to above as being responsible for what is done at his office, though the actual culprits appear to be the Vice-Consuls.)[50]

The Foreign Office view then hardened and a telegram was sent on 17 July to Henry G. Chilton, the British chargé d'affaires ad interim in Washington, instructing him to inform the US government that 'in view of this highly irregular procedure we contemplate withdrawal of exequatur of Consul Slater and recognition of Vice-Consul Brooks [...] adding that action will be deferred for one month from date of your communication in case state department prefer to remove these officers of their own accord'.[51] Chilton sent the note the following day to Charles E. Hughes, US secretary of state. And so began an unhappy period in US–UK consular relations.

The State Department immediately instructed the embassy in London and the consul general there to make a full investigation into the matter, and a member of the London consular staff was sent to Newcastle to examine all the circumstances. The embassy assumed that the proposed withdrawal of the officers' recognition would not be proceeded with until the US government had had an opportunity 'to develop and confirm the pertinent

Figure 19.1 Group photograph, staff of the Foreign Office 'American Department', 1885. It shows, seated, left to right: Richard P. Maxwell and Sir Harry Jervoise. Standing, left to right: Hon. Louis Greville, Charles Des Graz, James Sant and George Fairholme. Jervoise was senior clerk in charge of the department that was known officially as the American and Asiatic Department. It included China, hence the notice to that effect on one of the cupboard doors. The notice on the door behind Fairholme says 'U[nited] States.' It seems odd that Maxwell is smoking a cigarette in this fairly formal photograph. [Author's collection.]

facts'.[52] On 29 July, George Harvey, the US ambassador, sent Hughes a report by Consul Leslie Reed of his two days of investigations in Newcastle that exonerated both consular officers.[53] Hughes communicated this to Chilton on 11 August and informed him that he would not voluntarily transfer the officers and trusted that the British government would not withdraw the exequatur and recognition before submitting specific evidence to the US government and before giving it an opportunity to present its views.[54] In view of this it is odd that more than two weeks previously on 19 July and unknown to the FO, the State Department had telegraphed the embassy in London: 'Slater [...] transferred to Martinique, West Indies. Should proceed immediately upon arrival his successor, Consul [John] Corrigan now Havre. Brooks assigned Vice Consul Havre, should proceed immediately upon arrival his successor [Alman F] Rockwell, now Vice, Clerk, Brussels. [...] Inform Slater and Brooks and request recognition Corrigan and Rockwell.'[55]

Nevertheless, by 18 August the FO had prepared the necessary draft documents for revoking the exequatur and recognition, one of the officials commenting that 'the action proposed is so rare that we can only produce the one concrete precedent' and that it related to 'foreign consular officers of enemy nationality at the time we were at war'.[56] And on 28 August, Lord Curzon, the Foreign Secretary, sent a long letter to the US ambassador reminding him that the State Department had been informed on 18 July of the circumstances in which the British government had felt bound to withdraw the exequatur and recognition of the consular officers at Newcastle. The reason given for Slater's exequatur being withdrawn was that 'he must be responsible for the action of his subordinate'. It had been hoped that the State Department would have withdrawn both men, hence the reason for giving a month's deferral. Instead, the Department were now asking for evidence, which Curzon said the FO would have readily furnished and were somewhat surprised that no request had been made. As the month's deferral had already lapsed he regretted that the FO's action could no longer be further deferred. However, 'as an act of courtesy' he enclosed three statements made by people who had encountered difficulties when obtaining visas at Newcastle. The local authorities at Newcastle were being informed of the action being taken against Slater and Brooks. Curzon concluded his letter: 'I should add that His Majesty's Government are not objecting to Consul Slater's practice of handing applicants for visas cards of introduction to the agents of the United States lines, although His Majesty's consular officers abroad do not at present take advantage of applications for visas to issue such recommendations in favour of the British steamship lines.'[57] This seems to have put the cat among the pigeons and William Phillips, the under secretary of state in the State Department, who had apparently not yet seen Curzon's note of 28 August, sent for Chilton on 30 August and told him that the consulate would be closed for the present.[58] George Post Wheeler, the chargé at the US embassy in London sent a note to the FO on 31 August saying 'we are just in receipt of a telegram from the Department of State instructing us to close the Consulate at Newcastle at once and remove the archives. Consul Slater and Vice-Consul Brooks have been trans-ferred to other countries. We have no instructions as yet as to how the documents nor-mally authenticated at Newcastle shall be handled.'[59] Immediately, enquiries began to be received from firms in Newcastle about how their US export documentation would be processed. On the same day, Phillips sent for Chilton again to say that he had now learnt with pleasure from the ambassador in London the contents of Curzon's note of 28 August, particularly regarding the statements by the aggrieved passengers, and 'he wished to deal with the question in [a] most friendly spirit. He thought that both sides should lay their cards on the table and that [the] matter should be sifted to the bottom.' During the interview, Chilton mentioned the difficulties now being encountered by local firms, but Phillips said that he had no one he could send as consul to Newcastle at the moment. He did not let on that arrangements had already been made some six weeks earlier, on 19 July, identifying Slater's and Brooks's transfers and their replacements. So much for laying 'their cards on the table'.[60] The FO sent a telegram to the ambassador in Washington on 8 September, saying:

> We understand that archives and furniture are being removed from Newcastle consulate, and there appears to be every intention of closing it indefinitely. [...] Would it not be possible to arrange for some junior official to take charge of the consulate during investigations, which

we understand the United States government are making? Matter is urgent. You should make every effort to secure temporary arrangement on lines suggested.[61]

The FO were correct in their view that the consulate appeared to be closing indefinitely. On 30 August, Phillips had instructed Harvey, the ambassador in London, to close Newcastle immediately, transfer the archives and furniture to Hull, pay off the clerks and messenger with usual notice and compensation, pay the rent and terminate the lease and notify Slater to proceed to Corunna and Brooks to Dresden.[62] These are different locations from those set out in the Department's telegram to the embassy in London dated 19 July, mentioned earlier. John H. Grout, the consul at Hull, confirmed that Newcastle's property and archives had arrived in Hull on 15 September.[63] During the closure, Newcastle's consular business was handled by the Leeds consulate.

The State Department was unwilling to let matters rest, however. On 1 September, Phillips sent a six-page memo to the president (Warren Harding) saying that he had probably seen press reports about this case, and 'you may care to have before you the facts which have led up to this action'.[64] He followed this with another memo to the president on 14 September saying that subject to his approval, it was proposed to send Consul General Nelson Trusler Johnson to Britain on 15 September to conduct a full investigation into the case. The president agreed the following day.[65] In a letter to Herbert C. Hengstler, Chief of the Consular Bureau, on 11 October, Johnson reported that after his arrival in London he had met with Ambassador Harvey who had told him that 'I should not forget that we were in a very strong position as the Foreign Office had blundered, and knew it had blundered.' However, Johnson's own view was:

I do not believe that it is proper to use the visa office of a Consulate to press the advantages of American-owned ships and I am therefore convinced that had this not been done here in England and more especially at Newcastle we would never have been placed in the mess that we are now in. No matter how well meant their efforts were that does not, in my mind, clear away my belief that those efforts were extremely ill-timed and ill-judged; efforts which we have no reason to be proud of.

Despite this, he concluded that: 'While it is unethical for officers to mix the drumming up business for our steamships with their visa work, nevertheless the drumming up of such business is a highly proper commercial function of a consular officer and in no way deprecated by the Department.'[66]

On 17 November Johnson submitted a lengthy and comprehensive report of his investigations. He had questioned Slater and Brooks; visited the consulates at Birmingham, Liverpool, Hull and Southampton to acquaint himself with the methods they used in their visa work; had travelled to Newcastle where he had had interviews with prominent shipowners and steamship ticket agencies; and had visited the Foreign Office for informal discussion with Sperling. Based on all this, he had 'not found any evidence to show that Brooks had ever abused his powers as a consular officer authorised to issue visas, by making difficulties about the visas of applicants who did not give evidence of intention to travel by the United States lines'. He added that certain conditions at Newcastle 'might, and possibly may, have created in the suspicious minds of the agents of passenger steamers, and their clients, who presented themselves at the Consulate as applicants for visas, a belief that the difficulties which they encountered in obtaining a visa were connected with their attitude toward travel by the United States Lines'. He described the two conditions. First, with the exception of the American consulate and one other, all the consulates in the city were conducted by honorary consuls 'from whom shipping services are obtained practically on demand and to whom the shipping and business community at Newcastle have always expected to pay gratuities for services of various kinds'. Second, the consulate:

> appears to have been, prior to the appointment of Consul Slater, conducted in a somewhat loose fashion. The Vice Consul for a long time was a Mr Hetherington Nixon, who maintained a small private agency, located down on the river side, where he sold steamship tickets to the lowest class of emigrants. I was informed that Vice Consul Nixon had regularly accepted gratuities for services to the shipping community rendered after office hours, and that he was dismissed after an investigation into his activities. Vice Consul Nixon was succeeded by Vice Consul Campbell who was suspected of similar practices, but was dismissed for other reasons.

Brooks had arrived at Newcastle on 24 January 1921 and Slater and he had pulled things together to the extent that 'it would appear that the Consulate under [their] administration [...] was more active and alert in the effort to check up on the information given to it by applicants for visa [...] than was the case of the other offices in the United Kingdom'. However, as is further explained later on, Johnson also found that (a) in January 1922 the Department had sent consuls instructions to support American ships; (b) in the same month, representatives of the United States Lines had written to all consuls in Britain encouraging them to promote the use of American ships; and (c) the consulate general had sent a similar instruction to consuls the following month.[67]

The case generated a great deal of official correspondence at the very highest level on both sides of the Atlantic.[68] At one point, Sperling and William R. Castle (chief of the Division of Western European Affairs at the State Department) tried unsuccessfully to devise a form of words that would end the impasse 'to save the face of both Governments as far as possible'.[69] But the affair dragged on for a further 18 months, with disagreements about whether both governments should issue 'identic' instructions to their consuls, whether or not Slater and Brooks should be permitted to return to Newcastle, or be permitted to be assigned to posts within the British Empire, and whether Brooks should be permitted to be appointed to Belfast.[70] Lord Curzon, for example, was unhappy about assigning Brooks to Belfast. However, matters were finally settled, and in April 1924 notes were exchanged between the two governments announcing that an understanding had been reached, Slater had been transferred as consul at Fort William and Port Arthur in Canada, and Brooks as vice consul at Belfast. Charles Roy Nasmith, consul at Ghent, was assigned to Newcastle and on 10 April 1924 was instructed to proceed to Hull in order to obtain the Newcastle consulate's records, archives, seals, flags and so on, which had been stored there, and should then proceed to Newcastle to reopen the consulate. He was informed that a 'special allowance of not to exceed $300' had been granted 'for the purchase of desks, chairs, and other furniture and furnishings which are urgently necessary,' and 'All possible economy should be exercised in the expenditure of this allowance.' He was instructed to forward a copy of the lease, a plan of the accommodation, two photographs showing the exterior of the building and a street plan, and was also granted an allowance of $900 per annum for hiring two foreign clerks 'whose compensation should be divisible by five and twelve'.[71] Nasmith arrived in Newcastle in May 1924 and the consulate was reopened on 2 June in its new location, Mosley Chambers, 28 Mosley Street, rented for £150 annually.[72]

It is apparent from reading the mass of internal official documentation from the two sides more than ninety years later that the FO to a lesser extent but the State Department to a greater extent handled this affair badly. If Sperling in the Foreign Office had (a) accepted the advice of his colleague on 14 July to play things down or (b) taken the trouble to carry out as efficient and thorough an investigation of the circumstances as that carried out by US consul general Nelson Johnson, the FO might never have instituted the proceedings against Slater and Brooks. As instructed, on 18 July, Chilton the British chargé d'affaires in Washington had forwarded to Secretary of State Hughes the previous day's FO instruction about Slater and Brooks, and the following day the Department notified the embassy in London that both officers had been transferred, their replacements named and that the embassy should seek British approval to their appointments. This cannot have been a coincidence, so why did the incident not end there? It seems that the embassy did not follow up this instruction, which would have prevented Curzon writing to the ambassador on 28 August confirming withdrawal of the exequatur and recognition of Slater and Brooks. Also, on 28 September 1922, five days after his arrival in London, Johnson revealed in a personal and confidential letter to Hengstler, Chief of the Consular Bureau, that he had gone through the files of the consulate general in London, finding them 'extremely interesting and illuminating'. He reported that in January of that year the European Representative of the United States Lines had written to all the US consuls in the United Kingdom asking them to do everything possible to develop passenger traffic for the Lines; in February, the Department had sent a circular urging US consuls and diplomats to give support to the use of ships flying the American flag; and in the same month the consulate general had instructed all consuls in the UK 'to encourage the use of these lines by all passengers whom you have reason to suppose are intending to proceed to or return to the United States'. To make matters worse, on 30 May 1922 the consul general had sent a despatch to the Department stating that 'the members of the staff of the alien visa office had been under direction to bring the facilities of the American passenger service to the attention of intending immigrants without, of course, taking any steps to which objection might justly be raised by foreign shipping interests'. The consul general had also asked the Department for instructions for the guidance of consular officers in this work. However, the Department failed to follow-up his request.[73] These events all took place before the FO took its action in July. The State Department were fortunate that this did not become public knowledge as it would have considerably weakened their case. They should have recognized that the seeds of this problem had been sown early in the year and that they had failed to respond to the consul general's request for guidance on it. It is easy, of course, all these years later to criticize the handling of this affair when, as an author, one has the privilege of access to the internal papers of both parties.

The newly reopened consulate was inspected in October 1924 by Robert Frazer, Jr. In addition to Nasmith there was an American vice consul, Richard C. Beer, and three

Figure 19.2 Charles Roy Nasmith was born in Mannsville, New York, and after a short period as a teacher joined the Consular Service in 1907 as a clerk in the Limoges consulate. Vice consul appointments followed in Brussels, Amsterdam and Rotterdam until being appointed consul at Ghent in 1918. Subsequent posts as consul were in Newcastle upon Tyne (1924–1927); Porto Alegre, Brazil (1927–1931); Marseille (1931–1935) and Edinburgh (1935, from where he retired in 1946). During his time in Edinburgh he was a founder member and dean of the Consular Corps in Edinburgh and Leith. He had contemplated returning to America but he and his Scottish wife (who had been born in Belgium) had become so fond of Edinburgh that they decided to remain, and resided there until their deaths. [Harris & Ewing Collection, Library of Congress, Prints & Photographs Division, Reproduction Number LC-DIG-hec-19553.]

British clerkesses. Ratings for all of them ranged from high average to very good. The consulate's absence had obviously been missed because business was extremely brisk during the quarter ended 30 September 1924, as recorded in Frazer's report. Even after the running costs of the consulate had been met it was possible to send a profit of more than $7,000 to the Treasury Department. Most of this had been raised from visa work, with almost fifteen hundred cases processed. Almost eight hundred invoices were certified, five hundred bills of health issued, more than six thousand letters received and more than four thousand sent during the same period.[74] The next inspection took place in 1926, by Louis G. Dreyfus Jr. Nasmith was still in charge, but vice consul Beer had been replaced by Davis B. Levis and a messenger had also been hired. Dreyfus felt that the office was 'very liberally staffed indeed' and recommended losing one of the posts.[75] Nasmith was transferred to Porto Alegre, Brazil, in 1927.

At the end of 1927, William Furman Doty was assigned from St Michael's in the Azores. He was no stranger to Britain, having served previously at Cardiff and Stoke on Trent. Full details of his colourful career, and of his serious eyesight problem, are given in the history of the Stoke on Trent consulate (Chapter 21). He retired from Newcastle on 31 December 1932, at the age of 62.[76] He had announced his intention to retire a few months earlier that year 'in order to save the government his salary and to permit younger men to get ahead. Ordinarily he would not retire until 1936, when he will be 65, but his voluntary action will save more than half his salary.'[77] His replacement in 1932 was Paul Chapin Squire of Massachusetts. He had spent eight years working as a wholesale and retail provision dealer before joining the Consular Service as vice consul at St Nazaire in 1919. Prior to Newcastle, he was consul at Kingston, Jamaica. In 1933, Newcastle was inspected by Homer M. Byington. In addition to Squire, the staff consisted of vice consul Merlin E. Smith, three clerkesses and a messenger.[78] Squire transferred to Nice in 1936.[79] He obviously found the conditions in Nice agreeable, since some fourteen years later after his last posting to Dublin, he retired there and died in 1966.[80]

Harold Playter arrived from the consulship at Ponta Delgado in the Azores. Like many of his generation he had had a varied career before joining the Service, having spent 17 years as a miner, tax collector, farmer and writer of short stories before becoming consul at Saltillo, Mexico, in 1919.[81] He retired from the Service at Newcastle in 1942. Charles Roy Nasmith returned briefly on temporary duty from 1941 to 1942, when Charles Harrington Heisler took over. Further details of Nasmith's career are given in the Edinburgh consulate history (Chapter 15). Heisler joined the Service as a clerk in the Johannesburg consulate in 1914 after having served in the Delaware National Guard and been employed as an engineer with railroad and mining companies in various parts of the world. Before arriving at Newcastle he had been consul in Tunis.[82] Harold Denham Pease, who took over in 1949, had been a criminologist working for the state of California before joining as a clerk at the consulate general in Shanghai in 1929. Prior to his appointment at Newcastle he was consul at Puerto la Cruz, Venezuela.[83] The Newcastle consulate continued in business for only a few more years; Pease was appointed to Cork as consul on 22 September 1953 and the consulate was closed two weeks later on 7 October 1953.[84]

Chapter Twenty

SOUTHAMPTON

Southampton is an important and busy port in the south of England with a long maritime history. In 1620, the Pilgrim Fathers sailed from there, not from Plymouth as is generally thought, only putting in to Plymouth for repairs to their ships. The city was formerly an important port of call for transatlantic liners, and it was also from there on 10 April 1912 that the *Titanic* sailed on its ill-fated maiden voyage. Nowadays the port is popular with luxury cruise ships. The city has close links with the Isle of Wight, about ten miles distant, which is reached by frequent ferry services.

The US consular presence in the area was inextricably linked with Cowes, on the Isle of Wight, which was where Thomas Auldjo, a local British businessman was appointed vice consul in 1790. However, as we have seen, his appointment was not recognized by the British government on the grounds that there had never before been a foreign consul in Cowes. As a compromise, the government was prepared to recognize him at Poole, on the mainland, and to overlook the fact that he was residing in Cowes. His recognition as vice consul at Poole therefore dates from 1791. His status changed in 1816 when he was recognized as consul at Cowes.[1] Southampton came within the Cowes consular district. Auldjo's successors were Americans Robert R. Hunter, in 1823, and William Whetten in 1842. When visiting England in 1842 Joseph Rodney Croskey met his friend Whetten who decided that the consular post was not worth his retention and resigned it in favour of Croskey. Croskey had been born in Philadelphia but on his father's death had left there at the age of seven and under his London uncle's care was educated in England until the age of 16. Returning to the United States he embarked on a colourful career which included travel and business in Africa and Central America. He duly served as consul from 1844 until 1849, when he was removed from office by the newly elected President Zachary Taylor.[2] In 1850 Charles W. Fenton of New Jersey was appointed consul for both Southampton and Cowes, based in Southampton. However his appointment was short-lived, as he found the emoluments of the post inadequate and resigned later that year.[3] The emoluments were obviously regarded as satisfactory by Croskey, as he was reappointed in 1850 at a salary of $1,800[4] and served until 1857.[5] In 1862, he stood unsuccessfully in a parliamentary by-election in Southampton caused by the death of Brodie M. Willcox, the Liberal Party member, but was defeated by William Rose, the Conservative candidate.[6]

William Thomson of New York arrived in 1857. He appeared to have an unusually keen eye for women's fashions of the day. Writing in March 1858 to Virginia Tunstall Clay, a Washington and Alabama socialite, he said:

> I did think of sending you and Mrs Fitzpatrick one of the new style petticoats, so novel, it
> seems, at the seat of government; but, upon inquiry for the material, my bachelor wits were

quite outdone, for I could not even guess what size might suit both of you ladies! Since sending a few lines to you, I have spent a day at Brighton, which is in my [consular] district, and I saw quite a new style and decided improvement on the petticoat. A reversible crimson and black striped linsey-wolsey under a white cambric skirt, with five, seven, or nine tucks of handsome work, not less than ten or twelve inches deep. This style of new garment is very distingue [*sic*] to my feeble bachelor eye, and would attract amazingly in Washington just now.[7]

Thomson served until 1861 when he was replaced by Captain John Britton of New York.[8] Britton was a naturalized American citizen who had been born in Ireland. As a former steamship captain he was familiar with the needs and demands of a maritime consulate. During his time, consular agencies were established at Weymouth (1861), Cowes (1866) and Portsmouth (1867). He served until 1869 when Thomson was reappointed. By 1872, there were agencies only at Portsmouth and Weymouth.[9] When the post was inspected that year the inspector suggested abolishing it and creating in its place an agency under the consul general at London.[10] The suggestion was not implemented, and Thomson was reappointed for the third time in 1878.[11] By 1883, the consulate had relocated from 3 Canute Road to premises in Insurance Chambers, 71 High Street.[12] There was very little business; for example, during the year ending 31 December 1885 only nine invoices were authenticated; even its subordinate Weymouth agency had 12.[13] Thomson served until his death in January 1887 and 'was much respected for his urbanity of manners and courteous demeanour'.[14]

Henry H. Pendleton of West Virginia arrived in 1887. The office was once again in Canute Road, but at number 10. Pendleton was replaced in 1889 by fellow West Virginian Jasper P. Bradley, and in 1893 by Warner S. Kinkead of Kentucky. By now, the salary had been increased to $2,500.[15] In 1898, John Edward Hopley, also from Kentucky but appointed from Ohio, took over the consulship. The offices were now at 4 Washington Terrace, Queens Park, and were rented for $389 per year, and there were reported to be 'about 24 American citizens residing in Southampton'.[16] Hopley had been engaged in newspaper work for most of his life. Richard Jones, the vice and deputy consul, had been born in Wales but had become a naturalized American citizen in 1895. Prior to his appointment in 1898 he had been a purser on one of the steamships of the American Line.[17] Hopley remained until 1903, when he exchanged posts with Colonel Albert Winfield Swalm in Montevideo, Uruguay.[18] Swalm, although a native of Pennsylvania, had been proprietor and publisher of various Iowa newspapers, had served in the Iowa Infantry in the Civil War and in the Iowa National Guard, and had held several other public positions in the state before being posted to Montevideo in 1897. His salary at Southampton was $4,500. The first inspection under the 1906 legislation was undertaken by Horace Lee Washington in 1908. The offices were now at 17 Queens Terrace and occupied an entire eight-roomed, four-storey house, all lit by gas. In addition to Swalm, the staff consisted of Jones, the vice and deputy consul, and two British clerks. During the previous year, 52 steamships of the America Line had called at the port. The consulate was self-sufficient financially, with income for the year amounting to $1,328 and expenditure $716. Exports to the United States were almost $100,000, of which the largest item was automobiles. The office was rated as 'fair'.[19]

In March 1909, Swalm was reappointed to the post and a further inspection was undertaken, by Heaton W. Harris, less than three months later. Harris did not meet Jones, the vice consul, who was 'at present understood to be fatally ill of Bright's disease and not likely to live but a few weeks.'[20] The prognosis proved correct and his successor, John A. Broomhead, was appointed a month later. Like Jones, he had been born in England but during a long career as a master mariner had become a naturalized American citizen.[21] By 1910, only the Weymouth agency remained open, but two years later an agency was established in Jersey. Swalm was described as 'vigorous and active. He was in the army, had experience in the Far West with the Indians [...] and is a somewhat droll and unique character, careless in dress, blunt in speech but upright and capable. [...] He is kind-hearted and popular.' His American wife was 'an educated and attractive lady who has met many distinguished people and presides over her home with much charm and manner'. The office was rated as 'good'.[22]

Harris also carried out the next inspection in 1911. Swalm's salary remained at $4,500, and staff numbers remained the same. The consulate's financial viability began to cause concern, however; expenditure was $7,300 whereas income was only $1,628. Although there was a reasonable amount of business, salaries accounted for the bulk of the expenditure. Swalm was given a glowing report and the office was rated as 'good'. Harris noted that there were 34 consulates in the city, of which 12 were career posts.[23] A further inspection was carried out in 1914 by Ralph J. Totten. Swalm and the two clerks were rated as 'good'; Broomhead as 'excellent', the first time a member of staff had received this highest rating.[24] Swalm seemed ideally suited for the post of consul. In the early years of World War One, when the United States was neutral, he superintended the arrangements for the internment of German prisoners of war. But when the first contingent of American troops arrived in Southampton he proudly marched at their head through the city.[25] He also showed patience and good humour. For example, at the outbreak of the war a small group of Americans found themselves in Southampton trying to sail for Le Havre. Southampton docks were at that time a military zone and in order to sail for Le Havre Americans were required to have their passports visaed by the Belgian and French consuls general in London as well as the American consul in Southampton. The group arrived from London at two in the morning to learn that their ship was leaving two hours later. They hurried to the consulate but discovered, unsurprisingly, that it was closed and they were unable to rouse anyone there. Their activities attracted the attention of a police officer who arrested them for creating a disturbance (they had been throwing pebbles at the windows and the consular coat of arms), but he relented, told them that Swalm's residence was in another part of the city and bundled them into a taxi. They described their reception at Swalm's residence.

Scantily but decorously clad, Colonel Swalm received us, and greeted us as courteously as though we had come to present him with a loving-cup. He acted as though our pulling him out of bed at two in the morning was intended as a compliment. For affixing the seal to our passports he refused any fee. We protested that the consuls-general of other nations were demanding fees. 'I know', he said, 'but I have never thought it right to fine a man for being an American.'[26]

In 1917, the Weymouth agency was raised to a vice consulate under John Crouse Moomaw of Virginia. This was his first appointment since joining the Consular Service in that year; his previous career had been in education and law. It seems that the post was a personal one designed to give him basic consular experience, as he remained only until 1919 when he transferred to Bombay, still as vice consul.[27] Weymouth then closed.

The next inspection took place after the war, in 1919, and was undertaken once again by Totten. Staffing was the same as before. Swalm was described as 'an old man now in his 74th year. He is in excellent health for his age but he is neither strong nor rugged. He is surprisingly active for his years and would go out in any kind of weather in order to be of assistance to any one in trouble.' He is also 'one of the best loved and generally respected men in this inspection district. […] He is known by all in the city and the police salute him when he passes. He and his good wife were splendid in looking after our sick and wounded soldiers.' The consulate's expenditure during the previous year once again outstripped its income: $10,030 compared to $1,109. The inspector recommended that Swalm should be transferred to 'some milder climate for his last consular years'.[28] This was accepted, and at the end of the year he was transferred to Hamilton, Bermuda, as consul where he died three years later, at age 76.[29]

John Marbacher Savage of New Jersey arrived in 1919 from Sheffield. He had had previous consular experience in Belfast and Dundee, had left the Service between 1897 and 1914 to engage in business in Belfast and New York, and then rejoined in Sheffield in 1914. The next inspection of Southampton took place in 1921, once again by Totten. Staffing levels had increased; in addition to the American vice consul, Roy Bower, there was one American clerk and three British clerks (including, for the first time, a clerkess). Additional staff were required because of the substantial increase in the number of persons seeking visas for travel to the United States, some 12,500. This in turn had a positive effect on the consulate income. After expenditure was met, there was a surplus of $11,500.[30] Savage's salary in 1922 was $4,000.[31] Further inspections took place in 1923 and 1927. A small profit of $1,200 was made in 1923. In 1927, the numbers seeking visas increased once again, as did the numbers of staff required to process them. In addition to Savage, there were three vice consuls and seven British clerks. At the end of the year, the consulate showed a record profit of more than $17,000.[32] In July 1927 the consulate moved to a brand new block of modern offices at Havelock Chambers, 20–22 Queen's Terrace. The offices included 10 rooms on the third floor at an annual rent of $2,114, or £425. Savage retired from the Service in Southampton in 1929 by which time only the Jersey agency remained.[33]

For some reason, two consuls were appointed in 1929. John Herman Bruins of Michigan arrived in August and James Barclay Young of Washington, DC, arrived in November. Both were consuls but of different classes; Young was the senior officer, receiving a salary of $6,000 whereas Bruins' salary was $3,500.[34] During the First World War Bruins had served as an officer in military intelligence and afterwards had worked as a financial and credit reporter before joining the Service as a consular assistant in 1923. Subsequent postings were to Riga and then to Singapore from 1926 to 1929. He remained at Southampton until 1931 when he transferred to Hamburg.[35] Before joining the Service as a consular assistant in 1909, Young had been a newspaper reporter and secretary to a member of Congress. Prior to coming to Southampton he had been at Venice since 1920. He remained at Southampton until 1933 when he transferred to Callao-Lima, Peru, as consul general.[36] By now, there were no longer any agencies.

Howard Karl Travers of New York arrived in 1933 from Palermo. After a short career in business and military service he joined the Service in 1919 as vice consul at Hull. He remained at Southampton until 1936 when he transferred to Budapest.[37] His successor, George Kenneth Donald of Alabama was appointed consul general, the first time that Southampton had been headed by an officer of that class. He had joined the Service in 1914 as consul at Maracaibo, Venezuela. Prior to transferring to Southampton he had been consul general at Milan since 1934. His reports from war-ravaged Southampton are described in Chapter 4. At the end of 1940 he was transferred to Windsor, Ontario, and the consulate was closed.[38] Announcing its closure, the State Department said it was because 'the office has no functions, since no tourists from the United States now visit Southampton and no American vessels may apply there for cargo clearance'.[39] This was an almost Kafkaesque understatement, entirely avoiding the real reason, which was that Southampton was under constant attack by the Luftwaffe.

The consulate was reopened at the end of 1945 by William Hopkins Beck, of Washington, DC, also a consul general. He had 10 years' experience in a variety of careers, including military service and working for the National Geographic Society, before joining the State Department in 1920. Many of his subsequent assignments during the next nine years were accompanying secretaries of state on ad hoc missions, before being appointed consul general at Ottawa in 1931. Prior to arriving at Southampton he had been consul general at Hamilton, Bermuda.[40] During his time at Southampton there were three vice consuls. After Beck, the consulate was headed by a succession of consuls: Samuel Gale Ebling (1949–1950), Joseph P. Ragland (1950), John C. Pool (1954–1956), Robert J. Cavanaugh (1956–1957) and James F. Grady (1957), until in 1962 Roy L. Wade arrived as consul general.[41] He was assisted by William A. Mucci, consul, and by this stage there was little call for an American consular presence in the city. It was no great surprise, therefore, that the consulate was finally closed on 31 October 1965.

Chapter Twenty-One

STOKE ON TRENT

Stoke on Trent, in Staffordshire, known locally as Stoke, was formed in 1910 from an amalgamation of six towns – Tunstall, Burslem, Hanley, Stoke, Fenton and Longton – and became a city in 1925. The main industry in all these towns was the production of earthenware and stoneware, and among the dozens of companies were world-famous ones such as Royal Doulton, Spode and Wedgwood. Such was the concentration of these industries that the area was known as 'The Potteries'.

Over the years the location of the US consulate changed in line with the municipal changes, but it was always unique since there were no other consulates in any of the towns. The first consular office was an agency established in Tunstall in 1863 headed by Thomas Llewellyn; by 1869 it had been upgraded to a consulate headed by J. S. Runnels[1] and moved to Burslem in 1877 (although it still retained the name of Tunstall), and then finally to Stoke on Trent in 1910. Runnels was succeeded in 1871 by Josiah M. Lucas.[2] Lucas, a lifelong Illinois friend of Abraham Lincoln, had had a fairly chequered career before being appointed to Tunstall. He had been a clerk in the General Land Office, Postmaster of the House of Representatives, an army captain dealing with commissary matters and been nominated (unsuccessfully) for the post of consul at Singapore.[3] In 1873, John Copestake, a local Burslem man, joined the consulate as a junior clerk and began a career that lasted more than fifty-one years.[4] Lucas was followed in 1879 by Edward Ephraim Lane, of Connecticut, who served until 1886. He was evidently held in high regard locally and when he was recalled to the United States he was presented with a silver tea and coffee service by William Woodall, the Member of Parliament for Hanley, on behalf of a number of leading Staffordshire citizens.[5] He died two years after returning to America.

Jacob Schoenhof arrived in 1886.[6] He had been born in Germany but had moved to the United States in his early twenties and become a naturalized American citizen. He had been in the wholesale lace business for many years until retiring in 1884. An expert in textile tariffs, wages and economics he was appointed to Burslem by President Grover Cleveland 'under the belief that his observations there would be of value to the Government'.[7] The consulate offices were composed of two rooms in Queen Street, Burslem. Business was brisk, and in 1885 the consulate certified more than 3,100 invoices.[8] Schoenhof was succeeded in 1890 by William Burgess of New Jersey, a leading figure in the American pottery industry. In 1879, he had established the pottery firm of William Burgess and Company before moving to New Jersey where he founded the International Pottery Company. He accepted the consulship, his only foray into consular activities, 'because every manufacturing potter in the United States signed a petition requesting

President Harrison to appoint him'.[9] He was therefore a very partial observer comparing the English pottery industry with the American one. During their time in 'The Potteries' he and his wife participated in an unusual event that his son John recalled years later.

A big event that is particularly vivid in my recollection is the visit to our home [in Alsager] of Buffalo Bill. [...] The American Consul was the one to entertain him. [...] The great day of the big [Buffalo Bill] show followed close after 'Buffalo Bill's' visit to us. We proceeded to the nearby city [Stoke on Trent] and took our place on the large open stands. Soon someone came for Father and Mother and asked them to go with them to where the famous old 'Deadwood Coach' was getting ready for its drive across the large arena. They were to be the travellers in the old mail coach. [...] Presently we saw a little band of Indians creeping along one side of the grounds, and then from an opening at the far end came the 'Deadwood Coach' drawn by six horses and accompanied by a guard of scouts. We knew, of course, that Mother and Father were in the coach. When this group got to the middle of the grounds directly in front of us, we saw that the scouts scented danger. The Indians and their horses had been concealed but now they came out in the open and swooped down upon the coach and its guard. Terrific firing followed. Indians and scouts were 'killed' and their Indian or scout riders lay behind them and shot over their 'dead bodies'. [...] And we were glad to see our parents come back alive to their places by us. Father and we kids had enjoyed the whole affair. As I remember, Mother was thrilled but a little frightened when 'the Indians fired straight at her from right outside the window'. After the performance we were conducted to the tents of the Indians, they were prisoners of the US government under the custody of Buffalo Bill. This group had been in the battle of Wounded Knee and had taken part in the activities of Custer and his men. The chief 'Sitting Bull' was there, seated in his tent. He shook hands with us and grunted.[10]

On 3 March 1893, the day before President Cleveland was inaugurated, the departing consul Burgess issued a report on the state of the Tunstall pottery industry. The State Department delayed its publication for almost a year, before publishing it together with a report by Burgess's successor, Wendell C. Warner, dated 17 February 1894. When the two reports were compared it showed that Burgess had 'reduced every benefit that the English workman derived from his labor, and exaggerated every burden he has to bear'. On the other hand, Warner:

aiming only to report facts, has stated just what the circumstances are, lets the reader into the facts about the alleged burdens reported by his predecessor, and by giving some price lists of the same articles as reported by Mr Burgess has shrunk many of Mr Burgess's prices, and has supplied the believers in the Burgess report with a reasonable explanation of the failure of the Tunstall potters to emigrate at once to the United States upon the appearance of the Burgess report.

As another example of Burgess's partial reporting he 'did not tell the State Department, in his last report, what the Tunstall potters earn. In going into the "cost of living" in Tunstall, it might have occurred to him that the facts in regard to what a man spends to support himself and family depend for their interest to the student of political economy somewhat upon a knowledge of his earnings.'[11] As Burgess was so closely identified with

Figure 21.1 William Burgess of New York City was founder and president of the International Pottery Company of Trenton, New Jersey, and a leading lobbyist and supporter of the United States Pottery Manufacturers Association. His appointment as consul in Tunstall, in the heart of the English Potteries District, from 1890 until 1893 was therefore hardly that of an impartial observer. He used his time there to compare the pottery industries in the two countries. His final report on the local pottery industry in Tunstall was severely criticized, leading to the State Department issuing a more balanced and accurate one by his successor, Wendell Warner. The consulate moved to nearby Stoke on Trent in 1910. [Courtesy of Douglas Burgess, Fremont, California.]

and protective of the American pottery industry, the decision to appoint him to Tunstall was perhaps unwise.

As we have seen, Wendell C. Warner of New York succeeded Burgess in 1893. Unlike Burgess, his reports were always balanced. He remained until 1897 when William Harrison Bradley of Chicago arrived. The son of the late William H. Bradley, who for many years had been Clerk of the US Court at Chicago, his previous service had been as consul at Nice from 1889 until 1893. During his time in Nice he had been informed that he would be transferred to Copenhagen to replace the consul who had been removed because of alleged irregularities. However, Bradley had declined the appointment and retired from the Consular Service. After a four-year absence, he rejoined the Service in 1897 and was posted once again to Tunstall. Business activity there continued at a high level, and during the year ending 30 June 1901 the value of exports to the United States from the district was almost three million dollars. When he left in 1903 he transferred to Manchester where he served until 1907, three years as consul and one year as consul general.[12] William P. Smyth of Missouri arrived at Tunstall in 1903 from Hull, where he had been consul since 1897. Before joining the Consular Service he had been in charge of the Republican Party's press bureau at Chicago.[13] In 1905, the consulate relocated to Burslem, occupying rooms on the ground floor of a small building at 16 Moorland Road.

Edward B. Walker, a New York lawyer who succeeded Smyth in 1906, was the first holder of the post to experience an inspection under the 1906 Regulations. The inspector was Horace Lee Washington, who began his 1908 report by stating that if the legislation then going through Parliament to unify the six towns under the name of Stoke was enacted then the consulate should move from Burslem to Stoke, which it did in 1910. Exports to the United States from the consulate district remained high, exceeding three million pounds annually, and more than four thousand certificates had been certified, which had generated a fee income of almost $13,000. The consulate 'rates as an important office' and the post 'is not sufficiently recognized by a salary of $3,000 and might be graded as Class Six at a salary of $5,500'. Washington had few comments to make about Walker other than 'the consul's habits are good. His recreations are golf, and short trips at close of week with his family. He has been in poor health, and has suffered from neuritis.' However Walker's wife received a more positive report. 'His wife is of undoubted assistance to him in the community, as she has interested herself in local movements of a charitable nature, and is understood to be generally liked.' Copestake, the British vice consul, 'in good health, but slightly deaf', was regarded as 'not altogether suitable for the position of Vice Consul, and [...] the efficiency of the office would be increased by the appointment of another Vice Consul, making Mr Copestake Deputy [...] and continuing him, at a reduced salary, as Clerk'. He reinforced this by concluding 'It appears that the tone of this office, by reason of the influence of the Vice Consul who has been here so many years, is more British than American [and] appears to warrant a rating that can not be marked higher than FAIR.'[14] The Department agreed with this and later in the year sent a young American, J. Preston Doughten, to become vice and deputy consul. However, it added that 'the Department appreciates the faithful services of Mr Copestake and will retain him as Second Clerk in the office at a salary of $400 a year. He will also be appointed Deputy Consul when Mr Doughten is appointed Vice and Deputy Consul.'[15] This huge salary cut must have come as a blow to Copestake, as his salary at the time of the inspection was $800; it was softened slightly by an increase of a hundred dollars four months later.[16] The complaint about the consulate being more British than American was a fairly common one made by inspectors but it was inevitable, since in most cases there were always permanent British staff who provided essential continuity to keep offices running smoothly during the frequent changeovers of American consuls. A further inspection took place the following year, by Heaton W. Harris. The personnel remained unchanged and the office's rating remained as 'fair'. Doughten received a good report but Harris believed it 'a little doubtful whether the young man, who is understood to have well-to-do parents and to be an only son, will care to remain in the service when he discovers that the bulk of the work is clerical with a fair element of drudgery in it'.[17] The assessment proved wrong, however; although Doughten remained for less than two years he continued in the Service and his subsequent postings included Kobe, Calcutta, Moscow, Brussels, Washington, Warsaw and London.[18]

Harris inspected the consulate once again in 1911, by which time it had moved to Stoke on Trent and was accommodated in premises in King's Chambers, Wolfe Street. The personnel were unchanged except that Doughten had been replaced by a young female stenographer. The value of exports to the United States had decreased slightly to just under two and a half million dollars, with three thousand invoices certified. In overall terms the consulate was self-financing: office receipts were approximately $9,300, while expenditure was $4,700.[19] Walker resigned from the Service later that year.[20] The next inspection was in 1914 and was undertaken by Ralph J. Totten. The new consul was Robert S. S. Bergh, a naturalized American citizen who had been born in Norway. Originally a pharmacist, he had joined the Consular Service in 1898 in Gothenburg and had come to Stoke on Trent from Belgrade.[21] Totten felt that Bergh's 'efficiency would be doubled if he were sent to a post where his knowledge of languages could be used. [He could speak and read Norwegian, Swedish, German, Danish, Servian [sic], and French.] He is badly out of place in England and suffers from rheumatism due to dampness.' He and his American wife had five children and 'the family contribute favorably to his standing'. His personal rating was 'good'. By this date, Copestake's salary had been restored to $800 and he was rated as 'good'. Pattie Plant, the alliteratively named young female stenographer, was rated as 'excellent' and the overall rating of the office was now 'good'. There was little change in the value of exports and the office continued to be self-financing.[22]

Due to the First World War, the next inspection did not take place until 1919. It was carried out once again by Totten, and the personnel remained unchanged from his previous inspection. Bergh was now age 67, and his health was recorded as 'very poor'. Indeed, Totten reported that 'He is very miserable and unhappy in Stoke, which is one of the worst posts in the European inspection district. [...] To make matters worse the climate is bad and the smoke is horrible.' An idea of the smoke pollution created by the ceramics and stoneware industries may be gained from the following account.

> On average, bottle ovens were fired once a week. [...] It required about fifteen tons of coal to fire one bottle oven once, and almost half the heat generated would go up the bottle shaped chimney as smoke. The smoke, emerging sixty feet up, would eddy and curl down onto the buildings and street, even entering workshops and houses through ill-fitting windows and half open doors, so that the air became terribly polluted.[23]

Totten continued: 'Mr Bergh will almost certainly die, as his wife did, if he is left another year at Stoke. Besides the health and personal reasons for the transfer of this officer there is the Service reason, that his knowledge of languages and his training make him far more valuable for use on the continent than in an English speaking post.' He also noted that Bergh's two 'attractive daughters' who remained with him had 'great linguistic ability [and] would be a great help to him in such a post'. The office was rated 'very good' for the first time and Copestake, also for the first time, was rated as 'excellent', as was the stenographer once again. The value of exports to the United States for the year was just over three million dollars. Although Totten noted that 'This is one of the most economically administered offices in Britain,' the office's expenditure now exceeded income. The writing was on the wall. Despite all the high ratings that he had given, Totten began to signal the fate of the consulate:

> The office has become a most unimportant invoice post. [...] The work of the office, consisting as it does almost entirely of invoice work, could be divided among Birmingham, Liverpool, Nottingham and Manchester and none of these offices would realize any change had taken place. There are entirely too many inland British posts where the American interests and possibilities of trade extension are practically nil, and Stoke is one of the most useless.[24]

Bergh was assigned in September that year to a post in a warmer climate, Guadeloupe, but declined it and was assigned the following month to Stavanger where he died in 1923 at the age of 71.[25]

The next inspection took place in 1921 and was undertaken once more by Totten. Bergh's replacement was William Furman Doty, of Brooklyn, New York, although the officer in charge at the time of the inspection was shown as George W. Young. Copestake and Plant, the stenographer, were still in place. The office address was now Lloyd's Bank Building in Wolfe Street. Doty had an unusual background. He was educated at Princeton Theological Seminary; thereafter studied law; was a page in the US Senate; a teacher in Alaska; worked in a reindeer enterprise on St Lawrence Island, Alaska; and was a minister and missionary in the United States, Alaska (not part of the United States until 1959) and Tahiti. He became a clerk in the consulate at Tahiti and after passing the consular examination became consul there in 1902. His consular career after this took him to Riga, Nassau and Cardiff from where he was assigned to Stoke in 1920.[26] The consulate's financial situation had now improved: the value of exports to the United States increased to more than five and a half million dollars, and there was a surplus of almost $7,500 on the office's running costs; business activity also increased, with almost two thousand letters received and one thousand sent, and a significant amount of work generated by visa applications and notarial services. Nevertheless, Totten concluded, once again, that 'The office is a result of the old days when invoices had to be sworn to in person and has now no meaning or usefulness with the modern system of type samples for appraising.' He stopped this time at recommending closure but said that 'the office could easily be conducted by a Vice Consul de Carrière class III [a career officer as opposed to a civilian], provided he was unmarried'.[27]

The consulate was next inspected in 1924, by Robert Frazer Jr. Personnel remained the same as at the previous inspection but an additional clerk had been taken on. Business activity was still satisfactory and there was a small surplus on the office's running costs. The British staff all received very positive reports but Doty's eyesight was noted as a significant problem. Frazer reported: 'There is no doubt that Mr Doty, who is unquestionably most conscientious, industrious, and sincerely desirous of doing better trade promotion work, labors under several severe handicaps. His eyesight is so poor that he is obliged to use a magnifying glass, he said, of some 19 inches diameter, with the result that he is virtually unable to read or write except to a very limited extent.'[28] His problems had been highlighted years earlier when his consulate at Riga was inspected in 1911. The inspector, Alfred L. M. Gottschalk, noted at the time that Doty was 'an ex-drayman, almost blind and very nervous'.[29] The description of 'ex-drayman' seems odd. While in many careers these reports might have heralded compulsory retirement on medical grounds they did not do so for Doty. Less than two months after the inspection he was transferred from Stoke to the Azores, and three years later to Newcastle upon Tyne from where he eventually retired in 1932.[30] He appears again in the histories of the Cardiff and Newcastle upon Tyne consulates (Chapters 11 and 19). Frazer concluded his report with the now familiar note about the consulate's future: 'It is hardly felt that any considerable disadvantage would be entailed were the office closed altogether. It is only 37 miles from Manchester. [...] Services could be performed at Manchester as well as at Stoke.'[31]

The final inspection of the consulate took place in December 1926 and was undertaken by Louis G. Dreyfus Jr. The consul was Renwick S. McNiece, who had arrived from the consulship at Ponta Delgada in the Azores to where Doty had been transferred. The three British staff continued to receive positive reports, and the value of exports to the United States during the year remained high at more than three and a half million dollars. Almost five thousand invoices had been certified, more than two thousand letters had been received and more than fifteen hundred sent. The consulate's running costs also showed a surplus of almost $5,500, which was remitted to the Treasury. It was noted that the clerk, John Copestake, had by then given more than fifty-one years of service.[32] After McNiece's appointment, the consulate was headed by vice consuls, the last of whom was Davis B. Levis of Illinois, appointed in 1929. The consulate closed on 1 October of that year.[33]

Chapter Twenty-Two

AN EVOLVING, ADAPTIVE SERVICE

The book has provided a *tour d'horizon* of the early US Consular Service and its modern successor and of their activities in Britain from 1790 to the present day. There is no doubt that considerable improvements have been made in the institution over that period and that it continues to develop, taking advantage of new technological innovations. Despite this, there remains a feature that not only has never been tackled but on the contrary has seen an increase. Namely, political appointments.

Although the United States came late to establishing a consular service compared to European countries such as Britain, France, Portugal and the Netherlands it was a quick learner. Yet it was slow (a) to take account of the many criticisms levelled at the standards of its service by businessmen and others, and (b) to rid itself of the questionable practice of appointing its consuls on the basis of who they knew, rather than what they knew, and of making financial contributions to presidential campaigns, the so-called spoils system. Pioneers such as Wilbur Carr, chief of the Consular Bureau and later Director of the Consular Service, were well aware of the deficiencies of the service and managed slowly to raise professional standards to the level we now see and expect today. Their efforts were helped by the merger of the separate Consular Service and Diplomatic Service into the Foreign Service in 1924. Nowadays Foreign Service officers who have served as consuls, or in other career tracks, can and do go on to senior non-consular posts in embassies, and non-consular staff in embassies can and do go on to posts in consulates. We need only look at some of those officers who have served as consul general in Belfast to see how this works in practice, all of them career members of the Foreign Service. Kathleen Stephens (1995–1998) was later in her career appointed ambassador to the Republic of Korea; Barbara J. Stephenson (2001–2004) was later ambassador to Panama, and in 2010 was appointed Deputy Chief of Mission at the London Embassy; Susan M. Elliott (2007–2009) transferred to the Moscow Embassy as minister counselor for political affairs and was then appointed as ambassador to Tajikistan; Gregory S. Burton (2012–2015) came from a senior post at the embassy in Afghanistan.

Although the spoils system no longer applies to lower-level diplomatic appointments it continues to flourish today for ambassadorial appointments as well as for a large number of other federal appointments. The ambassador is the senior diplomat, the chief of mission, in an embassy, yet many are not career diplomats and owe their appointments to having contributed or 'bundled' a significant sum of money to the campaign coffers of the successful presidential candidate.[1] A small number may not have contributed financially but may be political allies of the candidate. Their appointments are overwhelmingly only to attractive Western European countries, never to dangerous or unhealthy countries such as Iraq or Afghanistan, or in Central Asia. Posts in those countries are given to career officers. As an indication of the interest shown in obtaining an ambassador appointment it was reported in 2001 that key donors to President Bush's campaign were 'jockeying for plum ambassadorships around the world. A list of 1,700 people scrambling for top diplomatic jobs has already been whittled down to 200. There are only 49 vacancies and the White House has been bombarded with candidates' letters of recommendation and other lobbying efforts.'[2] Only once since 1785 has the post of ambassador in London gone to a career diplomat – Raymond G. H. Seitz, who served there from 1991 to 1994. And what is the price for the Court of St. James's, the prestigious London embassy? According to an academic study in 2012 it 'appears to lie between $650,000 and $2.3 million'.[3]

Various bodies have expressed concern about this practice, such as the American Academy of Diplomacy, which reported in 2015:

> The increasing importance of what money can buy in American politics has exacerbated the practice of appointing political ambassadors without appropriate experience or credentials. From the earliest days of the Republic, America has called on the skills of highly talented citizens to serve as ambassadors. Some have served brilliantly. The practice of calling on such individuals should not justify sending abroad ambassadors so lacking in evident qualifications as to make themselves a laughing stock at home and abroad. The sale of office is contrary to law. That it appears to be happening is an embarrassment to the country and adds nothing to either the prestige or the quality of American diplomacy.

Furthermore:

> It is both ironic and tragic that the United States is now moving farther away from the principles of a professional career Foreign Service based on 'admission through impartial and rigorous examination', promotion on merit and selection out for low performance, and advice to political leaders based on extensive experience and impartial judgment. The problem, effectively a return to a nineteenth-century 'spoils system', is government-wide. [...] Other sovereign nations rely almost totally on career professionals to pursue their foreign policy interests. [...] [T]he US is virtually alone in delegating some of its most important and sensitive posts to those with little or no diplomatic experience.[4]

On the other hand, it cannot be denied that there have been many good political appointees over the years. They bring a different perspective to the role due to their varied backgrounds and are unafraid to do things that a career officer might hesitate to do because of career concerns. Even the American Foreign Service Association (AFSA), which is the professional and labour union of the US Foreign Service, says: 'We acknowledge that many talented individuals have come from outside the career ranks to ably serve as ambassadors; however, this practice should be exceptional and circumscribed.'[5] However, there is still a feeling among many career diplomats that the top posts are closed to them. Barbara Stephenson, a former Deputy Chief of Mission in the London embassy, voiced her feelings:

As one of my dear British colleagues said to me, 'I know it is great representing America, such a powerful country, as an American diplomat. But you know what? I can rise to the top of my profession. I can hope to be Ambassador in Washington. You could never hope to be Ambassador in London.' And I think that is one of the downsides of it, the way that we, unlike almost all other Western industrialized countries, have a lot less space for the career diplomats. So that is one of the negatives you start to feel when you are as senior as I am; there are few tracks left open.[6]

The former Consular Service took the lead early in the twentieth century to abolish the spoils system for consular appointments, with one exception, explained later in the chapter. At the time, this was a major shake-up for the political establishment. Consideration ought now to be given for ambassadorial appointments to follow this admirable precedent. It is also important to bear in mind, but is often overlooked, that the Foreign Service Act of 1980 states that: 'Contributions to political campaigns should not be a factor in the appointment of an individual as a chief of mission'.[7] And yet, it is exactly this factor that leads to many individuals being nominated for an ambassadorial appointment. According to AFSA, the number of political appointments between 2009 and 12 January 2016 was 32 per cent.[8] The spoils system goes to the heart of the system of funding presidential campaigns, and donors and others need to be rewarded when their successful candidate takes office. Hence why many federal appointments are filled by political appointees. Realistically, therefore, the system will continue. However, ambassadors, unlike most other federal appointees, represent the face of the United States abroad and it is essential that suitable persons are appointed. Perhaps a compromise could be reached by introducing a modest reduction in the number of political candidates. This is a view shared by, among others, Nicholas Burns, a retired very experienced career Foreign Service officer, who was formerly Under Secretary of State for Political Affairs and, earlier, ambassador to NATO and to Greece. 'I'm not against political appointees. [...] But, in the main, we ought to have – the great majority of our ambassadors ought to be career Foreign Service officers. The historic average is about 70%. I would like to see that at 80%.'[9] This would send the right message to foreign governments, especially close allies, that the United States was sending its best qualified candidates, a number of whom could continue to be political appointees, to their countries. It could also lead to a reduction in the numbers of unqualified candidates who appear before the Senate Foreign Relations Committee seeking confirmation of their nomination for an ambassador post and avoid some of the embarrassing performances given by a few of them when answering questions about the countries concerned. Similarly, it could prevent cases where political appointees had been successful in obtaining a post but a short time afterwards had been obliged to resign their ambassadorships. For example, during the Obama administration the ambassadors to Kenya, Luxembourg and Malta resigned in the wake of critical reports by the State Department's Office of the Inspector General. As an interesting and little-known footnote to this topic of the spoils system, the consulate general in Hamilton, Bermuda, which comes within the responsibility of the ambassador in London, is the only remaining consulate occasionally headed by a political appointee. The breakdown of appointees from 1994 until 2016 is: Robert Farmer, 1994–1999 (political); Lawrence Owen, 1999–2000 (political); Denis Coleman, 2002–2004 (political); Gregory Slayton, 2005–2009 (political); Grace Shelton, 2009–2012 (career); Robert Settje, 2012–2015 (career); and Mary Ellen Koenig, 2015– (career).[10]

Although there has been little sign of change in the ambassadorial appointment system, the United States has been very pro-active in consular-related areas. Consular relations legislation was slow to develop and relied mainly on bilateral consular conventions or treaties between countries. Various attempts were made to draw up multilateral consular conventions in the early twentieth century and the United States was at the forefront of those efforts. In 1925, a draft convention with 11 articles relating to consuls was adopted by the American Institute of International Law. The League of Nations also made a half-hearted attempt but merely 'noted' the question of the legal status of consuls in 1928 and took the matter no further. Arguably the most important initiative pre-World War II was that undertaken by Harvard Law School which in 1932 in its *Research in International Law* journal included a draft convention on the legal position and functions of consuls. While no action was taken on this initiative it was taken up by the newly established United Nations in 1949, although study of the topic by its International Law Commission (ILC) and its Sixth (Legal) Committee did not begin until 1955 when work began on a draft consular convention. The United States played an active role in all the many very detailed, and at times heated, deliberations.[11] It took several years of frequent sessions, during which detailed draft articles were thrashed out, sometimes word by word, before agreement was reached to hold a Conference in Vienna from 4 March until 22 April 1963. Conference delegates spent several weeks deliberating the draft consular convention prepared by the ILC before reaching agreement on 22 April 1963 to adopt the Vienna Convention on Consular Relations and its accompanying protocols. This has largely stood the test of time and is in use throughout the world today.[12] The United States did, however, have problems in convincing several of its own states that they had to observe the Convention, particularly in regard to the right of foreign detainees to have access to their consuls.[13]

The consular role continues to thrive and has changed considerably from the time when it involved mainly trading issues (especially invoice validating) and maritime problems (especially those of seamen). The principal functions nowadays relate to the travelling public, for example, issuing visas, passports, and so on, a service described as US citizen services. The volume of consular business has also greatly increased, notably in the area of visas, with more people travelling on holiday and business. For example, during peak seasons, the London Embassy's consular section can process up to one thousand non-immigrant visa applications and two hundred passport and citizenship cases on a daily basis.[14] The United States has developed new ways of dealing with the increase, particularly by using new technology. For example, it introduced the Electronic System for Travel Authorization (ESTA) for citizens of the United Kingdom and selected other countries to register their details online before travelling to the United States, thus making their entry easier. And in November 2015, it expanded its Global Entry scheme to UK citizens who travel frequently to the United States. This allows expedited clearance through US border controls of pre-approved, low-risk travellers, and has been particularly welcomed by the business sector. Also, as we have seen, the Virtual Presence Post opened in Cardiff in November 2000, and in other cities throughout the world, is a novel way of offering a relatively low-cost remote consular facility in cities that do not have an American consulate. A further initiative is American Corners, 'a physical public diplomacy outpost. This provides Internet access, a small reference collection, and discussion forum, sponsored by a host country's municipal or national government. The US Government only is required to fund the equipment and materials used. […] the host country pays for the staff and the rent of the facility. Security is minimal because no American staff is present.'[15] There are no American Corners in Britain.

The roles played by American consuls have therefore come a very long way since Thomas Jefferson's dismissive remark, quoted earlier in the book, that 'we do not find the institution of consuls very necessary'.

APPENDIX

LOCATIONS AND CATEGORIES
OF CONSULAR OFFICES

Over the years since 1790, the United States had an extensive network of 90 consular offices throughout Britain, including Ireland (part of Britain until 1922), that stretched from the Orkney Islands to the Channel Islands. There was scarcely a town or city that did not at one time have a representative, as may be seen from the following tables. In many cases, the presence was not a lengthy one, and this was particularly the pattern with consular agencies, most of which existed for only a few years. Also, the status of offices often changed, and this is indicated in the following table.

England					
Town or City	Consulate General	Consulate	Vice Consulate	Consular Agency	Commercial Agency
Barnsley				X	
Barnstable				X	
Bideford				X	
Birmingham	X				
Bradford	X			X	X
Bristol	X				
Brixham				X	
Burslem	X				
Carlisle				X	X
Coventry				X	
Cowes	X			X	
Dartmouth				X	
Derby				X	
Dover				X	
Exeter				X	
Falmouth	X				
Gloucester				X	X
Huddersfield	X			X	X

(continued)

England				
Town or City	Consulate General	Consulate	Vice Consulate	Consular Agency	Commercial Agency
Hull		X		X	X
Kidderminster				X	
Leeds		X			
Leicester				X	
Liverpool	X	X			
London	X	X			
Manchester	X	X			
Newcastle upon Tyne		X	X	X	
Nottingham		X		X	X
Old Hartlepool				X	
Plymouth		X			
Poole			X		
Portsmouth				X	
Ramsgate, Margate & Deal				X	
Redditch				X	
Sheffield		X		X	
Southampton	X	X			
St Helens				X	
Stoke on Trent		X			
Stowerbridge				X	
Stroud				X	
Sunderland				X	
Taunton				X	
Trowbridge				X	
Tunstall		X			
Wellington				X	
West Hartlepool				X	
Weymouth			X	X	
Wolverhampton				X	
Worcester				X	
Wotton Underedge				X	

Scotland					
Town or City	Consulate General	Consulate	Vice Consulate	Consulate Agency	Commercial Agency
Aberdeen				X	
Dundee		X			
Dunfermline		X		X	X
Edinburgh	X	X			
Galashiels				X	
Glasgow	X	X			
Greenock				X	
Kirkcaldy				X	
Kirkwall				X	
Leith		X			
Troon				X	

Wales					
Town or City	Consulate General	Consulate	Vice Consulate	Consulate Agency	Commercial Agency
Beaumaris				X	
Cardiff		X		X	
Carmarthen				X	
Holyhead				X	
Llanelly				X	
Milford Haven				X	
Newport				X	
Swansea		X		X	X
Tenby				X	

Northern Ireland					
Town or City	Consulate General	Consulate	Vice Consulate	Consulate Agency	Commercial Agency
Ballymena			X	X	
Belfast	X	X			
Londonderry				X	
Lurgan				X	
Newry			X		
Sligo			X	X	

Channel Islands					
Town or City	Consulate General	Consulate	Vice Consulate	Consulate Agency	Commercial Agency
Guernsey				X	
Jersey				X	

Isles of Scilly					
Town or City	Consulate General	Consulate	Vice Consulate	Consulate Agency	Commercial Agency
St Mary's				X	

Ireland (up to 1922)					
Town or City	Consulate General	Consulate	Vice Consulate	Consulate Agency	Commercial Agency
Athlone				X	
Ballina				X	
Cork		X			
Crookhaven				X	
Dublin		X			
Dundalk				X	
Galway		X		X	
Kingstown (renamed Dùn Laoghaire in 1921)		X			
Limerick				X	
Queenstown (renamed Cobh in 1922)		X			
Waterford				X	
Wexford				X	

NOTES

Introduction

1 J. H. Longford, 'The Consular Service and Its Wrongs', *Quarterly Review* 197 (April 1903), no. 394, 598, 606.

2 596 UN Treaty Series 261.

3 Lord Gore-Booth, ed., *Satow's Guide to Diplomatic Practice*, 5th ed. (London: Longman, 1979), chap. 26.2.

4 D. C. M. Platt, *The Cinderella Service: British Consuls since 1825* (London: Longman, 1971), ix.

5 Peter Bridges, 'Mr Carr Goes to Prague', *Diplomacy & Statecraft* 8, no. 3 (November 1997), 188.

6 Private letter from Sir Hughe Knatchbull-Hugessen to Sir Alexander Cadogan, Permanent Under Secretary, Foreign Office, 20 January 1939. Platt, 241. The grandly named Knatchbull-Hugessen was one of three Diplomatic Service members who served on the Foreign Office committee that was considering the merging of the Diplomatic and Consular Services. He and his colleagues were opposed to a merger and submitted a minority report. The private letter did not form part of their report.

7 See, for example, the title coined by Platt for his book.

8 Zara Steiner, 'The Last Years of the Old Foreign Office, 1898–1905', *The Historical Journal* 6, no. 1 (1963), 59–60.

9 The Secretary of State, Congressional Budget Justification 1 (Department of State Operations, Fiscal Year 2012), 313.

10 Examples of countries in which embassies are not located in their capital cities: Amsterdam is the capital of The Netherlands, but the seat of government and parliament is at The Hague. Hague. Jerusalem is the capital of Israel, but most countries have their embassies in Tel Aviv. In December 2017, President Trump announced that the United States now recognises Jerusalem as Israel's capital. 'The State Department will immediately begin the process to implement this decision by starting the preparations to move the U.S. Embassy from Tel Aviv to Jerusalem.' https://www.state.gov/secretary/remarks/2017/12/276304.htm (accessed 10 January 2018)

11 United Nations, 'Vienna Convention on Diplomatic Relations 1961', see in particular Article 29, http://legal.un.org/ilc/texts/instruments/english/conventions/9_1_1961.pdf, and 'Vienna Convention on Consular Relations 1963', see in particular Article 43.1, http://legal.un.org/ilc/texts/instruments/english/conventions/9_2_1963.pdf [both accessed 3 February 2016].

12 William Barnes and John Heath Morgan, *The Foreign Service of the United States: Origins, Development, and Functions* (Washington, DC: Department of State, 1961), 165; 34 Stat. 99.

13 Charles Stuart Kennedy. *The American Consul: A History of the United States Consular Service 1776–1924,* rev. ed. (Washington, DC: New Academia Publishing, 2015).

14 Department of State, *Toward a Stronger Foreign Service: Report of the Secretary of State's Public Committee on Personnel* (Washington, DC, 1954), Publication 5458.

15 https://uk.usembassy.gov/embassy-consulates/edinburgh/history/ [accessed 6 June 2017].

16 Francis Carroll, *The American Presence in Ulster: A Diplomatic History, 1796–1996* (Washington, DC: Catholic University of America Press, 2005); Bernadette Whelan, *American Government*

in Ireland: A History of the US Consular Service 1790–1913 (Manchester: Manchester University Press/Palgrave, 2000).

17 Sir Ivor Roberts, ed., *Satow's Diplomatic Practice*, 6th ed. (Oxford: Oxford University Press, 2009).

Chapter One Early Colonial History and American Independence

1 An equally historic event took place two days later when James issued a proclamation that the new Union flag, often described as the Union Jack, was to be flown for the first time.

2 For a detailed history of colonial agents and their impact see Michael G. Kammen, *A Rope of Sand: The Colonial Agents, British Politics, and the American Revolution* (New York: Vintage Books, 1974).

3 However, the new independent states continued to have different types of overseas representation over the years and to this day a number of them have offices in Europe looking after their interests, whether encouraging inward investment for their state or promoting tourism for their state. See, for example, the websites of the Council of American States in Europe and Visit USA.

4 Bernard Bailyn, *The Ideological Origins of the American Revolution*, Enlarged Edition (Cambridge, MA: Belknap Press of Harvard University Press, 1992), 1–2, 13–14.

5 Hugh Brogan, *The Penguin History of the USA* (London: Penguin, 2001), 173–74.

6 They are, as shown on the document: New Hampshire, Massachusetts Bay, Rhode Island and Providence Plantations, Connecticut, New York, New Jersey, Pennsylvania, Delaware, Maryland, Virginia, North Carolina, South Carolina and Georgia.

7 Brogan, *Penguin History of the USA*, 194.

8 Circular to Consuls and Vice-Consuls, 13 May 1791, The Papers of Thomas Jefferson, vol. 20, 1 April–4 August 1791, ed. Julian P. Boyd (Princeton University Press, 1982), 401–4.

Chapter Two Creation and Growth of the State Department

1 Samuel Flagg Bemis, *The Diplomacy of the American Revolution* (Bloomington: Indiana University Press, 1957), 32; Alexander DeConde, *The American Secretary of State: An Interpretation* (London & Dunmow: Pall Mall Press, 1963), 2.

2 Graham H. Stuart, *American Diplomatic and Consular Practice*, 2nd ed. (New York: Appleton-Century-Crofts, 1952), 18; David F. Trask, et al., 'A Short History of the U.S. Department of State, 1781–1981', *Department of State Bulletin* (January 1981): S1–S2; DeConde, *The American Secretary of State*, 2.

3 Henry Butterfield Ryan, *A Brief History of United States Diplomacy* (Arlington, VA: Association for Diplomatic Studies and Training, 1996), 4; DeConde, *The American Secretary of State*, 4–5, 7; State Department website http://www.state.gov/r/pa/ho/time/ar/91718.htm [accessed 6 October 2009].

4 Chris Cook and David Waller, *The Longman Handbook of Modern American History: 1763–1996* (Harlow: Longman, 1998), 229; State Department website http://www.state.gov/r/pa/ho/time/ar/91718.htm; Trask, 'A Short History', S3.

5 Trask, 'A Short History', S3; State Department website http://history.state.gov/departmenthistory/people/jefferson-thomas [accessed 6 October 2009].

6 Ryan, *A Brief History*, 8.

7 Bill Palmer, 'A Department on the Move', *State Magazine* (April 2005): 22–23.

8 William Barnes and John Heath Morgan, *The Foreign Service of the United States: Origins, Development, and Functions* (Washington, DC: Department of State, 1961), 131.

9 State Department website, 'Diplomacy: The State Department at Work'. http://www.state.gov/documents/organization/46839.pdf [accessed 4 January 2016].

10 Website of the United States Embassy, London. http://london.usembassy.gov/about-us.html [accessed 3 December 2015].

11 Department of State, Alphabetical List of Bureaus and Offices. http://www.state.gov/r/pa/ei/rls/dos/1718.htm [accessed 7 January 2016].

12 American Diplomacy at Risk (Washington, DC: American Academy of Diplomacy, April 2015), 15–16. http://www.academyofdiplomacy.org/publications/ADAR_Full_Report_4.1.15.pdf [accessed 6 January 2016].

13 Ibid., 51.

14 Gordan Adams and Shoon Murray, eds., Mission Creep: The Militarization of US Foreign Policy (Washington, DC: Georgetown University Press, 2014).

15 Ann Scott Tyson, 'Gates Warns of Militarized Policy', Washington Post, 16 July 2008. http://www.washingtonpost.com/wp-dyn/content/article/2008/07/15/AR2008071502777.html [accessed 7 January 2016].

16 Chairman of the Joint Chiefs of Staff Guidance for 2008–2009, Michael G. Mullen, November 2008. http://www.cfr.org/military-leadership/chairman-joint-chiefs-staff-guidance-2008–2009/p17862 [accessed 6 January 2016].

17 Memo dated 15 December 2009 and attached documents from Defense Secretary Robert Gates to Secretary of State Hillary Clinton. http://www.washingtonpost.com/wp-srv/nation/documents/Gates_to_Clinton_121509.pdf?sid=ST2009122303054 [accessed 7 January 2016].

18 Department of State, Policy Planning Staff. http://www.state.gov/s/p [accessed 7 January 2016].

19 Department of State Foreign Affairs Manual, vol. 6, Handbook 5, International Cooperative Administrative Support Services Handbook. http://www.state.gov/documents/organization/89197.pdf [accessed 6 January 2016].

20 Secretary of State Condoleezza Rice, speaking at Georgetown University, Washington, DC, on 18 January 2006. http://www.unc.edu/depts/diplomat/item/2006/0103/rice/rice_georgetown.html [accessed 6 January 2016].

Chapter Three Establishment and Development of the Consular Service

1 The Papers of Thomas Jefferson, ed. Julian P. Boyd, vol. 17, 6 July to 3 November 1790 (Princeton, NJ: Princeton University Press, 1965), 254n6; William Barnes and John Heath Morgan, The Foreign Service of the United States: Origins, Development, and Functions (Washington, DC: Department of State, 1961), 28.

2 Journals of the Continental Congress, vol. 29, 621.

3 Ibid., 722–24.

4 Ibid., 831–33.

5 Ibid., 850–51; Emory R. Johnson, 'The Early History of the United States Consular Service 1776–1792', Political Science Quarterly XIII, no. 1 (1898): 31.

6 Journals, 854–55; Johnson, 'The Early History', 31–32.

7 http://www.whitehouse.gov/about/presidents/thomasjefferson/ [accessed 3 February 2016].

8 Letter dated 22 October 1997 to the author from Henri Zuber, Ministère de la Culture, Direction des Archives de France, Centre historique des Archives nationales, Service de la Recherche, Paris.

9 Boyd, The Papers of Thomas Jefferson, vol. 14, 8 October 1788 to 26 March 1789 (Princeton NJ: Princeton University Press, 1958), 121–25. Jefferson's comments are dated 20 June 1788. Also available at the National Archives, Founders Online, http://founders.archives.gov/documents/Jefferson/01-14-02-0055-0006.

10 Letter dated 16 April 2007 to the author from Bruno Gravellier, Cultural and Commercial Delegate, US Consulate, Bordeaux; State Department website FAQs; Barnes and Morgan, *The Foreign Service of the United States*, 31.

11 Barnes and Morgan, *The Foreign Service of the United States*, 32; Senate Executive Journal, 9 February 1790, 40. Canton is now known as Guangzhou.

12 Senate Executive Journal, 9 February, 4 June, 2 August 1790, 40, 48 and 54, respectively.

13 Ibid., 23 February 1791, 76.

14 'Thomas Jefferson, Circular to American Consuls, New York, August 26, 1790', in Boyd, *The Papers of Thomas Jefferson*, vol. 17, 6 July to 3 November 1790 (Princeton NJ: Princeton University Press, 1965), 423–24.

15 Ibid., 423.

16 Ibid., 424.

17 The Barbary Coast was the term for the Mediterranean coast of North Africa.

18 Second Cong., Sess. I, ch. 24 (1792).

19 2 Stat. 203, 2 Stat. 433 and 3 Stat. 729.

20 *New York Times*, 7 June 1897, 7.

21 S. Doc. 83, 22d Cong., 2d Sess. (1833), (Serial 230).

22 34th Cong., 1st Sess., ch. 127 (1856).

23 http://memory.loc.gov/cgi-bin/ampage?collId=llrd&fileName=015/llrd015.db&recNum=452 [accessed 5 January 2018]

24 *United States Consular Regulations: A Practical Guide for Consular Officers and also for Merchants, Shipowners and Masters of American Vessels in All Their Consular Transactions*, 1868, United States Department of State, 3rd ed., revised and enlarged, Washington, French and Richardson, 1868.

25 https:fam.state.gov/FAM/FAM.aspx?ID=07FAM [accessed 12 June 2017].

26 Thomas Wilson to Secretary of State Louis McLane, 23 September 1833, RG 59, T199, Roll 1, National Archives and Records Administration.

27 Thomas Wilson to Secretary of State James Buchanan, 25 February 1848, RG 59, T199, Roll 1, National Archives and Records Administration. Wilson's father, Joseph, was of Scottish ancestry and had gone to America where he had become an American citizen. After taking part in the Civil War, he returned as consul in Dublin, an appointment he held from 1794 to 1809.

28 H.R. 630, 29th Cong., 2d Sess., a bill to revise the consular system of the United States.

29 10 Stat. 619.

30 Ibid.

31 An Act to regulate the Diplomatic and Consular Systems of the United States. 11 Stat. 52.

32 11 Stat. 60.

33 Report by William H. Seward, secretary of state, to President Abraham Lincoln, 24 December 1862. H.R. 38th Cong., 1st Sess., Mis. Doc. No. 77, at 4–5; Seward to Hon. William Pitt Fessenden, chairman of Senate Committee on Finance, 9 January 1864, H.R. 38th Cong., 1st Sess., Mis. Doc. No. 77, at 5–6.

34 An act making appropriations for the consular and diplomatic expenses of the government for the year ending 13 June 1865, and for other purposes. 13 Stat. 137.

35 Seward to Lincoln, 24 December 1862. H.R. 38th Cong., 1st Sess., Mis. Doc. No. 77, at 4.

36 Register of the Department of State (Washington, DC: Government Printing Office, 1874), 35.

37 Katharine Crane, *Mr Carr of State: Forty-seven Years in the Department of State* (New York: St Martin's Press, 1960), 55–56.

38 George McAneny, 'How Other Countries Do It: An Account of the Suggestive Results of an Inquiry by the State Department of the United States into the Consular System of Other Nations', *The Century Magazine* LVII, no. 4 (February 1899): 611.

39 William W. Rockhill, 'Evils to Be Remedied in Our Consular Service', *The Forum*, XXII (February 1897): 673, quoted in Barnes and Morgan, *The Foreign Service of the United States*, 123.

40 Quoted in Seward to Hon. William Pitt Fessenden, chairman of Senate Committee on Finance, 9 January 1864, H.R. 38th Cong., 1st Sess., Mis. Doc. No. 77, at 12.

41 Register of the Department of State (October 10, 1874), 56–58; *Act of June 11 1874* (18 Stat. 66); *Act of June 17 1874* (18 Stat. 77).

42 www.whitehouse.gov/history/presidents/aj7.html [accessed 12 September 2009].

43 *The Collected Works of Abraham Lincoln*, ed. Roy P. Basler, vol. IV (New Brunswick, NJ: Rutgers University Press, 1953), 284.

44 Ibid., 300. In the event, the recommendation was not followed and the post at Glasgow went to James S. Prettyman of Delaware.

45 William F. Wharton, 'Reform in the Consular Service', *The North American Review* 158, no. 449 (April 1894): 413.

46 George Makepeace Towle, 'Our Consular Service', *The Atlantic Monthly* 29, no. 173 (March 1872): 303.

47 Henry White, 'Consular Reforms', *The North American Review* 159, no. 457 (December 1894): 721.

48 Francis B. Loomis, 'The Foreign Service of the United States', *The North American Review* 169, no. 514 (September 1899): 349.

49 Frederic Courtland Penfield, *New York Times*, 11 March 1893.

50 Nicholas Kralev, 'Cuts urged in political ambassadorships.' *The Washington Times*, 2 July 2008.

51 'Thomas Jefferson, Circular to American Consuls, New York, August 26th 1790' in Boyd, *The Papers of Thomas Jefferson*, 423–24.

52 Department of State, circular dated 8 August 1815.

53 General Instructions to the Consuls and Commercial Agents of the United States, 1838. United States. *State Department Bulletin*, January 1981, S6.

54 *Association for Diplomatic Studies Newsletter*, November 1988. At that time the Association's name did not include 'and Training'.

55 Ghent, in Belgium, where the Treaty was signed in 1814 ending the War of 1812 between the United States and Britain.

56 *Association for Diplomatic Studies Newsletter*, November 1988.

57 Description of uniform worn by John Campbell White when second secretary in the American Legation, Petrograd, in 1915. Copy of letter dated 19 June 1989 from his widow, Elizabeth M. White, forwarded to the author by Marilyn Bentley, Association for Diplomatic Studies and Training, Arlington, VA, USA.

58 *A Brief History of United States Diplomacy* (Arlington, VA, Association for Diplomatic Study and Training, 1996), 7. It is odd that the order should refer to 'the diplomatic or consular service', since by the time of the order there had been a unified Foreign Service for 13 years.

59 Raymond Seitz, *Over Here* (London: Phoenix, 2001), p. 59. Seitz remains the only career US ambassador ever appointed to London, where he served from 1991 to 1994.

60 Wilbur J. Carr, 'The American Consular Service', pt II, *The American Journal of International Law* 1, no.4 (October 1907): 908.

61 McAneny, 'How Other Countries Do It', 605.

62 Ibid., 610.

63 Ibid., 611.

64 Carr, 'The American Consular Service', 891.

65 Ibid.

66 White, 'Consular Reforms', 712.

67 Ibid.

68 Towle, 'Our Consular Service', 306.

69 Ibid.

70 George M. Towle to Secretary of State Hamilton Fish, 4 November 1869; W. Yates Selleck to Fish, 16 October 1869; RG 59, T165, Roll 2, National Archives and Records Administration.

71 David Gould to Secretary of State William Seward, 12 July 1866; Neil McLachlan to Seward, 30 June 1866. Despatches from US Consuls, Leith, NARA, Roll 4, T396.

72 David C. Davies to Department of State, 12 October 1897; Griffith W. Prees to William R. Day, assistant secretary of state, 13 October 1897. Despatches from US Consuls, Swansea, NARA, Roll 1, T688.

73 Crane, *Mr Carr of State*, 54.

74 Towle, 'Our Consular Service', 302.

75 Ibid., 303.

76 Ibid., 304.

77 White, 'Consular Reforms', 711.

78 Carr, 'The American Consular Service', 905.

79 Herbert Hengstler, retired chief of the Consular Bureau, cited in Crane, *Mr Carr of State*, 56.

80 34 Stat. 99.

81 Carr, 'The American Consular Service', 908.

82 Ibid., 909, 912.

83 Edward N. Burns to Secretary of State Bryan, 15 March 1913, quoted in Crane, *Mr Carr of State*, 148–50, 152. Carr retired in 1939 as Minister to Czechoslovakia.

84 38 Stat. 805.

85 Memo dated 20 July 1922 from 'LCP' [Lowell Call Pinkerton] to Carr. State Department Records, National Archives, Record Group 59, 1910–1929, Decimal File FW125.655. Pinkerton at that time was a consul on secondment to the Department's Consular Bureau. Later in his career he held a number of senior appointments, retiring in 1957 as Ambassador to Sudan. https//history.state.gov/departmenthistory/people/pinkerton-lowell-call [accessed 9 January 2016].

86 43 Stat. 140.

87 Ulysses Grant-Smith, quoted in Crane, *Mr Carr of State*, 260–61.

88 Walter Burges Smith, *America's Diplomats and Consuls of 1776–1865: A Geographic and Biographic Directory of the Foreign Service from the Declaration of Independence to the End of the Civil War* (Washington, DC: Center for the Study of Foreign Affairs, Foreign Service Institute, Department of State, 1986), 36.

89 Barnes and Morgan, *The Foreign Service of the United States*, 206, 229–30, 303, 308–9, 363.

90 A similar amalgamation of services was not introduced into the British system until 1943, and took some time thereafter to be fully implemented.

91 Warren Frederick Ilchman, *Professional Diplomacy in the United States 1779–1939: A Study in Administrative History* (Chicago: University of Chicago Press, 1961), 187–243.

92 Homer L. Calkin, *Women in the Department of State: Their Role in American Foreign Affairs* (Washington, DC: Department of State, 1978), 41.

93 Ibid., 41.

94 Ibid., 22.

95 Ibid., 53.

96 Marilyn S. Greenwald, *A Woman of* The Times (Athens: Ohio University Press, 1999), 11.

97 Calkin, *Women in the Department of State*, 78.

98 In 1925 the Consulate General in Amsterdam consisted of Gale, a consul and two vice consuls. Register of the Department of State (January 1, 1925), 70. Gale was by this time aged 61 and had served since July 1906 in the Consular Service. Ibid., 131.

99 Calkin, Women in the Department of State, 78–79.

100 Ibid., 78–80.

101 Ibid., 80.

102 Ibid., 82–83; State Department, Office of The Historian, FAQs.

103 Calkin, *Women in the Department of State*, 83.

104 Ibid. They had four children; one of their sons also had a distinguished British diplomatic career. At the time that Stogsdall and Summerscale met he was a member of the Levant Consular Service. This was one of the separate, specialized regional British consular services that were based in China, Japan, Siam and the Levant. Personnel served their entire careers within these services, and all were fluent in the relevant languages. The services were eventually merged with the General Consular Service in 1936 and, later, in 1943 into the new Foreign Service.

105 Ibid., 83–84.

106 Ibid., 85.

107 Ibid., 107–8.

108 She was one of six women who had become Foreign Service Officers in 1939 without taking the Foreign Service examinations. This was because it had been agreed that the Commerce and Agriculture Departments would transfer their Foreign Service functions and personnel to the State Department. Molesworth was an assistant trade commissioner stationed in Guatemala in 1939. Ibid., 90–93.

109 Information from Foreign Service Lists and Biographic Registers for the years in question.

110 *The Times*, 5 July 1965, 13.

111 At the time of writing she is President of the American Foreign Service Association (AFSA).

112 Helga Ruge, *Flashbacks of a Diplomat's Wife* (Chico, CA: Clay & Marshall, 2001), 103.

113 60 Stat. 999.

114 Henry M. Wriston, at the time president of Brown University, Providence, Rhode Island.

115 Barnes and Morgan, *The Foreign Service of the United States*, 300.

116 94 Stat. 2071.

117 State Department, *Foreign Affairs Manual*, vol. 2, 133.1–133.5.

118 Ambassador, Embassy London to Secretary of State, *Information Age Diplomacy: Virtual Presence Post, Cardiff – A Model for Elsewhere?*, 28 February 2001.

119 David T. Jones, 'The Under-appreciated Consular Cone', *Foreign Service Journal* (March 2001), 20–24.

Chapter Four US Consular Representation in Britain

1 *Journals of the Executive Proceedings of the Senate of the United States of America, 1789–1805*, 4 June 1790, 48; 7 June 1790, 50; 17 June 1790, 51–52; 23 February 1791, 76; 24 February 1791, 76; and 2 & 3 August 1790, 54.

2 Despatches from United States Consuls in Liverpool, RG 59, letter dated 8 September 1790 James Maury to Thomas Jefferson, M141, Roll 1; Despatches from United States Consuls in Dublin, RG 59, letter dated 26 November 1790 William Knox to Thomas Jefferson, T199, Roll 1.

3 'Johnson to Jefferson, 2 November 1790', in *The Papers of Thomas Jefferson*, ed. Julian P. Boyd, vol. 17, 6 July to 3 November 1790 (Princeton, NJ: Princeton University Press, 1965), 667–68.

4 In order of their opening, the consulates and consular agencies were located in Liverpool (1790, James Maury), Dublin (1790, William Knox), London (1790, Joshua Johnson), Poole (1791, Thomas Auldjo), Bristol (1792, Elias Vanderhorst of South Carolina; came to Bristol in 1774 with his family, was appointed on 4 May 1792 and remained in post until his death in 1816), Plymouth (1792, John Hawker), Exeter (1793, Edmund Granger), Falmouth (1793, Edward Fox), Bideford (1795, Stephen Wilcocks), Hull (1796, George Knox), Belfast (1796, John Holmes), Cork (1797, John Church), Leith and Edinburgh (1798, Harry Grant of South Carolina), Carmarthen (1798, Thomas Morris), Milford Haven (1798, Hugh Falconer), and Glasgow (1801, John J. Murray). Charles Stuart Kennedy, *The American Consul: A History of the United States Consular Service 1776–1914* (Westport, CT: Greenwood Press, 1990), 20; documents forwarded to the author by the US Consuls General, Belfast and Edinburgh;

letter dated 19 January 2000 to the author from John S. Williams, city rchivist, Bristol Record Office; compilation by the author from 57–61 of Walter B. Smith II, *America's Diplomats and Consuls of 1776–1865*, Occasional Paper No. 2, Washington DC, Department of State, Center for the Study of Foreign Affairs, Foreign Service Institute, 1986; *Welcome to the National Archives Rotunda*, General Leaflet No. 18, National Archives and Records Administration, Washington, DC, 1996.

5   *Statistical Abstract for the United Kingdom in Each of the Last Fifteen Years from 1857 to 1871*, Nineteenth Number, Table No. 14, 20, C.609, 1872; *Statistical Abstract for the United Kingdom in Each of the Last Fifteen Years from 1872 to 1886*, Thirty-fourth Number, Table No. 23, 44, C.5173, 1887, respectively. A measure of how increased trade also meant increased work for the consuls can be gleaned from figures for a decade or so later showing the volume of invoices that had to be authenticated. For example, in the calendar year 1885, the London consulate general authenticated 20,486 invoices, Liverpool 10,437, Bradford 7,264, Manchester 6,708, Glasgow 4,166, Nottingham 3,335, Tunstall 3,150, Dundee 2,792 and Birmingham 2,745. *Inspection of United States Consulates in the United Kingdom by Thomas M. Waller, Consul General* (Washington, DC: Government Printing Office, 1887), 12–13.

6   Extract from report by Joseph Rodney Croskey, US Consul, Southampton, dated 31 July 1854. Senate Executive Document 107, 34th Cong., 1st Sess., 603.

7   Database compiled by the author from official published sources.

8   Consular Agent of the United States, Message from the President of the United States transmitting Report of De B. Randolph Keim, Agent, &c., 1872. H.R. 42nd Cong., 3d Sess., Executive Document No. 145, at 82.

9   Lindsay Sarah Krasnoff, Office of Historian, State Department, e-mail message to author, 16 March 2009; *Christian Science Monitor* (3 March 1976), 2.

10 Arlin Turner, *Nathaniel Hawthorne: Biography* (New York and Oxford: Oxford University Press, 1980), 273.

11 Report dated 28 November 1871 by the Hon. Francis J. Pakenham, British chargé d'affaires, Washington, Parliamentary Papers 1872 (c.498) LXII, 151.

12 www.usembassy.org.uk/scotland/history.htm [accessed 17 July 2008].

13 U.S. Department of State Foreign Affairs Manual Volume 3 Personnel, 3 FAM 8914.2. https://fam.state.gov/searchapps/viewer?format=html&query=consular%20agents&links =CONSULAR,AGENT&url=/FAM/03FAM/03FAM8910.html#M8914_2 [accessed 15 June 2017].

14 US Department of State, 2017 Foreign Service (FS) Salary Table, effective 8 January 2017. https://www.state.gov/documents/organization/266594.pdf [accessed 15 June 2017].

15 Isle of Wight History Centre, 'The Cowes Consuls', Newsletter, June 2004. http://www. iwhistory.org.uk/archive/newsapr4.htm [accessed 5 February 2016].

16 Auldjo to Jefferson, 4 November 1790, National Archives. http://founders.archives.gov/ documents/Jefferson/01-18-02-0002 [accessed 4 February 2016].

17 Auldjo to Jefferson, 14 September 1801, National Archives. http://founders.archives. gov/documents/Jefferson/01-35-02-0218 [accessed 4 February 2016]. Auldjo was later recognized as consul at Cowes in 1816. Walter Burges Smith, *America's Diplomats and Consuls of 1776–1865: A Geographic and Biographic Directory of the Foreign Service from the Declaration of Independence to the End of the Civil War* (Washington, DC: Center for the Study of Foreign Affairs, Foreign Service Institute, Department of State, 1986), 58.

18 Seward to Hon. William Pitt Fessenden, chairman of Senate Committee on Finance, 9 January 1864, H.R. 38th Cong., 1st Sess., Mis. Doc. No. 77, at 6.

19 United States v. Badeau, Circuit Court, New York, July 6, 1887. *The Federal Reporter*, Vol. 31, Cases Argued and Determined in the Circuit and District Courts of the United States. July-October, 1887, 697-700. Available online at: https://digital.library.unt.edu/ark:/67531/ metadc36360/m1/717/?q=573 [accessed 7 January 2018]

20 Until 1893 the senior United States diplomatic representative was styled minister and envoy plenipotentiary, based in the legation in London. The last holder of the title was Robert T. Lincoln. From that year onwards the representative was upgraded to ambassador extraordinary and plenipotentiary and the legation became an embassy. The first holder of that title was Thomas F. Bayard.

21 Thomas Jefferson to Thomas Pinckney, Philadelphia, 11 June 1792. [US] National Archives, Founders Online. http://founders.archives.gov/?q=11%20June%201792%20 Author%3A%22Jefferson%2C%20Thomas%22&s=1111311111&sa=&r=44&sr= [accessed 19 January 2016].

22 N. A. M. Rodger, *The Command of the Ocean: A Naval History of Britain 1649–1815* (London: Allen Lane, 2004), 566.

23 Despatches from US consuls in London, RG 59, Joshua Johnson to Mr William Wells, aboard the Victory at Spithead, 10 June 1791, T168, Roll 1.

24 Reliable figures of numbers of American prisoners of war detained in Dartmoor Prison are difficult to discover. One estimate is that there were 'more than 6500 American sailors; [and that] about fifteen percent were the black crews of privateers that had been plundering British merchants off the coasts of England and Europe'. http://www.pbs.org/wned/war-of-1812/essays/prisoners-war/ [accessed 5 February 2016].

25 Hundreds of American prisoners of war were held in Dartmoor Prison and in prison ships. Reginald Horsman, 'The Paradox of Dartmoor Prison', *American Heritage Magazine* 26, no. 2 (February 1975).

26 Reports from the consuls of the United States on the commerce, manufactures, etc., of their consular districts, No. 51, March 1885 (Washington, DC: Government Printing Office, 1885), 480–81, 548–53, 557–67, 621–31, respectively.

27 Message from the president of the United States, transmitting, in response to the Resolution of the Senate of March 2, 1901, a communication from the secretary of state submitting reports from consular officers of the United States giving an account of each consulate and consular agency, showing its principal industries and exports, the surrounding climatic conditions, the general cost of living and similar information (Washington, DC: Government Printing Office, 1902), 231–468.

28 Despatches from US consuls in Leith, RG 59, John Safford Fiske to William H. Seward, secretary of state, 2 January 1868, T396, Roll 4; despatches from US consuls in Bradford, RG 59, W. Yates Selleck to J. C. B. Davis, assistant secretary of state, Form dated 31 December 1869, T165, Roll 2; www.measuringworth.com [accessed 16 June 2017].

29 When the Hamilton Consulate General was inspected in 2006 it was recommended that responsibility for it should be transferred from the Bureau of European and Eurasian Affairs to the Bureau of Western Hemisphere Affairs, thus ending its link to the London Embassy. Obviously this recommendation was not followed. OIG Report No. ISP-1-06-48, Inspection of Consulate General Hamilton Bermuda, August 2006. https://oig.state.gov/system/files/146706.pdf [accessed 20 January 2016].

30 An act to regulate the Diplomatic and Consular System of the United States, August 18, 1856. 11 Stat. 52.

31 Quoted in William Barnes and John Heath Morgan, *The Foreign Service of the United States: Origins, Development, and Function* (Washington DC: Department of State, 1961), 124.

32 Consular Agent of the United States, Message from the President of the United States Transmitting Report of De B. Randolph Keim, Agent, &c. 1872, at 21. H.R. 42nd Cong., 3d Sess., Executive Document No. 145,

33 Ibid., 80.

34 William L. Duff, appointed 29 September 1866.

35 Consular Agent of the United States, Message from the President of the United States Transmitting Report of De B. Randolph Keim, 15.

36 Ibid., 16–17.

37 Ibid., 19.

38 Ibid., 79.

39 Ten years previously, Consul General Adam Badeau in London mentioned in his report for the year ending 30 September 1876 that 'under the orders of the State Department the visitation of subordinate consulates has been discontinued, except in special cases'. Report upon the Commercial Relations of the United States with Foreign Countries for the year 1876 (Washington, DC: Government Printing Office, 1877), 393.

40 Many of these 'Englishmen' were Scottish, Welsh or Irish.

41 Thomas M. Waller, Consul-General, *Inspection of United States Consulates in the United Kingdom* (Washington, DC: Government Printing Office), 1887.

42 The Hon. Robert Adams Jr., 'Faults in Our Consular Service', *The North American Review* 156, no. 437 (April 1893), 465.

43 Katharine Crane, *Mr Carr of State: Forty-Seven Years in the Department of State* (New York: St Martin's Press, 1960), 89.

44 An act to provide for the reorganization of the consular service of the United States, 5 April, 1906. 34 Stat. 99.

45 Prior to his appointment as consul-general at large, Horace Lee Washington had held consular appointments in Cairo, Alexandretta (Syria), Valencia, Geneva and Cape Town. He served as consul-general at large until 1908, when he was appointed consul general in Marseilles. The following year, he was transferred to Liverpool where, apart from a two-month assignment at the State Department, he served until 1924 when he transferred to London. He remained there until 1928, when he moved back to the State Department from which he retired in 1929. Register of the Department of State (January 1, 1930), 215–16.

46 Stoke on Trent Consulate, Inspection 1919, Inspection Reports on Foreign Service Posts 1906–1939, RG 59, NARA.

47 Letter dated July 16, 1911 from Heaton W. Harris, consul-general at large, to Herbert C. Hengstler, Chief of the Consular Bureau. Filed on the 1911 Inspection Report for Stoke on Trent. Harris was appointed consul general at Frankfurt, Germany, in 1912. In 1918 he was appointed consul general in Havana, Cuba, from where he retired in 1920. Register of the Department of State (January 1, 1926), p.136. The persons he mentions in his letter were colleagues; for example, John L. Griffiths, consul general in London; Benjamin Franklin Chase, consul at Leeds; Frank H. Mason, consul general at Paris; Alexander M. Thackera, consul general at Berlin; Robert P. Skinner, consul general at Hamburg.

48 The consulates inspected by Frazer in Britain in 1924 included Birmingham, Dundee, Dunfermline, Edinburgh, Newcastle upon Tyne and Stoke on Trent. He also inspected Dublin that year, by which time Ireland had become the Irish Free State. Register of the Department of State 1924, 55.

49 Register of the Department of State 1922, 52.

50 American Consular Bulletin 3, no. 2 (April 1921): 10.

51 United States Statutes at Large 46, pt. 2, at 1922. Seventy-first Cong., Sess. II, ch. 670 (1930).

52 An act for the reorganization and improvement of the Foreign Service of the United States, and for other purposes, 24 May, 1924. 43 Stat. 140.

53 Pub. L. No. 96–465; 94 Stat. 2071, section 209.

54 State Department website. http://oig.state.gov/about [accessed 9 January 2015].

55 Review of the New London Embassy Project. Statement by Steve A. Linick, inspector general for the Department of State and the Broadcasting Board of Governors before the Committee on Oversight and Government Reform. United States House of Representatives, December 8, 2015. https://oversight.house.gov/wp-content/uploads/2015/12/Linick-DOS-IG-Statement-12-8-London-Embassy.pdf [accessed 12 January 2016].

56 Fiona Reid, 'Grand Entrance', *The Scotsman*, 31 May 2007.

57 *Belfast Telegraph*, 8 September 2004.

58 State Department, Report of Inspection, Embassy London, United Kingdom, ISP/I-99-27 (September 1999), 47.
59 Privately produced handlist of G. C. Fox & Co. consular appointments supplied to the author by Charles Lloyd Fox, July 2001.
60 Ibid.
61 Robert J. Brugger et al., eds., *The Papers of James Madison.* Secretary of State Series, Vol. 1, 4 March–31 July 1801 (Charlottesville: University Press of Virginia, 1986), 248–49; www.state.gov/r/pa/ho/faq/#family [accessed 18 August 2008]; Charles S. Kennedy, *A History of the United States Consular Service 1776–1914* (Westport, CT: Greenwood Press, 1990), 46.
62 Email to the author dated 25 March 2009 from Tiffany T. Hamelin, Office of the Historian, Department of State.
63 Telephone call on 16 October 2001 from Charles L. Fox informing the author that he had submitted his resignation to the six embassies. Factors influencing his decision included ownership of the firm of G. C. Fox & Co. changing several times within a relatively short period, and a decrease in the amount of consular activities. This item is based on the author's unpublished PhD thesis, Nicholas Michael Keegan, 'Consular Representation in Britain: Its History, Current Status, and Personnel' PhD thesis, University of Durham, 2004, 148–50.
64 Pigot's Directory of Leeds, 1829 & 1834; Alfred Hunter, editor, *A Register of Officers and Agents, Civil, Military, and Naval in the Service of the United States* (Washington, DC 1853), 3.
65 Alma Howell Brown, 'The Consular Service of the Republic of Texas', *Southwestern Historical Quarterly* 33, no. 4 (April 1930): 299–315; *Boyle's Court Guide for January 1847*, London, 833–34; S. T. Bindoff et al., eds., *British Diplomatic Representatives 1789–1852* (London: Camden Third Series, Vol. 50, 1934), 163; Ashbel Smith to Lachlan M. Rate, 11 February 1845, Correspondence with Texan Consuls, RG 307, Folder 13, Texas State Archives, Austin, Texas. Ogden's 1843 letter of appointment as Texas Consul is in the Ogden Family Collection in Princeton University Library.
66 *Boyle's Court Guide, London, April 1849*, 877; Fran Hazelton, *London's American Past: A Guided Tour* (London, Papermac), 1991.
67 Foreign Office List and Diplomatic and Consular Year Book, July 1861, 203.
68 Foreign Office List, January 1872, 274. An interesting discussion of the topic has been written by Russell Clement, Special Collections Librarian at Brigham Young University, Hawaii Campus, entitled: *From Cook to the 1840 Constitution: The Name Change from Sandwich to Hawaiian Islands.* http://evols.library.manoa.hawaii.edu/bitstream/handle/10524/495/JL14054.pdf?sequence=2 [accessed 16 May 2012].
69 *Official Directory, Republic of Hawaii*, 91. http://www.cwru.edu/edocs/7/440.pdf [accessed 11 September 2008]; Foreign Office List and Diplomatic and Consular Year Book, 1900, 385.
70 Crane, *Mr Carr of State*, 170–71, 189.
71 Ibid., 172.
72 *New York Times*, 11 May 1915, 2.
73 Crane, *Mr Carr of State*, 172.
74 Ibid.,186.
75 Report dated 2 December 1940 by Philip Holland, consul general, Liverpool, Franklin Delano Roosevelt Digital Archives, Franklin Delano Roosevelt Presidential Library and Museum, Hyde Park, New York.
76 Memo, Philip Holland, American consul general, Liverpool, to Walter McKinney, consul, London, 9 December 1940, Great Britain Diplomatic Files, FDR Digital Archives.
77 Memo dated 16 December 1940 quoting a personal message received by Consul Walton C. Ferris from an intimate friend in Sheffield. FDR Digital Archives.
78 Memo dated 16 December 1940 by Walton C. Ferris, consul, London, reporting telephone call that day from Vice Consul Henry O. Ramsay, Sheffield. FDR Digital Archives.

79 Report dated 25 November 1940 by George K. Donald, consul general, Southampton, FDR Digital Archives.
80 Report dated 27 November 1940 by Donald.
81 Report dated 1 December 1940 by Donald.
82 Report dated 2 December 1940 by Donald.
83 Report dated 3 December 1940 by Donald.
84 Report dated 26 November 1940 by Roy W. Baker, consul, Bristol, FDR Digital Archives.
85 Report dated 3 December 1940 by Baker.
86 Report dated 23 November 1940 by James R. Wilkinson, consul, Birmingham, FDR Digital Archives.
87 Report dated 28 November 1940 by Henry M. Wolcott, consul, Plymouth, FDR Digital Archives.
88 Barnes and Morgan, *The Foreign Service of the United States*, 249.
89 Ambassador John G. Winant to Secretary of State Cordell Hull, 3 April 1941, FDR Digital Archives.
90 Ambassador William J. Crowe, Jr, giving the Belfast Bicentennial Speech at Queens University, Belfast, 20 May 1996.
91 Report dated 27 December 1940, by James R. Wilkinson, Consul, Birmingham. FDR Digital Archives.
92 Report dated 27 December 1940 by James R. Wilkinson, American consul, Birmingham, to Walter H. McKinney, consul in the American Consulate General, London; report dated 8 January 1941 by Herschel V. Johnson to Secretary of State Cordell Hull, FDR Digital Archives.
93 Barnes and Morgan, *The Foreign Service of the United States*, 249.
94 Consul General Walter M. McClelland, interviewed by Charles Stuart Kennedy on 20 November 1995, Foreign Affairs Oral History Program, available via the Library of Congress website, https://cdn.loc.gov/service/mss/mfdip/2004/2004mcc07/2004mcc07.pdf
95 University of Ulster. http://cain.ulst.ac.uk/othelem/incorepaper.htm [accessed 7 September 2008].
96 For an excellent and succinct account of the role of the consulate general during 'the troubles', see Francis M. Carroll, *The American Presence in Ulster: A Diplomatic History, 1796–1996* (Washington, DC: The Catholic University Press of America, 2005).
97 Ibid., 234.
98 Ibid., 215–19; Raymond Seitz, *Over Here* (London: Phoenix, 2001), 289–91.

Chapter Five Impact of the Civil War and the Role of American Consuls in Britain

1 Hugh Brogan, *The Penguin History of the USA* (London: Penguin, 1999), 317.
2 Quoted in William A. Blair, 'Extremists at the Gate: Origins of the American Civil War', in Aaron Sheehan-Dean, ed., *Struggle for a Vast Future: The American Civil War* (Oxford: Osprey, 2006), 21.
3 James M. McPherson, 'Volunteer Soldiers', in Brian Lamb, ed., *Booknotes: Stories from American History, Leading Historians on the Events that Shaped Our Country* (New York: Penguin, 2002), 81; James M. McPherson, review of Mark E. Neely, Jr, *The Civil War and the Limits of Destruction* (Cambridge, MA: Harvard University Press, 2007) in *The New York Review of Books* 55, no. 2 (14 February 2008); Philip Jenkins, *A History of the United States*, 2nd ed. (Palgrave Macmillan, 2003), 144; Brogan, *The Penguin History of the USA*, 345. In 'Volunteer Soldiers', McPherson makes the point that 620,000 dead amounted to 2 per cent of the American population in 1861 and that 2 per cent in 2002 would be five million; Niall Ferguson, *Colossus: The Rise and Fall of the American Empire* (London: Penguin, 2004), 304, table 2.

4 McPherson, 'Volunteer Soldiers', 81.

5 The consulates were in Charleston, New Orleans, Richmond, Mobile, Savannah and Galveston.

6 Frank Lawrence Owsley, *King Cotton Diplomacy: Foreign Relations of the Confederate States of America*, 2nd ed., revised by Harriet Chappell Owsley (Chicago: University of Chicago Press, 1958), 467–94.

7 Natalia Summers, *List of Documents Relating to Special Agents of the Department of State 1789–1906*, Special Lists, no. 7 (Washington, DC: The National Archives, 1951), 52.

8 Summers, *List of Documents*, 188.

9 Charles Francis Adams, Jr, to his father, 11 March 1862, in Worthington Chauncey Ford, ed., *A Cycle of Adams Letters 1861–1865*, vol. I (Boston and New York: Houghton Mifflin, 1920), 118–19.

10 Summers, *List of Documents*, 51, 195.

11 Laird's Contract Book, 187–188, ref. ZCL 005/0026, Cammell Laird Collection, Wirral Archives Service, Birkenhead.

12 James D. Bulloch, *The Secret Service of the Confederate States in Europe: Or, How the Confederate Cruisers Were Equipped* (New York: Random House, 2001. Originally published in 1884), 264.

13 Ibid., 266, 268.

14 Ibid., 292.

15 Ibid., 269, 303.

16 Ibid., 304.

17 Sarah Forbes Hughes, ed. *Letters and Recollections of John Murray Forbes*, vol. II (Boston: Houghton Mifflin, 1899), 5, 7–9.

18 Ibid., 9.

19 Ibid., 44–45.

20 Brian Jenkins, *Britain and the War for the Union*, vol. 2 (Montreal, McGill-Queen's University Press, 1980), 246–47.

21 Letter dated 10 July 1863 by Forbes and Aspinwall to Gideon Welles, Secretary of the Navy Department. Forbes Hughes, *Letters and Recollections of John Murray Forbes*, 64.

22 The *Rappahannock* never fired a shot in anger. Although condemned by the Admiralty 'as rotten and unserviceable', it was purchased by an agent acting on behalf of Confederate Commander Matthew F. Maury. Jenkins, *Britain and the War for the Union*, 323. Fearing it might be seized, Maury arranged for it to sail to Calais where it remained for the duration of the war. Bulloch, *The Secret Service of the Confederate States in Europe*, 491–94.

23 Bulloch, *The Secret Service of the Confederate States in Europe*, 47.

24 Gustavus Kroener was born in Germany in 1809 and emigrated to America in 1833. He was active in Illinois legal and political life and was a friend of Lincoln. In 1861 he sought a diplomatic post from Lincoln, suggesting Berlin, Switzerland or Vienna. However, he was appointed US minister to Spain in June 1862. This did not please him and he tried desperately to get Lincoln to agree to give him the Vienna post and even, a few days before being officially presented at the Spanish Court, pleaded to be appointed to Turin instead. His efforts were unsuccessful and he remained in Madrid until 1864, when he returned to his former pursuits in Belleville, Illinois. The following year he was one of the pallbearers who carried Lincoln's coffin. See, for example, letters from Kroener to Lincoln dated 5 April and 15 June 1861, 7 June and 22 September 1862, Abraham Lincoln Papers, Library of Congress, Washington, DC. In the letter dated 15 June 1861, he asked Lincoln to delay appointing Anson Burlingame. Burlingame had been appointed as minister to Austria but the Austrian government had declared him *persona non grata* because of the support he had given the Hungarian revolutionary, Lajos (Louis) Kossuth. Lincoln therefore appointed Burlingame minister to China, where he served from 1861 to 1867. Stewart Sifakis, *Who Was Who in the Union, Vol. 1 of Who Was Who in the Civil War: A Biographical Encyclopedia of More Than 1500 Union Participants* (New York: Facts on File, Inc., 1988), 55.

25 Nine-page manuscript account by Dudley, of his appointment and initial experiences as Liverpool Consul; includes account of his interview with Lincoln. Written 5 March [1884?], Ref. DU 1275, Thomas H. Dudley Papers, The Huntington Library, San Marino, California.
26 The American Chamber of Commerce in Liverpool was founded in 1801 largely through the efforts of Rathbone's father and James Maury, the US consul.
27 Nine-page manuscript account by Dudley.
28 George Reeser Prowell, *The History of Camden County, New Jersey* (Philadelphia: L. J. Richards, 1886), 221–22.
29 Jenkins, *Britain and the War for the Union*, 247.
30 Prowell, *The History of Camden County*, 221–22.
31 William John Potts, 'Biographical Sketch of the Hon. Thomas H. Dudley, of Camden, NJ, who Died April 15, 1893.' *Proceedings of the American Philosophy Society 1895*, 34, no. 147 (1895), 117.
32 Dudley's son Edward served as vice consul and acting consul in 1871 and 1872; thereafter he was a partner in his father's New Jersey law firm. Thomas H. Dudley Collection, Huntington Library, San Marino, California, available via Online Archive of California. http://www.oac.cdlib.org/view?docId=tf7c6005nh;developer=local;query=;style=oac4;view=admin [accessed 12 September 2009].
33 *Dictionary of American Biography*, vol. XIII (London: Oxford University Press, 1934), 243.
34 Johnson was appointed some two months after James Maury was appointed to Liverpool.
35 Obituary, *New York Times*, 23 May 1891.
36 Summers, *List of Documents*, 146.
37 *Intelligence in the Civil War* (Washington, DC, Central Intelligence Agency, c.2007), 43. In 1862, he presented a battery of cannons to the Minnesota militia for which he received an honorary commission as a major general. From then on, he was known as General Sanford. Henry Shelton Sanford Papers, Sanford Memorial Library, Sanford, Florida.
38 Register of Henry Shelton Sanford Papers, General Sanford Memorial Library, Sanford, Florida.
39 See, for example, a good description of the activities of the Belfast consul, Dr John Young, throughout the Civil War in Francis M. Carroll's *The American Presence in Ulster: A Diplomatic History, 1796–1996* (Washington, DC: The Catholic University of America Press, 2005), 62–84. Young also tried, unsuccessfully, to obtain funds from the State Department to pay for a secret agent. Kevin J. Foster, 'The Diplomats Who Sank a Fleet: The Confederacy's Undelivered European Fleet and the Union Consular Service', *Prologue* 33, no. 3 (Fall 2001), 186–87.
40 Neil McLachlan to Secretary of State William H. Seward, 27 September 1861, Washington DC, National Archives and Records Administration, Despatches from United States Consuls in Leith, 1858–1871, Record Group 59, Reel T396.
41 Foster, 'The Diplomats Who Sank a Fleet', 180–93. For a map showing the main blockade running routes and the areas patrolled by the Union's Blockading Squadrons, of which there were four, see Craig L. Symonds, 'Uncle Sam's Web-Feet: Winning the War at Sea', in *Struggle for a Vast Future: The American Civil War* ed., Aaron Sheehan-Dean (Oxford: Osprey, 2006), 120.
42 *New York Times*, 17 July 1863.
43 Bulloch, *The Secret Service of the Confederate States in Europe*, 496.
44 Roy Rawlinson's excellent website, 'When Liverpool Was Dixie: A Tribute to Commander James Dunwoody Bulloch'. http://www.whenliverpoolwasdixie.co.uk/index.html [accessed 13 September 2009]; State Department, Office of the Historian, Preventing Diplomatic Recognition of the Confederacy, and the *Alabama* Claims. http://www.state.gov/r/pa/ho/time/cw/# [accessed 13 September 2009].
45 Bulloch, *The Secret Service of the Confederate States in Europe*, 496.
46 Zebina Eastman, *Eight Years in a British Consulate, from 1861 to 1869*, 19. Lecture given in 1872, and published in Chicago in 1919 by his son.
47 David Paull Nickles, *Under the Wire: How the Telegraph Changed Diplomacy* (Cambridge, MA: Harvard University Press, 2003), 73, 215n20.

48 Spy Reports, March 1862–March 1863, *CSS Alabama* Collection, William Stanley Hoole Special Collections Library, University of Alabama; Dudley to Seward, 11 December 1861, Despatches from US Consuls in Liverpool, England, 1790–1906, National Archives and Records Administration, Microfilm M141, Roll 20 [underlining in the original].

49 Proceedings of the Central Criminal Court, 7 May 1860, 153; Freeman H. Morse to Henry Shelton Sanford, 29 June 1861, Henry S. Sanford Papers, Box 139, Folder 12, item 1, Sanford Museum, Florida.

50 *Intelligence in the Civil War*, 43.

51 Ignatius Pollaky to Henry Shelton Sanford, London, 11 October 1861, Henry Shelton Sanford Papers, Sanford Museum, Sanford, Florida.

52 ibid.

53 The freehold property in which Bulloch and his companions were based had long historic antecedents. It was, and still is, owned by the Crown Estate and came into its ownership in or around 1531 when the land was appropriated by Henry VIII from the Provost and College of Eton and Others and became part of the Bailiwick of St James. Crown Estate, Certificate of Title, dated 20 October 2006.

54 Post Office London Directory, 1862. Also, Isaac, Campbell & Co was declared bankrupt in 1869 with debts of almost £72,500, of which almost £27,500 was for outstanding loans. Papers filed by Saul Isaac, trading with Samuel Isaac as the firm of S. Isaac Campbell & Co., under The Bankruptcy Amendment Act 1868, DD/H/166/23, Nottinghamshire Archives.

55 Foster, 'The Diplomats Who Sank a Fleet', 185.

56 civilwarartillery.com.

57 Bulloch, *The Secret Service of the Confederate States in Europe*, 293.

58 Ibid., 341.

59 Ibid., 204.

60 Ibid., 525.

61 Ibid., 205.

62 *A Cycle of Adams Letters 1861–1865*, vol. I, ed. Worthington Chauncey Ford, (Boston and New York: Houghton Mifflin, 1920), 106, 114.

63 Eastman, *Eight Years in a British Consulate*.

64 Owsley, *King Cotton Diplomacy*, 9.

65 Ibid., 3.

66 Ibid., 42–44, 135–36.

67 Ibid., 551–52.

68 Ibid., 242–43.

69 Consul Chase to F. W. Seward, cited in Owsley, *King Cotton Diplomacy*, 254.

70 Bulloch, *The Secret Service of the Confederate States in Europe*, 76–88.

71 Ignatius Pollaky to Henry Shelton Sanford, London, 11 October 1861, Henry Shelton Sanford Papers, Sanford Museum, Sanford, Florida.

72 Foster, 'The Diplomats Who Sank a Fleet', 187–88.

73 *Intelligence in the Civil War*, 43.

74 Edward C. Anderson, *Confederate Foreign Agent: The European Diary of Major Edward C. Anderson*, edited with a prologue and epilogue by W. Stanley Hoole (Tuscaloosa, AL: Confederate Publishing, 1976); Bulloch, *The Secret Service of the Confederate States in Europe*, 38; Owsley, *King Cotton Diplomacy*, 154 et seq.

75 *Intelligence in the Civil War*, 44.

76 Jenkins, *Britain and the War for the Union*, 122–26.

77 Letter dated 28 April 1864 from Secretary of State Seward to the Hon. E. B. Washburne, chairman of the Committee on Commerce, House of Representatives, 38th Cong., 1st Sess., Misc. Document No. 77.

78 State Department, Office of the Historian, http://www.state.gov/r/pa/ho/time/cw/17610.htm [accessed 11 September 2009].

79 Eastman, *Eight Years in a British Consulate*, 21.
80 20 November 1861, Letters and Recollections of John Murray Forbes, etc. Vol. I, 252. Nassau Senior (1790–1864) was an English economist.
81 Adams to his son, Charles, 31 January 1862, Ford, *A Cycle of Adams Letters*, Vol. I, 107.
82 'America's Identity Crisis', *The Spectator*, 19 August 2017, 3.
83 Dudley to Seward, No. 96, 25 July 1862, Despatches from United States Consuls in Liverpool 1790–1906, Record Group 59, M141, NARA.
84 Adams to his son, Charles, 21 March 1862, Ford, *A Cycle of Adams Letters*, Vol. I, 123.
85 Henry Adams to his brother, Charles, 8 May 1862, Ford, *A Cycle of Adams Letters*, Vol. I, 140.
86 *The Times*, 9 October 1862, 7–8.
87 James Ford Rhodes, *History of the Civil War, 1861–1865* (New York: Macmillan, 1917), 270.
88 Adams to his son, Charles, 25 December 1862, Ford, *A Cycle of Adams Letters*, Vol. I, 220–21.
89 Adams to his son, Charles, 25 September 1863, Ford, *A Cycle of Adams Letters*, Vol. II, 85.
90 Henry Adams to his brother, 15 April 1864, Ford, *A Cycle of Adams Letters*, Vol. II, 126.
91 One of those thought, wrongly, to have been implicated was Dudley's eventual successor at Liverpool, Nathaniel Beverly Tucker.
92 William J. Cooper, Jr, *Jefferson Davis, American* (New York: Vintage Books, 2001), 626.
93 Register of the Department of State (Washington, DC: Government Printing Office, 1874), 128.
94 Bulloch, *The Secret Service of the Confederate States in Europe*, 600.
95 Naturalization papers of James Dunwoody Bulloch, January 1869, National Archives, Kew, ref. HO/1/154/6059 C320188.
96 *Intelligence in the Civil War*, 45.
97 Kathleen Burk, *Old World, New World: The Story of Britain and America* (London: Little, Brown, 2007), 270.
98 Olive Risley Seward, ed., *William H. Seward's Travels around the World* (New York: Appleton, 1873), 714–15.

Chapter Seven Belfast

1 Message from the president of the United States Transmitting Report of De B. Randolph Keim, Agent, &c., 1872, H.R. 42nd Cong., 3d Sess., Executive Document No. 145, 9–10.
2 Inspection of United States Consulates in the United Kingdom, by Thomas M. Waller, consul general (Washington, DC, Department of State: Government Printing Office, 1887), tables B & C.
3 Message from the President of the United States, Transmitting in response to the resolution of the Senate of March 2, 1901, a communication from the Secretary of State submitting reports from consular officers of the United States giving an account of each consulate and consular agency, showing its principal industries and exports, the surrounding climatic conditions, the general cost of living, and similar information (Washington, DC: Government Printing Office, 1902), 248.
4 The Irish Free State eventually became Eire in 1937 and then an independent republic in 1949.
5 Ambassador William J. Crowe, Jr, giving the Belfast Bicentennial Speech in Queens University, Belfast, 20 May 1996, and quoting from the *Belfast Telegraph* of 24 January 1946.
6 Lawrence H. Hydle, interviewed by Charles Stuart Kennedy, July/August 1994, Foreign Affairs Oral History Program, Association for Diplomatic Studies and Training, Arlington, VA. Frontline Diplomacy, Manuscript Division, Library of Congress, Washington, DC.
7 Charles R. Stout, 1977–1980; Michael A. G. Michaud, 1980–1983; Samuel Bartlett, 1983–1986.
8 Embassy London, United Kingdom, and its Constituent Posts, 0-89-39, November 1989, Report of Inspection, Department of State, Office of Inspector General, 8, 33, 35.

9 State Department, Compliance Followup Review of the Inspection of Embassy London, United Kingdom, and its Constituent Posts, ISP/S-91-12, November 1990, O-83, 24.

10 Embassy London, United Kingdom, and its Constituent Posts, ISP/I-93-43, September 1993, Report of Inspection, 9.

11 Ibid.

12 Ibid.

13 Ibid., 15.

14 Ibid., ii.

15 Later in her career Kathleen Stephens was ambassador to the Republic of Korea from 2008 until 2011.

16 Embassy London, United Kingdom, and its Constituent Posts, ISP/I-99-27, September 1999, Report of Inspection, 10.

17 Ibid.

18 Raymond Seitz, *Over Here* (London: Phoenix, 2001), 289.

19 Ibid.

20 Seitz, *Over Here*, 286–91; Francis M. Carroll, *The American Presence in Ulster: A Diplomatic History, 1796–1996* (Washington, DC: The Catholic University of America Press, 2005), 214–19; Richard Gilbert, 'Dissent in Dublin: For Two FSOs, Cable Drew Retribution and Frustration', *Foreign Service Journal* 73, no. 7 (July 1996), 28–35.

21 Gilbert, 'Dissent in Dublin'; Stephen Engelberg, 'US Says Envoy to Ireland Wrongly Punished 2 Colleagues', *New York Times*, 8 March 1996.

22 Ambassador William J. Crowe, interviewed by Charles Stuart Kennedy, 8 June 1998, Foreign Affairs Oral History Program, Association for Diplomatic Studies and Training, Arlington, VA. Frontline Diplomacy, Manuscript Division, Library of Congress, Washington, DC.

23 Inspection Report, 1999, 37; Department of State Foreign Affairs Manual, vol. 9, 40.37, N1, 1–14.

24 Embassy London, Inspection Report, 1999, 37.

25 In August 2010, after serving as ambassador to Panama she was appointed Deputy Chief of Mission at the London Embassy where she served until 2013; for the last few months she was Chargé d'Affaires ad interim.

26 Later assignments included ambassador to Tajikistan and Civilian Deputy and Foreign Policy Advisor at EUCOM (the US's European Command).

27 http://belfast.usconsulate.gov/consul_general.html [accessed 4 August 2015].

Chapter Eight Birmingham

1 Obituary, *New York Times*, 8 March 1879, 5.

2 Consular Agent of the United States, Message from the President of the United States, Transmitting Report of De B. Randolph Keim, Agent, &c., 1872. H.R. 42nd Cong., 3d Sess., Executive Document No. 145, at 74–75.

3 *New York Times*, 18 December 1878, 3. Schuyler is pronounced 'sky-ler'.

4 After leaving Birmingham in 1879, Schuyler was appointed consul general in Rome; the following year he was chargé d'affaires and consul general in Bucharest, and in 1882 he was appointed minister and consul general to Romania, Serbia and Greece. In March 1889 President Harrison nominated him for the post of assistant secretary of state but withdrew it as a result of opposition from the Foreign Affairs Committee. It seems that Schuyler had been severely critical of the performance of Elihu Washburne during the latter's 12-day appointment as secretary of state in March 1869. Washburne later served as minister to France from 1869 to 1877 and was the only official representative of a foreign government to remain in Paris during the siege of 1870–1871 and the days of the Commune. In 1888, following his unsuccessful nomination as assistant secretary of state, Schuyler was appointed agent and consul general,

Cairo. His time there was not long, however, as he contracted malaria and died the following year in Venice, at age 50. State Department, Former Secretaries of State. http://history.state.gov/departmenthistory/people/washburne-elihu-benjamin [accessed 13 September 2009]; *New York Times*, 19 July 1890, 5.

5 Rosamund Bartlett, *Tolstoy: A Russian Life* (London: Profile Books, 2010), 177.

6 Eugene Schuyler, *American Diplomacy* (New York: Charles Scribner's Sons), 1895.

7 John F. Jewell, A Veteran Consul, *American Consular Bulletin* V, no. 5 (May 1923), 135, 148–49.

8 Ibid., 148.

9 Ibid., 149.

10 Register of the Department of State (1931), 262.

11 Register of the Department of State (1889), 20.

12 Message from the President of the United States, transmitting, in response to the Resolution of the Senate of March 2, 1901, a communication from the secretary of state submitting reports from consular officers of the United States giving an account of each consulate and consular agency, showing its principal industries and exports, the surrounding climatic conditions, the general cost of living, and similar information. Senate, 57th Cong., 1st Sess., Document 411 (Washington, 1902), 256–58, 378.

13 Register of the Department of State (1933), 182; *New York Times*, 3 July 1908, 7.

14 Birmingham Consulate, Inspection 1908, Inspection Reports on Foreign Service Posts, 1906–1939, RG 59, NARA.

15 Inspection Report 1909.

16 Inspection Report 1911.

17 Inspection Report 1914.

18 Register of the Department of State (July 1933), 182. He ended his career as consul general in London from 1928 to 1932.

19 As Totten was not medically qualified it was rather unwise of him to give this layman's diagnosis of a disease and to enter it in an official inspection report. According to the Oxford English Dictionary, locomotor ataxia is 'The abnormal gait (unsteady and high stepping) associated with neurosyphilis of the posterior roots of the spinal cord (tabes dorsalis); (also) tabes dorsalis itself.'

20 *Le Soleil* (Quebec), 20 and 23 March 1931; *New York Times*, 21 and 23 March 1931; *L'Action Catholique* (Quebec), 23 March 1931; *The Globe* (Toronto), 23 March 1931; *Quebec Chronicle-Telegraph*, 24 March 1931; TIME magazine, 30 March 1931.

21 Inspection Report 1919.

22 Register of the Department of State (1922), 92.

23 John Franklin Jewell's previous post had been consul in Batavia, Java. It was reported in 1921 that he was 'suffering somewhat in health after three years of continuous service at tropical Batavia. He has been ordered to the United States'. *American Consular Bulletin* 3, no. 2 (April 1921): 6. He was unassigned from 8 February 1921 until being assigned to Birmingham from 18 January 1922. He died in Birmingham on 23 October 1927, at age 53. Register of the Department of State (1928), 222.

24 Inspection Report 1926.

25 Inspection Report 1934.

26 Inspection Report 1938.

27 Register of the Department of State (1950), 238–39.

28 William D. Morgan interviewed by Lester Elliot Sadlow, 23 June 1995. ADST Foreign Affairs Oral History Project. Frontline Diplomacy, Manuscript Division, Library of Congress, Washington, DC.

29 Ibid.

30 'American in the Midlands', *The Times*, 5 July 1965, 13; The Biographic Register, Department of State (July 1968), 124.

Chapter Nine Bradford

1 Foreign Office List, March 1868, 270.
2 Thomas S. Fiske, 'Emory McClintock: Obituary', *Bulletin of the American Mathematical Society* 23, no. 8 (1917): 353–57; McClintock to Julius Proeschel, Bradford, 16 February 1865, McClintock Collection, Dickinson College, Carlisle, Pennsylvania.
3 Despatches from US consuls in Bradford, Record Group 59, T165.
4 Private letter from Towle to Frederick W. Seward, 18 July 1868, Despatches from US consuls in Bradford, Record Group 59, T165.
5 Raymond to Seward, 22 August 1868, Despatches from US consuls in Bradford, Record Group 59, T165.
6 Towle to Seward, 29 October 1868; Towle to J. C. B. Davis, 2 October 1869, Despatches.
7 Towle to Hamilton Fish, 26 May 1869, Despatches.
8 Towle to J. C. B. Davis, 27 August 1869, Despatches.
9 Shortly after leaving office, Towle wrote an interesting article setting out his views on the deficiencies of the US consular service, in particular the procedures for selecting, appointing and replacing consuls. George M. Towle, 'Our Consular Service', *The Atlantic Monthly* 29, no. 173 (March 1872): 300–309.
10 Selleck to Fish, 3 December 1869, Despatches.
11 Selleck to Hamilton Fish, 14 December 1869, Despatches.
12 *Bradford Observer*, 18 November 1882.
13 Consular Agent of the United States, Message from the President of the United States, Transmitting Report of De B. Randolph Keim, Agent, &c., 1872. H.R. 42nd Cong., 3d Sess., Executive Document No. 145, at 10–11.
14 Register of the Department of State (March 1874), 21, and (October 1874), 21.
15 Grinnell became consul in Manchester in 1897.
16 Thomas M. Waller, consul general, 'Inspection of United States Consulates in the United Kingdom' (Washington, DC: Department of State, Government Printing Office, 1887), 5, 9, 12.
17 Report by William F. Grinnell, consul, Bradford, 25 March 1886, Consular Reports on Commerce, Manufactures, Etc., No. 71, November 1886, 349.
18 *New York Times*, 4 July 1889, 3.
19 Ibid., 22 July 1889, 2.
20 John Arnold Tibbits to Major Francis W. Frigout, vice and deputy consul general, London, 13 April 1893, John C. New Collection, Indiana Historical Society.
21 *New York Times*, 24 July 1893, 5.
22 Register of the Department of State (1893), 28.
23 *American Foreign Service Journal* VII, no. 2 (February 1930): 57.
24 C. B. Galbreath, 'Claude Meeker as Member of the Kit-Kat Club, and the Ohio State Archaeological and Historical Society', *Ohio History* 40, no. 4 (October 1931): 600–612; William Alexander Taylor, *Centennial History of Columbus and Franklin County, Ohio* (Chicago–Columbus: S. J. Clarke, 1909), 147–48.
25 *New York Times*, 4 July 1889, 3.
26 Message from the President of the United States, transmitting, in response to the Resolution of the Senate of March 2, 1901, a communication from the secretary of state submitting reports from consular officers of the United States giving an account of each consulate and consular agency, showing its principal industries and exports, the surrounding climatic conditions, the general cost of living, and similar information. Senate, 57th Cong., 1st Sess., Document 411 (Washington, 1902), 263–64.
27 Register of the Department of State (October 1, 1937), 290.
28 *American Foreign Service Journal* VII, no. 6 (June 1930): 200.

29 *New York Times*, 21 May 1914, 1.
30 *The Times*, 16 January 1937, 17.
31 Register of the Department of State (1948), 293.
32 Ibid., 271.
33 *Bradford Chamber of Commerce Journal* (May 1953): 47; letter by O. B. Stokes, *New York Times*, 18 May 1953, 20.
34 Bradford Telegraph and Argus, 7 May 1953. Biographic Register of the Department of State (1956), 301.

Chapter Ten Bristol

1 See, for example, a photograph of the plaque on the house. http://www.victoriacountyhistory.ac.uk/explore/items/american-consulate [accessed 31 January 2016]. An internet search reveals many other examples.
2 Appointment of Elias Vanderhorst of South Carolina as Consul of the USA for the Port of Bristol, 4 May 1792. Vanderhorst Collection, Bristol Record Office.
3 Elias Vanderhorst, Approbation of Consular Appointment, 10 February 1793. Vanderhorst Collection, Bristol Record Office.
4 John Quincy Adams to Vanderhorst, 6 October 1815. Vanderhorst Collection, Bristol Record Office.
5 Letter from Samuel F. B. Morse, 12 March 1814, Samuel F. B. Morse Papers, Library of Congress.
6 Pigot's Directory for Bristol, Gloucestershire, 1830.
7 *The Gentleman's Magazine* 103 (1833): 572.
8 Zebina Eastman, *Eight Years in a British Consulate, from 1861 to 1869* (Chicago; 1919), 9–10.
9 Abraham Lincoln to William H. Seward, 20 August 1861, the Abraham Lincoln Papers at the Library of Congress. Seward was stabbed at his home on the same night, 14 April 1865, that Lincoln was shot by John Wilkes Booth. Seward's attacker was an accomplice of Booth. Unlike Lincoln, Seward recovered.
10 Eastman, *Eight Years in a British Consulate*, 29.
11 Consular Agent of the United States, Message from the President of the United States, Transmitting Report of De B. Randolph Keim, Agent, &c., 1872, H.R. 42nd Cong., 3d Sess., Executive Document No. 145, at 11.
12 Carl Sandburg, *Abraham Lincoln: The Prairie Years and the War Years* (New York: Harcourt, 2002), 155.
13 Herbert Mitgang, 'Garibaldi and Lincoln,' *American Heritage Magazine* 26, no. 6 (October 1975).
14 Obituary, *New York Times*, 8 December 1885, 2.
15 *New York Times*, 28 October 1880, 2.
16 *New York Times*, 6 January and 27 March 1881, 8 and 5, respectively.
17 Register of the Department of State (1 January 1926), 153.
18 J. Perry Worden, 'Touring Europe on Next to Nothing', *Outing* 24, no. 3 (June 1894): 231.
19 'Court Circular', *The Times*, 2 January 1909, 11.
20 Stoke on Trent Consulate, Inspection 1914, Inspection Reports on Foreign Service Posts, 1906–1939, RG 59, NARA.
21 *New York Times*, 6 November 1945, 19.

Chapter Eleven Cardiff

1 Council Minutes: 1855–1862, Cardiff Records, vol. 4, 1903, 441–49.
2 Slater's Commercial Directory for Cardiff, 1858–1859; Pigot's London Provincial Directory, 1822–1823.

3 Inventory of the Cleveland Family Collection, The Pennsylvania State University, Special Collections Library; *New York Times*, 20 August, 1869.
4 Register of the Department of State (1866), 5.
5 Consular Agent of the United States, Message from the President of the United States, Transmitting Report of De B. Randolph Keim, Agent, &c., 1872, H.R. 42nd Cong., 3d Sess., Executive Document No. 145, at 78–79.
6 Ibid., 79.
7 Register of the Department of State (1874), 21.
8 *New York Times*, 6 May 1928.
9 Report of De B. Randolph Keim, 77, 79.
10 *New York Times*, 2 March 1880, 5.
11 Lady Cook was the former Tennessee Claflin, who married Sir Francis Cook in 1885. She was an ardent and eloquent campaigner for women's rights, as well as for other causes. She died in London in January 1923. *The Times*, 20 January 1923, 10.
12 *New York Times*, 29 April 1909, 9. Sikes remained as consul until his death in 1883.
13 Foreign Office List 1882, 309.
14 Thomas M. Waller, consul general, 'Inspection of United States Consulates in the United Kingdom' (Washington, DC: Department of State, Government Printing Office, 1887).
15 *New York Times*, 26 April 1891, 1, and 11 March 1894, 1.
16 *Encyclopedia Vermont Biography: A Series of Authentic Biographical Sketches of the Representative Men of Vermont and Sons of Vermont in Other States* (Burlington, VT: Ullery, 1912), 228.
17 Message from the President of the United States, transmitting, in response to the Resolution of the Senate of March 2, 1901, a communication from the secretary of state submitting reports from consular officers of the United States giving an account of each consulate and consular agency, showing its principal industries and exports, the surrounding climatic conditions, the general cost of living, and similar information. Senate, 57th Cong., 1st Sess., Document 411 (Washington, 1902), 280.
18 Ibid., 279–80.
19 'Obituary', *New York Times*, 4 January 1905; *The Times*, 4 January 1905, 8.
20 Register of the Department of State (1 January 1926), 153; *American Journal of International Law*, supp. to vol. 5, Official Documents, 1911, 142.
21 *New York Times*, 19 May 1911, 11.
22 Register of the Department of State (1 January 1926), 153.
23 *New York Times*, 21 May 1920, 6.
24 Register of the Department of State (December 1918).
25 State Department Biographical Register 1922, 102.
26 Register of the Department of State (December 1918).
27 Biographic Register of the Department of State (1945), 213.
28 *New York Times*, 13 May 1937, 25.
29 Register of the Department of State (1 October 1937), 291; *New York Times*, 28 September 1941.
30 Register of the Department of State (1951), 133. His commission, signed by President Truman on 23 June 1950, and his exequatur, signed by King George VI on 6 November 1950, are in the Ebling Collection at Georgetown University Library.
31 Chester Earl Beaman, interviewed in 1999 by Charles Stuart Kennedy, Foreign Affairs Oral History Program, Association for Diplomatic Studies and Training. Frontline Diplomacy, Manuscript Division, Library of Congress, Washington, DC.
32 Chester Earl Beaman, interviewed in 1999 by Charles Stuart Kennedy, Foreign Affairs Oral History Program, Association for Diplomatic Studies and Training. Frontline Diplomacy, Manuscript Division, Library of Congress, Washington, DC.
33 'Obituary', *Washington Post*, 22 May 2007.
34 Helga Ruge, email dated 4 September 2008 to the author.

35 Helga M. Ruge, *Flashbacks of a Diplomat's Wife* (Chico, CA: Clay & Marshall, 2001), 99–118; *Chico Statements*, Fall 2000, California State University, Chico; correspondence between the author and Mrs Ruge in September 2008.

Chapter Twelve Dublin

1 James Maury to Thomas Jefferson, 8 September 1790, RG 59, M141, Roll 1; William Knox to Thomas Jefferson, 26 November 1790, RG 59, T199, Roll 1, NARA.

2 Receipt dated 17 December 1790 from William Mossop, engraver, for two guineas, RG 59, T199, Roll 1.

3 Knox to Jefferson, 7 September 1791, RG 59, T199, Roll 1.

4 Knox to George Washington, 13 November 1791, RG 59, T199, Roll 1.

5 Knox to Jefferson, 17 January 1792, RG59, T199, Roll 1.

6 Knox to Jefferson, 28 May 1792, RG59, T199, Roll 1.

7 Francis R. Drake, *Life and Correspondence of Henry Knox, Major-General in the American Revolutionary Army* (Boston: Samuel G. Drake, 1873), 8, 9, 22.

8 Horace Elisha Scudder, ed., *Recollections of Samuel Breck, with Passages from his Note-Books (1771–1862)* (Philadelphia: Porter & Coates, 1877), 103.

9 Drake, *Life and Correspondence of Henry Knox*, 8–9.

10 Scudder, *Recollections of Samuel Breck*, 104–5.

11 Author's email correspondence in October 2008 with Stacey Peeples, Archivist of the Pennsylvania Hospital; Drake, *Life and Correspondence of Henry Knox*, 8–9.

12 *New York Times*, 22 May 1895, 3; Thomas Wilson to Secretary of State Louis McLane, 23 September 1833, RG59, T199, Roll 1.

13 Thomas English to Secretary of State Robert Smith, 15 July 1809, RG59, T199, Roll 1.

14 John English to Robert Smith, 10 July 1810, RG59, T199, Roll 1.

15 Thomas Wilson to Secretary of State James Monroe, 14 February 1815; Thomas English to Monroe, 14 February 1815, RG59, T199, Roll 1.

16 Isaac English to Secretary of State John Quincy Adams, 13 January 1825, T199, Roll 1.

17 Wilson to Secretary of State James Buchanan, 1 July 1847, T199, Roll 1.

18 Wilson to Buchanan, 25 February 1848, T199, Roll 1.

19 Hugh Keenan to Buchanan, 6 October 1847, T199, Roll 1.

20 Keenan to Buchanan, 17 December 1847, T199, Roll 1.

21 Keenan to Buchanan, 14 July 1848, T199, Roll 1.

22 Keenan to State Department, 8 January 1849, T199, Roll 1.

23 Keenan to State Department, 1 April 1849; James Foy to Secretary of State Daniel Webster, 18 November 1850, T199, Roll 1.

24 Walter Burges Smith, *America's Diplomats and Consuls of 1776–1865: A Geographic and Biographic Directory of the Foreign Service from the Declaration of Independence to the End of the Civil War* (Washington, DC: Center for the Study of Foreign Affairs, Foreign Service Institute, Department of State, 1986), 61.

25 List of Diplomatic and Consular Officers of the United States, 1866, 6; *Journal of the Executive Proceedings of the Senate of the United States of America*, 13 March–29 November 1867.

26 H.R. 1636, 42nd Cong., 2d Sess.

27 H.R. 43rd Cong., 1st Sess., Report 408 (11 April 1874).

28 *New York Times*, 28 September 1893, 4; John Howard Brown, ed., *Lamb's Biographical Dictionary of the United States*, vol. VII (Boston, MA: Federal Book Company of Boston, 1903).

29 John F. Jewell, 'A Veteran Consul', *American Consular Bulletin* V, no. 5 (May 1923): 135.

30 Consular Agent of the United States, Message from the President of the United States, Transmitting Report of De B. Randolph Keim, Agent, &c, 1872. H.R. 42nd Cong., 3d Sess., Executive Document No. 145, at 13.

31 Report of De B. Randolph Keim, 13.
32 *New York Times*, 31 December 1910, 9.
33 Thomas M. Waller, consul general, 'Inspection of United States Consulates in the United Kingdom' (Washington, DC: Department of State, Government Printing Office, 1887), 9.
34 *New York Times*, 4 June 1889, 3; 20 January 1910, 11.
35 'Dublin Vice Consul's Death', *The Times*, 13 April 1914, 8; John Howard Brown, ed., *Lamb's Biographical Dictionary of the United States*, vol. VII (Boston, MA: Federal Book Company of Boston, 1903).
36 *The Collected Works of Abraham Lincoln*, ed. Roy P. Basler, vol. VIII (New Brunswick, NJ: Rutgers University Press, 1953–55), 337.
37 Clare Dowler, 'John James Piatt, Representative Figure of a Momentous Period', *The Ohio Archeological and Historical Quarterly* 45, no. 1 (January 1936): 1–26.
38 Paula Bernat Bennett, ed., *Palace Burner: The Selected Poetry of Sarah Piatt* (Champaign: University of Illinois Press, 2005), 43–44, 169n43, 169n44; Mary McCartin Wearn, *Negotiating Motherhood in Nineteenth-Century American Literature* (London: Routledge, 2007), 105–35.
39 *The Times*, 13 April 1914, 8.
40 Ibid.
41 Telegram dated 18 February 1898 by Robert S. Chilton Jr., Chief of the Consular Bureau, Robert S. Chilton, Jr, Papers, Box 1, Folder 11, Georgetown University Library.
42 Message from the President of the United States, transmitting, in response to the Resolution of the Senate of March 2, 1901, a communication from the secretary of state submitting reports from consular officers of the United States giving an account of each consulate and consular agency, showing its principal industries and exports, the surrounding climatic conditions, the general cost of living, and similar information. Senate, 57th Cong., 1st Sess., Document 411 (Washington, 1902), 302.
43 *New York Times*, 13 March 1902, 9.
44 Foreign Office List 1905, 457.
45 Dublin Consulate, Inspection 1908, Inspection Reports on Foreign Service Posts, 1906–39, RG 59, NARA.
46 Inspection Report 1908.
47 Wilbur Carr to Alfred K. Moe, 18 November 1908, filed within the inspection report.
48 Inspection Report 1909.
49 Ibid.
50 Inspection Report 1911.
51 Ibid.
52 Inspection Report 1914.
53 State Department Biographical Register (1922), 102.
54 Register of the Department of State (1 January 1924), 89; (1 January 1926), 83.
55 Foreign Office List 1922, 493.
56 Register of the Department of State (October 1938), 107; Preliminary Guide to the Charles M. Hathaway, Jr, Papers, Davidson Library, University of California, Santa Barbara.
57 Inspection Report 1924.
58 Memo to Hengstler, 25 September 1924, filed with Inspection Report.
59 Inspection Report 1926.
60 Embassy website. http://dublin.usembassy.gov/index/embassy-news/about-the-embassy2/former-ambassadors.html [accessed 14 September 2009].

Chapter Thirteen Dundee

1 Robert Grieve, consul at Leith and responsible for Dundee, forwarded to the State Department on 6 January 1834 a statement of Dundee's consular fees for the period 10 to 31 December

1833, signed by Edward Baxter as vice consul for Dundee. Grieve to Secretary of State Louis McLane, 6 January 1834, Despatches from United States Consuls, Leith, Record Group 59, T396, NARA.

2 *Journal of the Executive Proceedings of the Senate of the United States of America*, 22 March 1834, 372; 'From the London Gazette, Tuesday, July 29', *The Times*, 30 July 1834, 3.

3 *The Collected Works of Abraham Lincoln*, ed. Roy P. Basler, vol. VI, 1862–1863 (New Brunswick, NJ: Rutgers University Press, 1953–1955), 51–52.

4 Ibid., 58.

5 *New York Times*, 3 November 1921.

6 *New York Times*, 2 August 1871.

7 Consular Agent of the United States, Message from the President of the United States, Transmitting Report of De B. Randolph Keim, Agent, &c., 1972, H.R. 42nd Cong., 3d Sess., Executive Document No. 145, at 14–15.

8 Leslie M. Scott, 'History of the Narrow Gauge Railroad in the Williamette Valley', *The Quarterly of the Oregon Historical Society* XX, no. 2 (June 1919), 141–158.

9 *Aberdeen Almanac* 1830, 248.

10 Register of the Department of State (1874), 22; Report of De B. Randolph Keim, 15.

11 Thomas M. Waller, consul general, 'Inspection of United States Consulates in the United Kingdom' (Washington, DC: Department of State, Government Printing Office, 1887), 14.

12 Message from the President of the United States, transmitting, in response to the Resolution of the Senate of March 2, 1901, a communication from the secretary of state submitting reports from consular officers of the United States giving an account of each consulate and consular agency, showing its principal industries and exports, the surrounding climatic conditions, the general cost of living, and similar information. Senate, 57th Cong., 1st Sess., Document 411 (Washington, 1902), 305–7.

13 'De B. Randolph', *The Times*, 4 January 1894, 5; Register of the Department of State (1915), 115.

14 Message from the President, 1902, 305–7. It is not known whether Allan Baxter was related to Edward Baxter, the first consular officer.

15 *New York Times*, 15 February 1897, 7; Register of the Department of State (1 January 1930), 196.

16 Dundee Consulate, Inspection 1908, Inspection Reports on Foreign Service Posts, 1906–1939, RG 59, NARA.

17 *American Journal of International Law*, supp. to vol. 1, 1907, 331 and vol. 5, 1911, 142.

18 Chief Clerk to Higgins, 25 November 1908, on Inspection Report 1908 file.

19 Inspection Report 1909.

20 Register of the Department of State (1922), 132; *New York Times*, 19 June 1924.

21 Charles Stuart Kennedy, *The American Consul: A History of the United States Consular Service 1776–1914* (Westport, CT: Greenwood Press, 1990), 223.

22 Register of the Department of State 1922, 133. Later, while consul general in London, Hollis returned to Dundee and in the presence of consul Henry A. Johnson married Alice Davidson, a hospital nurse from Arbroath. It was his second marriage. He died on 8 June 1930 and was buried in Arlington National Cemetery with full naval honours. Marriage certificate dated 18 May 1918 in the author's possession; *American Foreign Service Journal*, July 1930, 255.

23 Dunfermline, Inspection Report, 1909.

24 *New York Times*, 10 May 1914.

25 Inspection Report 1911. For more about Dennison's lameness, see the account of the Birmingham consulate in Chapter 8.

26 List of US Consular Officers 1789–1939, National Archives and Records Administration, M587, Roll 10; Foreign Office List, 1916, 595; my correspondence with Alison Fraser, Principal Archivist, The Orkney Library & Archive, Kirkwall, 17 and 18 March 2009.

27 Inspection Report 1914. The author has been unable to trace the fate of the consuls' photographs.

28 Register of the Department of State 1922, 194; The Aberdeen Almanac and Northern Register 1916 and 1922, 104 in each.

29 *Evening Express*, Aberdeen, 1 October 1909; *Aberdeen Daily Journal*, 30 September and 1 October, 1912; Minutes and Proceedings of Aberdeen Town Council 1917–1918, 107, 135; (Aberdeen, Aberdeen City Library and Cultural Services, Sutton Publishing Ltd., 1997), 66.

30 *New York Times*, 4 November 1917. Although the firm is not named in the article it is likely to be James Keiller & Sons.

31 Register of the Department of State (1922), 139.

32 Inspection Report 1919; List of US Consular Officers 1789–1939, National Archives and Records Administration, M587, Roll 10.

33 Poindexter's brother, Miles, was a senator for Washington state from 1909 to 1922; he was unsuccessful in gaining re-election and was appointed ambassador to Peru, where he served from 1923 until 1928. His vice consul brother's activities, if he was aware of them, must have been an embarrassment. Biographical Directory of the United States Congress.

34 Inspection Report 1921.

35 Herbert C. Hengstler to Robert Frazer Jr., 7 June 1924, copy on Inspection Report 1924 file.

36 Inspection Report, 1924.

37 https://www.findagrave.com/cgi-bin/fg.cgi?page=gr&GRid=49288745   [accessed   23 August 2017].

38 Inspection Report 1924.

39 Inspection Report 1926.

40 Register of the Department of State (1922), 193.

41 *New York Times*, 14 September 1932, 21.

42 Register of the Department of State (1922), 14; *New York Times*, 23 October 1932, 19.

43 Register of the Department of State (1942), 243.

44 Ibid., 170–1.

45 *New York Times*, 4 February 1940, 43.

Chapter Fourteen Dunfermline

1 Robeson to Davis, 13 February 1871, Record Group 59, NARA, Roll 4, T396.

2 Robeson to Davis, 24 April 1871, T396; Register of the Department of State 1872, 24.

3 Consular Agent of the United States, Message from the President of the United States, Transmitting Report of De B. Randolph Keim, Agent, &c., 1972, H.R. 42nd Cong., 3d Sess., Executive Document No. 145, at 19–20.

4 Doig later moved to America and appears to have prospered. He applied for naturalization. In 1891 he is described as 'a visitor and American barrister residing at 232 and 231 Strand, St Clement Danes, London, England with his wife Florence and 3 servants'. http://www.dcedin.co.uk/TNG/getperson.php?personID=I1212&tree=tree1 [accessed 24 August 2017].

5 Message from the President of the United States, transmitting, in response to the Resolution of the Senate of March 2, 1901, a communication from the secretary of state submitting reports from consular officers of the United States giving an account of each consulate and consular agency, showing its principal industries and exports, the surrounding climatic conditions, the general cost of living, and similar information. Senate, 57th Cong., 1st Sess., Document 411 (Washington, 1902), 309.

6 Register of the Department of State (1874), 22.

7 Thomas M. Waller, consul general, 'Inspection of United States Consulates in the United Kingdom' (Washington, DC: Department of State, Government Printing Office, 1887), 6, 9.

8 *New York Times*, 9 March 1883, 1.

9 Register of the Department of State (1915), 116.

10 Waller, 'Inspection of United States Consulates', 6–14; *New York Times*, 24 November 1886.

11 Registers of the Department of State (1893 and 1901), 50, 15, respectively.

12 *New York Times*, 23 November 1889, 13 September 1896, 29 April 1901.

13 Register of the Department of State (1922), 149.

14 Message from the President, 309.

15 Ibid., 308.

16 Ibid., 309.

17 NARA, List of US Consular Officers, 1789–1939, M587, Roll 10.

18 Ibid.

19 'Commercial Markets. Flax and Jute Textiles, Dunfermline, Jan. 16', *The Times*, 17 January 1908, 23.

20 Dunfermline Consulate, Inspection 1908, Inspection Reports on Foreign Service Posts, 1906–1939, RG 59, NARA.

21 Department to Blake, 21 October 1908, filed with Inspection Report.

22 Inspection Report 1909.

23 Blake's residency in Edinburgh raises an interesting situation. As there was a consulate in that city, this meant that two American consuls for different districts lived in the same city. I have not come across a similar case.

24 Inspection Report 1909.

25 Register of the Department of State (1916), 74.

26 Register of the Department of State (January 1926), 204.

27 *New York Times*, 21 December 1902.

28 Inspection Report 1911.

29 *New York Times*, 20 June 1915.

30 Inspection Report 1911.

31 Register of the Department of State (1915), 128.

32 Inspection Report 1914.

33 Register of the Department of State (1922), 61, 177.

34 Inspection Report 1920.

35 Dundee Consulate, Inspection Report 1921.

36 Dunfermline, Inspection Report 1924.

37 *New York Times*, 12 August 1925.

38 Inspection Report 1924; *Dunfermline Press*, 5 September 1925, 4; *New Jersey Courier*, October 1925; Register of the Department of State (January 1926), 204; Nancy Bierbrauer, Ocean County Historical Society, Toms River, New Jersey, letter to the author, dated 25 May 2009.

39 Email correspondence to the author from Lyndsay Sarah Krasnoff, Office of the Historian, Department of State, 16 March 2009.

40 Van Sant's years in Dunfermline were marred by personal tragedy as well as by ill health. His second wife, Arvilla, died in 1920 at age 38, a year after the death of their two-year-old son Howard. In 1923, Van Sant married once more; his marriage to Marion Wilson Russell or Ford took place in Edinburgh. *Scotland's People* (a partnership between the General Register Office for Scotland, the National Archives of Scotland and the Court of the Lord Lyon. GROS references 424/00 0293, 424/00 0354 and 685/02 0270, respectively).

Chapter Fifteen Edinburgh and Leith

1 Harry Grant to B. Dandridge, 1 November 1798, Despatches from United States Consuls in Leith, Record Group 59, T396, NARA; *The London Gazette*, 5 December 1798.

2 Grant to Rufus King, 30 July 1799, and other letters between January 1800 and June 1801, Despatches, T396.

3 The practice of government officials disappearing from their posts seems to have remained popular over the centuries. For example, it was reported in 2010 that an official in the European Commission was dismissed, and even then only reluctantly it seems, after having 'been absent from work, without explanation, for several years'. Another was dismissed after 'a prolonged unauthorised absence for almost two years'. Simon McGee, 'Eurocrats Kept Brothels', *The Sunday Times*, 7 November 2010, 1–2.

4 William Pinkney to Robert Grieve, 8 November 1810; *Journal of the Executive Proceedings of the Senate of the United States of America*, 1817, vol. 3, 74, and 1834, vol. 4, 344–55; Grieve to Secretary of State Louis McLane, 10 and 21 August, 5 December 1833; Grieve to Secretary of State John Forsyth, 1 July 1837, Despatches, T396.

5 Grieve to McLane, 7 July 1834, Despatches, T396.

6 Grieve to Telfair, 5 June 1835; Grieve to Forsyth, 1 July and 1 October 1835, Despatches, T396.

7 Grieve to Forsyth, 1 July 1837, Despatches, T396; *The London Shipping Gazette*, 24 November 1836.

8 Act of 11 June 1874 (18 Stat. 66).

9 James McDowell to Secretary of State Cass, 10 January 1860, Despatches, T396.

10 James McDowell, Jr, to State Department, 1 July 1861, Despatches, T396.

11 Neil McLachlan to Lincoln, 23 August 1861, Despatches, T396.

12 Despatches, T396.

13 David Gould to Secretary of State Seward, 6 November 1866, Despatches, T396.

14 Gould to Department, undated, but in May 1867; also 28 June 1867; William Gould and James Galloway to Seward, 22 and 26 July 1867. Despatches, T396.

15 John S. Fiske to Seward, 24 September and 8 November 1867, 9 April 1868, Despatches, T396; *The Annual Register: A Review of Public Events at Home and Abroad, for the Year 1871*, new series (London: Rivingtons, 1872), 221.

16 *The Annual Register*, 220–24.

17 Ibid., 224.

18 Fiske to Fish, 24 June 1870, Despatches, T396.

19 Despatches from US ministers to Great Britain, 1791–1906, Record Group 59, M30, Rolls 99–100, 1870, NARA.

20 James Galloway to Fish, 5 August 1870, Despatches, T396.

21 John Robeson to Davis, 26 August 1870, Despatches, T396.

22 J. Smith to Pratt, internal State Department memo, undated but probably late November 1870; Robeson to Davis, 2 December 1870; Galloway to Davis, 2 December 1870; Robeson to Davis, 19 January 1871, Despatches, T396.

23 Robeson to Davis, 13 February 1871, Despatches, T396.

24 Robeson to Davis, 24 April 1871, Despatches, T396.

25 Consular Agent of the United States, Message from the President of the United States, Transmitting Report of De B. Randolph Keim, Agent, &c., 1872, H.R. 42nd Cong., 3d Sess., Executive Document No. 145, at 20.

26 Commercial Relations of the United States with Foreign Countries for the Year 1879, vol. II, (Washington, DC: Government Printing Office, 1880), 384–91; Henry E. Mattox, *The Twilight of Amateur Diplomacy: The American Foreign Service and Its Senior Officers in the 1890s* (Kent, OH, and London: The Kent State University Press, 1989), 147.

27 Register of the Department of State, 10 November 1913, 123; Commercial Relations of the United States with Foreign Countries during the years 1887 and 1888 (Washington, DC: Government Printing Office, 1889), 480–90.

28 Wallace Bruce to Quincy, 18 July 1893, Despatches from United States Consuls in Edinburgh, T602. His request was refused.

29 Bruce to Quincy, 31 August 1893, Despatches, T602. General Fremantle's presence was particularly fitting. Early in his career he had obtained three-months leave of absence and spent it travelling through the Confederate states meeting many prominent military and civil leaders. He

also witnessed the battle of Gettysburg. On his return he published an account of his trip. See Walter Lord, ed., *The Fremantle Diary: Being the Journal of Lieutenant Colonel James Arthur Lyon Fremantle, Coldstream Guards, and His Three Months in the Southern States* (London: Andre Deutsch, 1956).

30 Bruce to Quincy, 8 August 1893, Despatches, T602.

31 Francis Underwood to Quincy, 5 September 1863; Underwood to Strobel, Assistant Secretary of State, 21, 26, and 27 September 1893, Despatches, T602.

32 Underwood to Alvey Adee, second assistant secretary of state, 15 June 1893, Despatches, T602.

33 *The Scotsman*, 8 August 1894.

34 State Department memo, Consular Bureau to Edwin F. Uhl, assistant secretary of state, 3 May 1894, Despatches, T602.

35 Richard Lees to Secretary of State Gresham, 20 April 1894, Despatches, T602.

36 Frederick Piatt to Uhl, 27 September 1894, Despatches, T602.

37 Underwood to Uhl, 20 June 1894, Despatches, T602.

38 Piatt to Uhl, 7 August 1894, Despatches, T602.

39 *The Scotsman*, 8 August 1894.

40 Piatt to Uhl, 9 August 1894, Despatches, T602.

41 Piatt to Uhl, 10 August 1894, Despatches, T602; *The Scotsman*, 8 and 11 August 1894.

42 Robert MacBride to Secretary of State, 7 September 1894; MacBride to Uhl, 23 October 1894, Despatches, T602.

43 MacBride to Uhl, 15 November 1894, Despatches, T602.

44 MacBride to Uhl, 21 September 1895, Despatches, T602.

45 https://www.measuringworth.com/ukcompare/relativevalue.php [accessed 24 August 2017].

46 Piatt to Uhl, 6 December 1895; MacBride to Rockhill, 22 May 1897; MacBride to Day, 17 August 1897, Despatches, T602.

47 Piatt to Uhl, 21 December 1895, Despatches, T602. Stuyvesant was well-connected diplomatically. The guests at his wedding in London to the Comtesse de Warranaer on 16 June 1902 included senior members of the American Embassy, such as Ambassador Joseph Choate, First Secretary Henry White (he was Stuyvesant's brother-in-law), Second Secretary John R. Carter, and former Third Secretary William C. Eustis. *New York Times*, 17 June 1902, 7. https://www.measuringworth.com/ukcompare/relativevalue.php [accessed 24 August 2017].

48 Rufus Fleming to William R. Day, Assistant Secretary of State, 11 October and 1 December 1897, Despatches, T602; Register of Department of State, May 1922, 119.

49 Fleming to David J. Hill, assistant secretary of state, 17 May 1899; State Department manuscript memo, 6 April 1900, Despatches, T602.

50 Fleming to Hay, 29 July; Fleming to Assistant Secretary of State Francis B. Loomis, 30 July, 6 and 24 August; Wingate to Fleming, 16 August; Fleming to Wingate, 19 August, all 1903, all Despatches, T602.

51 Fleming to Loomis, 29 August 1904; Fleming to assistant secretary of state, 15 March and 3 July 1905, and 28 June 1906, Despatches, T602.

52 Edinburgh and Leith Consulate, Inspection 1908, Inspection Reports on Foreign Service Posts, 1906–1939, RG 59, NARA.

53 NARA, List of US Consular Officers, 1789–1939, M587, Roll 10.

54 Inspection Report 1909.

55 Inspection Report 1911.

56 Ibid.

57 Inspection Reports, 1909 and 1911.

58 Wilbur Carr to Fleming, 8 January 1912, 30 January 1915; included among the 1914 inspection papers.

59 Inspection Report, 1914.

60 'Death of Mr Rufus Fleming. American Consul in Edinburgh', *The Scotsman*, 5 April 1920, 4. A similar account was contained in 'Death of U.S. Consul in Edinburgh', *The Edinburgh Evening News*, 5 April 1920, 5.

61 Inspection Report, 1919.

62 Inspection Report, 1921.

63 Inspection Report, 1924.

64 Inspection Report, 1926.

65 Ibid.

66 *The Scotsman*, 11 February 1927, 12.

67 Inspection Report, 1933.

68 Register of the Department of State (1945), 212; Handbook of the Consular Corps of Edinburgh-Leith, 1949–1950, National Archives of Scotland, HH41/576, 25.

69 'An American Who Retired in Edinburgh', *Edinburgh Evening News*, 6 December 1954; 'Former U.S. Consul in Edinburgh. Late Mr C.R. Nasmith', *The Scotsman*, 6 December 1954.

70 Handbook of the Consular Corps of Edinburgh-Leith, 1949–1950, 25.

71 Edward L. Killham, interviewed by Robert Martens, December 1992, Foreign Affairs Oral History Program, Association for Diplomatic Studies and Training, Arlington, VA. Frontline Diplomacy, Manuscript Division, Library of Congress, Washington, DC. Handbook of the Consular Corps of Edinburgh-Leith, 1949–1950, 18.

72 Register of the Department of State (1945), 212; Handbook of the Consular Corps of Edinburgh-Leith, 1949–1950, National Archives of Scotland, HH41/576, 25.

73 Robert Bruce Houston, interviewed by Horace G. Torbert, 14 May 1990, Foreign Affairs Oral History Program, Association for Diplomatic Studies and Training, Arlington, VA. Frontline Diplomacy, Manuscript Division, Library of Congress, Washington, DC.

74 NARA, RG59, Management Staff Files, Lot 69, D.434; Miscellaneous Subject Files 1960–1967; Marginal Consular Posts, 1961.

75 Paul F. DuVivier interviewed by Charles Stuart Kennedy, 20 February 1990, Foreign Affairs Oral History Program, Association for Diplomatic Studies and Training, Arlington, VA. Frontline Diplomacy, Manuscript Division, Library of Congress, Washington, DC.

76 State Department, Foreign Service List, September 1967, iv, 19.

77 Foreign Service List, October 1970.

78 NARA, Central Foreign Policy Files, 1973–1976, Record Group 59, General Records of the Department of State (Retrieved from Access to Archival Databases, 5 January 2012), Document Number 1975EDINBU00074, 3 April 1975.

79 Ibid., Document Number 1975EDINBU00081, 9 April 1975.

80 Ibid., Document Number 1976EDINBU00037, 30 January 1976.

81 Allison Klein, 'Man Fatally Shoots Wife, Self at Retirement Home', *Washington Post*, 16 May 2008.

82 Douglas H. Jones, 'Lockerbie, Ten Years Later,' *Foreign Service Journal*, December 1998, 13–14, 46–48; Inspection Report 1989, 8.

83 Inspection Report 1989, 8.

84 Inspection Report 1999, 15.

85 State Department, Daily Press Briefing, 18 July 1995, DPB # 106, Briefer: Nicholas Burns; Cathy L. Hurst, 'Edinburgh: Celebrating 200 Years of Consular History', *State Magazine* (October 1998): 32–35.

86 Inspection Report 1999, 12–13.

87 Speech by Ambassador Philip Lader at Duke University, Durham, North Carolina, 11 October 2000. www.usembassy.org.uk/ukamb22.html [accessed 18 February 2001].

88 Consulate General website, http://www.usembassy.org.uk/scotland/officer_bio.html [accessed 15 September 2009].

89 http://edinburgh.usconsulate.gov/about-us/principal.html [accessed 2 August 2012].

90 Document dated 20 February 2013, previously classified 'Secret/No Foreign Nationals'. American Embassy London to State Department. Scenesetter for Secretary Kerry's visit to London on 24–25 February 2013. Among documents made available to the author by the State Department under a Freedom of Information Act request.

91 Document dated 12 September 2014 by Consul Bazarnic: 'EAC Convened to Discuss Security Posture Ahead of Independence Referendum'. Made available to the author by the State Department under a Freedom of Information Act request.

92 Letter dated 7 July 2017 to the author from Alesia Y. Williams, chief, FOIA and Declassification Services Office.

93 The United States has embassies in many other similarly sized countries as Scotland, for example, Luxembourg, Ireland, Iceland, Latvia, Lithuania and Estonia.

94 See, for example, First Minister Nicola Sturgeon's address to the Irish Parliament on 29 November 2016 when she repeated that the question of Scottish independence remains firmly on the table. www.bbc.co.uk/news/uk-Scotland-scotland-politics-38139630 [accessed 29 November 2016]. This continues to be her Party's policy.

95 http://edinburgh.usconsulate.gov/about-us/principal.html [accessed 18 August 2015].

Chapter Sixteen Falmouth

1 Nicholas Michael Keegan, 'Consular Representation in Britain: Its History, Current Status, and Personnel', PhD thesis, University of Durham, 2004, 149; *Consular Documents and Posts Held at Various times by Partners and Others, G. C. Fox & Co.,* privately printed, 1984, given to the author by Charles L. Fox, July 2001.

2 *Senate Executive Journal,* 19 February 1793, 129–30; 20 February 1793, 130.

3 *Senate Executive Journal,* 29 May 1794, 158; 30 May 1794, 159.

4 *Oxford Dictionary of National Biography.*

5 Charles Stuart Kennedy, *The American Consul: A History of the United States Consular Service 1776–1914* (Westport CT: Greenwood Press, 1990), 46.

6 *Senate Executive Journal,* 26 January 1819, 170; *Oxford Dictionary of National Biography.*

7 Rollin R. Winslow, 'The History of the American Consulates at Plymouth and Falmouth from 1792 to 1936,' *Annual Reports and Transactions of the Plymouth Institution and Devon and Cornwall Natural History Society,* vol. 18 (1944 for 1936–1937), 58. Winslow was appointed US consul in Plymouth in 1934.

8 Despatch No. 112, dated 4 January 1856, cited in *The Works of James Buchanan: Comprising His Speeches, State Papers, and Private Correspondence,* ed. John Bassett Moore, vol. X, 1856–1860 (Philadelphia & London: J. B. Lippincott, 1910).

9 Blue Book for 1853, containing the salaries of all the US ministers to foreign courts, the fees of the US consuls in all parts of the world, etc. (Philadelphia, 1853), 5.

10 Winslow, 'History of the American Consulates', 59.

11 Register of the Department of State (1874), 22.

12 Consular Agent of the United States, Message from the President of the United States, Transmitting Report of De B. Randolph Keim, Agent, &c., 1872, H.R. 42nd Cong., 3d Sess., Executive Document No. 145, at 15.

13 Message from the President of the United States, transmitting, in response to the Resolution of the Senate, March 2, 1901, a communication from the secretary of state submitting reports from consular officers of the United States giving an account of each consulate and consular agency, showing the principal industries and exports, the surrounding climatic conditions, the general cost of living, and similar information. Senate, 57th Cong., 1st Sess., Document 411 (1902), 313.

14 The last member of the family to serve as consul at Plymouth was Thomas W. Fox IV, who served there from 1884–1897; Winslow, 'History of the American Consulates', 49.

15 Message from the President of the United States, 313.

16 Thomas M. Waller, consul general, 'Inspection of United States Consulates in the United Kingdom' (Washington, DC: Department of State, Government Printing Office, 1887), 6.

17 Ibid., 13.

18 Ibid., 6.
19 Typed list given to the author by Charles Fox in July 2001.
20 Message from the President of the United States, 312.
21 Email dated 25 March 2009 to the author from Tiffany T. Hamelin, Historian, Policy Studies Division, Office of the Historian, Department of State.
22 Typed list given to the author by Charles Fox in July 2001.
23 *New York Times*, 11 March 1868, 1.
24 *New York Times*, 21 July 1901, 1.
25 Telephone call on 16 October 2001 from Charles L. Fox informing the author that he had submitted his resignation to the relevant embassies. Factors influencing his decision included ownership of the firm of G. C. Fox & Co. changing several times within a relatively short period, and a decrease in the amount of consular activities.

Chapter Seventeen Liverpool

1 The Rev. Maury was said by some to have narrow views. He 'denounced anyone who did not belong to the Church of England, and he eventually took Britain's side in disputes with her American colonies.' Richard B. Bernstein, *Thomas Jefferson* (New York: Oxford University Press, 2005), 3.
2 Although no longer president but still nevertheless deeply engaged in political life, Jefferson found time to write to Maury a few weeks before America declared war on Britain: 'Our two countries are to be at war, but not you and I. And why should our two countries be at war, when by peace we can be so much more useful to one another? Surely the world will acquit our government from having sought it.' Thomas Jefferson to James Maury, 25 April 1812. In *The Writings of Thomas Jefferson*, ed. Paul Leicester Ford, vol. IX, 1807–1815 (New York and London: G. P. Putnam's Sons, 1898), 348.
3 Anne Fontaine Maury, ed., *Intimate Virginiana: A Century of Maury Travels by Land and Sea* (Richmond, VA: Dietz Press, 1941).
4 Julian P. Boyd, ed., *The Papers of Thomas Jefferson*, vol. 10 (Princeton, NJ: Princeton University Press, 1954), 387–8.
5 Ibid., vol. 17, 1965, 252n.
6 Maury's Commission of Appointment, dated 7 June 1790, is in the Virginia Historical Society, Richmond, Virginia. It is signed by George Washington and countersigned by Thomas Jefferson. (Mss2 M4484 a 1). On the same date, the Senate approved the appointment of William Knox of New York as consul in Dublin 'in the kingdom of Ireland'. Journal of the executive proceedings of the Senate of the United States of America 1789–1805, 7 June 1790, 49. Notice of the royal approval of Maury's appointment was published in *The London Gazette*, 2–6 November 1790, 659.
7 *Senate Executive Journal*, 4 and 7 June 1790, 48–49; James Maury to Thomas Jefferson, 8 September 1790, Despatches from United States Consuls in Liverpool, 1790–1906, Record Group 59, M141, Roll 1, NARA; William Knox to Thomas Jefferson, 26 November 1790, Despatches from United States Consuls in Dublin, 1790–1906, Record Group 59, T199, Roll 1, NARA.
8 *Senate Executive Journal*, 4 June 1790, 48; 7 June 1790, 50; 17 June 1790, 51–52; 23 February 1791, 76; and 24 February 1791, 76.
9 'Diplomatic relations and the American Legation in London were established on June 1, 1785, when John Adams presented his credentials as Minister Plenipotentiary to King George III. Adams, however, became so frustrated with the cool reception that he closed the legation in 1788 and the post remained vacant for four years.' A Guide to the United States' History of Recognition, Diplomatic, and Consular Relations, by Country, since 1776: The United Kingdom, Department of State. https://history.state.gov/countries/united-kingdom [accessed 26 January 2016].

10 *Senate Executive Journal*, 2 August 1790, 54.
11 Joshua Johnson to James Maury, 1 November 1790, Despatches from United States Consuls in London, 1790–1906, Record Group 59, T168, NARA.
12 Gore's 1790 Directory for Liverpool.
13 Roger Hull, Researcher, Liverpool Record Office, email to the author, 22 April 2009.
14 Ibid.
15 Ron Jones, *The American Connection: The Story of Liverpool's Links with America, from Christopher Columbus to the Beatles* (Moreton, UK: Wirral, 1986, printed privately), 9–27.
16 Paul Webster, Librarian, Liverpool Record Office, email to the author, 7 May 2009, quoting from Baines' History of Lancashire 1824.
17 Jones, *The American Connection*, 29.
18 National Museums Liverpool, U.S. consulate eagle takes up residence at Museum of Liverpool, 21 May 2014. http://www.liverpoolmuseums.org.uk/about/mediacentre/2014/eagle-sculpture-displayed.aspx [accessed 26 January 2016].
19 *Senate Executive Journal*, 10 February 1790, 40.
20 William Barnes and John Heath Morgan, *The Foreign Service of the United States: Origins, Development, and Functions* (Washington, DC: Department of State, 1961), 32.
21 Number 4 Rodney Street is now part of the administrative offices of Liverpool John Moores University.
22 Merseyside Painters, People and Places, Catalogue of Oil Paintings, 1978, 159.
23 Maury to Jefferson, 9 September 1790, NARA, Record Group 59, M141.
24 Margaret Maury to William Maury, 22 June 1819. Maury, *Intimate Virginiana* 43–44.
25 *Senate Executive Journal*, 2 March 1815, 626; Barnes and Morgan, *The Foreign Service of the United States*, 64n, 105n.
26 Maury, *Intimate Virginiana*, 153–158.
27 Ibid., 15.
28 Ibid., 14. A silver tureen from the dinner service is in the Fredericksburg Area Museum and Cultural Center, Virginia, and a silver platter inscribed by the Liverpool merchants is in the Virginia Historical Society, Richmond, Virginia.
29 *Dictionary of American Biography*, Vol. 13 (New York: Charles Scribner's Sons, 1934), 639.
30 Schuyler is pronounced 'Sky-ler'.
31 Doreen Bolger, 'Ambrose Andrews and His Masterpiece "The Children of Nathan Starr"', *American Art Journal* 22 (Spring 1990): 5.
32 'Foreign Office, November 11, 1844', *London Gazette*, 15 November 1844, 4059.
33 Allen Johnson, ed., *Dictionary of American Biography*, vol. IV (London: Oxford University Press, 1930), 549.
34 Arlin Turner, *Nathaniel Hawthorne: Biography* (New York and Oxford: Oxford University Press, 1980), 265.
35 Bradford Torrey, ed., *The Writings of Henry David Thoreau*, vol. XV (Boston: Houghton Mifflin, 1909), 37.
36 Turner, *Nathaniel Hawthorne*, 265.
37 Nathaniel Hawthorne, 'Consular Experiences', in *Our Old Home: A Series of English Sketches*, centenary edition of the works of Nathaniel Hawthorne, vol. V (Athens: Ohio State University Press, 1970), 35–36.
38 Ibid., 9.
39 Turner, *Nathaniel Hawthorne*, 306.
40 The religious order is now known as the Dominican Sisters of Hawthorne. Rose's name in religion is Mother Mary Alphonsa. Her cause for sainthood is currently (2017) being considered in the Vatican.
41 Turner, *Nathaniel Hawthorne*, 274.
42 Barnes and Morgan, *The Foreign Service of the United States*, 124.

43 'Abuses in the Consular Service', ibid.; Consular Agent of the United States, Message from the President of the United States Transmitting Report of De B. Randolph Keim, Agent, &c., 1872, H.R. 42nd Cong., 3d Sess., Executive Document No. 145, at 80–81; *New York Times*, 'Mr Hawthorne and His Consulate', 2 October 1857; 'The Liverpool Consulate', *New York Times*, 16 August 1861. John B. Floyd was a former US secretary of war who was accused of financial irregularities while in office, although he was later cleared. During the Civil War he became a Confederate general.

44 Beverley Tucker Family Papers, Special Collections Research Center, Earl Gregg Swarm Library, College of William and Mary, Williamsburg, Virginia.

45 Robert M. Magraw of Maryland, George McHenry of Pennsylvania and De Witt C. Littlejohn of New York. *Senate Executive Journal*, 7 January 1861, 243; 6 February 1861, 258; 11 March 1861, 293.

46 *The Collected Works of Abraham Lincoln*, ed. Roy P. Basler, vol. IV (New Brunswick, NJ: Rutgers University Press, 1953–1955), 466.

47 Dudley's handwritten narrative, 5 March, 1884, Papers of Thomas H. Dudley, 1841–1893, DU1275, Manuscripts Department, Huntington Library, San Marino, California; Brian Jenkins, *Britain and the War for the Union*, vol. 2 (Montreal: McGill-Queen's University Press, 1980), 120.

48 Papers of Thomas H. Dudley, 1841–1893, DU1275, Manuscripts Department, Huntington Library.

49 Foreign Office List and Diplomatic and Consular Year Book 1872, 286.

50 Report of De B. Randolph Keim, 21.

51 'Obituary', *The Times*, 6 May 1893, 6.

52 Register of the Department of State 1874, 23.

53 *New York Times*, 5 March 1883.

54 Ibid.

55 *New York Times*, 1 April 1885.

56 Thomas M. Waller, consul general, 'Inspection of United States Consulates in the United Kingdom', (Washington, DC: Department of State, Government Printing Office, 1887), 6–7, 14.

57 Cited in Henry E. Mattox, *The Twilight of Amateur Diplomacy: The American Foreign Service and Its Senior Officers in the 1890s* (Kent, OH, and London: The Kent State University Press, 1989), 59.

58 John Howard Brown, ed., *Lamb's Biographical Dictionary of the United States*, vol. VII (Boston, MA, Federal Book Company of Boston, 1903).

59 Gore's Directory of Liverpool 1900.

60 *New York Times*, 7 May 1899.

61 Message from the President of the United States, transmitting, in response to the Resolution of the Senate of March 2, 1901, a communication from the secretary of state submitting reports from consular officers of the United States giving an account of each consulate and consular agency, showing its principal industries and exports, the surrounding climatic conditions, the general cost of living, and similar information, Senate, 57th Cong., 1st Sess., Document 411 (Washington, 1902), 346–49.

62 Foreign Office List and Diplomatic and Consular Year Book 1905, 458.

63 Message from the President of the United States, 349; *American Journal of International Law*, supp. to vol. 1, 1907, Official Documents, 332.

64 Dom Julian Stead, OSB, letter to the author, 22 May 2006; undated note by Dom Julian in the Stead Collection, Mills Memorial Library, McMaster University, Hamilton, Ontario, and used with his permission.

65 Register of the Department of State (1 January 1930), 215–16.

66 Register of the Department of State (1929), 166.

67 Memo, Political Observations, Philip Holland, American Consul General, Liverpool, 28 February 1942, Great Britain Diplomatic Files, Box 36, Franklin Delano Roosevelt Digital Archives, Franklin Delano Roosevelt Presidential Library and Museum, Hyde Park, New York.

68 *New York Times*, 18 October 1955.

69 Walter M. McClelland, interviewed by Charles Stuart Kennedy, 20 November 1995, Foreign Affairs Oral History Program, Association for Diplomatic Studies and Training, Arlington, VA. Frontline Diplomacy, Manuscript Division, Library of Congress, Washington, DC. http://memory.loc.gov/ammem/collections/diplomacy/.

70 Stanley D. Schiff, interviewed by Charles Stuart Kennedy, 9 November 2000, Foreign Affairs Oral History Program.

71 J. Edgar Williams, letter to the author, 28 November 2006.

72 Service gave a lengthy and revealing series of interviews in 1977 and 1978, the transcripts of which can be accessed via the Library of Congress at http://memory.loc.gov/ammem/collections/diplomacy/.

73 John Kifner, 'John Service, a Purged "China Hand", Dies at 89', *New York Times*, 4 February 1999.

74 The other consulates were Edinburgh, Manchester and Southampton. Memorandum from the Deputy Under Secretary of State for Administration (Jones) to Secretary of State Rusk, Washington, February 14, 1961. National Archives and Records Administration, RG 59, Management Staff Files: Lot 69, D434, Miscellaneous Subject Files, 1960–1967, Marginal Consular Posts, 1961.

75 NARA, Central Foreign Policy Files, 1973–1976, Record Group 59, General Records of the Department of State (Retrieved from Access to Archival Databases, 4 January 2012), Document Number 1976LONDON02909, 25 February 1976.

76 Ibid., 1976LONDON02975, 26 February 1976; 'US closes Liverpool consulate', *Christian Science Monitor*, 3 March 1976, 2.

77 NARA, Central Foreign Policy Files, 1973–1976, Record Group 59, General Records of the Department of State (Retrieved from Access to Archival Databases, 4 January 2012), Document Number 1976Rome02805, 20 February 1976; letter dated 7 July 2009 from Normand W. Redden to the author.

Chapter Eighteen London

1 Kent's Directory for the Year 1794, Cities of London and Westminster, and Borough of Southwark.

2 John Adams, the first US minister plenipotentiary, served in London from 1785 until 1788. There was a break of almost four years before his successor, Thomas Pinckney, was appointed in January 1792.

3 Jefferson to Johnson, 7 August 1790. In *The Papers of Thomas Jefferson*, ed. Julian P. Boyd,vol. 17, 6 July to 3 November 1790 (Princeton, NJ: Princeton University Press, 1965), 119.

4 Johnson to Jefferson, 2 November 1790, Boyd, *The Papers of Thomas Jefferson*, 667–68; also in Despatches from United States Consuls in London, 1790–1906, Record Group 59, T168, NARA.

5 Despatches from United States Consuls in London, 1790–1906.

6 Jacob M. Price, 'Johnson, Joshua (1742–1802)', in *Oxford Dictionary of National Biography*, (Oxford: Oxford University Press, 2004). http://www.oxforddnb.com/view/article/60692 [accessed 4 June 2009].

7 The Royal Kalendar for the Year 1801, 116.

8 Bird, Savage and Bird were the London banking agents of the US government. When the bank failed in 1803 the US government business was taken over by Barings. Philip Zeigler, *The Sixth Great Power: Barings 1762–1929* (London: Collins, 1988), 68–69.

9 James Madison to Samuel Williams, 29 June 1801. In Robert J. Brugger et al., eds., *The Papers of James Madison, Secretary of State Series*, vol. 1, 4 March–31 July 1801 (Charlottesville: University Press of Virginia, 1986), 357–38.

10 Samuel Williams to James Madison, 21 August 1801. In Mary Hackett, et al., eds., *The Papers of James Madison, Secretary of State Series*, vol. 2, 1 August 1801–28 February 1802 (Charlottesville: University of Virginia Press, 1993), 59.

11 Biographical Directory of the United States Congress.

12 Charles C. Smith, 'Memoirs of Colonel Thomas Aspinwall', in *Proceedings of the Massachusetts Historical Society*, November 1891, second series, vol. VII, 1891, 1892, 32–38; Money Market and City Intelligence, *The Times*, 7 March 1854, 11.

13 The Royal Blue Book Fashionable Directory for 1827, xvii; Blue Book for 1853, containing the salaries of all the US ministers to foreign courts, the fees of the US consuls in all parts of the world, Philadelphia, 4.

14 Biographical Directory of the United States Congress.

15 Freeman H. Morse, consul, London, to Henry Shelton Sanford, minister, Brussels, 29 June 1861. H. S. Sanford Papers, Box 139, Folder 12, Item 1, Sanford Museum, Florida.

16 List of Diplomatic and Consular Officers of the United States, together with their compensation, places of official residence, states where born and whence appointed, and dates of appointment (Washington, DC: Department of State, Government Printing Office, 1866), 5.

17 Obituary, *The Times*, 7 February 1891, 10; *Dictionary of American Biography*, vol. XIII (London: Oxford University Press, 1934), 243.

18 We have seen earlier that there was little or no movement between the Diplomatic Service and the Consular Service. This is why Badeau had to resign from the legation post (Diplomatic Service) to become consul general (Consular Service).

19 Consular Agent of the United States, Message from the President of the United States Transmitting Report of De B. Randolph Keim, Agent, &c. 1872. H.R. 42nd Cong., 3d Sess., Executive Document No. 145, at 23–24.

20 Register of the Department of State (1874), 23; *Whitaker's Almanack* (1879), 289.

21 *Dictionary of American Biography*, 485.

22 United States v. Badeau, Circuit Court, New York, July 6, 1887. *The Federal Reporter*, Vol. 31, Cases Argued and Determined in the Circuit and District Courts of the United States. July–October, 1887, 697-700. Available online at: https://digital.library.unt.edu/ark:/67531/metadc36360/m1/717/?q=573 [accessed 7 January 2018].

23 *Lamb's Biographical Dictionary of the United States* (Boston: Federal Book Company of Boston, 1903).

24 *New York Times*, 31 July 1881, 12.

25 Graham H. Stuart, *American Diplomatic and Consular Practice*, 2nd ed. (New York: Appleton-Century-Crofts, 1952), 339.

26 Foreign Office List and Diplomatic and Consular Year Book 1885, 311.

27 Thomas M. Waller, consul general, *Inspection of United States Consulates in the United Kingdom* (Washington, DC: Department of State, Government Printing Office, 1887); Message from the President of the United States, transmitting, in response to the Resolution of the Senate of March 2, 1901, a communication from the secretary of state submitting reports from consular officers of the United States giving an account of each consulate and consular agency, showing its principal industries and exports, the surrounding climatic conditions, the general cost of living, and similar information. Senate, 57th Cong., 1st Sess., Document 411 (Washington, 1902), 350.

28 Webster's Royal Red Book, or Court and Fashionable Register for May 1889 (London: A. Webster & Co., 1889), 953.

29 *New York Times*, 3 May 1889, 1.

30 *Lamb's Biographical Dictionary of the United States*; Henry E. Mattox, *The Twilight of Amateur Diplomacy: The American Foreign Service and Its Senior Officers in the 1890s* (Kent, OH, and London, Kent State University Press, 1989), 149.

31 Letter dated 11 April 1893 from Francis W. Frigout, vice and deputy consul general, London, to US consuls in Britain and Ireland asking them to send him 'a cabinet photograph of yourself, with your autograph thereon' for inclusion in the album. A cabinet photograph was

usually 4 by 6 inches, slightly larger than a carte de visite. Frigout's letter and all the replies from the consuls, enclosing or promising to send photographs, are in the John C. New Collection held by the Indiana Historical Society. Unfortunately, there is no trace of the presentation photograph album.

32 Register of the Department of State (1893), 31.

33 Foreign Office List and Diplomatic and Consular Year Book 1895, 361.

34 *New York Times*, 30 April 1902, 9; Rossiter Johnson, ed., *The Twentieth Century Biographical Dictionary of Notable Americans, Vol. VIII* (Boston: The Biographical Society, 1904); Message from the President of the United States, 351.

35 Message from the President of the United States, 350.

36 Ibid.

37 Biographical Directory of the United States Congress; *New York Times*, 13 December 1921, 19.

38 34 Stat. 99.

39 *New York Times*, 13 July 1907, 4.

40 *New York Times*, 1 December 1907, C2.

41 Emily Bax, *Miss Bax of the Embassy* (Boston: Houghton Mifflin, 1939), 168–69.

42 Ibid., 68.

43 *New York Times*, 1 December 1912, S5.

44 *New York Times*, 20 March 1910, C3.

45 American Consular Bulletin 1, no. 4 (June 1919): 5.

46 *New York Times*, 24 May 1914, C4.

47 *New York Times*, 1 June 1914.

48 *New York Times*, 10 October 1915, 17, and 14 November 1915, 5.

49 Katharine Crane, *Mr Carr of State: Forty-Seven Years in the Department of State* (New York: St Martin's Press, 1960), 190.

50 Register of the Department of State (January 1930), 200; Department of State, Office of the Historian.

51 *New York Times*, 26 May 1919, 14.

52 Register of the Department of State (1929), 159.

53 Russell Rhodes, 'A Yankee Consul in London Towne', *The Hartford Courant*, 18 March 1928. Richard Westacott was born in Boston, Massachusetts, on 26 March 1849, and was in the wholesale iron business for 30 years. He was appointed vice and deputy consul general at London on 24 May 1897, and after passing an examination was appointed consular clerk on 21 November 1898, then consular assistant on 1 July 1908 and finally vice consul on 6 February 1915. He died on 29 January 1922. All his consular service was undertaken in London. Register of the Department of State (December 19, 1917), 148; *New York Times*, 1 February 1922, 17.

54 American Consular Bulletin IV, no. 3 (March 1922): 70.

55 William Barnes and John Heath Morgan, *The Foreign Service of the United States: Origins, Development, and Functions* (Washington, DC: Department of State, 1961), 206, 229–30, 303, 308–9, 363.

56 *New York Times*, 28 October 1928, 5.

57 'A Day in the London Consulate General', *American Consular Bulletin* (1921), 14.

58 Register of the Department of State (1942), 127.

59 Court Circular, *The Times*, 25 October 1932, 17.

60 Register of the Department of State (1942), 147.

61 Register of the Department of State (1941), 148; 'US Consul-General's Promotion', *The Times*, 8 June 1939, 15.

62 Memo, Sumner Wells to Franklin D. Roosevelt, July 19, 1937, President's Secretary's Files (PSF) Safe Files: State Department, 1937, Franklin D. Roosevelt Digital Archives.

63 Register of the Department of State (1942), 140.

64 Register of the Department of State (1950), 494; *New York Times*, 6 June 1947, 19; 'Marriages. Mr. G. Tait and Miss M. Percival', *The Times*, 7 June 1947, 6; *Pittsburgh Post Gazette*, 25 August 1952, 22.

65 The integration of the State Department and the Foreign Service had been recommended by the Wriston Report in 1954 and was completed in 1957. Barnes and Morgan, *The Foreign Service of the United States*, 300.

66 Register of the Department of State (1950), 22–23.

67 Ibid., 287–88.

68 Register of the Department of State (1950), 467; Foreign Office List and Diplomatic and Consular Year Book 1962, 531.

69 Register of the Department of State (1950), 113.

70 Ibid., 231.

71 David Young and Derek Harris, 'UK provides best base for Europe', *The Times*, 11 December 1975, III.

72 Charles Stuart Kennedy in course of interviewing Ambassador Mary A. Ryan, 26 March 2003, Foreign Affairs Oral History Program, Association for Diplomatic Studies and Training, Arlington, VA. Frontline Diplomacy, Manuscript Division, Library of Congress, Washington, DC.

73 Ibid.

74 Ambassador David L. Hobbs, interviewed by Charles Stuart Kennedy, 4 March 1997, Foreign Affairs Oral History Program.

75 National Archives and Records Administration, Central Foreign Policy Files, 1973–1976, Record Group 59, General Records of the Department of State, (Retrieved from Access to Archival Databases, 5 January 2012), Document Number 1974LONDON13818, 23 October 1974.

76 Ibid., Document Number 1974PARIS24358, 16 October 1974.

77 Register of the Department of State (1950), 136.

78 Ambassador David L. Hobbs, interview.

79 Letter dated 7 July 2009 from Normand W. Redden to the author.

80 Ambassador David L. Hobbs, interview.

81 'La Dolce Visa', Time magazine, 22 June 1981.

82 Consul General Diane Dillard, interviewed by Charles Stuart Kennedy, 7 March 1990, Foreign Affairs Oral History Program.

83 Letter dated 1 June 2009 from Robert W. Maule to the author.

84 Ibid.

85 Ibid.

86 Ibid. 'The composer Benjamin Britten was inspired by the vast skies and moody seas of the Suffolk coast, and in 1948, along with singer Peter Pears and writer Eric Crozier, he founded the Aldeburgh Festival. [...] At first the Festival used local halls and churches but in 1967, Britten and Pears created a permanent home at Snape, 5 miles from Aldeburgh, by converting a Victorian maltings into an 832-seat venue. Within five years Britten and Pears had reclaimed more buildings on the site to establish a centre for talented young musicians. This is the legacy behind the flourishing organisation known today as Aldeburgh.' http://www.aldeburgh.co.uk/about_us/history [accessed 27 January 2016].

87 London Diplomatic List, June 1989; Barnes and Morgan, *The Foreign Service of the United States*, 206, 229–30, 303, 308–9, 363.

88 Department of State, Office of Inspector General, Report of Inspection, Embassy London and Its Constituent Posts, November 1989, 29–30.

89 https://uk.usembassy.gov/embassy-consulates/embassy/offices/ [accessed 21 June 2017].

90 Office of the Minister-Counselor of Consular Affairs, American Embassy London, Consular Briefing Package, 19 March 1991.

91 Department of State, Office of Inspector General, Report of Inspection, Embassy London, United Kingdom and Its Constituent Posts, September 1993, 19–21.

92 Elizabeth Ann Swift, interviewed by Charles Stuart Kennedy, 16 December 1992, Foreign Affairs Oral History Program.

93 'Elizabeth Cronin, Ex-Hostage in Iran', *New York Times*, 11 May 2004, B10. It was reported in 2015 that all those Americans taken hostage in Iran would receive financial compensation and could 'claim restitution of up to $4.4 million each, or $10,000 for each day that they were held. The funding will come from the penalties paid by companies that violated sanctions and conducted illegal business with Iran and other nations. Fifteen of the 53 hostages are no longer alive.' 'Hostages compensated decades after Iran ordeal', *The Times*, 26 December 2015, 46.

94 Speech by Ambassador Philip Lader at Duke University, Durham, North Carolina, 11 October 2000. www.usembassy.org.uk/ukamb22.html [accessed 18 February 2001].

95 Department of State, Office of Inspector General, Report of Inspection, Embassy London, United Kingdom and Its Constituent Posts, September 1999, 32, 34.

96 National Commission on Terrorist Attacks upon the United States, Staff Monograph on 9/11 and Terrorist Travel (Washington, DC: US Government Printing Office, 2004), 124, 126–27, 129. http://govinfo.library.unt.edu/911/staff_statements/911_TerrTrav_Ch5.pdf [accessed 13 June 2009].

97 National Commission on Terrorist Attacks upon the United States, Staff Monograph on 9/11 and Terrorist Travel (Washington, DC: US Government Printing Office, 2004), 124, 126–27, 129. http://govinfo.library.unt.edu/911/staff_statements/911_TerrTrav_Ch5.pdf [accessed 13 June 2009].

98 Jeff Goodell, 'How to Fake a Passport', *New York Times Magazine*, 10 February 2002.

99 Embassy press release, 2 October 2008.

100 Embassy press release, 3 November 2009. http://london.usembassy.gov/ukpapress99.html/ [accessed 6 November 2009].

101 Embassy press release, 23 February 2010. http://www.usembassy.org.uk/new_embassy/ new_embassy5.html [accessed 1 March 2010].

102 State Department, Office of Inspector General, Inspection of Consulate General Hamilton, Bermuda, August 2006. OIG Report No. ISP-1-06-48, Recommendation 4, 8.

103 Email dated 25 January 2016 to the author from Astrid C. Black, US Consulate, Hamilton, Bermuda.

Chapter Nineteen Newcastle upon Tyne

1 *A General Directory for Newcastle, Gateshead and Places Adjacent, 1824*, 69.

2 Email dated 5 August 2009 to the author from Sarah Mulligan, Library Information Officer, City Library, Newcastle upon Tyne.

3 Various returns, in Despatches from United States Consuls in Leeds-upon-Hull, 1797–1838, Record Group 59, T474, NARA.

4 In 1834, Albert Davy, the consul at Hull, established a consular agency at Sunderland. Albert Davy to Secretary of State Louis McLane, 7 April 1834, Despatches from United States Consuls in Leeds-upon-Hull, 1797–1838, Record Group 59, T474.

5 Undated statement in January 1832, in Despatches from United States Consuls in Leeds-upon-Hull, 1797–1838, Record Group 59, T474.

6 *The Law Times*, 'Reports' XI, New Series, 26 November 1864, 323.

7 Albert Davy to William L. Marcy, Secretary of State, 6 December 1855, Despatches from United States Consuls in Newcastle upon Tyne, 1854–1906, Roll 1, Record Group 59, T416.

8 Albert Davy to Lewis Cass, Secretary of State, 21 July 1857, Despatches from United States Consuls in Newcastle upon Tyne, 1854–1906, Roll 1, Record Group 59, T416; Lawrence H. Officer and Samuel H. Williamson, 'Computing "Real Value" Over Time with a Conversion between UK Pounds and US Dollars, 1830 to Present', *Measuring Worth*, 2009. http://www.measuringworth.com/exchange/ [accessed 27 January 2016].

9 Herbert Davy to William Marcy, Secretary of State, 10 June 1856, Despatches from United States Consuls in Newcastle upon Tyne, 1854–1906, Roll 1, Record Group 59, T416.

10 Dr John M. Hoffman, University of Illinois Library, email message to the author, 14 July 2009. He cites the source of the letter as in the Nicolay part of the Robert Todd Lincoln Collection of the Papers of Abraham Lincoln at the Library of Congress: Ser. 2, Reel 97, Frames 43209–43210 and versos.
11 *New York Times*, 17 January 1920, 11.
12 Register of the Department of State (1871), 22.
13 Robinson Locke, to his mother, 4 March 1884, Robinson Locke Collection, Rutherford B. Hayes Presidential Center, Fremont, Ohio.
14 Locke, to his mother, 4 March 1884, Robinson Locke Collection.
15 Locke to David Ross Locke, 31 March 1884, Robinson Locke Collection.
16 David Ross Locke to Robinson Locke, 10 September 1884, Robinson Locke Collection.
17 David Ross Locke to Robinson Locke, 21 September 1884, Robinson Locke Collection. James G. Blaine was secretary of state in the cabinets of James Garfield and Chester Arthur and was the Republican Party's unsuccessful presidential nominee in 1884, losing to the Democrat Grover Cleveland.
18 Robinson Locke to John Davis, Assistant Secretary of State, 1 May and 27 November 1884; 5 January and 24 February 1885, Despatches from United States Consuls in Newcastle upon Tyne, Record Group 59, Roll 8, T416, NARA.
19 Locke to Davis, Assistant Secretary of State, 24 February 1885.
20 Locke to James D. Porter, Assistant Secretary of State, 1 June 1885, Despatches from United States Consuls in Newcastle upon Tyne, Record Group 59, Roll 8, T416.
21 Evan Rowland Jones to Robinson Locke, 8 July 1885, Robinson Locke Collection.
22 Thomas M. Waller, *Inspection of United States Consulates in the United Kingdom* (Washington, DC: State Department, 1887), 13–14.
23 Herbert Davy to James D. Porter, Assistant Secretary of State, 18 September 1885, Despatches from United States Consuls in Newcastle upon Tyne, Record Group 59, Roll 8, T416.
24 Jasper Smith to Robinson Locke, 4 February 1887, Robinson Locke Collection.
25 Smith to Assistant Secretary of State, 7 January and 6 September 1889, Despatches from United States Consuls in Newcastle upon Tyne, Record Group 59, Roll 8, T416.
26 Smith to William F. Wharton, Assistant Secretary of State, 14 June 1889, Despatches from United States Consuls in Newcastle upon Tyne, Record Group 59, Roll 8, T416.
27 Horace C. Pugh to William F. Wharton, Acting Secretary of State, 27 July & 7 November 1889, Despatches from United States Consuls in Newcastle upon Tyne, Record Group 59, Roll 8, T416; C. C. Oakey, *Greater Terre Haute and Vigo County: Closing the First Century's History of City and County, Showing the Growth of Their People, Industries and Wealth, Vol. 2* (New York: Lewis, 1908), 567–68.
28 Register of the Department of State (November 10, 1913), 124.
29 Register of the Department of State (1893), 32.
30 *New York Times*, 23 June 1893, 12; Register of the Department of State (1 July 1893), 47.
31 Message from the President of the United States, transmitting, in response to the Resolution of the Senate of March 2, 1901, a communication from the secretary of state submitting reports from consular officers of the United States giving an account of each consulate and consular agency, showing its principal industries and exports, the surrounding climatic conditions, the general cost of living, and similar information. Senate, 57th Cong., 1st Sess., Document 411 (Washington, 1902), 368–71.
32 *American Journal of International Law*, supp. to vol. 1, 1907, Official Documents, 333.
33 Newcastle upon Tyne Consulate, Inspection 1908, Inspection Reports on Foreign Service Posts, 1906–1939, RG 59, NARA.
34 Inspection Report 1909.
35 Inspection Report 1911.
36 Ibid.

37 Register of the Department of State (10 November 1913), 124.

38 State Department Records, National Archives, Record Group 59, Decimal File, 1910–1929, File 125.655, Metcalf to the Department, Despatch 377 of 19 March 1912; Department's action, undated, doc. 125.6552.

39 *New York Times*, 30 June 1903, 6.

40 Inspection Report 1914.

41 State Department Records, National Archives, Record Group 59, Decimal File, 1910–1929, File 125.655, Hamm to the Department, Despatch 142 of 17 March 1919; Department's action, 129 of 5 April 1919.

42 Inspection Report 1919.

43 Register of the Department of State (1922), 128.

44 Ibid., 180.

45 Ibid., 96.

46 Presumably 'section' meant the British Isles, as there were no other consular offices in the Newcastle consulate district. Totten's area of responsibility was Europe, excepting European Russia, the Balkan States and Greece.' Register of the Department of State (1 May 1922), 53.

47 Inspection Report 1921.

48 G. E. Baker, Board of Trade, to Foreign Office, 26 June and 5 July 1922, FO 371/7300, File 1133, ff.173 & f.189, The National Archives (TNA), Kew.

49 Minute dated 14 July 1922, FO 371/7300, File 1133, f.193, TNA.

50 R. Sperling, 4 July 1922, FO 371/7300, f.178–79, TNA.

51 Code telegram from Foreign Office to Chilton, Washington, 17 July 1922, FO 371/7300, f.194, TNA.

52 Post Wheeler, Chargé, US Embassy, London to Sperling, 26 July 1922, FO 371/7300, f.196, TNA.

53 Papers Relating to the Foreign Relations of the United States 1922, Vol. II (Washington, DC: Government Printing Office, 1938), 392. Hereafter referred to as PRFRUS.

54 Hughes to Chilton, 11 August 1922, FO 371/7300, ff.253–54, TNA.

55 Telegram from State to London, 19 July 1922, Record Group 59, Decimal File, 1910–1929, File FW125.655, NARA.

56 Minute by G. Mounsey, 18 August 1922, FO 371/7300, f.232, TNA.

57 Curzon to US Ambassador George Harvey, 28 August 1922, FO 371/7300, ff.242–45, TNA. The United States Lines was wholly owned by the US government.

58 Sir Archibald Geddes, British Ambassador, Washington to Foreign Office, 30 August 1922, FO 371/7300, f.270, TNA.

59 Post Wheeler to H. J. Seymour, FO, 31 August 1922, FO 371/7300, f.287, TNA.

60 Geddes to Foreign Office, 31 August 1922, FO 371/7300, ff.272 & 275, TNA.

61 FO to Geddes, 8 September 1922, FO 371/7300, f.279, TNA.

62 Phillips to Harvey, PRFRUS, 394.

63 John H. Grout, Consul, Hull, Despatch No. 112 of 23 October 1922, Record Group 59, Decimal File 1910–1929, File 125.6552/39, NARA.

64 Phillips to President Harding, 1 September 1922, Record Group 59, Decimal File 1910–1929, File 125.655/556, NARA.

65 Phillips to President Harding, 14 September 1922, Record Group 59, Decimal File 1910–1929, File 125.655/138, NARA.

66 Johnson to Hengstler, 11 October 1922, Record Group 59, Decimal File 1910–1929, File 125.655/142, NARA.

67 Nelson Trusler Johnson to secretary of state, 17 November 1922, Record Group 59, Decimal File 1910–1929, File 125.655/40, NARA.

68 Much of the official correspondence on this topic in the National Archives in the United States and the United Kingdom is filed out of chronological order, which makes it difficult to follow the sequence of events as they occurred in both countries.

69 Memo by Sperling, 10 October 1922, FO 371/7301, f.345, TNA.

70 'Identic' is a term used in diplomacy for notes that contain essentially the same message, but may be expressed differently.

71 Wilbur J. Carr to Charles Roy Nasmith, 10 April 1924, Record Group 59, Decimal File 1910–1929, File 125.655/127b, NARA.

72 Inspection Report 1924.

73 Johnson to Hengstler, 28 September 1922, Record Group 59, Decimal File 1910–1929, File 125.655/143, NARA.

74 Inspection Report 1924.

75 Inspection Report 1926.

76 Register of the Department of State (1 July 1933), 158–59.

77 *Washington Post*, 30 September 1932, 7.

78 Inspection Report 1933.

79 Register of the Department of State (1948), 412.

80 *New York Times*, 23 November 1966, 39; Foreign Service List, 1 October 1949, 40.

81 Register of the Department of State (1942), 224.

82 Register of the Department of State (1948), 249–50.

83 Register of the Department of State (1950), 394.

84 Email dated 16 March 2009 to the author from Lindsay S. Krasnoff, State Department, Office of the Historian; Foreign Service List, 1 October 1954, 37.

Chapter Twenty Southampton

1 *Senate Executive Journal*, 16 April 1816, 43.

2 John Livingston, *Eminent Americans Now Living, with Biographical and Historical Memoirs of Their Lives and Actions* (New York: Sampson Low, Son & Co., 1854), 297–304.

3 *Senate Executive Journal*, 4 January 1850, 112; 18 September 1850, 234.

4 *Senate Executive Journal*, 18 September 1850, 234; 25 September 1850, 250.

5 *Senate Executive Journal*, 22 December 1857, 275.

6 'The Representation of Southampton', *The Times*, 10 November 1862, 6; 'The Representation of Southampton', *The Times*, 6 December 1862, 12.

7 Ada Sterling, *A Belle of the Fifties: Memoirs of Mrs Clay, of Alabama, Covering Social and Political Life in Washington and the South, 1853–1866*. Put into narrative form by Ada Sterling (London: William Heinemann, 1905), 85–86.

8 *Senate Executive Journal*, 22 December 1857, 275; 11 January 1858, 285; *London Gazette*, 24 May 1861, 2206.

9 Foreign Office List and Diplomatic and Consular Hand Book, 1872.

10 Consular Agent of the United States, Message from the President of the United States Transmitting Report of De B. Randolph Keim, Agent, &c., 1872, H.R. 42nd Cong., 3d Sess., Executive Document No. 145, at 27.

11 *London Gazette*, 8 November 1878, 5937; Foreign Office, 6 November 1878.

12 William Thomson to Admiral John Worden, US Navy, 16 August 1875, The Library at the Mariners' Museum, Newport News, VA; Thomas M. Waller, consul general, 'Inspection of United States Consulates in the United Kingdom' (Washington, Department of State: Government Printing Office, 1887), 9.

13 Ibid., 13.

14 Obituary, *The Times*, 6 January 1887, 9.

15 Register of the Department of State (1893), 33.

16 Message from the President of the United States, transmitting, in response to the Resolution of the Senate of March 2, 1901, a communication from the secretary of state submitting reports from consular officers of the United States giving an account of each consulate and consular

agency, showing its principal industries and exports, the surrounding climatic conditions, the general cost of living, and similar information. Senate, 57th Cong., 1st Sess., Document 411 (Washington, 1902), 420.

17 Message from the President of the United States, transmitting, in response to the Resolution of the Senate of March 2, 1901, a communication from the secretary of state submitting reports from consular officers of the United States giving an account of each consulate and consular agency, showing its principal industries and exports, the surrounding climatic conditions, the general cost of living, and similar information. Senate, 57th Cong., 1st Sess., Document 411 (Washington, 1902), 420.

18 Nevin O. Winter, *A History of Northwest Ohio* (Chicago: Lewis, 1917), 394.

19 Southampton Consulate, Inspection 1908, Inspection Reports on Foreign Service Posts, 1906–39, RG 59, NARA.

20 Inspection Report 1909.

21 Register of the Department of State (1918), 90.

22 Inspection Report 1909.

23 Inspection Report 1911.

24 Inspection Report 1914.

25 Journalist and US Consul, *The Times*, 16 September 1922, 11.

26 Richard Harding Davis, *With the Allies* (New York: Charles Scribner's Sons, 1914), 145–47.

27 Register of the Department of State (1919), 157.

28 Inspection Report 1919.

29 Register of the Department of State (1922), 186; *The Times*, 16 September 1922, 11.

30 Inspection Report 1921.

31 Register of the Department of State (1922), 64.

32 Inspection Report 1927.

33 Inspection Report 1938; Register of the Department of State (1930), 196.

34 Register of the Department of State (1930), 42.

35 Register of the Department of State (1950), 66. He died in December 1954 at the Naval Medical Center in Bethesda, Maryland, to where he had returned for emergency treatment from his post as counselor in the embassy in Beirut. He is buried in Arlington National Cemetery. http://www.arlingtoncemetery.net/jhbruins.htm [accessed 29 June 2010].

36 Register of the Department of State (1933), 286.

37 Register of the Department of State (1950), 508.

38 Register of the Department of State (1946), 203.

39 *New York Times*, 5 January 1941.

40 Register of the Department of State (1950), 33–34.

41 Register of the Department of State (1951), 133. Ebling's Commission, signed by President Truman on 4 April 1949, and his exequatur signed by King George VI on 28 November 1949 are in the Ebling Collection at Georgetown University Library.

Chapter Twenty-One Stoke on Trent

1 Smith, Walter Burges, *America's Diplomats and Consuls of 1776–1865: a Geographic and Biographic Directory of the Foreign Service from the Declaration of Independence to the End of the Civil War* (Washington, DC: Center for the Study of Foreign Affairs, Foreign Service Institute, Department of State, 1986), 59; Register of the Department of State, 1870, 20. Pigot & Co's 1828/9 Directory of Staffordshire has an entry on page 724 for Hugh Brown, described as an attorney and agent to the American consulate. His address is given as Union Street, Shelton, which is a suburb of Stoke on Trent. I have been unable to discover further details about him. I suspect that he acted as an occasional agent, without operating an agency.

2 Register of the Department of State, 1874, 25.
3 *Senate Executive Journal*, 19 May 1871; *Journal of the Executive Proceedings of the House of Representatives of the United States*, 1859–1860, 6 February 1860; Thomas F. Schwartz, 'An Egregious Political Blunder: Justin Butterfield, Lincoln, and Illinois Whiggery', *Journal of the Abraham Lincoln Association* 8 (1986): 16; Library of Congress, Abraham Lincoln Papers, Reel 28.
4 Message from the President of the United States, transmitting, in response to the Resolution of the Senate of March 2, 1901, a communication from the secretary of state submitting reports from consular officers of the United States giving an account of each consulate and consular agency, showing its principal industries and exports, the surrounding climatic conditions, the general cost of living, and similar information. Senate, 57th Cong., 1st Sess., Document 411 (Washington, 1902), 440; Stoke on Trent Consulate, Inspection 1926, Inspection Reports on Foreign Service Posts, 1906–39, RG 59, NARA.
5 *New York Times*, 9 February 1886, 1.
6 *The Times*, 6 February 1886, 12. Unattributed article: 'Foreign Office, February 4.'
7 *New York Times*, 15 March 1903, 7.
8 *The Times*, 6 February, 1886, 12; Thomas M. Waller, consul general, 'Inspection of United States Consulates in the United Kingdom' (Washington, DC: Department of State, Government Printing Office, 1887); *New York Times*, 15 March 1903, 7.
9 *New York Times*, 19 April 1891, 9.
10 Unpublished autobiography by John Stewart Burgess II, written in 1940, 28–29. Sent to the author by Susan Kimes Burgess.
11 *New York Times*, 25 March 1894.
12 *New York Times*, 19 August 1892, 2; Message from the President of the United States, 439–40; Register of the Department of State 1910, 58.
13 *New York Times*, 30 July 1897, 5.
14 Burslem Consulate, Inspection 1908, Inspection Reports on Foreign Service Posts, 1906–39, RG 59, NARA.
15 Letter dated 14 October 1908 from department to consul, on 1908 inspection file.
16 Letter dated 18 February 1909 from department to consul, on 1908 inspection file.
17 Inspection Report 1909.
18 Register of the Department of State (1929), 134.
19 Inspection Report 1911.
20 Register of the Department of State (10 November 1913), 130.
21 Register of the Department of State (1 January 1924), 210.
22 Inspection Report 1914.
23 How the Bottle Kiln Works. 'From the 18th century until the 1960s, bottle ovens were the dominating feature of the Staffordshire Potteries. There were over two thousand of them standing at any one time and they could be seen everywhere one looked.' Both in Notes on the History of Stoke on Trent. www.thepotteries.org [accessed 28 January 2016].
24 Inspection Report 1919.
25 Register of the Department of State (1 January 1924), 210.
26 Register of the Department of State (1 July 1933), 158–59.
27 Inspection Report 1921.
28 Inspection Report 1924.
29 Cited in Charles Stuart Kennedy, *The American Consul: A History of the United States Consular Service, 1776–1914* (Westport, CT: Greenwood Press, 1990), 222.
30 Register of the Department of State (1 July 1933), 158–59.
31 Inspection Report 1924.
32 Inspection Report 1926.
33 Register of the Department of State (1929), 53; email dated 16 March 2009 to the author from Lindsay Sarah Krasnoff, Historian, Department of the Historian, Department of State.

Chapter Twenty-Two An Evolving, Adaptive Service

1 A bundler is someone who raises money for a campaign from a number of sources and collects them into a 'bundle' which is paid to the campaign in a single lump sum.

2 Laura Peek, Bush's donors plead for payback as envoys, *The Times*, 20 March 2001, 14.

3 J. W. Fedderke & D. Jett, What Price the Court of St James? Political Influences on Ambassadorial Postings of the United States of America, Economic Research Southern Africa, ERSA Working Paper, 234, September 2012, 22. http://www.econrsa.org/system/files/publications/working_papers/working_paper_234.pdf [accessed 15 December 2015].

4 American Diplomacy at Risk, American Academy of Diplomacy, April 2015, 11, 10, 20, respectively. https://www.academyofdiplomacy.org/wp-content/uploads/2016/01/ADAR_Full_Report_4.1.15.pdf [accessed 19 July 2017].

5 http://www.afsa.org/afsa-statement-ambassadors [accessed 11 July 2017].

6 The Politic, An Interview with Barbara Stephenson, Former U.S. Charge d'Affaires to the United Kingdom, 24 August 2013. http://thepolitic.org/an-interview-with-barbara-stephenson-former-u-s-charge-daffaires-to-the-united-kingdom/ [accessed 7 February 2016].

7 HR 6790 (96th): Foreign Service Act of 1980.

8 http://afsa.org/list-ambassadorial-appointments [accessed 20 January 2016].

9 PBS Newshour. 'Recent confirmation hearings raise eyebrows at ambassador nomination criteria.' www.pbs.org/newshour/bb/questioning-wisdom-politically-appointed-ambassadors/ [accessed 11 July 2017].

10 Email dated 25 January 2016 to the author from Astrid C. Black, US Consulate, Hamilton, Bermuda.

11 This was at the height of the Cold War and many of the discussions became heated because committee membership was restricted to member states of the United Nations. At that time this excluded the People's Republic of China (PRC), the German Democratic Republic, and the Democratic Republic of Vietnam. Delegates from the USSR and the other Soviet bloc countries complained frequently about this, in particular saying that it was unfair and illogical to have China represented on the committees by the Republic of China (Taiwan) rather than by the PRC.

12 Nicholas M. Keegan, Consular Representation in Britain: Its History, Current Status, and Personnel, PhD thesis, University of Durham, 2004.

13 See, for example, the LaGrand case, Germany v. the United States of America, heard before the International Court of Justice in 1999. http://www.icj-cij.org/docket/files/104/8552.pdf [accessed 16 December 2015].

14 http://london.usembassy.gov/hrd/15102.html [accessed 14 December 2015].

15 The New Diplomacy: Utilizing Innovative Communication Concepts that Recognize Resource Constraints. A Report of the US Advisory Commission on Public Diplomacy, July 2003. https://www.state.gov/documents/ organization/22956.pdf [accessed 15 July 2017].

SOURCES

National Archives and Records Administration, Maryland

Documents

Record Group 59, Decimal File 1910–1929.
Record Group 59, Inspection Reports on Foreign Service Posts, 1906–1939.
Record Group 59, Central Foreign Policy Files, 1973–1976.

Microfilms

Despatches from United States Consuls in Bradford, 1865–1906, RG59, T165.
Despatches from United States Consuls in Dublin, 1790–1906, RG59, T199.
Despatches from United States Consuls in Edinburgh, 1893–1906, RG59, T602.
Despatches from United States Consuls in Leeds upon Hull, 1797–1906, T474.
Despatches from United States Consuls in Leith, 1798–1893, RG59, T396.
Despatches from United States Consuls in Liverpool, 1790–1906, RG59, M141.
Despatches from United States Consuls in London, 1790–1906, RG59, T168.
Despatches from United States Consuls in Newcastle upon Tyne, 1854–1906, RG59, T416.
Despatches from United States Consuls in Plymouth, 1793–1906, RG59, T228.
Despatches from United States Consuls in Swansea, 1892–1906, RG59, T688.
Despatches from US Ministers to Great Britain, 1791–1906, M30, Rolls 99–100.

The National Archives, Kew

FO 371/7300 Foreign Office, Political Department, General Correspondence, 1906–1966.
FO 371/7301 Foreign Office, Political Department, General Correspondence, 1906–1966.
FO 371/8184 Foreign Office, Political Department, General Correspondence, 1906–1966.
FO 371/8485 Foreign Office, Political Department, General Correspondence, 1906–1966.
FO 372/1941 Foreign Office, Treaty Department and Successors, General Correspondence, 1906–1962.

Papers Held in Public Archives

Beverley Tucker Family Papers, Earl Gregg Swarm Library, College of William and Mary, Williamsburg, Virginia.
Charles M. Hathaway, Jr, Papers, Davidson Library, University of California, Santa Barbara.
Elias Vanderhorst Collection, Bristol Record Office, Bristol.
Henry Shelton Sanford Papers, Sanford Memorial Library, Sanford, Florida.
John C. New Collection, Indiana Historical Society, Indianapolis.
Robert S. Chilton, Jr, Papers, Georgetown University Library, Washington, DC.
Robinson Locke Collection, Rutherford B. Hayes Presidential Center, Fremont, Ohio.
Samuel F. B. Morse Papers, Library of Congress.
Samuel Gale Ebling Collection, Georgetown University Library, Washington, DC.
Thomas H. Dudley Papers, The Huntington Library, San Marino, California.

Reports, Directories, Year Books and Miscellaneous Publications

A Register of Officers and Agents, Civil, Military, and Naval in the Service of the United States, Washington, 1853.

Aberdeen Almanac, 1830, 1916, 1922.

Aberdeen Post Office Directories, 1912–1913, 1917–1918.

Almanach de Gotha: Annuaire Généalogique, Diplomatique et Statistique, 1911.

Ambassador, Embassy London to Secretary of State, *Information Age Diplomacy: Virtual Presence Post, Cardiff – A Model for Elsewhere?* 28 February 2001.

American Consular Bulletin. Various issues.

Baines Liverpool Directory, 1824.

Birmingham Post Year Book and Who's Who 1955–56, Birmingham, 1955.

Birmingham Post Year Book and Who's Who 1957–58, Birmingham, 1957.

Birmingham Post Year Book and Who's Who 1962–63, Birmingham, 1962.

Blue Book for 1853, containing the salaries of all the US ministers to foreign courts, the fees of the US consuls in all parts of the world, Philadelphia, 1853.

Board of Trade Wreck Report for 'River Garry', 1894, No. 4833. Available at: http://www.plimsoll.org/resources/scclibraries/wreckreports/16355.asp (accessed 11 January 2018)

Boyle's Court Guide, London, April 1849.

Bradford Chamber of Commerce Journal, 1953.

Commercial Relations of the United States with Foreign Countries, Washington, DC, Annual Series.

Compliance Follow-up Review of the Inspection of Embassy London, United Kingdom, and Its Constituent Posts, ISP/S-91-12, November 1990, State Department, Washington, DC.

Consular Agent of the United States, Message from the President of the United States Transmitting Report of De B. Randolph Keim, Agent, &c. 1872. House of Representatives, 42nd Congress, 3rd Session, Executive Document No. 145.

Consular Documents and Posts Held at Various Times by Partners and Others, G. C. Fox & Co., privately printed by the Fox family, 1984.

Council Minutes: 1855–1862, Cardiff Records, Vol. 4, 1903.

Department of State, *Toward a Stronger Foreign Service; Report of the Secretary of State's Public Committee on Personnel*, Washington, DC, 1954, Publication 5458.

Dundee Directories, 1915–1921.

Foreign Affairs Oral History Program, (FAOH), Association for Diplomatic Studies and Training, Arlington, Virginia.

Foreign Service Journal. Various issues.

Franklin D. Roosevelt Presidential Library, Hyde Park, New York.

http://www.plimsoll.org/resources/SCCLibraries/WreckReports/16355.asp   [accessed   13 June 2012].

Inspection of United States Consulates in the United Kingdom, by Thomas M. Waller, Consul-General. Washington, Department of State, Government Printing Office, 1887.

Inspection Reports on Foreign Service Posts 1906–1939, Record Group 59. Special List No. 37, compiled by George Brent and Kent Carter, National Archives and Records Administration, College Park, Maryland. NARA, Washington, DC, 1974.

Keegan, Nicholas Michael. 'Consular Representation in Britain: Its History, Current Status, and Personnel.' PhD thesis, University of Durham, 2004.

Kelly's Directory, Durham and Northumberland, 1938.

Kelly's Directory, Liverpool, 1933.

Kennedy's St Louis City Directory, 1860.

Kent's Directory for the Year 1794, Cities of London and Westminster, and Borough of Southwark.

Message from the President of the United States, transmitting, in response to the Resolution of the Senate of March 2, 1901, a communication from the Secretary of State submitting reports from consular officers of the United

States giving an account of each consulate and consular agency, showing its principal industries and exports, the surrounding climatic conditions, the general cost of living, and similar information. Senate, 57th Congress, 1st Session, Document 411, Washington, 1902.

Minutes and Proceedings of Aberdeen Town Council, 1917–1918.

National Commission on Terrorist Attacks upon the United States, Staff Monograph on 9/11 and Terrorist Travel, Washington, DC, US Government Printing Office, 2004.

Oxford Dictionary of National Biography.

Papers Relating to the Foreign Relations of the United States, 1922, Vol. II, Washington, DC, Government Printing Office, 1938.

Papers Relating to the Foreign Relations of the United States, 1923, Vol. II, Washington, DC, Government Printing Office, 1938.

Papers Relating to the Foreign Relations of the United States, 1924, Vol. II, Washington, DC, Government Printing Office, 1939.

Peace's Orkney and Shetland Almanac.

Pigot's Directory for Bristol, Gloucestershire, 1830.

Pigot's London Provincial Directory, 1822–1823.

Register of Debates, 22nd Congress, 2nd Session, 1833, S.Doc.83.

Register of the Department of State, annual series, Washington, DC.

Report of Inspection, Embassy London, United Kingdom, and Its Constituent Posts, November 1989, State Department, Washington DC.

Report of Inspection, Embassy London, United Kingdom, and Its Constituent Posts, ISP/I-93-43, September 1993, State Department, Washington, DC.

Report of Inspection, Embassy London, United Kingdom, ISP/I-99-27, September 1999, State Department, Washington, DC.

Report on the Commercial Relations of the United States with All Foreign Nations, Vol. III, Consular Returns, Washington, 1857.

Reports from the Consuls of the United States on the Commerce, Manufactures, etc., of their Consular Districts, No. 51, March 1885, Washington, Government Printing Office, 1885.

Samuel F. B. Morse: His Letters and Journals. Samuel F. B. Morse Papers at the Library of Congress, Washington, DC.

Senate Executive Journal. Various issues.

Slater's Commercial Directory for Cardiff, 1858–1859.

Slater's Directory of North and South Wales, Monmouthshire, and the Cities of Bristol and Cheltenham, 1880.

Statistical Abstract for the United Kingdom in each of the last 15 years from 1857 to 1871, Nineteenth Number, London, Her Majesty's Stationery Office, C.609, 1872.

Texas State Archives, Correspondence with Texan Consuls, Liverpool, 28 February 1842–14 July 1844, RG 307, Folder 12.

Texas State Archives, Correspondence with Texan Consuls, London, 18 May 1841–11 February 1845, RG 307, Folder 13.

Texas State Archives, English Diplomatic Correspondence, 8 January 1845–4 February 1846, RG 307, Folder 12.

The Annual Register: A Review of Public Events at Home and Abroad, for the Year 1871, New Series, London, Rivingtons, 1872.

The Biographic Register, Department of State, July 1968.

The Cincinnati Directory for 1842.

The Federal Reporter, First Series, 1880–1924.

The Foreign Office List and Diplomatic and Consular Year Book, 1852–1965. Annual series, London, Harrison & Sons.

The Gentleman's Magazine, Vol. 103, 1833.

The London Gazette.

The London Kalendar for the Year 1801, London.

The Royal Blue Book Fashionable Directory for 1827, London.

The Royal Blue Book of London, 1860.

The Royal Kalendar for the Year 1799, London.

The United States Consuls Manual, United States Department of State, Washington, 1863.

United Nations. Vienna Convention on Consular Relations 1963, UN Treaty Series, Vol. 596, New York, United Nations.

United States consular regulations: a practical guide for consular officers and also for merchants, shipowners and masters of American vessels in all their consular transactions, 1868, United States Department of State, 3rd ed., revised and enlarged, Washington, French and Richardson, 1868.

United States Statutes at Large, Vol. 46, Part 2, p. 1922. 71st Congress, Sess. II, Ch. 670, 1930.

US Department of State, Foreign Affairs Manual.

Webster's Royal Red Book, or Court and Fashionable Register, 1889 & 1910, London.

Whitaker's Almanack, 1879, London.

BIBLIOGRAPHY

Abbot, George Jacob. *The United States Consular System: A Manual for Consuls, and Also for Merchants, Shipowners and Masters, Etc.* Washington, DC: Department of State, 1856.

Adams, Gordon, and Shoon Murray, eds. *Mission Creep: The Miltarization of US Foreign Policy.* Washington, DC: Georgetown University Press, 2014.

Adams, William Edwin *Memoirs of a Social Atom.* London: Hutchinson, 1903.

Allen, Walter, ed. *Transatlantic Crossing: American Visitors to Britain and British Visitors to America in the Nineteenth Century.* London: Heinemann, 1971.

Bailyn, Bernard. *The Ideological Origins of the American Revolution*, enlarged ed. Cambridge, MA: Belknap Press of Harvard University Press, 1992.

Barnes, William, and John Heath Morgan. *The Foreign Service of the United States: Origins, Development, and Functions.* Washington, DC: Department of State, 1961.

Bartlett, Rosamund. *Tolstoy: A Russian Life.* London: Profile Books, 2010.

Basler, Roy P., ed. *The Collected Works of Abraham Lincoln.* Brunswick, NJ: Rutgers University Press, 1953–55.

Bax, Emily. *Miss Bax of the Embassy.* Boston: Houghton Mifflin, 1939.

Bemis, Samuel Flagg. *A Diplomatic History of the United States*, 3rd ed. New York: Henry Holt, 1950.
———. *The Diplomacy of the American Revolution.* Bloomington: Indiana University Press, 1957.

Bennett, Paula Bernat, ed. *Palace Burner: The Selected Poetry of Sarah Piatt.* Champaign: University of Illinois Press, 2005.

Bernstein, Richard B. *Thomas Jefferson.* New York: Oxford University Press, 2005.

Berwanger, Eugene H. *The British Foreign Service and the American Civil War.* Lexington: University Press of Kentucky, 1994.

Biographical Directory of the United States Congress. Washington, DC: Government Printing Office, 2006.

Blancké, W. Wendell. *The Foreign Service of the United States.* New York: Frederick A. Praeger, 1969.

Boyd, Julian P., ed. *The Papers of Thomas Jefferson*, Vol. 14, 1958; Vol. 17, 1965; Vol. 20, 1982. Princeton, NJ: Princeton University Press.

Brogan, Hugh. *The Penguin History of the United States of America*, 2nd ed. London: Penguin, 2001.

Brown, John Howard, ed. *Lamb's Biographical Dictionary of the United States*, Vol. VII. Boston: Federal Book Company of Boston, 1903.

Brugger, Robert J., Robert Rhodes Crout, Dru Dowdy, Robert A. Rutland and Jeanne K. Sisson, eds. *The Papers of James Madison, Secretary of State Series*, Vol. 1, 4 March–31 July 1801. Charlottesville: University Press of Virginia, 1986.

Bryant, William Cullen. 'Railway Travel in England'. In *Transatlantic Crossing: American Visitors to Britain and British Visitors to America in the Nineteenth Century*, edited by Walter Allen. London: Heinemann, 1971.

Bulloch, James D. *The Secret Service of the Confederate States in Europe: Or, How the Confederate Cruisers Were Equipped.* New York: Random House, 2001. Originally published in 1884.

Burk, Kathleen. *Old World, New World: The Story of Britain and America.* London: Little, Brown, 2007.

Calkin, Homer L. *Women in the Department of State: Their Role in American Foreign Affairs.* Washington, DC: Department of State, 1978.

Carroll, Francis M. *The American Presence in Ulster: A Diplomatic History, 1796–1996.* Washington, DC: Catholic University of America Press, 2005.

The Consular Corps in Edinburgh and Leith, 1942–1992, Golden Jubilee Handbook.

Cook, Chris, and David Waller. *The Longman Handbook of Modern American History: 1763–1996.* Harlow, UK: Longman, 1998.

Cooper, William J. Jr. *Jefferson Davis, American.* New York: Vintage Books, 2001.

Crane, Katharine. *Mr Carr of State: Forty-Seven Years in the Department of State.* New York: St. Martin's Press, 1960.

Davis, Richard Harding. *With the Allies.* New York: Charles Scribner's Sons, 1914.

Davis, William C. *The Civil War: A Historical Account of America's War of Secession.* London: Salamander Books, 1996.

De Goey, Ferry. *Consuls and the Institutions of Global Capitalism, 1783–1914.* London, Routledge, 2016.

DeConde, Alexander. *The American Secretary of State: An Interpretation.* London and Dunmow: Pall Mall Press, 1963.

Dickie, John. *The British Consul: Heir to a Great Tradition.* London: C. Hurst Co., 2007.

Dictionary of American Biography. New York: Charles Scribner's Sons, 1934.

Drake, Francis R. *Life and Correspondence of Henry Knox, Major-General in the American Revolutionary Army.* Boston: Samuel G. Drake, 1873.

Eastman, Zebina. *Eight Years in a British Consulate, from 1861 to 1869.* Lecture given in 1872, and published in Chicago in 1919 by his son.

Encyclopedia Vermont Biography: A Series of Authentic Biographical Sketches of the Representative Men of Vermont and Sons of Vermont in Other States. Burlington, VT: Ullery, 1912.

Ferguson, Niall. *Colossus: The Rise and Fall of the American Empire.* London: Allen Lane, 2004.

Ford, Paul Leicester, ed. *The Writings of Thomas Jefferson,* Vol. IX, 1807–1815. New York and London: G. P. Putnam's Sons, 1898.

Ford, Worthington Chauncey, ed. *A Cycle of Adams Letters 1861–1865,* 2 vols. Boston and New York: Houghton Mifflin, 1920.

Foreman, Amanda. *A World on Fire: An Epic History of Two Nations Divided.* London: Allen Lane, 2010.

Gore-Booth, Lord, ed. *Satow's Guide to Diplomatic Practice,* 5th ed. London: Longman, 1979.

Greenwald, Marilyn S. *A Woman of the Times: Journalism, Feminism, and the Career of Charlotte Curtis.* Athens: Ohio University Press, 1999.

Gunning, Lucia Patrizio. *The British Consular Service in the Aegean and the Collection of Antiquities for the British Museum.* London, Routledge, 2016.

Hackett, Mary, et al., eds. *The Papers of James Madison, Secretary of State Series,* Vol. 2, 1 August 1801– 28 February 1802. Charlottesville: University of Virginia Press, 1993.

Handbook of the Consular Corps of Edinburgh-Leith, 1949–1950.

Hawthorne, Nathaniel. 'Consular Experiences'. In *Our Old Home: A Series of English Sketches,* centenary edition of the works of Nathaniel Hawthorne, Vol. V., 6–40. Columbus: Ohio State University Press, 1970.

Hazelton, Fran. *London's American Past: A Guided Tour.* London: Papermac, 1991.

Hochschild, Adam. *King Leopold's Ghost: A Story of Greed, Terror and Heroism in Colonial Africa.* London: Pan Books, 2006.

Hughes, Sarah Forbes, ed. *Letters and Recollections of John Murray Forbes,* 2 vols. Boston: Houghton, Mifflin, 1899.

Ilchman, Warren Frederick. *Professional Diplomacy in the United States 1779–1939: A Study in Administrative History.* Chicago: University of Chicago Press, 1961.

Intelligence in the Civil War. Washington, DC: Central Intelligence Agency, 2007.

Jenkins, Brian. *Britain and the War for the Union,* Vol. 1, 1975; Vol. 2, 1980. Montreal: McGill-Queen's University Press.

Jenkins, Philip. *A History of the United States,* 2nd ed. Basingstoke, UK: Palgrave Macmillan, 2003.

Jett, Dennis C. *American Ambassadors: The Past, Present, and Future of America's Diplomats.* New York: Palgrave Macmillan, 2014.

Johnson, Allen, ed. *Dictionary of American Biography,* Vol. IV. London: Oxford University Press, 1930.

Johnson, Rossiter, ed. *The Twentieth Century Biographical Dictionary of Notable Americans*, Vol. VIII. Boston: The Biographical Society, 1904.

Jones, Chester Lloyd. *The Consular Service of the United States: Its History and Activities*. Philadelphia: John C. Winston, 1906.

Jones, Ron. *The American Connection: The Story of Liverpool's Links with America, from Christopher Columbus to the Beatles*. Self-Published: 1986.

Kammen, Michael G. *A Rope of Sand: The Colonial Agents, British Politics, and the American Revolution*, New York, Vintage Books, 1974.

Kennedy, Charles Stuart. *The American Consul: A History of the United States Consular Service 1776–1924*, revised ed. Washington, DC, New Academia, 2015.

King, Dean. *A Sea of Words: A Lexicon and Companion to the Complete Seafaring Tales of Patrick O'Brian.*, 3rd ed. New York: Henry Holt, 2000.

Livingston, John. *Eminent Americans Now Living, with Biographical and Historical Memoirs of Their Lives and Actions*. New York: Sampson Low, Son & Co., 1854.

Lord, Walter, ed. *The Fremantle Diary: Being the Journal of Lieutenant Colonel James Arthur Lyon Fremantle, Coldstream Guards, on His Three Months in the Southern States*. London: Andre Deutsch, 1956.

Mahin, Dean B. *One War at a Time: The International Dimensions of the American Civil War*. Washington, DC: Brassey's, 2000.

Mattox, Henry E. *Twilight of Amateur Diplomacy: The American Foreign Service and Its Senior Officers in the 1890s*. Kent, OH: Kent State University Press, 1989.

Maury, Anne Fontaine, ed. *Intimate Virginiana: A Century of Maury Travels by Land and Sea*. Richmond, VA: Dietz Press, 1941.

Mays, James O'Donald. *Mr. Hawthorne Goes to England: The Adventures of a Reluctant Consul*. Ringwood, Hampshire: New Forest Leaves, 1983.

McCullough, David. *1776: America and Britain at War*. London: Penguin, 2006.

Merli, Frank J., and David M. Fahey. *The Alabama, British Neutrality, and the American Civil War*. Bloomington: Indiana University Press, 2004.

Milton, David Hepburn. *Lincoln's Spymaster: Thomas Haines Dudley and the Liverpool Network*. Mechanicsburg, PA: Stackpole Books, 2003.

Moore, John Bassett, ed. *The Works of James Buchanan: Comprising His Speeches, State Papers, and Private Correspondence*, Vol. X, 1856–1860. Philadelphia and London: J. B. Lippincott Company, 1910.

Morgan, Edmund S. *Benjamin Franklin*. New Haven, CT: Yale University Press, 2003.

Mowat, R. B. *The Diplomatic Relations of Great Britain and the United States*. London: Edward Arnold, 1925.

Newmarch, Rosa. *Mary Wakefield, a Memoir*. Kendal: Atkinson and Pollitt, 1912.

Nickles, David Paull. *Under the Wire: How the Telegraph Changed Diplomacy*. Cambridge, MA: Harvard University Press, 2003.

Oakey, Charles C. *Greater Terre Haute and Vigo County: Closing the First Century's History of City and County, Showing the Growth of Their People, Industries and Wealth*, Vol. 2. New York: Lewis, 1908.

Owsley, Frank Lawrence. *King Cotton Diplomacy: Foreign Relations of the Confederate States of America*, 2nd ed., revised by Harriet Chappell Owsley. Chicago: University of Chicago Press, 1959.

Phillips, William. *Ventures in Diplomacy*. London: John Murray, 1955.

Platt, D.C.M. *The Cinderella Service: British Consuls since 1825*. London: Longman, 1971.

Plischke, Elmer. *U.S. Department of State: A Reference History*. Westport, CT: Greenwood Press, 1999.

Price, Jacob M., ed. *Joshua Johnson's Letterbook 1771–1774: Letters from a Merchant in London to His Partners in Maryland*. London: London Record Society, 1979.

Prowell, George Reeser. *The History of Camden County, New Jersey*. Philadelphia, PA: L. J. Richards, 1886.

Rhodes, James Ford. *History of the Civil War, 1861–1865*. New York: Macmillan, 1917.

Roberts, Sir Ivor, ed. *Satow's Diplomatic Practice*, 6th ed. Oxford: Oxford University Press, 2009.

Rodger, N. A. M. *The Command of the Ocean: A Naval History of Britain 1649–1815.* London: Allen Lane, 2004.

Rodgers, Augustus C., ed. *United States Diplomatic and Consular Service. Our Representatives Abroad: Biographical Sketches*, 2nd ed. New York: Atlantic Publishing and Engraving, 1876.

Ruge, Helga. *Flashbacks of a Diplomat's Wife.* Chico, CA: Clay & Marshall, 2002.

Ryan, Henry Butterfield. *A Brief History of United States Diplomacy.* Arlington, VA: Association for Diplomatic Studies and Training, 1996.

Sandburg, Carl. *Abraham Lincoln: The Prairie Years and the War Years.* New York: Harcourt, 2002.

Sarolea, Charles. 'The Consular Corps of Edinburgh-Leith and the Service of the City: A retrospect and a Forecast', In *Handbook of the Consular Corps of Edinburgh-Leith, 1950–1951.*

Schuyler, Eugene, *American Diplomacy*, New York, Charles Scribner's Sons, 1895.

Scudder, Horace Elisha, ed. *Recollections of Samuel Breck, with Passages from his Note-Books (1771–1862).* Philadelphia, PA: Porter & Coates, 1877.

Seitz, Raymond. *Over Here.* London: Phoenix, 2001.

Seward, Olive Risley, ed. *William H. Seward's Travels around the World.* New York: Appleton, 1873.

Sheehan-Dean, Aaron, ed. *Struggle for a Vast Future: The American Civil War.* Oxford: Osprey, 2006.

Sifakis, Stewart. *Who Was Who in the Union, Vol. 1 of Who Was Who in the Civil War: A Biographical Encyclopedia of More Than 1500 Union Participants.* New York: Facts on File, Inc., 1988.

Smith, Walter Burges. *America's Diplomats and Consuls of 1776–1865: A Geographic and Biographic Directory of the Foreign Service from the Declaration of Independence to the End of the Civil War.* Washington, DC: Center for the Study of Foreign Affairs, Foreign Service Institute, Department of State, 1986.

Stein, Douglas L. *American Maritime Documents 1776–1860: Illustrated and Described.* Mystic, CT: Mystic Seaport Museum, 1992.

Sterling, Ada. *A Belle of the Fifties: Memoirs of Mrs. Clay, of Alabama, Covering Social and Political Life in Washington and the South, 1853–1866.* Put into narrative form by Ada Sterling. London: William Heinemann, 1905.

Strang, Lord. *The Foreign Office.* London: George Allen and Unwin Ltd., 1955.

Stuart, Graham H. *American Diplomatic and Consular Practice*, 2nd ed. New York: Appleton-Century-Crofts, 1952.

Summers, Natalia. *List of Documents Relating to Special Agents of the Department of State 1789–1906*, Special Lists, Number 7. Washington, DC: The National Archives, 1951.

Taylor, William Alexander. *Centennial History of Columbus and Franklin County, Ohio.* Chicago and Columbus: S. J. Clarke, 1909.

Torrey, Bradford, ed. *The Writings of Henry David Thoreau*, Vol. XV. Boston, MA: Houghton Mifflin, 1909.

Turner, Arlin. *Nathaniel Hawthorne: Biography.* New York and Oxford: Oxford University Press, 1980.

Van Dyne, Frederick. *Our Foreign Service: The ABC of American Diplomacy.* Rochester, NY: The Lawyers Co-operative, 1909.

Wearn, Mary McCartin. *Negotiating Motherhood in Nineteenth-Century American Literature.* London: Routledge, 2007.

Weatherill, Lorna. *The Pottery Trade and North Staffordshire, 1660–1760.* Manchester: Manchester University Press, 1971.

Werking, Richard Hume. *The Master Architects: Building the United States Foreign Service, 1890–1913.* Lexington: University Press of Kentucky, 1977.

Whelan, Bernadette. *American Government in Ireland: A History of the US Consular Service 1790–1913.* Manchester, UK: Manchester University Press/Palgrave, 2000.

Winant, John G. *A Letter from Grosvenor Square: An Account of a Stewardship.* London: Hodder & Stoughton, 1947.

Winter, Nevin O. *A History of Northwest Ohio.* Chicago: Lewis, 1917.

Zeigler, Philip. *The Sixth Great Power: Barings, 1762–1929.* London: Collins, 1988.

Journals

Adams, Robert Jr. 'Faults in Our Consular System'. *The North American Review* 156, no. 437 (April 1893): 461–66.

Anonymous. 'Some Account of a Consulate'. *Harper's New Monthly Magazine* 10, no. 59 (April 1855): 628–39.

Bolger, Doreen. 'Ambrose Andrews and His Masterpiece, "The Children of Nathan Starr"'. *The American Art Journal* 22, No. 1 (1990): 5–19.

Bridges, Peter. 'Mr Carr Goes to Prague'. *Diplomacy & Statecraft* 8, no. 3 (November 1997): 187–98.

Brown, Alma Howell. 'The Consular Service of the Republic of Texas'. *Southwestern Historical Quarterly* 33, no. 4 (April 1930): 184–230.

Carr, Wilbur J. 'The American Consular Service'. *The American Journal of International Law* 1, pt. II, no. 4 (October 1907): 891–913.

Chambers, George. 'The Early Years of American Consular Representation in Belfast'. *Familia: Ulster Genealogical Review* 2, no. 12 (1996): 1–13.

Cornwallis, K. 'History of the Crisis'. *Lippincott's Magazine of Popular Literature and Science* XII, no. 33 (December 1873): 681–84.

Dowler, Clare. 'John James Piatt, Representative Figure of a Momentous Period'. *The Ohio Archeological and Historical Quarterly* 45, no. 1 (January 1936): 1–26.

Fedderke, Johannes W., & Dennis Jett. 'Ambassadorial Postings of the United States of America. Economic Research Southern Africa', ERSA Working Paper 234 (September 2012).

Fiske, Thomas S. 'Emory McClintock: Obituary'. *Bulletin of the American Mathematical Society* 23, no. 8 (1917): 353–57.

Foster, Kevin J. 'The Diplomats Who Sank a Fleet: The Confederacy's Undelivered European Fleet and the Union Consular Service'. *Prologue* 33, no. 3 (Fall 2001): 181–93.

Galbreath, Charles B. 'Claude Meeker as Member of the Kit-Kat Club, and the Ohio State Archaeological and Historical Society'. *Ohio History* 40, no. 4 (October 1931): 600–12.

Gilbert, Richard. 'Dissent in Dublin: For Two FSOs, Cable Drew Retribution and Frustration'. *Foreign Service Journal* 73 (July 1996): 28–35.

Horsman, Reginald. 'The Paradox of Dartmoor Prison'. *American Heritage Magazine* 26, no. 2 (February 1975).

Howells, William D. 'A Memorial Tribute Essay in Honor of John James Piatt, Written Shortly after His Death'. *Harper's Monthly Magazine* 135, no. 1306 (July 1917): 291–93.

Hurst, Cathy M. 'Edinburgh: Celebrating 200 Years of Consular History'. *State Department*, (October 1998): 32–35.

Johnson, Emory R. 'The Early History of the United States Consular Service, 1776–1792'. *Political Science Quarterly* XIII, no. I (March 1898): 19–40.

Jones, David T. 'The Under-appreciated Consular Cone'. *Foreign Service Journal* 78, no. 2 (March 2001): 20–24.

Jones, Douglas H. 'Lockerbie, Ten Years Later'. *Foreign Service Journal* 75, no. 12 (December 1998): 13–14, 46–48.

'List of Consular Officers of the United States, Corrected to July 23, 1907.' Supplement. Official Documents. *American Journal of International Law* 1, no. S3 (1907): 321–47.

'List of Consular Officers of the United States, Corrected to March 20, 1911', Supplement. Official Documents. *American Journal of International Law* 5, no. S2 (1911): 133–59.

Longford, Joseph H. 'The Consular Service and Its Wrongs'. *Quarterly Review* 197, no. 394 (April 1903): 598–626.

Loomis, Francis B. 'The foreign service of the United States'. *The North American Review*, Vol. 169, Issue 514 (September 1899): 350–361.

McAneny, George. 'How Other Countries Do It: An Inquiry into the Consular System of Other Nations'. *The Century Illustrated Monthly Magazine* LVII, no. 4 (February 1899): 604–11.

Mitgang, Herbert. 'Garibaldi and Lincoln'. *American Heritage Magazine* 26, no. 6 (October 1975).

Palmer, Bill. 'Stately Homes: A Department on the Move'. *State Magazine* (April 2005): 22–23.

Parker, George F. 'The Consular Service of the United States'. *The Atlantic Monthly* 85, no. 510 (April 1900): 455–66; and no. 511 (May 1900): 669–83.

Pearson, Lee M. 'The "Princeton" and "The Peacemaker": A Study in Nineteenth-Century Naval Research and Development Procedures'. *Technology and Culture* 7, no. 2 (Spring 1966): 163–83.

Ridgely, Ben H. 'The Comedies of a Consulate'. *Scribner's Magazine* 19, no. 5 (May 1896): 625–37.

Rockhill, William W. 'Evils to Be Remedied in Our Consular Service'. *The Forum* XXII (February 1897): 673–83.

Schwartz, Thomas F. 'An Egregious Political Blunder: Justin Butterfield, Lincoln, and Illinois Whiggery'. *Journal of the Abraham Lincoln Association* 8 (1986): 16.

Scott, Leslie M. 'History of the Narrow Gauge Railroad in the Williamette Valley'. *The Quarterly of the Oregon Historical Society* XX, no. 2 (June 1919): 141–58.

Sebrell, II, Thomas E. 'The American Civil War Ended in England'. *American Studies Today*, no. 19 (September 2010): 3–8.

Smith, Charles C. 'Memoirs of Colonel Thomas Aspinwall'. Second series, *Proceedings of the Massachusetts Historical Society, Nov. 1891*, VII (1891, 1892): 32–38.

Smout, Thomas C. 'American Consular Reports on Scotland'. *Business History* 23, no. 3 (1981): 304–8.

———. 'US Consular Reports: A Source for Scottish Economic Historians'. *Scottish Historical Review* 58 (1979): 179–85.

Steiner, Zara. 'The Last Years of the Old Foreign Office, 1898–1905', *The Historical Journal* 6, no. 1 (1963), 59–60.

Towle, George M. 'Our Consular Service'. *The Atlantic Monthly* 29, no. 173, (March 1872): 300–309.

Trask, David F., David M. Baehler, and Evan M. Duncan. 'A Short History of the U.S. Department of State, 1781–1981'. *Department of State Bulletin* (January 1981): S1–S8.

Washburn, Albert H. 'Some Evils of Our Consular Service'. *The Atlantic Monthly* 74, no. 442 (August 1894): 241–52.

Wharton, The Hon. William F. 'Reforms in the Consular Service'. *The North American Review* 158, no. 449 (April 1894): 412–22.

White, Henry. 'Consular Reforms'. *The North American Review* 159, no. 457, (December 1894): 711–21.

Winslow, Rollin R. 'The History of the American Consulates at Plymouth and Falmouth from 1792 to 1936'. *Annual Reports & Transactions of the Plymouth Institution & Devon & Cornwall Natural History Society* 18 (1944 for 1936–37): 48–60.

Worden, J. Perry. 'Touring Europe on Next to Nothing'. *Outing* 24, No. 3 (June 1894): 231.

Newspapers and Magazines

Aberdeen Daily Journal
Belfast Telegraph
Birmingham Post
Bradford Observer
Edinburgh Evening News
Evening Express (Aberdeen)
Globe and Mail (Toronto)
Hartford Courant (Connecticut)
Herald (Glasgow)
Illustrated London News
International Herald Tribune
L'Action Catholique (Québec)
Le Soleil (Québec)
Liverpool Daily Post

New Jersey Courier
New York Herald
New York Times
Orkney Herald
Quebec Chronicle-Telegraph
Republican-American (Waterbury, Connecticut)
Scotsman
Spokane Daily Chronicle
Spokesman-Review
Time Magazine
Times (London)
Washington Post

INDEX

www.ingramcontent.com/pod-product-compliance
Lightning Source LLC
Chambersburg PA
CBHW020655270326
41928CB00005B/133